Advanced Information and Knowledge Processing

Series Editors
Professor Lakhmi Jain
lakhmi.jain@unisa.edu.au

Professor Xindong Wu
xwu@cs.uvm.edu

Also in this series

Gregoris Mentzas, Dimitris Apostolou, Andreas Abecker and Ron Young
Knowledge Asset Management
1-85233-583-1

Michalis Vazirgiannis, Maria Halkidi and Dimitrios Gunopulos
Uncertainty Handling and Quality Assessment in Data Mining
1-85233-655-2

Asunción Gómez-Pérez, Mariano Fernández-López and Oscar Corcho
Ontological Engineering
1-85233-551-3

Arno Scharl (Ed.)
Environmental Online Communication
1-85233-783-4

Shichao Zhang, Chengqi Zhang and Xindong Wu
Knowledge Discovery in Multiple Databases
1-85233-703-6

Jason T.L. Wang, Mohammed J. Zaki, Hannu T.T. Toivonen and Dennis Shasha (Eds)
Data Mining in Bioinformatics
1-85233-671-4

C.C. Ko, Ben M. Chen and Jianping Chen
Creating Web-based Laboratories
1-85233-837-7

Manuel Graña, Richard Duro, Alicia d'Anjou and Paul P. Wang (Eds)
Information Processing with Evolutionary Algorithms
1-85233-886-0

Colin Fyfe
Hebbian Learning and Negative Feedback Networks
1-85233-883-0

Yun-Heh Chen-Burger and Dave Robertson
Automating Business Modelling
1-85233-835-0

Dirk Husmeier, Richard Dybowski and Stephen Roberts (Eds)
Probabilistic Modeling in Bioinformatics and Medical Informatics
1-85233-778-8

Ajith Abraham, Lakhmi Jain and Robert Goldberg (Eds)
Evolutionary Multiobjective Optimization
1-85233-787-7

K.C. Tan, E.F. Khor and T.H. Lee
Multiobjective Evolutionary Algorithms and Applications
1-85233-836-9

Nikhil R. Pal and Lakhmi Jain (Eds)
Advanced Techniques in Knowledge Discovery and Data Mining
1-85233-867-9

Amit Konar and Lakhmi Jain
Cognitive Engineering
1-85233-975-6

Miroslav Kárný (Ed.)
Optimized Bayesian Dynamic Advising
1-85233-928-4

Yannis Manolopoulos, Alexandros Nanopoulos, Apostolos N. Papadopoulos
and Yannis Theodoridis
R-trees: Theory and Applications
1-85233-977-2

Sanghamitra Bandyopadhyay, Ujjwal Maulik, Lawrence B. Holder and Diane J. Cook (Eds)
Advanced Methods for Knowledge Discovery from Complex Data
1-85233-989-6

Marcus A. Maloof (Ed.)
Machine Learning and Data Mining for Computer Security
1-84628-029-X

Sifeng Liu and Yi Lin
Grey Information
1-85233-995-0

Samuel Pierre (Ed.)

E-Learning Networked Environments and Architectures

A Knowledge Processing Perspective

With 169 Figures

 Springer

Samuel Pierre, PhD
Department of Computer Engineering
Ecole Polytechnique de Montreal
Canada

British Library Cataloguing in Publication Data
A catalogue record for this book is available from the British Library

Library of Congress Control Number: 2006921440

AI&KP ISSN 1610-3947
ISBN-10: 1-84628-351-5   Printed on acid-free paper
ISBN-13: 978-1-84628-351-2

9 8 7 6 5 4 3 2 1

Springer Science+Business Media, LLC
springer.com

Contents

List of Contributors

Marie-Hélène Abel
UMR CNRS 6599
BP 20529 60205 Compiègne cedex,
    France
Email: Marie-Helene.Abel@utc.fr

Ahcene Benayache
UMR CNRS 6599
BP 20529 60205 Compiègne cedex,
    France
Email: Ahcene.Benayache@hds.utc.fr

Caitriona Bermingham
Department of Electronic and
    Computer Engineering
University of Limerick
Co. Limerick
Ireland
Email: caitriona.bermingham@ul.ie

Rubby Casallas
Software Construction Group
University of Los Andes
Carrera 1 N° 18A 10
Bogotá, Colombia
Email: rcasalla@uniandes.edu.co

Julien Contamines
Laboratory on Cognitive Informatics
    and Learning Environments, LICEF
Telé-university of Quebec, TELUQ
4750, Avenue Henri-Julien
Montreal H2T 3E4
Quebec, Canada
Email: jcontami@licef.teluq.uquebec.ca

Dario Correal
Software Construction Group
University of Los Andes
Carrera 1 N° 18A 10
Bogotá, Colombia
Email: dcorreal@uniandes.edu.co

Timmy Eap
School of Interactive Arts and
    Technology
Simon Fraser University
13450 102 Avenue
Surrey, BC V3T 2W1 CANADA
Email: teap@sfu.ca

Abdulmotaleb El Saddik
Multimedia Communications Research
    Laboratory, University of Ottawa
800 King Edward, Ottawa, Ontario,
    K1N 6N5, Canada
Email: abed@mcrlab.uottawa.ca

Sylvain Giroux
Laboratoire DOMUS
Département d'informatique
Université de Sherbrooke
2500 boul. Université
Sherbrooke, Qc

Canada J1K 2R1
Email: Sylvain.Giroux@USherbrooke.ca

Allyson Hadwin
Educational Psychology & Leadership
  Studies
University of Victoria
PO Box 3010, STN CSC
Victoria, BC, V8W 3N4, Canada
Email: hadwin@uvic.ca

Timothy Hall
EMRC-Educational Media Research
  Centre
Dept ECE, University of Limerick
Limerick, Ireland
Email: Timothy.hall@ul.ie

Khaled Hammouda
Systems Design Engineering
University of Waterloo
200 University Ave West
Waterloo, Ontario N2L 3G1
Canada
Email: hammouda@pami.uwaterloo.ca

Kate Han
SIAT
Simon Fraser University—Surrey
  Campus
13450—102 Ave
Surrey, BC, V3T5X3, Canada
Email: kate_han@hsbc.ca

Marek Hatala
Laboratory for Ontological Research
School of Interactive Arts and
  Technology
Simon Fraser University
13450 102 Avenue
Surrey, BC V3T 2W1 CANADA
Email: mhatala@sfu.ca

M. Anwar Hossain
Multimedia Communications Research
  Laboratory, University of Ottawa
800 King Edward, Ottawa, Ontario,
  K1N 6N5, Canada
Email: anwar@mcrlab.uottawa.ca

Dianne Jamieson-Noel
Center for Online and Distance
  Education
Simon Fraser University
1300 West Mall Complex
8888 University Drive
Burnaby, BC, V5A 1S6, Canada
Email: djn@sfu.ca

Kevin Johnson
Dept of Computer Science and
  Information Systems (CSIS)
University of Limerick,
Limerick, Ireland
Email: Kevin.Johnson@ul.ie

Mohamed Kamel
Electrical & Computer Engineering
University of Waterloo
200 University Ave West
Waterloo, Ontario N2L 3G1
Canada
Email: mkamel@pami.uwaterloo.ca

Vivekanandan Kumar
SIAT
Simon Fraser University—Surrey
  Campus
13450—102 Ave, Suite 1400
Surrey, BC, V3T5X3, Canada
Email: vivek@sfu.ca

Dominique Lenne
UMR CNRS 6599
BP 20529 60205 Compiègne cedex,
  France
Email: Dominique.Lenne@utc.fr

A.E. Mahdi
Department of Electronic and
    Computer Engineering
University of Limerick
Co. Limerick
Ireland
Email: hussain.mahdi@ul.ie

Mauro Marinilli
Università Roma Tre
via della Vasca Navale 79
00184 Roma, Italy
Email: marinil@dia.uniroma3.it

Olga Marino
Laboratory on Cognitive Informatics
    and Learning Environments,
    LICEFTelé-university of Quebec,
    TELUQ
4750, Avenue Henri-Julien
Montreal H2T 3E4
Quebec, Canada
Email: omarino@licef.teluq.uquebec.ca

Anis Masmoudi
Télé-Université
100, Rue Sherbrooke Ouest,
Montréal, H2X 3P2
Quebec, Canada
Email: masmodi@licef.teluq.uquebec.ca

Stefan Mihaila
Télé-Université
100, Rue Sherbrooke Ouest,
Montréal, H2X 3P2
Quebec, Canada
Email: smhaila@licef.teluq.uquebec.ca

Claude Moulin
UMR CNRS 6599
BP 20529 60205 Compiègne cedex,
    France
Email: Claude.Moulin@utc.fr

John Nesbit
Faculty of Education
Simon Fraser University—Burnaby
    Campus
8888 University Drive
Burnaby, BC, V5A1S6, Canada
Email: nesbit@sfu.ca

Gilbert Paquette
Télé-Université
100, Rue Sherbrooke Ouest,
    Montréal, H2X 3P2
Quebec, Canada
Email: gpquett@licef.teluq.uquebec.ca

Samuel Pierre
École Polytechnique de Montréal
C.P. 6079, Succursale Centre-Ville
    Montréal, H3C 3A7
Québec, Canada
Email: samuel.pierre@polymtl.ca

Alejandro Quintero
École Polytechnique de Montréal
C.P. 6079, Succursale Centre-Ville
Montréal, H3C 3A7
Québec, Canada
Email: alejandro.quintero@polymtl.ca

Griff Richards
Laboratory for Ontological Research
School of Interactive Arts and
    Technology
Simon Fraser University
13450 102 Avenue
Surrey, BC, CANADA V3T 5X3
Email: griff@sfu.ca

Ioan Rosca
Télé-Université
100, Rue Sherbrooke Ouest,
Montréal, H2X 3P2
Quebec, Canada
Email: irosca@licef.teluq.uquebec.ca

Ashok Shah
School of Interactive Arts and
    Technology
Simon Fraser University
13450 102 Avenue
Surrey, BC V3T 2W1 CANADA
Email: teap@sfu.ca

Maryam Shokri
Pattern Analysis and Machine
    Intelligence Lab
Department of Systems Design
    Engineering
University of Waterloo, 200 University
    Avenue West
ONTARIO, N2L 3G1, Canada
Email: mshokri@engmail.uwaterloo.ca

David Tassy
École Polytechnique de Montréal
C.P. 6079, Succursale Centre-Ville
Montréal, H3C 3A7
Québec, Canada
Email: David.Tassy@polymtl.ca

Hamid R. Tizhoosh
Pattern Analysis and Machine
    Intelligence Lab
Department of Systems Design
    Engineering
University of Waterloo, 200 University
    Avenue West
ONTARIO, N2L 3G1, Canada
Email: tizhoosh@uwaterloo.ca

Jorge Villalobos
Software Construction Group
University of Los Andes
Carrera 1 N° 18A 10
Bogotá, Colombia
Email: jvillalo@uniandes.edu.co

Philip Winne
Faculty of Education
Simon Fraser University—Burnaby
    Campus
8888 University Drive
Burnaby, BC, V5A1S6, Canada
Email: winne@sfu.ca

1
E-Learning Networked Environments: Concepts and Issues

Samuel Pierre and Gilbert Paquette

Abstract. This chapter presents the basic concepts and main issues that characterize the e-learning network environments from a knowledge management standpoint. Knowledge management is essentially focused on the concept of knowledge, and specifically concerns the competencies of those working for organizations. It involves two important processes: knowledge extraction and knowledge assimilation. The main issues of e-learning network environments include the design of knowledge scenarios that can be integrated into knowledge environments yet to be built, as well as the design of knowledge networks dedicated to supporting these environments and enabling the retrieval of learning resources. In this chapter, the problematic of building knowledge scenarios and knowledge environments is first presented. Then, the principles, methods, and tools required to build knowledge networks are summarized, and the problems associated with retrieving resources and knowledge in networked environments are addressed.

1.1 Introduction

Over the last decade, researchers and practitioners have developed a wide range of knowledge related to *electronic learning* or *e-learning*. This movement has affected different elements and components: infrastructures, tools, content-oriented applications, human–computer interactions, pedagogical issues, methodologies and models, case studies, and projects. This phenomenal development is particularly inspired by the opportunities generated by the Internet, a sophisticated computer network. As computer networks evolve, the variety and quantity of machines available and the quantity of links used is increasing. In fact, each type of network has its own specific logical setting, switching mode, data format, and level of quality of service (QoS). This explains, in part, the existence of heterogeneous environments for public and private networks of boundless dimensions giving rise to many problems of incompatibility [30]. E-learning environments must address such problems.

Over the last few years, an increasing number of organizations have recognized the importance of learning technologies and knowledge management [31].

The knowledge-based economy entails a movement toward Web-based distance education, which benefits from the enormous possibilities offered by the Internet [34]. Hence, tremendous investments in e-learning and telecommunication infrastructures are being made all over the world, yielding a proliferation of knowledge elements and learning components. As a result, it became necessary to identify, formalize, organize, and sustain the use of knowledge and learning components [4].

Despite this enthusiasm and growing interest, many problems remain to be solved before e-learning is widely adopted and deployed by organizations. Initial training in the public education sector, professional training, and personal training at home are merging. Any useful, computer-based training solution must provide flexible learning systems, outside and inside the education system, before, during, and after office hours. In all sectors, simplistic or inefficient use of the Web has yet to be overcome in order to offer an interesting alternative to the eyes of the client organizations. Currently, most e-learning material is focused on transmitting information. While this is undoubtedly useful, a shift to knowledge-intensive learning/training environments has yet to be made in order to address knowledge and skill shortages in a rapidly changing economy.

To unleash the power of new learning technologies, new research-based solutions are needed to ensure accessible, reusable, and high-quality Web-based learning materials and activities. For this purpose, it is necessary to go beyond the simple reusability of material in repositories of learning objects and find solutions in order to build significant learning scenarios or programs that enable learners to achieve real competency gains while reinvesting small learning objects [33]. Many enthusiastic predictions are also based on the use of broadband networks for full multimedia delivery of high-level three-dimensional/virtual-reality simulations and real-time telepresence interactions. Such services are now available only through a small number of communication link types, but they will generalize rapidly through cable modems, DSL telephone lines, satellites, or non-wired terrestrial communication, and their full potential for education has yet to be reached.

One of the most critical issues related to e-learning technologies remains the *knowledge management* paradigm, which constitutes an important concern for many major organizations. Knowledge management incorporates and extends traditional document or data management in many ways. It embeds concepts such as *intellectual capital, learning organization, business intelligence, process re-engineering, decision support, competency management*, and so on. It is a multidisciplinary field that uses methods and technologies from cognitive science, expert systems and knowledge engineering, data and text mining, library and information sciences, document management, computer supported collaborative work (CSCW), communities of practice, and organizational science. Its goal is to promote the systematic identification, production, formalization, availability, and sharing of knowledge within an organization, and it also aims to increase the competencies of its personnel, rather than simply offering them information consultation support. Knowledge management integrates the processing of higher-level knowledge, beyond raw data or factual information. It underlines the importance of principles, models, theories, processes, and methods, and helps uncover the tacit knowledge of experts to make it available for learning, working, and decision-making processes.

From a knowledge management standpoint, the main issues pertaining to e-learning networked environments include the design of knowledge scenarios that can be integrated into knowledge environments, the building of knowledge networks dedicated to supporting these environments, and the mechanisms enabling the retrieval of learning resources or useful knowledge. This introductory chapter characterizes the e-learning environments and analyzes these issues. Section 1.2 presents the basic concepts and background information concerning these environments. Section 1.3 exposes the problematic of building knowledge scenarios (discussed in Part I). Section 1.4 analyzes the process of building knowledge environments (Part II). Section 1.5 summarizes the principles, methods, and issues related to the design of knowledge networks (Part III). Section 1.6 addresses the problem of retrieving resources and knowledge from networked environments (Part IV). Section 1.7 concludes the chapter.

1.2 Basic Concepts and Background

A learning object can be defined as any entity, digital or not, that can be used, reused, or referenced during technology-supported learning activities. From an object-oriented programming standpoint, learning resources can be understood as objects in an object-oriented model, having methods and properties. These properties are generally described using metadata, i.e., structured data about data. Due to various methods, the learning objects can become interactive or adaptive [26]. Even though the term *knowledge object* takes precedence as it refers to uses other than formal learning, the terms *learning object* and *learning resource* are used as synonyms in this chapter.

Learning objects or resources can be distributed over different servers. They can be of any size and type: text, audiovisual material, educational software, multimedia presentations, or simulations. They also carry information to be explicitly used by persons in order to acquire knowledge and competencies. They can be described and gathered in such a way that facilitates their storage, publication, and retrieval. Such an organization is called a *learning object repository* (LOR).

A networked virtual environment can be defined as a software system within which multiple users, possibly located worldwide, interact with one another in real time [30]. Such an environment can be used for education and training, engineering and design, and, commerce and entertainment. When hardware, software, and communication tools, as well as the teaching, coaching, and assistance services offered to the users of the computer network are integrated together in a coherent way, they constitute an *e-learning networked environment*. Figure 1.1 shows the three main components of such an environment: the access infrastructure, the network infrastructure, and the content infrastructure.

In large networked environments, learning takes place under a variety of technical constraints. It is important that each learning object be adapted to these

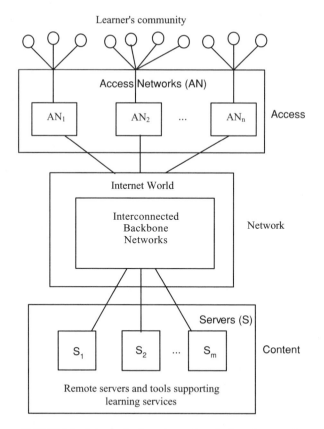

FIGURE 1.1. A typical e-learning networked environment.

constraints. Thus, the various computations carried out by a learning object must have an "anytime" flavor [13]. For this reason, among others, learner modeling remains active, considering only the information available and computing only as deeply as time and space constraints permit. Instructional planning must also be sensitive to these time and resource limitations.

One of the advantages of a LOR is that it allows any instructional designers or any person acting as an editor to track down interesting learning objects created in a learning context in order to reuse them or adapt them for use in another environment. For this purpose, interoperability and metadata protocols are needed.

One of the main purposes of interoperable learning objects is that they can be aggregated and integrated into a knowledge management or learning environment. Such an environment sometimes emerges from peer-to-peer interaction and can be designed by a team of instructional engineers by creating and implementing a delivery model that depicts interactions between users and the learning system components, activity descriptions, and learning objects [19,20]. The main challenge for the interoperability of learning objects consists of their design rather than the platform interoperability issues that initially motivated their development.

From a knowledge management standpoint, learning objects need to be encapsulated into abstract resources in order to provide designers with a scripting language to produce aggregations and launch resources in all different technical situations. Tools also need to be defined in order to associate knowledge models to resources, operations, and actors' competencies, which would facilitate the integrated search for useful resources and ensure the design consistency of a learning management system.

Interoperability involves several degrees of focus:

- digital packaging of the learning object itself, using the emerging metadata standards to catalogue it for local and global identification;
- providing different organizations with search tools;
- finding and interchanging information with one another;
- transporting objects for use in different contexts.

Learning objects can embody both educational content and learning activities and the traditional approaches to labeling and transporting containers of digital content are being challenged by emerging abilities to express content, processes, and metadata as semantically rich ontologies [32]. This leads to the concept of semantic Web services. In the same vein, the emergence of autonomous agents allows for the creation of learning environments where learners interact with or deploy multiple agents to help define and navigate individualized learning paths that are dynamically created and interactively shaped.

Learning objects can be active or adaptive. In fact, they generally consist of raw material that ideally can be used in different ways, for different purposes, and in different contexts. For these purposes, it is necessary for designers to be able to adapt original learning objects in order to reuse them properly in new contexts. However, it is difficult to make learning objects actively able to adapt to the context of their use, to the pedagogical goals of the learner or learning environment, to the nature and needs of the learners involved, to the level of detail needed to reach the pedagogical objectives, and to the technical constraints. This time-consuming task constitutes a serious bottleneck in the development of e-learning materials. In fact, making learning objects readily adaptable to various contexts, various learner capabilities, and various pedagogical needs would be a useful extension of their current capacities.

Learning object repositories are distributed and highly dynamic, in that new learning objects are being created all the time, while others may be withdrawn or modified. For this reason, it would be impossible to ensure the consistency of any central registry. Other challenges consist of providing learning objects with sufficient autonomy to enable them to discover other learning objects and perhaps self-organize, as well as with the capability to seek out complementary learning objects in order to automatically aggregate or adapt to each other. Methods already developed in the areas of autonomous agents, multiagent systems, planning, machine learning, and knowledge representation could be extended and adapted to solve these problems.

Learning objects can also be of an advanced multimedia type including three-dimensional (3D) or virtual-reality components. *Multimedia* refers to objects that contain a combination of "media" such as audio, video, text, graphics, and animation. In recent years, and with the advent of the MPEG-4 standard, *virtual reality* (VR) has become a new "medium" of advanced multimedia [17].

Virtual reality is a term defined as a computer-generated, interactive, three-dimensional environment in which a person is immersed [1]. This definition includes three key elements:

- the virtual environment is a computer-generated three-dimensional scene, which requires high-performance computer graphics to provide an adequate level of realism;
- the virtual world is interactive, i.e., both the user and the system provide each other with real-time responses in order to be able to interact with it in an effective manner;
- the user is immersed in this virtual environment.

One of the unique characteristics of a virtual-reality system is the head-mounted display worn by users. These displays block out the entire external world and show the user a scene that is entirely under the control of the computer. As a result, the user is completely immersed in an artificial world and becomes disconnected from the real environment. To ensure that this immersion appears realistic, the VR system must accurately monitor the user's movements and determine the result to be rendered on the screen of the head-mounted display.

Augmented reality (AR) is a growing area of virtual-reality research [27]. An augmented-reality system generates a composite view for the user. It combines and projects an authentic scene to the user with a computer-generated virtual scene thereby enhancing the real scene with additional information. In all applications, the improved reality presented to users enhances their performance and perception of the world. The ultimate goal is to create a system so that the user cannot tell the difference between the real world and the virtually enhanced version. Advanced multimedia includes VR and AR simulations that are used to provide advanced computer-based instruction and training.

Another relevant concept pertains to a *Virtualized Reality*^{TM} *Environment* (VRE): a generalization of the essentially synthetic virtual environment concept. While still being a computer-generated multimedia world model, VRE is based on information about the real/physical world objects and phenomena as captured by a variety of sensors.

Creating, searching, and delivering enhanced multimedia learning objects constitute important challenges since these objects are composed of a spatial and/or temporal synthesis of time-dependent (audio, video, animation, virtual reality) and time-independent media (text, image, data). Simulations, such as virtual reality, undoubtedly create a very rich learning environment [8,9]. The creation of these objects requires advanced authoring tools, particularly when such objects must be stored in different versions or be appropriately coded to accommodate users' preferences, contexts, situations, and network quality of service (QoS) conditions.

1.3 Building Knowledge Scenarios

At the heart of any knowledge-based learning system is the *knowledge scenario component* that provides many possible work plans for the user/learner. The learning scenario is the common point of reference and the workflow of interaction between the different actors in a typical e-learning environment, i.e., learners, trainers, content experts, designers, managers, etc.

Knowledge scenarios are basically networks of learning events (curriculum, courses, units, activities) with learning objects, material, and resources used or produced within the context of these events. Each actor follows, supports, coaches, manages, and/or designs a certain learning scenario. All users have their own view of the learning scenario and the learning objects they need to use or produce according to their role. Thus, each learning object document or tool can be configured differently for each user. Furthermore, each tool and document can accumulate data pertaining to its users.

Process-based learning scenarios are the main focus of instructional engineering. The approach proposed by Paquette et al [25] is based on the fact that specific knowledge of a subject matter and generic skills are constructed at the same time. A learning unit without an associated skill is analogous to a set of data without any process acting on it. Consider, for example, a training unit for electronic technicians. These learners must acquire knowledge pertaining to electronic devices. They must also be able to identify various kinds of electronic components and they need the competencies required to diagnose a defective electronic device. The first goal corresponds to a generic classification task, a generic skill that can be applied to any knowledge domain. The second goal corresponds to another generic skill, diagnosis, also applicable to any knowledge domain. Of course, a training unit in electronics will be very different if the course designer only wants learners to classify components, compared to a designer who wishes to train learners to diagnose malfunctions.

A learning scenario for a unit should be based, whenever possible, on a generic process corresponding to a generic skill. In other words, if instructional material designers want to develop knowledge in any subject matter along with skills like classification, diagnosis, induction, or modeling, they should propose classification, diagnosis, induction, and modeling problems or projects to the learner. Then, the collaborative activities, as well as the information, production, and assistance resources, will be chosen accordingly. For example, in a classification task, sorting tools in a spreadsheet and collaborative classification activities could be embedded in the scenario, coupled with guidance taking the form of methodological advice to support the classification process.

Building a learning scenario can be described as a three-step process. For example, the generic task of collaborative writing, corresponding to a synthesis generic

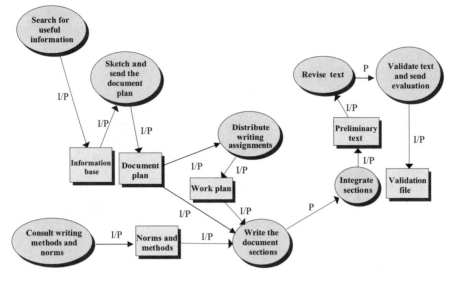

FIGURE 1.2. Building a knowledge scenario (step 1).

skill, can be part of a virtual conference scenario that can be used in most knowledge domains.

- *For the first step, the activities and the learner's productions are described in a graph*, for example using the MOT knowledge representation technique [20] leading to Figure 1.2. The activities in the scenario are linked to the learner's production (rectangles) by input-output (I/P) links. Typically, the learners search for information and consult writing methods and norms. Then, a plan of the document is sketched and a work plan to distribute tasks among learners is built. Finally, the sections are written. The integration of these sections yields a preliminary text that will be revised and evaluated.
- *For the second step, the actors and their roles are described, in relation to each activity*, as shown in Figure 1.3. In this example, these actors belong to a team of writers, composed of a leader and other learners. The tutor or trainer is also an actor and plays the role of an evaluation expert or a client who will validate the text at the end. All of these actors are linked as ruling (R) agents to the activities in the scenario. In this case, the team controls the search for information and the distribution of writing assignments, while the project leader dictates the sketch of the plan for the document, and the tutor validates the final text before sending an evaluation to the learners.
- *For the third step, tools, resources, or learning objects are assigned to the activities in the scenario*, taking into account the productions in progress, the learning resources serving as input for the activity, and the actors involved, as shown in Figure 1.4. In this example, a Web search engine and an annotation tool are used to search for input information and to consult writing methods and norms. Access to a human content expert can be provided to advise users about writing

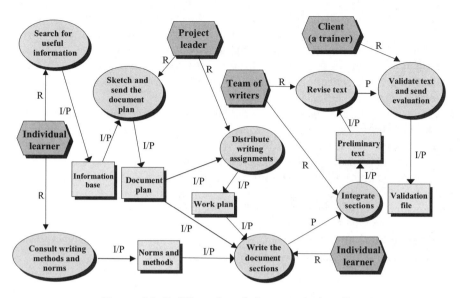

FIGURE 1.3. Building a knowledge scenario (step 2).

methods and norms for these kinds of documents. Teleconferencing could be added to sketch the plan and distribute the writing assignments. A collaborative text editor is used for the activities where the sections are integrated and, later on, when the text is revised in its final form. Finally, the tutor acting as the client annotates the text and sends an evaluation through Web email.

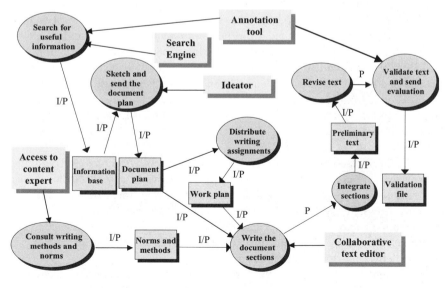

FIGURE 1.4. Building a knowledge scenario (step 3)

An intensive knowledge scenario, such as the one presented above, is in itself a learning object that can easily be adapted in many ways to generate new learning/working scenarios by rearranging the activity network, redefining the learner's productions, changing the actor's roles for a new cooperative approach or a completely individual scenario, and, adding or deleting learning objects, resources, or tools to adapt it to particular situations.

Note also that this scenario is generic, based on a generic collaborative writing task and an information synthesis generic skill. To be used in a specific knowledge domain, it must be instantiated within the domain. To do this, activity assignments are described according to the domain under study, for example "find information about atomic physics" or "find information about Impressionist paintings." Also, learning objects specific to the domain can be inserted into the scenario graph as inputs for certain activities, for example, a document pertaining to the norms used to write acceptable documents in physics or an adequate document in art history. Finally, different tools, human experts, or other resources can also be chosen from various fields while preserving the scenario structure.

1.4 Building Knowledge Environments

As indicated above, modeling learning scenarios is a central issue when it comes to designing and delivering e-learning or knowledge environments. From the scenario, the Web site can be designed and the resources selected and integrated into the interaction spaces that will constitute a knowledge environment for the learners or for other actors.

There are many possible knowledge environment models: "high-tech" classrooms, distributed classrooms, hypermedia self-training, asynchronous "on-line" training, communities of practice, and performance support systems.

"High-tech" classrooms gather students and trainers at a single location that provides sophisticated multimedia and network equipment. Studying in a classroom for a certain period of time does not mean learners are isolated from the outside world. Networked computers can provide access to Web sites and Internet multimedia presentations. Videoconferencing can also bring new expertise into the classroom. Many universities and organizations have built electronic campuses from this model to help manage the various possible transitions from a predominant classroom presentation model to more interactive and flexible ways to learn and teach.

Distributed classrooms are quite similar to high-tech classrooms except for the fact that learners and trainers are physically located in two or more distant locations. Learning events use specialized and sometimes costly real-time videoconferencing systems. Alternatively, desktop videoconferencing software can be used for real-time communication. This model and the previous one bear a resemblance to the traditional classroom, although some specialists claim that they offer much hype without delivering significant pedagogical gains.

Hypermedia self-training refers to the use of learning materials accessible through the Web or CD-ROMs to support an individualized learning approach to education. In the "pure" model, neither trainer support nor collaboration among learners in the system is provided. A training manager supplies the learning resources: self-training units, interactive or passive Web sites, and multimedia material on CD-ROMs or DVDs. The main benefit of this model is that it enables learners to progress at their own pace according to the time and place of their choice.

Asynchronous "on-line" training departs from this individualistic view. It is organized and led by a trainer or a teacher, allowing for interaction with the trainer or among learners during teamwork and discussion groups [14,15]. Unlike those occurring in the aforementioned classroom-like models, these interactions are asynchronous, retaining some of the flexibility of self-training, with the exception that the pace between modules is decided on by the teacher/trainer. The main tools and activities are forums, emails, and file transfers, together with less frequent audio or videoconferencing, on-line presentations, and real-time collaborative activities.

Communities of practice put the main emphasis on professional tasks [28]. The learners are basically content experts who wish to extend their knowledge through asynchronous exchanges of information via forums, emails, or document transfers. They progress through collaborative problem solving and shared project know-how. Contrary to the previous model, communities of practices are devoid of trainers acting as content experts or pedagogical coaches. Group leaders are provided; however, they possess less knowledge of the subject matter than the learners, although they are more knowledgeable when it comes to the methods used to support group interactions.

Performance support systems integrate training even more closely with the actual work processes and tasks in an organization [11]. Extensive use of the organization's databases and support software occur both ways: training material is used to enhance on-the-job performance, and authentic problems and tools are used to support training at the workplace and outside of it. On-line help, advisory systems, and human supervisors support these training/work activities. This model promotes just-in-time information to help users focus on real-life problems whether individually or in teams.

Wouldn't it be interesting to create an environment that supports any combination of these different knowledge environment models? Paquette [23,24] describes how an object-oriented model was designed to create a Virtual Learning Center built for such a purpose. This system integrates the best features of the four models presented above.

The Virtual Learning Center architecture supports five types of actors, an approach now embedded in other delivery systems. Each actor is personified through different characters or media agents playing a variety of roles and relying on a variety of resources, documents, communication tools, and interaction services.

- The *learner's* main function is to transform information into personal knowledge. The learner achieves knowledge acquisition and construction by managing a learning environment planned by another actor, the designer, in collaboration with other learner agents and with assistance from other actors.
- The *informer or content expert* makes information available to the learner. The corresponding content agents may provide information, but also books, videos,

TABLE 1.1. Actors' roles in typical delivery models

	Learner	Informer	Trainer	Manager	Designer
High-tech or distributed classroom	Attending presentations, completing exercises	Teacher presenting information	Teacher responding to learners' questions	Teacher preparing tech environment	Teacher designing plan and materials
Web/multimedia (MM) self-training	Navigating through MM content	Sites and MM material	Help components, FAQs	Manager organizing events and support	Team designing Web sites or MM
On-line training	Getting information, interacting in a forum	Teacher referring to learning material	Teacher leading forums	Manager organizing events and support	Teacher designing activities
Community of practice	Exchanging expertise and know-how	Learners themselves and various documents	Group leader	Manager organizing events and support	Designing process- based scenarios
Performance support	Solving situated real-life problems	Organization's documents and databases	Intelligent help systems	Manager supervises learners	Designing process- based scenarios

courseware, etc. Learners can also make information available to others as a result of their production activities, thus becoming an informer agent.

- The *designer* is the actor who plans, adapts, and sustains a telelearning system that integrates information sources (human informers or learning materials) and self-management, assistance, and collaboration tools for other actors.

- The *trainer* provides pedagogical assistance or coaching by advising learners about their individual processes and the interactions that may be useful to them, based on the learning scenarios defined by the designer.

- Finally, the *manager* provides organizational assistance to the learner (and other actors) by managing actors and events, creating groups and making teleservices available in order to ensure successful learning processes based on the scenarios defined by the designer.

At the time of delivery, all of these actors interact within their own computer-based environment. The Explor@ implementation[1] [12,22] is a Web-based system built on this conceptual framework that helps with the construction of a learning environment for each actor. This environment gathers resources that enable the actors to play their roles within a course Web site.

Table 1.1 underlines only the main roles of each actor for all of the delivery models previously presented. It is possible to support a combination of the

---

[1] Note that this first architecture is being extended in the TELOS system being built by the LORNET project. The extended architecture designed to create knowledge environments is presented in Chapter 4.

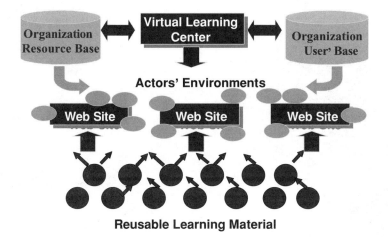

FIGURE 1.5. Three-level architecture.

components of these models through a Web-based Virtual Learning Center [23]. Within the same program, course, or learning event, certain units could be based on autonomous training, others on a community of practice, and even others on some form of distributed or high-tech classroom.

For this to happen, an open, flexible, extensible, and interoperable architecture is needed (see Fig. 1.5). This conceptual architecture is based on three levels. At the bottom, learning material (knowledge resources) are selected, adapted, digitized, or constructed to support content delivery of a subject matter.

Then the material is integrated into a Web site that gives access to a network of activities, resources, and productions to be realized. It is at this second level that the pedagogical strategy embedded in a knowledge scenario will be implemented.

For example, a business process simulation integrated into a management course could also be used to analyze learning material in a course offered to trainers. The learning scenarios implemented into the Web site determine how a learning tool such as this one will be used for learning in various situations or different application domains.

Finally, at the upper level, the designer adds one or more e-learning environments to the course Web site—one for each actor in the training delivery process. Each environment will group resources for self-management of activities, information search and consultation, production of new content (homework), collaboration between learners or trainers, and assistance in the form of users' guides, FAQs, resource persons, or intelligent agents.

Figure 1.6 shows a concrete view of what happens at delivery time.[2] From an organization portal, users move to the VLC home page and provide their user

---

[2] Parts of this course within the Explor@ environment can be viewed at http://www.licef.teluq.uquebec.ca/explorademo.

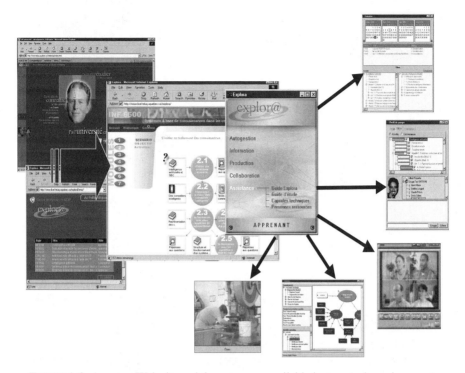

FIGURE 1.6. A course Web site and the resources available in an actor's environment.

names and passwords. The system then displays a list of the VLC learning events they can access, along with the roles they are authorized to play. Once they choose the event and a role, a window display composed of the learning event Web site and an Explor@ tool bar allows access to an actor's environment.

This environment gathers a set of knowledge resources according to the actor's role within the Web site. The resources are distributed over interaction spaces. Although this chapter presents a distribution over five spaces, other distribution patterns can be used. Each space is concerned with certain types of interactions: self-management of the e-learning system, interaction with information sources and production tools, collaboration with other learners or similar actors, and, finally, assistance from other types of actors such as trainers, informers, managers, or designers.

As shown in Figure 1.6, a resource can be any tool, multimedia document, or support service provided to the users according to their roles in the learning event. In this example, learners can access a calendar and a progress report for the management of their activities, view a video-streamed information source, collaborate with teammates through desktop videoconferencing, and produce a knowledge model to fulfill a course assignment.

To create such an environment, designers must clearly and thoroughly define the actors' roles, and the resources must be chosen accordingly. The previous example shows a hybrid delivery model that combines hypermedia self-training, on-line training, and community of practice activities. The resources were chosen for a typical learner from a description of the learning scenario, its activities and input resources, and the productions the learner must accomplish according to the assignments associated with the activities. The designer would carry out similar analyses for the trainer and the other actors in order to plan out their environments.

1.5 Designing Knowledge Networks

A networked environment is composed of the five following features [30]: a shared sense of space, a shared sense of presence, a shared sense of time, means of communication, and ways to share. A shared sense of space refers to the fact that all participants have the impression that they are located at the same place, real or fictional, such as in the same room, building, or vehicle. In this context, the same characteristics must be presented to all participants. A shared sense of presence refers to the fact that when they enter the shared place, each participant takes on a virtual persona, called an avatar, which includes a graphical representation, a body structure model (like the presence of arms, legs, antennae, tentacles, joints, etc.), a motion model, a physical model (height, weight, etc.), and other characteristics. A shared sense of time enables the participants to see each other's behavior in real time. Communicating in a networked environment consists of using gestures, typed text, or voice in order to enable some interaction among the participants. According to a fundamental component of engineering or training systems, ideally all communication mechanisms must seem authentic within a virtual environment. In a networked environment, sharing requires specific devices to provide users with a high-quality video conferencing system and the ability to interact realistically with each other but also with the environment itself.

A networked environment essentially consists of four basic components that work together to provide the sense of immersion among users located at different sites: graphic engines and displays, communication and control devices, processing systems, and communication networks.

Graphic engines and displays constitute a key component of the user interface in a networked environment. The display provides the user with a 3D window into the environment and the engine generates the images on display. This component can be enhanced by adding more sophisticated devices to improve the quality of the imagery and extend the user's experience. For these purposes, a CAVE can be used as a more immersive graphical display. This is a cube in which the participants stand in the middle in order to see images that are projected onto the walls in front, above, below, and on both sides of them. As the users move through the virtual environment, updated images are projected onto the CAVE's walls to give the sensation of smooth, continual motion.

The control and communication devices are necessary to allow users to communicate with other participants in the networked or virtual environment.

The processing system includes processor units that receive events from the users' input devices and compute how such input impacts the users' position within the environment and the location of other objects found in the same environment. The communication network is needed to allow users to exchange information (text, audio, and video communication) among themselves.

Typically, knowledge networks are environments that can be used for learning and training purposes. The design and development of such networks are complex due to the multiple aspects that must be taken into account: the network bandwidth, the heterogeneity of the components, the distributed nature of the interactions, the real-time system design, the resource management, the failure management, the scalability, and the configuration.

Network capacity constitutes a limited resource in a networked environment. For this reason, the network designer must carefully determine how to assign this capacity in order to avoid congestion, which would result in a decrease of network quality of service. The designer must also take into account the network heterogeneity, which refers to the fact that different users may be connecting to the networked environment using different communication networks with different capacities. This issue is particularly relevant in interactive learning or training applications where a lack of equality can lead to unrealistic training. Heterogeneity issues also arise with regard to the graphical display and computational and audio capabilities. The network designer's challenge consists of deciding whether to use minimal resources to ensure equality among participants or whether to attempt to expose these differences and address the resulting fairness issue.

To fully use the capacities of broadband networks in e-learning networked environments, content-based and context-based search and delivery methods for advanced multimedia learning objects are required [10]. These objects can be described using MPEG-7 (Moving Picture Expert Group 7) descriptors, an emerging standard for the specification of descriptors for a variety of multimedia information. MPEG-7 and XML can provide multimedia content capacities similar to those offered by IMS/CANCORE for textual content. The MPEG-4 standard can be used to deliver, render, and interact with multimedia learning objects, using their metadata description in MPEG-7. MPEG-4 has been developed to provide solutions for the new multimedia applications through characteristics like composition of presentation of structured and related objects, streaming, error resilience, powerful compression, and synchronization. The MPEG-4 streams are decoded in a way that allows object separation and reconstitution, making it possible for users to interact with the objects in the scene.

Another issue that must be taken into account by the network designer pertains to the distributed interactions. To be effective, the networked environment must provide users with the impression that the entire environment is located on their local machine and that their actions have an immediate impact on the environment.

Other design issues, like real-time system design and failure management, are related to the capability of the networked environment to perform many tasks concurrently, in a reasonable time frame, while ensuring that it remains operational in spite of component failures. Scalability is measured by the number of entities that may be processed simultaneously by the environment. It can also be a measure of the number of hosts that may be simultaneously connected to the environment. It depends on a variety of factors, including network capacity, processor capabilities, rendering speeds, the speed, and the throughput of shared servers. Finally, deployment and configuration issues are related to the fact that the software used in a networked environment may be dynamically downloaded to suit the changing needs of the executing environment. As a result, there is an impact on the software design, the choice of implementation language, and the set of supported execution platforms. The complexity of deployment issues increases if the networked environment must be executed within Web browsers over the Internet. More than software distribution, deployment also involves the participants' need to access configuration information, including network addresses to send data, the location of servers, security encryption keys and access codes, graphic images, computational models for different types of participants, and so on.

1.6 Retrieving Resources and Knowledge

Retrieving knowledge resources is a central process for any knowledge environment. It is used by learners to carry out tasks, solve problems or manage projects, by trainers looking for resources to facilitate learning, and by designers seeking resources to build knowledge environments.

The increased need to reuse learning objects or knowledge resources and the increasing necessity to integrate e-learning systems have led to a vast movement toward international standards for *learning objects* (LOs). Duval and Robson [5] present a review of the evolution of standards and specifications starting with the Dublin Core Metadata Initiative in 1995. The IEEE Learning Technology Standards Committee (LTSC) and its joint work with organizations like ARIADNE and IMS finally produced, in June 2002, a metadata standard for Learning Object Metadata (IEEE LOM) which is now being widely used by most e-learning systems.

Figure 1.7 presents a very high-level view of a learning system architecture that supports interactions among four types of entities: actors, learning objects (or knowledge resources), knowledge description referentials (metadata or ontologies), and knowledge scenarios (for courses or learning events). Actors operate scenarios composed of operations (or activities) where knowledge resources (LOs) are used or produced. Knowledge referentials (metadata or ontologies) describe the information owned or processed by actors, processed through operations, or contained in LOs: the properties of the knowledge resource. Four corresponding managers store and retrieve information in a database, construct information structures, and present information to users.

The knowledge resource manager is used to retrieve knowledge resources, reference new ones, or build aggregated resources for the actors' environments.

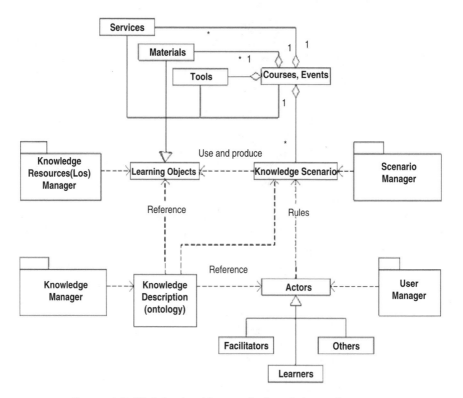

FIGURE 1.7. High-level architecture for knowledge environments.

Figure 1.8 presents the main components[3] of a knowledge resource manager and the relationships between them. The two upper components, the *LO aggregator* and the *LO launcher*, operate knowledge resources (LOs) that were previously retrieved from one or more learning object repositories located somewhere on the Web.

The six other components relate to a central metadata repository, and a set of files in a relational/XML database that respect a LOM (learning object metadata) model such as the IEEE LOM used to describe the properties of the knowledge resources or LOs. A central component is the *metadata editor* that enables users to associate a LOM file to any knowledge resource and store it in the system's permanent relational/XML database.

The five other components are specific user services for a metadata repository:

- The *metadata repository builder* helps find the location of interesting LOs on the Web or in a local area network and creates a LOM entry in a metadata repository

---

[3] Implemented in the Explor@-2 e-learning delivery system, this architecture is described in more details in [19].

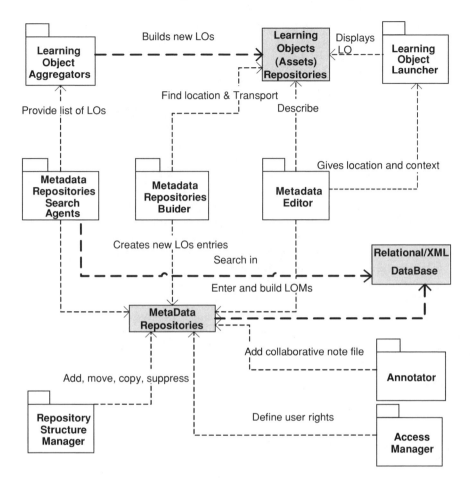

FIGURE 1.8. Main components of a knowledge resource manager.

for the resource that can be filed later using the metadata editor. Sometimes, in order to make an LO more widely accessible, this component transports the resource to a predefined location on a server.

- The *repository structure manager* selects a folder or grouping that contains a LOM record. It can move a metadata record from one folder to another, copy an alias onto another folder, delete a record or a folder, and duplicate a record to speed up the meta-referencing of a similar LO.
- The *repository search agents* apply user-defined constraints involving metadata attributes to find and display a set of corresponding metadata records from which resources can be viewed or launched.
- The *access manager* helps define a user's profile, access rights to folders, metadata files, and resources described by the metadata file. Rights include viewing, adding, modifying, deleting, and granting rights to other users.

- The *collaborative annotator* manages a local user group forum where users can exchange messages about a resource. It is integrated into the LO repository. These messages can also be stored in the metadata repository database.

Based on an extensive work developed by the instructional design team for the MISA–Learning Systems Engineering Method [21], a knowledge resource taxonomy was developed to distinguish four major classes: material/document, tool/application, service provider, and course/events.

- The material/document class has further subcategories that categorize resources according to the type of information, the type of media elements it contains, the type of media support, its usage context, or its aggregation mode.
- The tool/application class includes the resources used to navigate, communicate, produce/design, assist, search, and manage tools and applications.
- The service provider category aims to classify human resources that provide service to other actors or other types of resources. Subclasses are based on whether the actor provides technological, informational, organizational, student support, public relations, or training location support in a classroom, a laboratory, a virtual library, or an external location.
- The course/events class is subdivided according to the type of instructional structure (course, activity, workshop, etc.), the type of the delivery model (technological class, Web self-learning, community of practice, etc.), the type of instructional method (presentation and exercise, case study, problem-based instruction, etc.), and the type of knowledge scenario structure.

The actual IEEE LOM standard seems more adapted to describe materials and documents than other LO categories. An improvement should not consist of extending the official standard with more metadata entries until it becomes impracticable. A possible solution involves distinguishing metadata attributes by taking into account the LO granularity. Hodgins [16] proposes a five-level content hierarchy to classify LOs, where each level is characterized by its own metadata. The lowest level includes raw data and media elements, qualified as the "most" reusable, and the upper level is composed of courses and collections, which are the least reusable. The taxonomy presented in this chapter also proposes different LO levels, the course/events class being aggregates of the other three categories.

Instead of extending the number of LOM attributes, a more effective approach would rely on ontologies to provide new metadata elements and classification schemes that are widely accepted in certain fields, ontologies specifying a resource context, content, and structure [29]. Metadata records in LO repositories should make some semantic description available to computer search agents. According to the W3C Semantic Web proposal [2], such semantics are expressed using XML files structured within the resource description framework (RDF) in the form of subject-attribute-value triples or using the Ontology Web Language (OWL), which is now a Web standard.

Another important international problem, especially prominent in Canada and Europe, concerns bilingual and multilingual metadata editing. Due to the global distribution of LOs over the Internet, it is indispensable to provide translation possibilities by providing multilingual equivalents for all vocabulary-based metadata. There should be an effective control of the indexing language, covering selected concepts and interlanguage equivalency among descriptors. Controlled multilingual vocabulary increases discoverability and interoperability by enabling terms that are "interpreted" in the same way. Many initiatives in Europe (European SchoolNet4, CEN/ISS5) and Canada (CanCore) are working on standardizing the translations of IMS vocabulary. However, standards have yet to be made readily available, and further collaboration is needed between groups and developers.

The main challenge for LO interoperability lies more in the advances of instructional engineering [18] than in the metadata standardization initiatives that actually triggered their initial development. It is believed that instructional engineering is the key to sound and practical solutions to LO aggregation and interoperability.

1.7 Conclusion

This chapter presented some basic concepts and background related to e-learning networked environments from a knowledge management standpoint. After exposing the problematic of building knowledge scenarios and knowledge environments, the principles, methods, and issues related to the design of knowledge networks were summarized. Finally, the problem pertaining to retrieving resources and knowledge in networked environments was addressed.

Knowledge plays a central role in e-learning networked environments. Knowledge management, which promotes structured and higher-level knowledge, puts significant emphasis on the knowledge and the competencies of persons working for the organization. It uses two important processes: knowledge extraction and knowledge assimilation. Knowledge extraction transforms the experts' knowledge of a given domain into organized information or knowledge that can be made available to the entire organization. Knowledge assimilation by those who belong to the organization is the reverse process: transforming organizational information and knowledge into new competencies to be internalized by individual staff members through learning. This is where knowledge engineering meets instructional engineering and learning object production and management. Knowledge models are produced through knowledge engineering and are used as inputs to knowledge and competency acquisition by persons involved in formal or informal training activities. Knowledge modeling also helps represent use cases of a computerized learning or knowledge management system by describing the actors, the operations they perform, and the resources or learning objects they use or produce while processing knowledge of a domain. Conversely, actors involved in these use cases help test, validate, or identify improvements and extensions to the knowledge model or the ontology of a domain.

In the process of designing knowledge networks, considerable effort is spent on critical tasks including the modeling, aggregation, and coordination of learning objects. From the standpoint of a design team or a learning services provider who wants to build a network-based multiactor learning or knowledge management application in a certain context, actors or types of users need to attain some level of competency as defined in reference to a knowledge model. To do this, they must find, obtain, adapt, and launch resources (i.e., documents, applications, services, courses, or learning events), obtained from a network of learning object repositories. The resources can be compounded and integrated into the repository of the application. For this to happen, a design team needs to perform a number of activities including combining aggregation types and methods, controlling and integrating resources in the actors' environments, integrating operations with the resources that are used or produced into executable and visible processes to provide contextual operational interfaces to the actors, among others. Since the components of an e-learning networked environment interact in complex ways, the designer must consider this environment as a unified system dedicated to global learning or knowledge management.

Since current technologies do not support the automation of this task, the need for computer-based systems that support learning object adaptation and repurposing constitutes a real challenge [26]. To make learning objects active and adaptive, one approach consists of imbuing them with some degree of autonomy, i.e., to promote the idea that these objects can become software agents capable of interacting and adapting to meet the knowledge needs of learners.

To efficiently use or reuse learning objects stored in LOR, effective tools need to be developed to discover, extract, and share them. These tools help facilitate interactions, efficient organization, delivery, navigation, and retrieval. In this context, some key problems to tackle are related to the learning object content representation [32], the classification and clustering techniques to learn the categorization of a collection of learning objects, and the extraction of common knowledge.

To fully exploit the potential of images as a source of information, one would have to examine images based on their lower level features and look for hidden characteristics that would explain the behavior of domain level experts as they come into contact with these images. Unlike traditional data mining, considerable complexity is associated with image data mining mainly due to the difficulty of having a proper representation of information about the image [3]. In this context, research on shape-based retrieval [6], image data mining and content based retrieval [7] must be conducted to adapt these technologies to learning object repositories.

References

1. Aukstakalnis, S., Blatner, D. (1992) Silicon Mirage—The Art and Science of Virtual Reality. Berkeley, CA: Peachpit Press.
2. Berners-Lee, T., Hendler, J., Lassila, O. (2001) The semantic web. Scientific American, May.
3. Bimbo, A. (1999) Visual Information Retrieval. San Francisco: Morgan Kaufmann.
4. Davenport, T.H., Prusak, L. (1998) Working Knowledge: How Organizations Manage What They Know. Cambridge, MA: Harvard Business School Press.

5. Duval, E., Robson, R. (2001) Guest editorial on metadata. Interactive learning environments. Special issue. Metadata 9(3): 201–206.
6. El Badawy, O., Kamel, M. (2002) Shape-based image retrieval applied to trademark images. International Journal of Image and Graphics, 2(3): 375–393.
7. El Badawy, O., El-Sakka, M.R., Hassanein, K., Kamel, M. (2001) Image data mining from financial documents based on wavelet features. In: Proceedings of the International Conference on Image Processing, ICIP '2001, Vol. 1., Thessaloniki Greece: IEEE, pp. 1078–1081.
8. El Saddik, A. (2001) Interactive Multimedia Learning. Berlin: Springer-Verlag.
9. El Saddik, A., Fischer S., Steinmetz R. (2001) Reusable multimedia content in Web-based learning systems. IEEE Multimedia, July/September, pp. 30–38.
10. Georganas, N.D. (1997) Advanced Distributed Simulation and Collaborative Virtual Environments. Technical Report by Communications Research Centre, Industry Canada.
11. Gery G. (1997) Granting three wishes through performance-centred design. NATO Communications of the ACM, 40(7): 54–59.
12. Girard J., Paquette, G., Miara, A., Lundgren, K. (1999) Intelligent Assistance for Web-Based TeleLearning. In: S. Lajoie and M. Vivet (eds.), AI in Education—Open Learning Environments. IOS Press.
13. Grass, J. (1998). Reasoning about computational resource allocation: an introduction to anytime algorithms. http://info.acm.org/crossroads/xrds3-1/racra.html.
14. Harasim, L. (1990) Online education: an environment for collaboration and intellectual amplification. In: Harasim, L (ed.), Online Education: Perspectives on a New Environment. New York: Praeger Publishers.
15. Hiltz, R. (1990) Evaluating the virtual classroom. In: Harasim, L (ed.), Online Education: Perspectives on a New Environment. New York: Praeger Publishers, pp. 133–184.
16. Hodgins, H.W. (2002) The future of learning objects. e-Technologies in Engineering Education. A United Engineering Foundation Conference, 11–16 August, Davos, Switzerland.
17. Hosseini, M., Georganas, N.D. (2002) MPEG-4 based recording and replay of collaborative virtual reality sessions. In: Proceedings of the IEEE Virtual Reality 2002 Conference, Orlando, March.
18. Merrill, D. (1994) Principles of Instructional Design. Englewood Cliffs, NJ: Educational Technology Publications.
19. Paquette, G. (2004) Instructional Engineering in Networked Environments. San Francisco: Pfeiffer.
20. Paquette, G. (2004) Instructional Engineering for Network-Based Learning. San Francisco: Pfeiffer/Wiley.
21. Paquette, G. (2002) TeleLearning systems engineering—towards a new ISD model. Journal of Structural Learning, 14(4): 319–354.
22. Paquette, G. (2001) Designing virtual learning centers. In: Adelsberger H., Collis B., Pawlowski J. (Eds.), Handbook on Information Technologies for Education & Training. International Handbook on Information Systems. New York: Springer-Verlag, pp. 249–272.
23. Paquette, G. (1997) Virtual learning centres for XXIst century organisations. In: Verdejo, F., Davies, G. (eds.), The Virtual Campus. London: Chapman & Hall, pp. 18–34.

24. Paquette, G. (1995) Modeling the virtual campus. In: Collis, B., Davies, G. (eds.), Innovating Adult Learning with Innovative Technologies. Amsterdam: Elsevier Science B.V.

25. Paquette G., Aubin C., Crevier, F. (1997) Design and implementation of interactive telelearning scenarios. In: Proceedings of ICDE'97 (International Council for Distance Education). College Park, PA: Penn State University.

26. Paramythis, A., Loidl-Reisinger, S. (2004) Adaptive learning environments and e-learning standards. Electronic Journal of e-Learning, 2(1): 181–194.

27. Reitmayr, G., Schmalstieg, D. (2001) Mobile collaborative augmented reality. In: Proceedings of the 2nd IEEE/ACM International Symposium on Augmented Reality (ISAR'2001), NY, October. http://www.cs.columbia.edu/graphics/isar2001/. http://www.augmented-reality.org/isar2001.

28. Ricciardi-Rigault, C., Henri, F. (1994) Developing tools for optimizing the collaborative learning process. In: Proceedings of the International Distance Education Conference. College Park, PA: Penn State University, June.

29. Staab, S., Studer, R., Schnurr, H.P., Sure, Y. (2001) Knowledge processes and ontologies. IEEE Intelligent Systems, January/February, pp. 26–34.

30. Singhal, S., Zyda, M. (1999) Networked Virtual Environments: Design and Implementation. New York: ACM Press.

31. Stav, J.B., Tsalapatas, H. (2004) Open, dynamic content and e-learning management infrastructure for engineering and natural sciences. Electronic Journal of e-Learning, 2(2):263–272.

32. Tsalapatas, H., Stav, J.B., Kalantzis, C. (2004) Content management middleware for the support of distributed teaching. Electronic Journal of e-Learning, 2(2):263–272.

33. Vossen, G., Westerkamp, P. (2004) Maintenance and exchange of learning objects in a web services based e-learning system. Electronic Journal of e-Learning, 2(2): 292–304.

Part I
Building Knowledge Scenarios

2
Bridging the Gap Between E-Learning Modeling and Delivery Through the Transformation of Learnflows into Workflows

OLGA MARIÑO, RUBBY CASALLAS, JORGE VILLALOBOS, DARIO CORREAL, AND JULIEN CONTAMINES

Abstract. E-learning pedagogical models are described in terms of educational modeling languages (EMLs). IMS-LD is accepted as the standard EML. It allows for the description of multiactor adaptable learning processes. Although some IMS-LD–compatible editing tools are being developed, no delivery platform is yet available. This chapter proposes to bridge this gap by looking at business process modeling languages and execution engines, in particular the Workflow Management Coalition Standard, XPDL. The first two sections of the chapter give the introduction and the context of the work. Section 3 describes IMS-LD as well as existing editing and delivery tools. Section 4 describes XPDL and some editing tools and execution engines. Section 5 proposes a transformation from IMS-LD to XPDL, and Section 6 describes the application developed to implement this transformation. The chapter ends with some conclusions on the work done and on the possibilities it opens to further research and applications.

2.1 Introduction

A unit of learning in a virtual learning environment relates various different models: the actors' model, the resources or learning objects (resources and services) model, the knowledge and competency model, and the learning process model. The last one, also called pedagogical model or learnflow model, is the integrating model, the one that orchestrates all the others. It is through this model that the learning strategy is described in the system. In a structured learning situation, learners follow the process described by this learnflow. Other actors, as well as resources and services, are coordinated by this workflow as well.

To describe those models in a platform-independent language, some educational modeling languages (EML) have been proposed. In 2003, the IMS Global Learning Consortium released the IMS Learning Design specification [15]. IMS-LD is becoming an accepted EML standard specification. This specification allows for the description of the pedagogical process or learnflow of a unit of learning in an educational multiactors workflow called the method. Using a theatrical metaphor, a method can be realized by different plays. Each play is composed of sequential acts; each act includes parallel role-parts, which are associations between roles and activity. Roles are played by one person or a group of persons. Initial role classification distinguishes between learner and staff. The activity is the core of the model. It can be simple or complex (activity structure). It uses an environment composed of learning objects and services and may produce outcomes (products) that enrich the environment. Levels B and C of the specification add variables (properties) and rules to allow for personalization and annotation.

IMS-LD tends to bridge the gap between the design of a course, mainly an on-line course, and its delivery, and opens the way to reuse not only learning objects but also learning scenarios and strategies.

In spite of those promises, IMS-LD raises new challenges, both for the e-learning design and for the e-learning delivery. Although some delivery platforms like COW [44], LAMS [22], and Explor@ [38] are being modified to be level A compatible, no system is yet fully IMS-LD compatible. The IMS-LD community is working on the definition of a standard IMS-LD delivery platform architecture [20,45].

Looking at an apparently different context, business processes are also composed of activities played by actors using resources. Workflow management systems improve business processes by automating tasks, getting the right information to the right place for a specific job function, and integrating information in the enterprise [11]. The integrating component of a workflow management system is the workflow model. A workflow model is an abstraction of a business process. It is a structured organization of individual steps called tasks or activities. An agent or actor is a human being or a machine that can perform a task (enact an activity). Roles are a logical abstraction of one or more actors, usually in terms of functionality. Dependencies determine the execution sequence of activities and the data flow between them [6,23].

Workflow management systems and learning management systems both deal with common issues such as multiactor process modeling and execution, activities synchronization, services and objects integration, role instantiation, etc. Furthermore, both research communities are addressing new challenges such as the process life cycle management, the process evolution, and flexible and open process definition.

In this chapter, we make a comparison of workflow management systems and learning management systems. We focus our discussion on the process (workflow and learnflow) and on the existing tools to support both editing and enacting the process. Section 2 gives the context and the goals of this work. In section 3, we look closer at the learning design standard IMS-LD, both in terms of the language and in terms of the existing tools, while in section 4 we describe this same state of the art for workflow standard, XPDL. We have established a correspondence between IMSLD and XPDL elements, we have developed a transformation from IMSLD to XPDL based on this correspondence, and we have implemented this transformation in an application called LDX. The fifth part describes the transformation and the sixth the LDX set of tools. The chapter ends with a broader view on how this transformation allows us to support automatically the e-learning process, and with some conclusions at the model and language level as well as at the practical tool level.

2.2 Context

This section gives the context and a broad description of the work presented in the chapter. We start by describing and comparing the two problems we are dealing with: e-learning support and business process support. Although different in nature and domain, these problems establish some common requirements to supporting tools, while still having particular specific requirements. Section 2.2 sketches the main differences between e-learning and workflow management tools. The third section states the goal of our research, while in the fourth section we present the approach we took to develop this work. We end by summarizing the main results of our work, which will be detailed in the rest of the chapter.

2.2.1 Looking at the Problem

Both e-learning system and workflow system tend to solve the same very general problem of having an (or many) actor(s) executing an activity or graph of activities and producing something (Fig. 2.1). Therefore, the three main components of such a system in both cases are actor, activity, and product.

The goal of an e-learning system is the "learning." The main actor, the learner, is expected to learn, to acquire new knowledge and competencies, through the execution of different structured learning activities. E-learning systems' main component is the actor-learner. This emphasis on the actor-learner establishes particular requirements on e-learning systems: the process should be defined taking into account the learner's profile; the system should allow for run-time process adaptation based on conditions of the learner; the learner model must be rich and known to the process. Even resources proposed to the actor to execute an activity should take into account the actor profile.

In the business process context, on the other hand, what matters most is the product, the final outcome of the process. The main aspects of a workflow system are the product and the efficiency of the process regarding this production. Actors are secondary components; they are seen as resources whose importance lies in helping produce the final product. Particular requirements in this context include finding an assignment function from people to roles, decomposing the process in an efficient way, and optimizing the actor's participation. There are also particular requirements concerning the product: version management, satisfaction of a set of required properties, the possibility to be used and consulted outside the workflow system, etc.

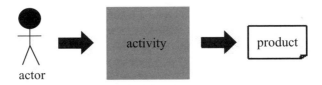

FIGURE 2.1. E-learning and workflow conceptualization.

In terms of the process or main activity, there are also some common issues. Both processes can be described by a graph of activities. Each activity is done by a particular type of actor, called a role. Normally, more than one role (actor) is involved in a process. Multiactor coordination and synchronization is thus required. Time events as well as other external events may affect the process execution.

However, there are also some differences. E-learning processes represent pedagogical models. While an e-learning pedagogical model might be inspired in an existing face-to-face training, new models can exist without a corresponding face-to-face model. In addition, when taking into account personal differences, the model of a same unit of learning is instantiated in different ways for different students. In the business world, on the other hand, workflows do normally represent existing documented enterprise processes. Different instances of the same workflow are identical copies except for the actors' assignment to roles and timing information, and they should produce quite identical products.

2.2.2 Looking at the Solution

The requirements identified in the preceding section are translated in some properties of the corresponding support systems. Both e-learning and workflow management systems have a formal way to describe multiactor processes. Activities in these processes may be organized with different patterns (sequence, choice, parallelism, and synchronization points). Responsibility for the execution of activities in the processes is defined in terms of actor types, also called roles. In an instantiation of the process, those roles are associated with actual actors. To do an activity, the actor has available services and resources that are partially or completely determined in the process model. To execute (enact/deliver) the multiactor process, both e-learning and workflow systems have to have control and synchronization mechanisms.

Having the actor as the heart of the process imposes particular requirements for e-learning systems. The model of the learner is normally part of the system, or at least there are ways to pass learner information into the system. Learner information must include knowledge and competencies. The whole process and possibly each activity should also have a reference on prerequisites and objectives. Thus, e-learning system should have some kind of knowledge modeling component.

Having the product and its production inside a business context, as the heart of the process, imposes particular requirements for the workflow management systems. To satisfy those requirements, workflow management systems normally include product management as well as different services and tools to manipulate the process (evaluation, measurement, audit, etc.). To support a broad variety of business processes, workflow management systems and workflow models offer a large span of control and synchronization patterns. Finally, they offer well-defined interfaces to communicate with other business applications.

From a practical point of view, the workflow management community has well-established process languages and various open-source enactment tools. On the other hand, the e-learning community is actively working on the development of pedagogical model editing tools that help produce IMS-LD models, but no e-learning platform is yet fully compatible with the standard e-learning modeling language, IMS-LD.

2.2.3 The Goal: Bridging the Gap Between E-Learning Editing and Delivery

The goal of our research is to benefit e-learning systems from advances made by the workflow management systems community, and at the same time to explore personalization and knowledge management integration in workflow management systems.

The work presented in this chapter addresses the first goal: more precisely, to bridge the currently existing gap between learnflow editing and learnflow execution by allowing a learnflow expressed in a standard educational modeling language to be executed by a workflow engine, capable of executing the process described in a standard process description language. To reach this goal we have defined three subgoals:

– To study e-learning and workflow models so as to identify common issues and differences and to establish a common vocabulary to describe them
– To define a translation schema, allowing us to express the control aspects of e-learning models in terms of the richer set of control elements of process models.
– To build a tool to implement this translation and to validate the results

2.2.4 Methodological Approach

Our starting hypothesis is twofold: we propose that pedagogical models can be described and delivered using the standard educational modeling language IMS-LD, and that workflow processes can be described and executed using the standard business process definition language, XPDL.

Based on this hypothesis, we have defined the following project steps:

– To express both languages (IMS-LD and XPDL) in a common language to facilitate their comparison and translation from one to the other
– To abstract all components that are not part of the control model, and to propose a translation schema from IMS-LD to XPDL. This translation is guided by IMS-LD syntactical structures; it takes into account every important aspect of the source language (IMS-LD).
– To identify IMS-LD elements that do not have a direct and natural translation into XPDL, and to propose a way of using XPDL extended attributes to describe them so that an XPDL compatible tool may handle the document.

2.2.5 Main Results

The main results of our project, which will be detailed in sections 5 and 6 of this chapter, include:

- A translation schema to translate IMS-LD into XPDL
- A clear identification of the principal difficulties of this translation
- The implementation of a set of tools to support the learning design lifecycle

2.3 IMS-Learning Design as an Educational Modeling Language

This section presents the educational modeling languages that allow for the description of e-learning processes and more specifically the IMS-LD specification. We start by giving a generic reference model for e-learning systems, one of whose components is the learnflow or pedagogical model. The pedagogical model is described by an educational modeling language (EML). The second section describes the main elements of an EML. In section 3.3, we present the particular case of the educational modeling language standard IMS-LD. Section 3.4 presents some of the tools to support course design using IMS-LD and its delivery.

2.3.1 E-Learning System Reference Model

There is no widely accepted e-learning reference model. In spite of that, most e-learning systems include the following components, not always well differentiated: A kernel, is the e-learning operating system, the learnflow execution engine. This engine executes a process described by a pedagogical modeling component. Actors are described elsewhere and actors' profiles are taken into account by the engine too. Resources, tools, and services are managed by one or more components in charge of finding, installing, launching them when needed. Finally, some systems also include a more or less elaborated knowledge component to describe at a knowledge level the activities, the resources, and the actors. Figure 2.2 shows this conceptual reference architecture model.

2.3.2 Educational Modeling Languages

A learnflow or pedagogical model is described using an EML, which includes a vocabulary or set of words to describe a process like activity, activity structure, role, and outcome, as well as pedagogical concepts like objectives, learner, and support activity. It also includes a grammar, a set of relations between these concepts, as well as consistency rules. An EML normally has an XML representation. The XML representation is used by the delivery system or learning management systems to run the described e-learning process. Thus, the XML file is the interface between the modeling of a learning process and its execution.

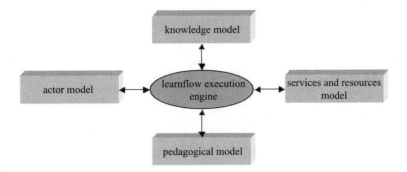

FIGURE 2.2. E-learning conceptual architecture model.

The main elements of an EML are the concepts of process, also called method, activity graph, or unit of learning, and the activity.

– The process is the structure describing the learnflow, the way in which activities are organized. It reflects a pedagogical strategy and is the backbone that connects the other elements of the model. Most EMLs allow the modeling of sequences of activities, of choice and decomposition structures, and of distribution and synchronization of parallel activities.
– The activity is the building element of the process. It describes the actual pedagogical action. An activity is related to other elements such as the type of actor who must execute the activity and the resources and services proposed to him to do it. The activity information includes pedagogical objectives and prerequisites, proposed time and eventually outcome information, and evaluation criteria and weight.

The EMLs are expected to have the expressive power required to describe any pedagogical model and to be neutral regarding pedagogical theories. Although it is true that any model can be described in terms of activities, relations between activities, roles and actors, resources and services, and objectives [14], EMLs' focus on process and activities makes them more suitable to represent pedagogical models centered on the activity than, for instance, those centered on collaboration and actors' interaction [27].

Languages such as MISA-MOT [36], COWL [43], and EML [21] are educational modeling languages in the sense that they offer a vocabulary to describe pedagogical models, a grammar to relate this vocabulary, and an XML binding. Nevertheless, their scope is local: their XML binding is understandable only by their own delivery platforms.

In the next section, we describe the educational modeling language IMS-Learning Design (IMS-LD) [15], which is a specification proposed as an EML standard by the IMS Global Consortium in 2003 [15]. As the IMS Global Consortium groups the main players in the e-learning community, one might expect that IMS-LD will be widely accepted and that model editing tools as well as e-learning delivery platforms will be developed or transformed to be compatible with this new standard.

2.3.3 Conceptual Elements of IMS-LD

IMS-LD is the standard educational modeling language approved by the IMS Learning Consortium in 2003 [15]. It is inspired by the educational modeling language EML [21], developed by the Open University of the Netherlands. Its goal is to provide a framework for the formal description of any education and learning process. It helps relate other specifications such as LOM [12] for the learning objects, RDCEO [13] for competency modeling, and LIP [17] and e-Portfolio [16] for the learner model.

To ease the implementation of these tools, the standard defines three levels. Level A ensures a basic behavior, level B adds properties and conditions, and level C adds notifications. The basic concepts of IMS-LD are shown in Figure 2.3.

Process (or the method): The process or learnflow is built into IMS-LD on a theatrical metaphor. A learning situation called a *method* in IMS-LD corresponds in the metaphor to a theatrical piece. As such, a piece can be played in different ways (the plays). A *play* is composed of sequential acts. In an *act*, the different roles or characters of the piece execute in parallel their script. In IMS-LD, the script to be executed can be an *activity* or a group of structured activities (*activity-structure*).

Activity: IMS-LD distinguishes between two types of activity: *learning activity* and *support activity*. The people involved in a learning situation may thus be

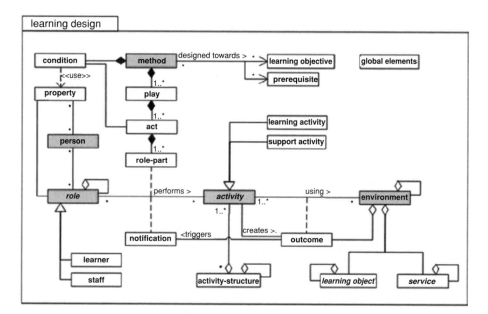

FIGURE 2.3. IMS-LD conceptual model [15].

assigned the role of a *learner* or a supporting role as *staff* member. Each activity is executed by a role (role-*part* association) using an *environment* composed of *learning objects* and services. The product of an activity, its *outcome*, may be integrated into the environments of other activities. A set of *prerequisites* and *learning objectives* may be tied both to the method and to the activities.

Role: The role *learner* can be modeled in a more explicit and rich way using other standards such as the portfolio, the LIP, or the competency model. IMS-LD allows for the description of learner information through the elements called properties. As explained in the next section, properties may be local or global and thus they help describe, among other data, learner information that is passed to or from the process and learner information that is generated and used only inside the process, possibly to personalize the training. During execution, the group of data that correspond to the learner properties is called the *dossier*.

Local Properties, Global Properties, and Conditions: Properties and conditions are part of the level B specification. Local properties allow for the management of information of persons, of roles, and of the learning process during the delivery of a learning situation (the execution of an LD run), while global properties act as parameters to interface the execution of the process with its context (institutional norms and conditions, learner portfolios, academic program data, etc.). Property values may be changed when an act or an activity is finished or when a rule is activated—its condition is satisfied. The modification of a property value may activate further changes, such as the ending of an activity, the hiding or showing of an activity, the generation of a notification, or the modification of other properties. In this way, by combining rules (called conditions in IMSLD) and properties, one can personalize the e-learning process and synchronize activities inside an act [27].

Notifications: Level C of the specification adds the concept of notification. A notification is a message sent automatically to a role when a condition is satisfied. This condition may be the ending of an activity, an act, a play or the whole method, the modification of the value of a property, or having an expression evaluated as true in the if part of a condition.

2.3.4 Tools for Learnflows

Many initiatives are being developed around the IMS-LD specification since its release in 2003. Research and development teams are working on the development or adjustment of editing, visualization, and delivery tools. Yet no full set of tools exists to support the whole process, and much of the work is still in a prototyping phase. In this section, we present some already-available tools for creating, manipulating, and delivering LD.

Editing Tools: Editing tools are applications that produce an IMS-LD document, that is, an XML document that is IMS-LD compliant. This document describes a learning design in terms of its different components: its global or pedagogical structure, which includes the method, the plays, the acts, the activities, and the activity structures; its learning environments with the associated learning objects and services; and its properties, prerequisites, learning objectives, expressions, notifications, and roles.

Editors may also produce partial IMS-LD documents. It may produce a "content independent" pedagogical structure, that is, an XML document still compliant with IMS-LD but with only the pedagogical structure and possibly the roles, the services, and the properties defined; neither the prerequisites nor the objectives or the learning objects are specified. We call this content-independent LD an LD template. Its main interest concerns the possibility of having a repository of frameworks of pedagogical strategies from which to create a learning unit. Actually, there is no editing tool supporting the management of LD templates. The LAMS system [22] use templates, but the system is not yet fully compliant with IMS-LD.

MOT+ Editor

At the Laboratoire en Informatique Cognitive et Environnements de Formation (LICEF) research center, development efforts have been placed on authoring methods editors and tools to facilitate delivery. The Méthode d'Ingénierie pédagogique de formations à distance (MISA) method is a mature instructional design method produced and refined in the last 10 years [37]. It uses a graphic educational graphical modeling tool, MOT, and it is supported by a Web-based design system, Atelier distribué d'ingénierie de systèmes d'apprentissage (*ADISA*).

In the context of the *Lornet project* [26], the IMS-LD learning level A specification has been transposed using the MOT+ [4] graphical modeling tool to develop an IMS-LD editor (Fig. 2.4). All IMS-LD objects [method, play, act, activities (three types), roles (two types), environment with services and learning objects] have been specified. Parallel to this work, a built-in parser to the MOT+ tool is being completed to produce an IMS-LD–compliant XML output.

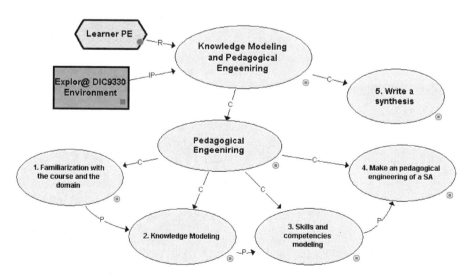

FIGURE 2.4. An LD in MOT+ editor.

Besides that, work will be undertaken, on the one hand, to adapt the MISA method to help designers produce compliant IMS-LD designs and, on the other hand, to extend the Explor@2 delivery system to support the production of run-time design instances. Currently, this delivery platform is not fully compliant with IMS-LD, although it does already take into account some multiactor issues. The goal is to enable Explora@2 to import IMS-LD–compliant courses.

Mot+ allows exporting LD in the XML format-compliant IMS-LD but not in a content package compliant with *IMS Content package* specification. In addition, the user cannot describe resources with *LOM specification* or plug a learning object stored in a learning object repository (LOR). However, the *LICEF research center* developed a learning object repository within the *eduSource project* [8] and a LOM editor (*LomPad* [24]). In the future, these three systems will be linked.

The validation process happens during the exportation in XML format compliant with IMS-LD schema. In addition, a manual is available that presents the graphical language and a light methodology to develop an LD.

RELOAD Editor

RELOAD [19] is a project funded by the *Joint Information Systems Committee* (JISC) of Great Britain. RELOAD is also the name of the project tools. RELOAD is initially dedicated to the development of learning object management tools and to research on learning object management in collaborative online environments. During 2003, plans to develop a LD editor based on their SCORM [39] editor were put forth. Now, this editor supports all the three levels (A, B, and C) of IMS-LD.

RELOAD allows describing resources with LOM metadata, using these resources to elaborate an instructional model. This model can be compliant with SCORM 1.2 or IMS-LD. Besides, it makes it possible to generate the package in according to *IMS content package* specification.

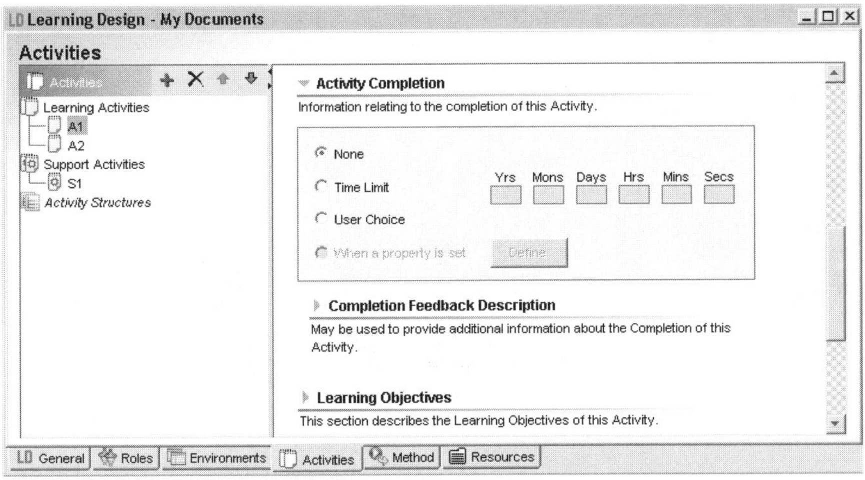

FIGURE 2.5. An LD in RELOAD editor.

As opposed to MOT+, RELOAD is a frame-based editor, not a graphical one. Different tabs allow defining the different components of the LD (Fig. 2.5). The editing process is constraint with frame-based solution. There is no validation functionality because syntax mistakes are inhibited. For help, a manual is available in which users can find a light process[1] to build an LD.

Alfanet Editor

Alfanet Editor [41] is being developed by UNED (Madrid, Spain) within the European *Alfanet project*. Alfanet aims to create methods and tools for active and adaptable learning. Alfanet Editor is a module of the Alfanet LMS prototype. The user can create courses compliant with e-learning standards. Like RELOAD, this editor is frame-based (Fig. 2.6); users can produce a content package, and local resources are managed with LOM specification. The first difference is that there is a connection with a learning object repository. During the editing process, the user can retrieve resources within this repository. The second difference is that Alfanet editor is only compliant with the level A of the IMS LD specification. A user manual explains the editor functionalities; no methodological design approach is proposed in the manual.

Whereas MOT+ and RELOAD installations are easy and without specific preliminary setup, the user must install the *Groove Workspace* application to launch Alfanet Editor. On the other hand, once installed, this system proposes communication tools and allows collaborative work.

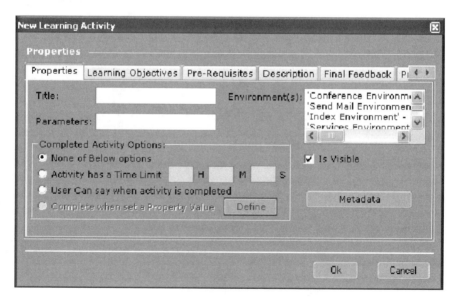

FIGURE 2.6. An LD in Alfanet editor.

---

[1] Light process is a process to construct main IMSLD components and elements.

Execution tools: A valid IMS-LD document may be used to actually produce a learning environment. The same IMS-LD document can be used to produce many particular learning environments in the same way as the same face-to-face course may be offered in different sessions at different times, for different groups of students with different teachers. As for those courses, a process of describing the particular session is needed. In terms of IMS-LD, this production process makes the association between an LD document and a session or run: starting time, learning community, etc. Such a session is called an *IMS-LD instance* or an *IMS-LD run*. This production stage can be supported by a specific tool or by the execution tool itself.

An IMS-LD run is executed or delivered to the different members of the learning community (learners, teachers, tutors, experts, etc.) through a delivery platform. Each one of these actors has his/her own view of the run, which includes his/her personal properties, activity trace, etc. Each of these views is called an *IMS-LD personalized run* or *IMS-LD personalized instance*.

Finally, all those states may be applied to IMS-LD in all three levels, A, B, and C, thus having, for instance, IMS-LD instantiations of IMS-LD documents that are level A compliant.

Efforts were concentrated on edition tools since 2003. In the last years, some companies and research centers start adapting their delivery system in order to import LD documents and execute them. For example, Blackboard Inc. is adapting EduBox Player [7] and integrating it in its popular e-learning platform. EduBox Player is an execution environment for EML-compliant pedagogical model. IMS-LD was inspired in EML, so adapting EduBox Player to be IMS-LD compliant should be straightforward.

In Canada, the e-learning delivery system Explor@2 of LICEF research center is being modified to import the LD documents produced by the MOT+ Editor.

Probably the most advanced effort in this direction is CopperCore [32]. CopperCore application is a sequel to research and tool development carried out by OUNL (Open University of the Netherlands) researchers in the EduBox project, sponsored by the EU AlFanet project, and launched in February 2004. Copper-Core is an open-source project, consisting of a set of Application Program Interface (APIs) allowing the production and delivery of an IMS-LD unit of learning. These APIs cover publication, administration, and a run-time engine for all levels of IMS-LD. With the collaboration of SLED Project [40], CopperCore can be used like a Web service simple object access protocol (SOAP). For the time being, no available e-learning delivery system embeds CopperCore engine.

2.4 XPDL as a Business Process Language

There exist many languages and models for representing business processes. Some of the most widely known are BPMN [3], BPEL4WS [1], WSBPEL [31], and XPDL [46]. These languages have different notations to describe data flows, transitions, and control of the process being modeled. Some of these notations describe these elements with graphical languages. Most of them propose an XML binding to facilitate the export of the process to different enactment engines.

Various groups and associations are actively working on the definition of standard models and languages that allow for the description of both the business process and of its instantiation and execution. OASIS [31] is refining the language WSBPEL, WfMC [11] has proposed XPDL, and BPMI [2] is responsible of a notational model for process description called BPMN [3].

As for e-learning systems, the main interest of workflow or business process modeling languages is to provide a vocabulary and a grammar sufficiently rich as to express any business model in a way that can be understood and implemented by a workflow management system.

In this section, we study in detail the process modeling language XPDL, XML Process Description Language. XPDL is the language proposed by the Workflow Management Coalition and it is part of a broader architecture proposed as the reference model for the definition, implementation, and interrelation of application intended to support the modeling and execution of business process workflows. Section 2.4.1 presents the WfMC reference model. Section 2.4.2 presents the XPDL language, and in section 2.4.3, we describe various existing support tools.

2.4.1 Workflow Reference Model

The Workflow Management Coalition (WfMC) [11] defines a workflow as being the total or partial automatization of an industrial process. The workflow helps automatically support processes that include the circulation of information, documents, or tasks between participants based on a set of rules. A workflow management system defines, manages, and executes workflows. Workflow execution, also called enactment, consists of the execution of its composing activities as well as of the applications and environments associated with these activities. The workflow control model determines the execution order of those elements.

The workflow reference model proposed by the WfMC is described in terms of a central component, the system engine or workflow enactment service, and of five interfaces between this engine and the other components of the system (Fig. 2.7). Interface 1 makes the link between the engine and process definition tools. It is through this interface that a process description—an XPDL document—is passed to the engine to be executed. Interface 2 makes the link with the client applications. Interface 3 helps connect and launch the tools that are used in the different activities of the workflow. Interface 4 allows for the interaction between different enactment engines. Finally, interface 5 describes the process audit and management services.

2.4.2 Process Description Languages or Workflow Models

Interface 1 of the workflow reference model gives the enactment engine the definition of a process it has to execute. The definition of a process is "the representation of a business process in a form that support automated manipulation, such as modeling, or enactment by a workflow management system" [46]. This definition or model includes a structured organization of individual steps called tasks or activities; the definition of agents or human actors who can execute a particular task;

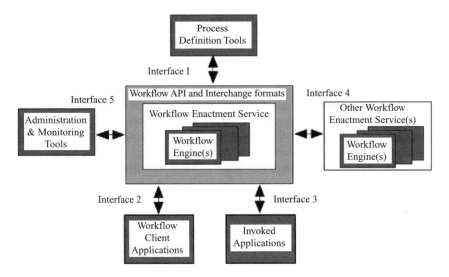

FIGURE 2.7. Workflow reference model [11].

the roles or actor types and the dependencies or transitions that describe the activities' execution order and conditions, and finally the resources; and the external
applications that are available to the actor of an activity [6,23].

The main component of the workflow model is the workflow itself. This flow
includes all the activities of the process as well as the transition rules between these
activities and the data flow between them. The concept of transition and control
pattern is central to the model. Definition process languages propose different
kinds of transitions and control pattern (sequence, parallel paths, synchronization,
multiple choice, single choice, etc.).

2.4.3 The Conceptual Elements of XPDL

The XML Process Definition Language (XPDL) was produced by the Workflow
Management Coalition (WfMC) in 2002 [46]. Version 2.0 of the language is being
defined and a draft was published in February 2005. This new version is fully
compatible with version 1.0 and its main modification is its intended compatibility
with the Business Process Modeling Notation (BPMN) defined by BPMi [2].

The goals of XPDL are (1) to provide a business process representation language in a way that allows for automated manipulation: modeling, instantiation,
simulation, visualization, audit, documentation, etc., and (2) to clearly distinguish
between the process definition and the process execution and to provide an interface between the process modeling and the process execution so as to be able to
link different modeling tools with different execution engines.

XPDL describes the high-level entities that appear in a process definition
(Fig. 2.8).

The rest of this section presents the main elements of the XPDL language, in
its version 1.0. First, we present the elements that have a scope global to various

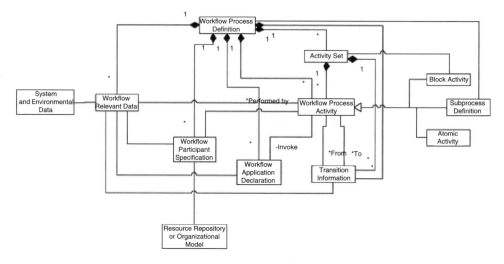

FIGURE 2.8. XPDL metamodel [46].

process definitions, then the ones that are local, whose scope is only one process definition.

The Package Structure: In a XPDL definition, the element with the broader scope is the package. It contains elements shared by all the processes inside it as well as the definition of each of these processes. Table 2.1 describes the most relevant elements of a package.

The Structure of a Process: The building piece of a process is the activity. A *workflow process activity* represents a task to be made. An activity is executed by a participant or by a resource (link with the *workflow participant specification* or with the *workflow relevant data)* eventually using an application (link with the *workflow application declaration*).

An activity may be a whole subprocess having its own activities and related to the main process by the subprocess definition elements. An activity may be a structured

TABLE 2.1. Elements of a XPDL package. The graphic icons are the graphical representation of these elements in the graphical editor, JaWE [9]

Element	Name	Description /Use
	Workflow Participant Specification	Participants are part of the organization model.
	Workflow Application Declaration	XPDL allows the declaration of tools or applications that will be invoked by the workflow process.
	Workflow Relevant Data	Represents the variables in a package definition, used by activities, processes, and subprocesses.
	External Packages	Definitions in other XPDL packages that could be referenced in this package.

TABLE 2.2. Elements of an XPDL process. The graphic icons are the graphical representation of these elements in the graphical editor, JaWE [9]

Element	Name	Description /Use
	Workflow Process	This element represents a workflow process definition.
	Generic Activity	Represents indivisible steps in a workflow process.
	Route Activity	This kind of activity is used for control flow and synchronization of other activities.
	Block Activity	Set of activities and transitions enclosed in a single activity.
	Subflow	This kind of activity represents a new process definition. This process could be invoked in a synchronous or asynchronous way.
	Transition Information	A transition represents the link between two activities. It contains a condition to determine if it will be activated or not.

block of activities, the *activity block*, composed of a set of more basic activities, the *activity set*. Finally, an activity can be an atomic task, the atomic activity. Activities can be *generic*, if they make part of the process, or *route* activities, used for control purposes. One particular route activity is the empty activity (Table 2.2).

Participants and Roles: *Workflow participant specification* contains information on the potential actors of the different activities. These participants may be human or machine agents. The specification includes the possibility of linking this element with a bank of participants or resources. Another concept, the *workflow application declaration* establishes the interface between the workflow and the applications and services it needs to call to support a particular task.

Relevant Data: XPDL specifies two types of data: the workflow relevant data, which are data generated during the enactment of the process, and the system and environment data, which help describe the execution context. Both types of data can be used in the activities and in the transition condition as well as interface parameters to pass data to other system components.

Extended Attributes: These elements represent information that can be interpreted and used by the tools, allowing for the particularization of the process to some tool properties.

2.4.4 Tools for Workflows

In this section, we analyze some existing tools that help define and execute process described in XPDL. Each tool is described in terms of its functionality. For each one, we present the main extended attributes used to implement particular aspects not specified in the standard.

JaWE: A Process Editing Tool: XPDL representation of processes may be complex and difficult to visualize and trace in a textual way. Graphical editing tools should be used. The new version (version 2.0) of XPDL includes information that helps manipulate the display of the process main elements by any design tool. Each application will be able to create a special element called *nodegraphinfo* to store information on the presentation of the elements. Information generated by one application could be reused by another one.

However, existing process editors still work with version 1.0 of XPDL. In this version, the only way to deal with the presentation of elements is the use of extended attributes.

Enhydra JaWE [9] is a tool to design workflows compatible with XPDL version 1.0. JaWE is a graphical workflow editor. With JaWEi+ is possible to design a process in a graphical way and generate its XPDL representation. It is also possible to import XPDL process description and to visualize them graphically.

Being built on Java 1.4, JaWE installation requirements are minimal. It runs on UNIX and Windows. Additional required libraries are distributed with the application.

A process in JaWE is contained into a project. The definition of a process in JaWE is made top-down in two steps. Entities at the package level, such as workflow application declaration, workflow relevant data, workflow participant specification, extended attributes, external packages, and data types, are defined in the first step. In the second step, one can create workflow processes inside this package. Inside a workflow process, one can define the following entities: process definition, application declaration, relevant data, transitions, and process activities.

JaWE offers the possibility of validating the process defined, according to XPDL version 1.0 specification. Thus, while building the package and the composing process flows, the designer may validate it and identify the wrong parts.

JaWE uses extended attributes for the activities, the transitions, and the workflow process. These attributes are explained in Table 2.3.

TABLE 2.3 XPDL extended attributes in JaWE

Extended attributes in the activities	Use
Participant ID	Role in charge of the activity
X Offset	Offset in the x axis of the activity
Y Offset	Offset in the y axis of the activity
Extended attributes in transitions	Use
Routing Type	Transition type
Extended attributes in the process	Use
Start of workflow	Initial activity of the workflow
End of workflow	Final activity of the workflow
Participant visual order	Order of presentation of the participants in the editor

Process Execution Tools: A second group of workflow tools concern workflow execution engines. These engines can import business process definitions, described in XPDL, and launch and execute an instance of the process described.

There are quite a few workflow-editing tools, and various execution engines have been developed, many of which are GPL licensed, and many others are commercial products. In this section, we describe two of these execution models: WFMOpen [5] and Enhydra Shark [10]. Both are widely used; they are GPL and LGPL licensed, respectively, and both use J2EE technology in their implementation.

WFMOpen

WFMOpen is a tool developed on J2EE that offers a component for process execution based on a set of Java interfaces. This component is based on the WfMC specifications as well as on the specification *Workflow Management Facility* V 1.2 of OMG [34].

From a functional perspective, WFMOpen offers services to import process definitions defined in XPDL, to instantiate them, to manage the created instances, to assign participants to the instances, to assign products to the activities, to call external tools, and to control the workflow of these instances. In addition, it offers workflow monitoring and management services as well as some services for the construction of client applications. The workflow components may manage an unlimited number of instances of the original process. These instances, once launched, are independent of the original process definition.

From a logical perspective, the tool has a central component called Danet's Workflow Component that offers the basic functionalities of the execution engine in charge of the execution of the process instances. This component has three sub-components: Workflow Core, Workflow Engine, and Resource Assignment Facility.

The Workflow Core facilitates process creation and instantiation and controls the execution of the created instances. The Workflow Engine subcomponent is in charge of the activation of the activities, and the subcomponent Resource Assignment Facility is in charge of the resource assignments.

The main component, as well as its subcomponents, is implemented through five packages that compose the API of the Workflow Engine. Those APIs are the component workflow API, the workflow management system API, an API for the invocation of application control agents, an API to use the resource assignment service, and an API to use the resource management system.

The workflow component uses a set of extended attributes inside the imported XPDL process definitions. The list of extended attributes used by this component is presented in the Table 2.4.

Enhydra Shark

Enhydra Shark is a workflow engine based on WfMC and object management group (OMG) specification; thus, it used XPDL 1.0 as the process description language.

TABLE 2.4 XPDL Extended attributes used by the WFMOpen workflow component

Attribute	Use
Implementation	Extension used inside the declaration of applications. This attribute is used to specify the behavior of the tool to be used.
Remove Closed Process	Establishes how the engines will discard the ended processes.
Debug	Indicates if the processes are started in a debugging mode or not.
Audit Event Selection	Indicates which events will be audited during the process execution.
Store Audit Events	Indicates if the selected events will persist in an event log or not.
Deferred Choice	Indicates if a transition AND-Split must be executed following the pattern Deferred Choice.

Shark may be used as an embedded library in different types of applications, either in Web environments or in more traditional client/server applications.

The most important feature of Shark is the fact that it does not use extended attributes for the process definitions. The process definitions handled by Shark are easily transferred to other editing or execution tools.

Moreover, thanks to its common object request broker architecture (CORBA) [33] interface, Shark may be used by different clients. It offers also a mechanism to make the integration with LDAP [25] for the use of information on established organizational structures.

2.5 Translation Scheme

The scope of the translation scheme is the model of control from IMS-LD to XPDL. Only level A is considered.

This section presents a common vocabulary in order to describe, in the same terms, the subjacent models of control of IMS-LD and XPDL. The reason to introduce this vocabulary is to avoid the ambiguities raised because of the use of the same terms with different meanings in the models.

The first subsection presents the elements of the static model; the second subsection presents the elements of the dynamic model; the third subsection describes the model of control of IMS-LD; the fourth subsection describes the model of control of XPDL; and, finally, the fifth subsection shows the proposed translation.

2.5.1 Static Aspects of the Common Model

This subsection introduces some static elements of a process model. They are an abstraction of the main characteristics of the e-flows and the w-flows:

Role: A role defines a type of actor by characterizing its responsibilities and/or abilities, and by associating a name. An actor can play various roles and many actors can play the same role.

Datatype: A datatype defines the structural characteristics (syntactical) that represent the possible elements in the domain of application. There are (predefined) simple datatypes and complex datatypes defined by the use. A simple datatype has a name and a set of values. A complex datatype has a name and a description of its composition.

Activity: An activity is a discrete task with a start, an end, and a well-defined objective. The activity has associated a role, which describes the responsible actor of the task, and, it can have a set of services and tools to be used by the actor, if required. Moreover, an activity is characterized by a set of input data (to be used by the actor) and a set of output data (to be produced by the actor). An activity can be instantiated only once or multiple times simultaneously.

Transition: A transition defines an order relationship between two activities.

Process: A process is a structured set of activities that share a defined common objective. *Structured* means that the activities are executed following an established order defined by some rules in the model of control and based on transitions. A process has an execution context consisting of a set of data (name and type). This context allows the manipulation of information shared by all the activities in the process; the data in the context are used to make decisions at run time.

Services and Tools: Services and tools are elements not controlled by the execution engine; nevertheless, an actor can use them, based on his own decisions, to achieve the objective of the activity. The tools are used by the actor to transform data, whereas the services are used by the actor to acquire knowledge, communicate something, participate in a discussion, etc.

2.5.2 Dynamic Aspects of the Common Model

This subsection introduces some concepts that appear at run time.

Actor: The actor is responsible for transforming or creating data to accomplish the objective of an activity by means of services and tools to perform the associated task. The execution model should include a policy to assign actors to instances of activities.

Data: Data are the values that elements in the application domain can assume. These elements are typed and have a name.

Process Instance: A process can have several instances at run time, and each one serves to accomplish the defined objective in the process definition. Each instance has its own execution to be used by the activity instances of the process.

Activity Instance: When a process is instantiated, at the same time all its activities are instantiated too. An activity instance can be in one of the three states: inactive, active, or finished. Each activity instance has its own execution context consisting of the received input data and the global data of the process instance to which the activity belongs.

The execution engine follows the order defined by the transitions and uses the process and activity context to determine if a transition can take place or not. The set of transitions arriving at an activity determines if the activity can be initiated

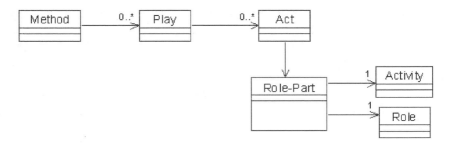

FIGURE 2.9. Conceptual structure of the model of control in IMS-LD.

or not. Furthermore, it should be defined if the activity instance will be executed in sequential or parallel mode.

Model of Control: The model of control includes the elements whose life cycle is administrated by the execution engine. It means that the elements whose execution is controlled by the actor are not part of the model of control.

2.5.3 Model of Control of IMS-LD

IMS-LD uses a theatrical metaphor to define pedagogical processes in a standard way. Furthermore, the metaphor predefines some control structures assuming similar to every pedagogical model.

In the theatrical metaphor, the notion of transition is not explicit, although the metaphor establishes an organization among the activities, given as a result a predefined topology of control. Figure 2.9 shows the conceptual structure of the model of control in IMS-LD.

The execution engine interprets the structure shown in Figure 2.10 as follows: the plays, in a method, are executed simultaneously. The acts in a play are executed in a sequential way following the order in which they were defined, i.e., an act is not initialized until its predecessor was finished. The role-parts are executed in parallel. The activity-structure, in a role-part, can have *sequential* or *selection* type. If the type is *sequential*, the set of activities associated with the activity-structure is

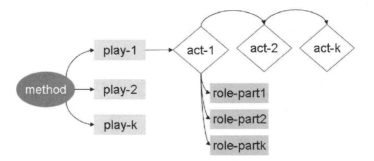

FIGURE 2.10. Execution of a method.

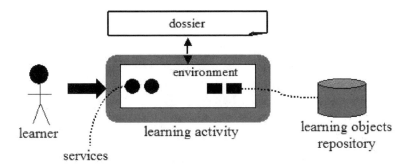

FIGURE 2.11. Execution of a learning activity.

executed in a sequential way. If, on the contrary, the type is *selection*, the role-part finishes when a number of activities, greater or equal to a predefined minimum, finishes. Finally, if any of the activities in the role-part is a support activity and this has associated a group of actors, the execution engine has to create an instance for each actor in the group, and the support activity finishes when all the instances finish.

Figure 2.11 illustrates a learning activity being performed by a learner. In a structure called the *environment*, the actor has available services, tools, and learning objects. The use of the elements in the environment is decided on and controlled by the learner and not by the execution engine. The input data to the activity are values of *properties* and they are in a set called a *dossier*. The actor performing the activity can modify the data in the dossier. The actor decides when the activity is finished.

Levels B and C of IMS-LD imply an extension to the model of control. In that case, the execution engine should take into account that some elements, in particular, the activities can become visible or invisible inside a process instance. It means that the graph of control is changed at runtime.

2.5.4 Model of Control of XPDL

The XPDL model does not have a common metaphor because there are a vast number of application contexts for the workflow process. It can range from a process to fulfill a request for a credit in a financial company, to a process to develop software. For this reason, the language has to provide the necessary structures to describe different control flows.

In XPDL a process is defined as a set of activities and a set of transitions, where the transitions define a partial order among the activities. There are four types of basic activities: (1) simple, which represents a punctual activity or a routing activity; (2) a block activity, which is a group of activities perceived as a unit, (3) a subflow, which represents a synchronic or asynchronic execution of an independent process; and (4) an application, which encapsulates the execution of an external application.

A transition relates two activities and has a condition associated with it. At run time, if the evaluation of the condition is true, the transition can be done.

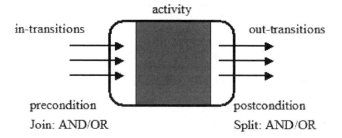

FIGURE 2.12. Model of control of XPDL.

The model of control of XPDL is described inside the activities by means of preconditions and postconditions (Fig. 2.12). A precondition determines if an activity can be initiated, taking into account the set of transitions arriving to it. There are two possible cases: (1) the activity is initiated when, for all the transitions arriving to it, the condition is true (Join-AND); or (2), when for at least one transition, its condition is true (Join-OR).

A postcondition determines the set if activities to be executed after the current activity. There are two possibilities: (1) all activities reached by a transition from the current activity are executed (Split- AND); or (2) only the activities reached by a transition from the current activity, whose condition is true, are executed (Split-OR).

2.5.5 The Proposed Translation Scheme

Our translation scheme is centered on the model of control. This subsection describes the translation of the theatrical used by IMS-LD to the XPDL language constructors and the limitations of a direct translation.

Translation of the Theatrical Metaphor: This subsection presents the translation scheme in a top-down approach. Furthermore, we use the workflow patterns proposed in [42] to help explain the translation.

Method

A method is translated to a Block Activities in XPDL; each activity represents one of the plays defined in the method. Block Activities are executed in parallel and do not need to be synchronized. Figure 2.13 illustrates the translation. This is an

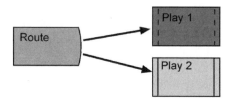

FIGURE 2.13. Translation of a method to XPDL.

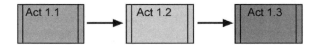

FIGURE 2.14. Translation of a play to XPDL.

example of a method with two plays executed in parallel. This type of execution corresponds to the parallel split pattern, and to the implicit termination pattern [42].

Play

A play is translated to a Block Activities in XPDL; each activity represents one of the acts defined in the play. The activities are executed in a sequential order, using the sequence pattern [42]. Figure 2.14 presents a play composed by three acts; they are executed in sequence. The conditions of the transitions are all true, the pre-condition is a Join-OR and the postcondition a Split Join-OR.

Act

An act is translated to a set of Block Activities in XPDL; one for each role-part. They are executed in parallel and synchronized when all are finished. Figure 2.15 shows an act composed of two role-parts and synchronized using two routing activities. This translation follows the parallel split and synchronization merge patterns [42].

The first routing activity has as its postcondition a Split-AND on the role-parts included in the act. The second routing activity synchronizes the termination of the role–parts executed in parallel, and its precondition is a Join-AND.

Role-Part

A role-part is translated as a Block Activity that contains the activities of its activity structure. There are two cases to be considered according to the activity-structure type (*sequence* or *selection*).

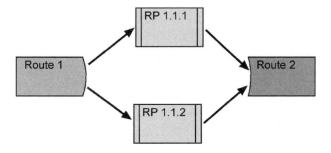

FIGURE 2.15. Translation of an act in XPDL.

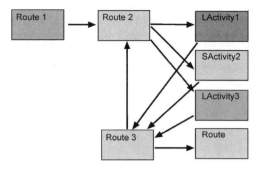

FIGURE 2.16. Translation of an activity structure (selection type) in XPDL.

In the *sequence* case, the activities in the Block Activity are executed according to the sequence pattern [42]. In the *selection* case, the translation uses the arbitrary cycle's pattern [42], as shown in the example of Figure 2.16.

Figure 2.16 shows a role-part composed of three activities: two learning-activities (LActivity1, LActivity3) and, one support activity (SActivity2). The flow of control starts with a routing activity (Route 1) followed by a second routing activity (Route 2). Route 2 uses a Split-Or postcondition (with exclude conditions) to choose during an iteration, with only one possible transition. Once the selected activity is finished, Route 3 is initiated. Route 3 decides if a new iteration has to be executed or not, by verifying if all the selected activities have been executed.

In the case of multiple and simultaneous instances at run time, it is possible to make the translation but with a restriction: a predefined maximum number of instances to be created at run time has to be known. This scheme follows the multiple-instances run-time pattern [42].

Limitations of the Direct Translation: There are at least two characteristics of the model of control of IMS-LD that cannot be translated directly to XPDL: the possibility to create at run time an arbitrary number of instances of the same activity, and the possibility to modify the visibility of the activities at run time.

To solve the first problem, we have defined the restriction on the maximum number of instances to create. The second problem appears in levels B and C of IMS-LD, which are out of the scope of our work.

2.6 LDX-Flow Tools

This section describes LDX-Flow. This is a set of tools to support the life cycle of a learning design. The strategy used to define the tools was the transformation of learnflows into workflows. The tools were developed as a part of a collaborative project between the University of Los Andes and the Téléuniversité du Québec (TELUQ).

The section has four subsections: the first three describe the functional, logical, and physical architectures, and the fourth presents some of the results achieved during the experimentation.

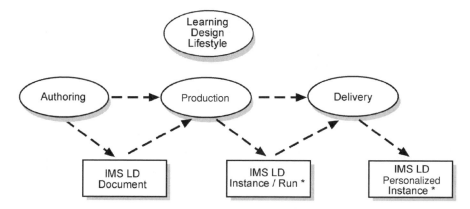

FIGURE 2.17. Learning design life cycle.

2.6.1 Functional Architecture

Figure 2.17 presents the life cycle of a learning design.

LDX-Flow allows the creation, editing, translation, and execution of a unit of learning defined using IMS-LD. LDX-Flow is a set of five tools that support the life cycle presented in Figure 2.17. In Table 2.5, we summarize their main functionality. Currently, our tools are limited to manage learning design descriptions compatible with level A of IMS-LD. Levels B and C are not yet supported.

Functionality of the LDX-Editor: By means of the LDX-Editor (Fig. 2.18), it is possible to create and edit learning designs using the IMS-LD standard. A user (for example, the instructor) can manipulate, in an interactive way, concepts like method, play, component, activity structure, learning activity, support activity, etc. LDX-Editor facilitates the visualization of the course through a graphical

TABLE 2.5 The set of tools of LDX-Flow and their relationship with the process in the life cycle of a learning design

Process	Tool	Description
Authoring	LDX-Editor	Allows the editing of learning designs using the IMS-LD elements. Once the information is edited, this could be stored in an XML file following the standard specification.
Production	LDX-Translator	Partially supports the production of a learning design. It corresponds to the translation of the control model defined in IMS-LD and to the control model of the XPDL language.
Delivery	LDX-Enactor	Executes instances of XPDL processes, which were generated using the LDX-translator tool.
	LDX-Client	Allows the diverse actors of a learning unit to interact with their execution instances.
	LDX-Admin	Offers services of administering and monitoring the elements involved in the execution.
	LDX-Resource	Offers services of assigning resources to the activities.

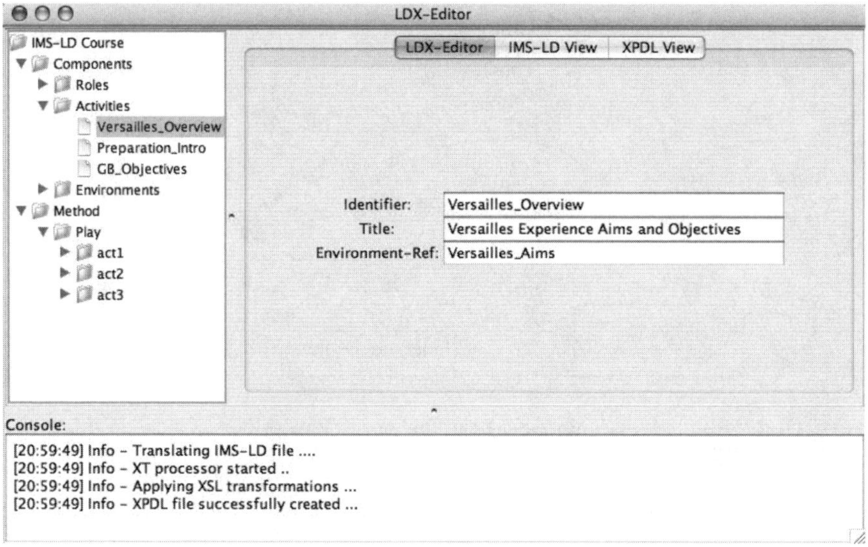

FIGURE 2.18. LDX-Editor.

presentation based on a tree that shows the composition of the different elements. Furthermore, the tool guarantees that the course built are structurally correct with respect to the standard.

Functionality of the LDX-Translator: LDX-Translator performs the translation from IMS-LD to XPDL. The translations are done according to the schema presented in section 2.5. Moreover, the tool can add to the output XPDL file the set of extended attributes required for the JaWe editor to visualize the XPDL process.

Functionality of the LDX-Enactor: This tool allows the instantiation and execution of the processes created in the LDX-Editor and translated by the LDX-Translator. The tool is responsible for the management of the enactment of the processes. This offers services to import XPDL process definitions. Once the tool imports the processes, they can be instantiated and executed.

Functionality of the LDX-Resource: This tool offers services to manage resources. These resources are the participants (human actors) in the activities.

Functionality of the LDX-Client: This tool offers services to allow actors to interact with an instance of a process being executed by the LDX-Enactor. Using this tool, users can know the instance of the process in which they are participating, the assigned activities already finished, and the assigned activities pending initialization.

The tool has a specialized interface according to the type of role. For instance, if the user is an instructor (staff role), he can consult the state of advancement of every learner in his course.

Functionality of the LDX-Admin: This tool offers services for the administration and monitoring of the LDX-Enactor using JMX technology [30]. For example,

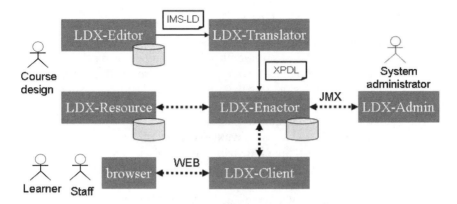

FIGURE 2.19. Logical architecture of LDX-Flow.

by using this tool, it is possible to consult how many instances are in execution, to review the log of the system, and to monitor the communication between the connected clients.

2.6.2 Logical Architecture

Figure 2.19 shows the logical architecture of the suite of tools of LDX-Flow.

The goal of the design of the architecture was to allow each tool to support a process in the life cycle of a learning design. The editor allows the edition of learning units in IMS-LD and the connection to the translator to produce XPDL files. The translator receives learning designs and applies the transformation needed to produce correct XPDL documents. The enactor imports these documents and allows the instantiation and execution of processes defined there.

The LDX-Enactor tools serves as a bridge between the other tools composing the architecture. First, the enactor offers services to the client components (LDX-Client). Users through a browser access the client components. Second, the LDX-Enactor offers services to the administration and resource tools.

2.6.3 Physical Architecture

The logical architecture, presented in the preceding section, has been implemented using the Java 2 Platform, Enterprise Edition (J2EE) platform [28], specifically on the JBoss Application Server (JBoss) container [18].

We used session and entity Enterprise Java Beans (EJB) components to implement the tools: LDX-Translator, LDX-Enactor, and LDX-Resources. Oracle database [35] is in charge of the management of the persistence data. The LDX-Client was implemented as a set of Web components (JSPs and Servlets). The LDX-Admin was implemented using JXM technology [30]. Finally, we used Java [29] and the swing framework to implement the LDX-Editor.

2.6.4 Evaluation of the Tools

The master's program of the systems and computing engineering department of the University of Los Andes offers a seminar whose purpose is for the students to describe the state of the art of their research topic. The process defined, to achieve the goal, consists of a series of activities performed by instructors, students, and teaching assistants. The mechanics are based on the sequential assignment of a set of readings, preparation of reviews, discussion of the reviews in small groups, and publication, for the whole class, of a synthesis. The instructors have as task, the assignment of the readings, the participation in the discussion sessions, and the validation of the results. The teaching assistants have the administrative support to everybody in the class as their task.

During the first semester of 2005, we defined, using IMS-LD, a learning design to model the process described above. The process was executed with a group of 15 students, two teaching assistants, and four instructors. We followed a completed process of production and delivery using the LDX-Flow tools. This exercise allowed us to validate the translation scheme and to test the implementation of the tools in a real context.

From the gained experience until now, we have defined three lines for our future work on this project. In the first place, we know that it is necessary to perform a validation on a larger scale, to consolidate the tools, and to validate, in other contexts, the translation scheme proposed. In the second place, we would like to evolve the translation scheme to use the version 2.0 of XPDL. Finally, we would like to study some ways to use the extended attributes of XPDL to support levels B and C of IMS-LD.

2.7 Conclusion

Current educational modeling languages, in particular the standard IMS-LD, offer a rich framework for the description of multiactors and adaptable pedagogical models. These properties create new requirements for e-learning delivery engines. While some IMS-LD editing tools are being released, no delivery engine is yet fully IMS-LD compatible.

On the other hand, workflow management systems also manipulate workflow modeling languages to describe business processes. One broadly accepted process description language is XPDL, the language proposed by the Workflow Management Coalition. XPDL is supported by various commercial and shareware editing and execution tools.

This chapter has explored the differences and similarities between e-learning and workflow systems. The establishment of a common vocabulary between IMS-LD and XPDL has helped identify translation possibilities, has shown the expressive power of workflow control pattern, and has clearly identified particular elements of the e-learning world that might be difficult to translate into workflow modeling languages and to execute by workflow enactment engines.

The translation schema proposed as well as the LDX-Flow set of tools that have been developed, although reduced to level A IMS-LD components, are a first attempt to implement the support of the whole life cycle of an IMS-LD–compatible learning design: design, production, and delivery are automatically supported by LDX-Flow. The evaluation made has proven the validity of the process and the compatibility with the standards involved.

It is worth noting that the translation step opens broad possibilities for both e-learning and workflow management communities. In fact, one can imagine various life cycle paths such as editing an LD with the graphical editor MOT+, publishing it with LDX-Flow, and delivering on a workflow process engine.

The new process engine will take advantage of the analysis we have done to understand the subjacent models of IMS-LD and XPDL. The classification of concepts as the static ones and as those that only appear at run time has allowed us to better understand the requirements a process engine should meet to fully support the execution of an LD expressed on IMS-LD.

More conceptual research concerns the analysis of the differences encountered and of the possibilities of enriching both models with features included in the other model.

References

1. Andrews, T., Curbera, F., Dholakia, H., et al. (2003) Business process execution language for Web services version 1.1. Technical report. ftp://www6.software.ibm.com/software/developer/library/ws-bpel.pdf
2. Business Process Management Initiative (BPMi). http://www.bpmi.org.
3. Business Process Modeling Notation (BPMN). http://www.bpmn.org.
4. Centre de Recherche LICEF : Mot+ Editor. http://www.licef.teluq.uquebec.ca/francais/real/demot.htm (20 Jun. 2005).
5. Danet.: WFMOpen Project. http://wfmopen.sourceforge.net.
6. Eder, J., Gruber, W. (2002) A meta model for structured workflows supporting workflow transformation. In: Lecture Notes on Computer Science, 2435.
7. EduBox. http://www.ou.nl/info-alg-edubox.
8. eduSource Project. http://www.edusource.ca.
9. Enhydra Java Workflow Editor (JaWE). http://jawe.objectweb.org.
10. Enhydra Shark Open Source Workflow. http://shark.objectweb.org.
11. Hollingsworth, P. (1995) The workflow reference model. Technical Report TC00-1003, Workflow Management Coalition (WfMC).
12. IEEE. (2002) Draft standard for learning object metadata 1484.12.1.
13. IMS Global Learning Consortium. (2002) IMS Reusable Definition of Competency or Educational Objective Information Model. Version 1 Final Specification.
14. IMS Global Learning Consortium. (2003) IMS Learning Design Best Practice and Implementation Guide. Version 1. Final Specification.
15. IMS Global Learning Consortium. (2003) IMS Learning Design Information Model. Version1 Final Specification.
16. IMS Global Learning Consortium. (2004) IMS ePortfolio Information Model. Version 1.0 Public Draft.

17. IMS Global Learning Consortium. (2005) IMS Learner Information Package—Information Model Specification. Version 1.0.1 Final Specification.
18. JBoss Inc.(2005) Jboss Enterprise Middleware System. http://www.jboss.org/products/index.
19. Joint Information Systems Committee (JISC). Reload editor. http://www.reload.ac.uk.
20. Kluijfhout, E. (2002) Stimulating the widespread use of EML. OTEC2002/22, http://hdl.handle.net/1820/200.
21. Koper R. (2001) Modeling units of study from a pedagogical perspective, the pedagogical meta-model behind EML. Technical report first draft, version 2. Educational Technology Expertise Center—Open University of Netherlands, Heerlen, Netherlands.
22. Learning Activity Management System (LAMS). http://www.lamsinternational.com/.
23. Lei, K., Singh, M. (1997) A Comparison of Workflow Metamodels, Proceedings of the ER-97 Workshop on Bahavioral Modeling and Design Transformations: Issues and Opportunities in Conceptual Modeling, Los Angeles, November 1997.
24. LICEF : Lompad. http://demo.licef.teluq.uquebec.ca/LomPad/en/index.htm.
25. Lightweight Directory Access Protocol (LDAP). ftp://ftp.rfc-editor.org/innotes/rfc3928.txt (2004).
26. Lornet. Lornet Project. http://www.lornet.org.
27. Marino, O., Contamines, J. (2004) La modélisation de Scénarios Collaboratifs d'apprentissage: possibilités et limites du standard IMS-LD. Communication au Colloque CIRTA, Congres ACFAS.
28. Sun Microsystems. Java 2 Platform Enterprise Edition (J2EE). http://java.sun.com/j2ee.
29. Sun Microsystems. Java API Specification. http://java.sun.com/reference/api.
30. Sun Microsystems. Java Management Extensions (JMX). http://java.sun.com/products/JavaManagement.
31. OASIS. Web Services Business Process Execution Language (WSBPEL). http://www.oasis-open.org/committees.
32. Open University of the Netherlands (OUNL). CopperCore. http://www.coppercore.org.
33. OMG. CORBA. http://www.corba.org.
34. OMG. (2000) Workflow Management Facility Specification Version 1.2. Needham, MA: Document number bom/00-05-02.
35. Oracle Corporation. Oracle Database. http://www.oracle.com/database.
36. Paquette, G. (2002) La Modélisation des Connaissances et des Compétences, pour Concevoir et apprendre. Presses de l'Université du Québec, 2002, 352 pages.
37. Paquette, G. (2003) Using learning object repositories: the eduSource suite of tools. eduSource Industrial Forum communications. http://www.edusource.ca/english/resources/eduSource-Moncton-AN.ppt.
38. Paquette G., Marino, O., de la Teja, I., Léonard, M., Lundgren-Cayrol, K. (2005) Delivery of learning design: The explor@ system case. In: Koper, R., Tattersall, C. (eds.), Learning Design: A Handbook on Modelling and Delivering Networked Education and Training. New York: Springer-Verlag.
39. SCORM. Sharable Content Object Reference Model (SCORM). http://www.adlnet.org/scorm/index.cfm.
40. SLED. http://www.jisc.ac.uk/?name=sblds.
41. UNED.: Alfanet Editor. http://rtd.softwareag.es/alfanet.
42. Van der Aalst, W. (2003) Patterns and XPDL: A Critical Evaluation of the XML Process Definition Language. QUT Technical report, FIT-TR-2003-06, http://www.citi.qut.edu.au/pubs/ce-xpdl.pdf, Queensland University of Technology, Brisbane, 2003.

43. Vantroys, T., Peter, Y. (2002) Un système de workflows flexible pour la formation ouverte et à distance. In: Frasson, C., Pecuchet, J.-P. (Dir.), Technologies de l'Information et de la Communication dans les Enseignements d ingenieurs et dans l industrie. Villeurbanne, France: Institut National des Sciences Appliquees de Lyon.
44. Vantroys, T., Peter, Y. (2004) Cow, a flexible platform for the enactment of learning scenarios. International Workshop on Groupware CRIWG 2003, Lecture Notes on Computer Science. New York: Springer-Verlag.
45. Vogten, H. (2005) Designing a learning design engine as a collection of finite state machines. International Journal on E-Learning. http://hdl.handle.net/1820/303.
46. Workflow Management Coalition (WfMC). (2002) Workflow Process Definition Interface—XML Process Definition Language. Version 1. Final Draft WFMC-TC-1025.

3
A Toolkit for Building Geo-Referenced Lessons: Design, Implementation, and Praxis

SYLVAIN GIROUX

Abstract. We coined the term *mobile lessons* for lessons held outside traditional classrooms. During these lessons, all actors are mobile and must move to perform the required tasks. Themes tackled in such lessons may be as varied as geography, history, ecology, dialects in linguistics ... Mobile lessons are not a new teaching strategy, but mobile devices may render them more efficient and more attractive. The aim is to put students in conditions germane to the ones in which experts work. We implemented in Java a toolkit for creating and using mobile lessons and for monitoring students on the field. Contents and questions are described in XML. Using this software, teachers of a high school in Sardinia (Italy) developed and experienced a mobile lesson on the archaeological site of Nora. In light of this experiment, a wireless, distributed, and more sophisticated version of the software was implemented.

3.1 Introduction

The real world is a marvelous teacher. Why not use it as a complement to lessons in classrooms? Students would acquire better knowledge by going into the field, looking for information, and observing the real phenomenon. They would feel more involved and autonomous. Long ago, field lessons were generally presented on sheets of paper. A predetermined sequence of questions and actions was planned in advance and the questions were the same for all students. Recent advances in technology in wireless communication, mobile devices, location-based services, geo-referenced information, and pervasive computing enable to envision the world as an interactive environment. In this chapter we show how technology, pedagogy, and learning can meet to transform the field into an interactive personalized playground for students. They can use such a playground to learn and deepen their knowledge. We call this approach "mobile lessons."

Field lessons are not a new teaching strategy, but mobile devices and information systems may render them more efficient and more attractive. Moreover, since device prices drop regularly, schools can afford the required material. However, the implementation, the configuration, and the management of distributed applications over mobile devices are too complex for teachers. So we designed and implemented `MobileLessons`, a toolkit that basically offers:

- tools to help teachers create lessons capitalizing on mobile devices and geo-referenced information;
- tools enabling students to perform mobile lessons in the field; these tools are available through laptops, personal digital assistants (PDAs), and cellular phones;
- tools allowing teachers to monitor students in real time in the field.

The toolkit is implemented in Java. Lesson content and questions are described in XML. The whole implementation relies on `e-mate` [5]. E-mate is a framework for the delivery of mobile personalized geo-referenced services over many channels (PCs, PDAs, cellular phones ...) and using multimodality (text, image, sound ...). The platform provides distributed services over the Internet. `E-mate` made these services accessible from a computer, a PDA, or a cellular phone. A very interesting feature of `e-mate` is the generation on the fly of a user interface for any device. Multiple releases of `MobileLessons` were implemented. They were used to experiment in classrooms and with students, or to test and prove concepts. We believe that this toolkit is easy and intuitive to use for teachers and students, easy to maintain and deploy, and should not burden a school budget.

In this chapter, we first describe an experiment in 2001 of a mobile lesson with the first release of `MobileLessons`. In this experiment students used laptops connected to GPS to explore a Roman archaeological site in Sardinia, Italy (§3.2). This experiment is then analyzed from different perspectives: pedagogy (§3.3), content (§3.4), system administration (§3.5), and technology (§3.6). In light of this experiment, new tools were added and the distributed infrastructure was set. A mobile lesson became then a set of distributed components called services, accessible through the Internet. These services can be reached from different devices.

3.2 Experimentation

Thanks to `MobileLessons`, teachers at a high school in Sardinia, Italy, developed and experienced a mobile lesson for the archaeological site of Nora.[1] This site is very interesting from an historical perspective because it contains both Punic and Roman ruins. The lesson was performed in June 2001 with a class of 12- to 13-year-old students.

History courses are usually done using textbooks and sometimes videos. If lucky, students may visit a museum as a "field lesson". Seldom the study of history becomes a practical lesson by going onto the field. In many cities there are many artifacts still visible and tangible as testimonies of national history. Archaeologists use these artifacts to rebuild and interpret history.

---

[1] http://www.nora.it/.

In Italy, part of the history curriculum of the first year of high school addresses Roman civilization. So we decided to prepare a mobile lesson on the structure of ancient Roman cities. This lesson has to be integrated into the general curriculum; therefore, courses on Roman civilization were given before the mobile lesson to prepare students for the field they were about to explore. Courses were also given after the mobile lesson to help them reflect on their field observations and to deepen their knowledge, as it would be the case in any science laboratory.

Sardinia is incredibly rich in archaeological and historical sites. With respect to the content under study, Nora was the perfect site. It has a rich history and the structure of the city is well apparent:

In 238 B.C., Sardinia was conquered by the Romans, therefore also Nora passed under the Roman domain. It started off as the main town of the island and the governorship's site, but soon Karalis took its place. Anyhow also later on Nora remained an important town: it was "Caput Viae" (town cape of a road, from which distances were calculated). The importance of the town was testified by the presence of four (not one) Thermal Buildings, of a theatre and an amphitheatre (not yet excavated) and of some elegant villas situated at a certain distance from the urban centre of the town. The common people's houses were quite small and usually consisted in a single room at the bottom with a wooden intermediate floor on top used as bedroom. The archaeological findings preserved in Pula Museum give a good idea of the daily routine of the town: there are common use objects built in Nora or imported from the various Mediterranean coasts. The slow decline of Nora began in the IV century A.C., with the falter of the Roman Empire and when the seas became unsafe. The Vandals (455 A.D.) the town ended its vital cycle and was gradually abandoned by the people who chose safer inland areas. [6]

Once the content and the site were chosen, teachers started to prepare the mobile lesson. They first identified zones of interest (agora, common people's quarter, rich quarter, hospital . . .), and then "hot spots" for each zone were selected (Fig. 3.1). A hot spot corresponds to a precise location to which significant information can be attached. The objective was to bring students to discover these points in the field and to infer the global structure of the city. Knowing the exact position of a student will enable the system to ask precise questions, helping him to reflect on what he sees. Questions may focus on

- *specific artifacts visible from his position*. For instance, when standing in front of the theater, a student can see huge urns. A question asks if their purpose was to amplify voices and sounds, to keep the wine fresh for the actors, or to store and preserve oil and grains.
- *how the place was used by people*. For instance, in front of the forum the student is asked if the forum was a place where citizens talked about politics, a place where to take refreshing walk in the summer, or a place where one could watch the sea to check for the arrival of vessels.
- *where the place is located with respect to another one*. For instance, in front of a small thermal building, the student is asked if the drainage was in the direction of the street and the gutter toward the sea, or toward the hills.

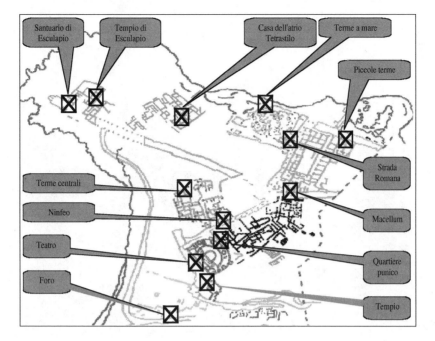

FIGURE 3.1. Hot spots chosen by teachers for the Nora mobile lesson.[2]

So teachers first went to the chosen site with a GPS system and recorded the coordinates of each hot spot. The information given by the GPS is a 2-tuple (longitude, latitude),[3] for instance East, 38° 59' 3,80"; North, 09° 00' 59,72". Each hot spot was then associated with other information to produce geo-referenced information. Basically the information is stored in the XML files and contains a label, a description, the GPS coordinates, questions (multiple choices, true or false, etc.), and sometimes hints that may help to find a location or answer a question.

Students have to find a significant place, for example the theater, and not a GPS position. But this is not enough, because the theater is indeed a squared area whose side is more than 40 meters long. The students must find the right position picked up by the teacher, near the theater. So the search is more than being around the theater, but what are the relevant locations related to a theater? When some difficulties occur in finding the right place, explanations, help, or hints are supplied progressively.

---

[2] The map is adapted from http://www.isolasarda.com/nora-itinerario.htm.
[3] Latitude and longitude were used to represent a GPS position. For convenience, it might be possible to transform them into UTM coordinates expressed in meters using a specific algorithm, but for our purpose it was not necessary. We made many tests about the precision of GPS data and we accepted a position as right with an 8- to 10-meter uncertainty.

FIGURE 3.2. The first release of `MobileLesson` runs on a laptop connected to a GPS. In the background there is a view of the Nora site.

They may be as wide-ranging as the teacher's imagination can sustain: charade, riddle, description, etc.

As stated previously, the theme of the lesson—the structure of cities of Ancient Rome—was introduced to the students in the classroom to prepare them for the mobile lesson. But no indication was given on the exact format the lesson would take, neither on the software nor on the devices that will be used. Only once on the field, the structure of the lesson, devices, and software were presented. Teams of two or three students were given laptops connected to a Garmin GPS system (Fig. 3.2). We wanted to motivate students and give them the feeling of a game. Hence the mobile lesson structure was akin to a "treasure hunt." Students had to discover as many as possible of the significant hot spots in a limited amount of time (45 minutes[4]). When they found a hot spot, they could also answer questions related to it. A score was associated with each hot spot found and each correct answer to questions. Each trial decreases the value of a hot spot or a question. If students asked for hints, a question was worth less. Students could wander wherever they want. Since the site is surrounded by fences and by the sea, letting them roam freely was not an issue.

---

[4] The software reads the time allowed in a property file, so duration can be easily changed and even personalized.

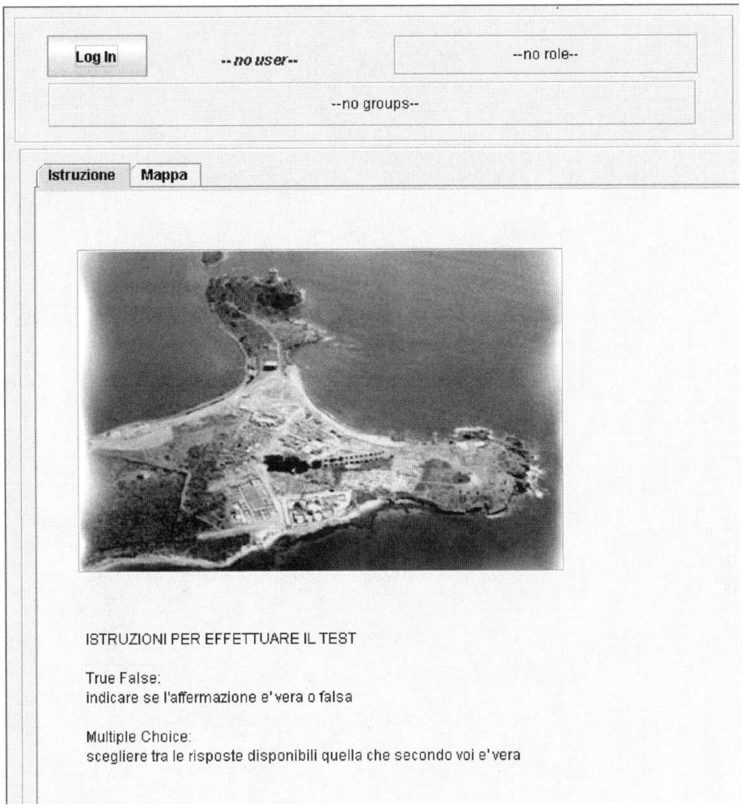

FIGURE 3.3. Start-up window gives access to login instructions.

The start-up window gives access to the login panel, the instruction panel (Fig. 3.3), and the map panel (Fig. 3.4). To login, a user has to provide a login name and a password. According to his roles, different tab panels are then shown. Three roles were defined: teacher, student, and administrator. A user may fill more than one role (Fig. 3.5). Students have access to the "Corsa al tesoro" panel (Fig. 3.6). Teachers have access to the "Locations Editor" panel (Fig. 3.7) and the "Tests Editor" panel. Administrators have access to the "Applications Properties" panel (Fig. 3.9), the "Users Properties" panel, and the "All Users" panel.

Once students are logged on, a list of hot spots appears (Fig. 3.6). They can search them in random order. When students believe they are at the right location, that is the one identified by teachers, they ask the MobileLesson for confirmation by clicking on the "Eureka" button. The current GPS position is then compared to the GPS position taken by the teacher. If the current GPS position is close enough, students get access to questions related to this hot spot. They may be general questions about the place, but often they are questions about what the students can see from this precise location. Students have only to turn or move slightly to

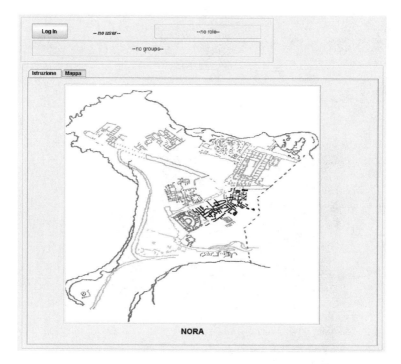

FIGURE 3.4. Start-up window gives access to a map.

observe the place and discover or infer the correct answers. If the position was wrong, more information about the place is supplied. Students have to search again and ask the software again if they are at the right place or not.

As exemplified by the experimentation at the Nora site, mobile lessons are based on geo-referenced data. Geo-referenced data link information to a location. Not surprisingly, mobile lesson are designed and organized along three dimensions: pedagogy, content, and technology. The next sections further describe these axes.

3.3 Pedagogical Strategies

A mobile lesson should not be an isolated element but rather a part of a pedagogical sequence. One of our objectives is to integrate in a lesson factors that might help learners to build their knowledge in a constructivist spirit [3]. We believe that, to foster the effective construction of their knowledge, students should go into the field, look for information, and, above all, observe the real phenomenon, and therefore act in a more personal and autonomous way. Mobile personalised and geo-referenced systems [5] seem to be a very appropriate means to implement approaches based on experimentation [8].

To prepare a mobile lesson, a teacher selects a zone and identifies a set of hot spots. Students will have to discover these points when they will be in the

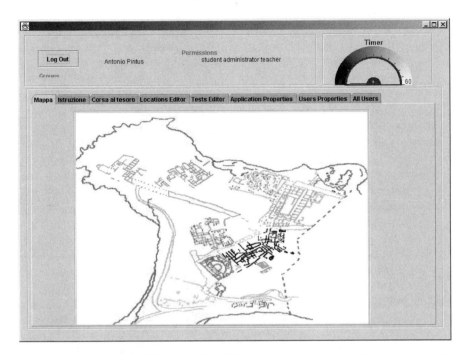

FIGURE 3.5. A user may fill many roles. When a user is a student, a timer is displayed. Since this user fills all the available roles, this snapshot shows all the tab panels available in the system.

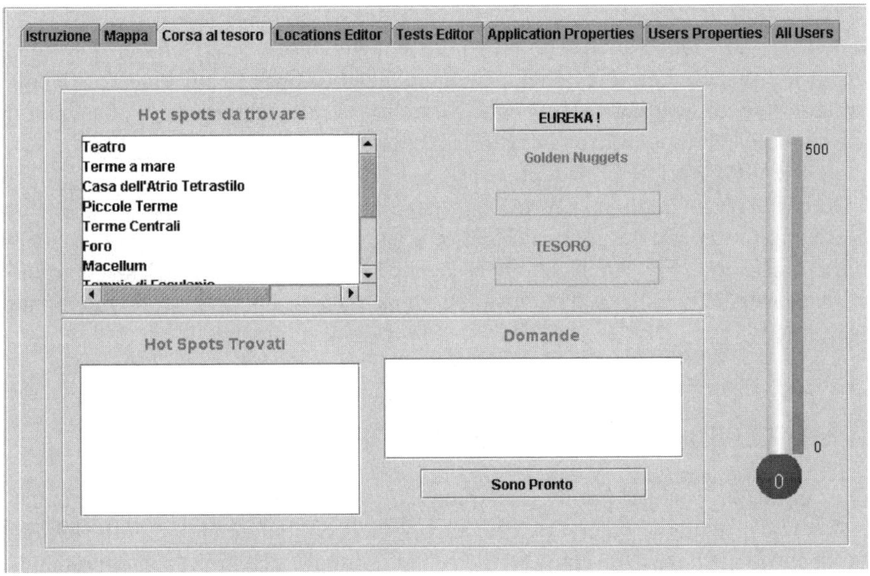

FIGURE 3.6. The panel that students use to participate in a mobile lesson.

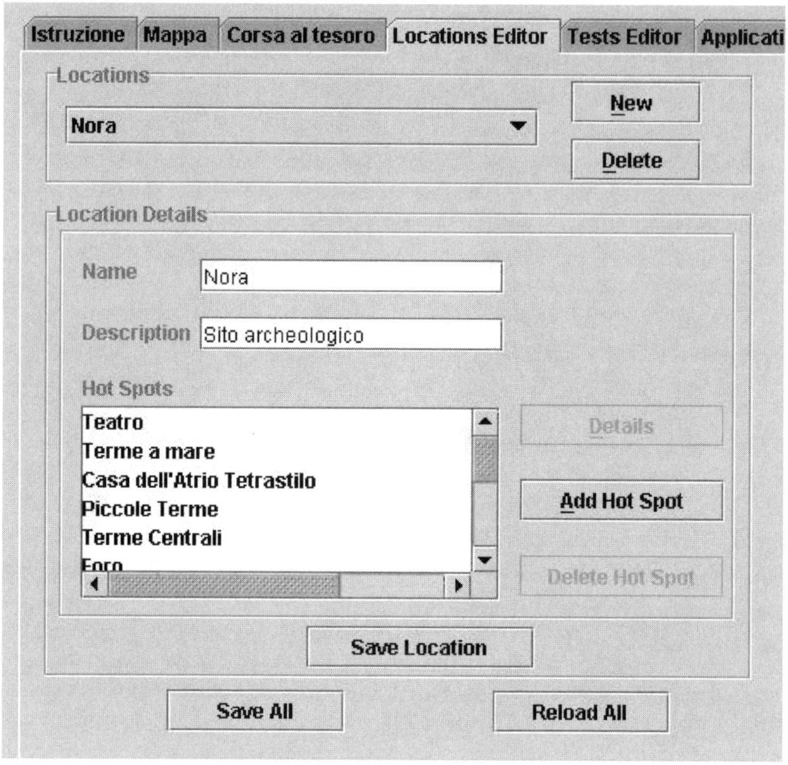

FIGURE 3.7. Hot spots editor.

field (Fig. 3.1). Once having found a hot spot, students have to answer questions about the place where they stand. Students have to observe all kinds of details around them to give correct answers. Mixing general questions with observation questions leads students to deduce the behavior of people of an ancient civilization, their scientific level, their arts, etc.

In our experimentation at Nora, a decisive means to motivate students [1] was by giving the lesson the look and feel of a game. Time constraints (Fig. 3.5, top right) and scores (Fig. 3.6, right) are associated with the discovery of hot spots and with answers to questions. The fewer attempts made to find a hot spot, the higher the score is.

3.4 Content in a Mobile Lesson

Our approach is not a purely constructivist one. A mobile lesson is part of a pedagogical sequence where traditional courses occur before and after the lesson. Students do not have to discover all the content by themselves. Yet content remains always at the center of the activities. Accordingly, the four steps of a mobile lesson life cycle of are (1) identification of relevant content by teachers (§3.4.1),

(2) introduction of content to students (§0), (3) acquisition of content by students (§3.4.2), and (4) reflection on content in the classroom (§3.4.3).

3.4.1 Design of the Lesson: Identifying Content

As a first step in mobile lesson life cycle, teachers design the lesson and prepare pedagogical material. A synopsis is made defining the theme—*the structure of an ancient Roman city*—and the objectives—*to discover the main buildings (Forum, theater, temple . . .), their use (politics, religion . . .), and their relative location in a Roman city (poor quarter, rich quarter, marketplace . . .)*. An appropriate site is identified—*Nora was chosen*. Two teachers went to the Nora site to get a better idea of the archaeological elements that were present and to discuss the lesson organization and structure. Later teachers went to the site to gather geo-referenced data. They bring a laptop equipped with a GPS. Using the "Locations Editor" panel of MobileLessons (Fig. 3.7), they named and collected GPS coordinates of relevant spots. This information was saved in XML files. Back at school, they prepared location-based questions using the "Tests Editor" panel (Fig. 3.8). Finally, the teachers prepared helpful hints that students might receive, and completed the lesson description. During this step, a scenario describing tasks to perform was also elaborated. A free-wandering approach was selected: no order was imposed on the hot spots to discover.

3.4.2 Presentation to Students: Introducing Content

Once the lesson was ready, teachers introduced basic related content to the class. They informed students of the forthcoming mobile lesson without giving too many details. They also presented to students a map of Nora.

3.4.3 Lesson on the Field: Acquiring Content

Then students went onto the field. Once on site, the tasks to do, rules of the game, device manipulation, and software were explained. The lesson was carried out in teams of two or three students. As explained before, they had to find the places spotted by teachers (Fig. 3.6). We noted that, while teachers were reluctant to use devices and software, being afraid of breaking them, students had no problems with the technology and were rather eager to use it.

Learning in the field is not restricted to history. Themes addressed by mobile lessons may be of great variety: geography, linguistics, botany . . . For instance, to study the evolution of a language, students can track traces of a dialect in everyday-artifacts, for instance by identifying the Sardinian origin of shop names, products, streets . . . To study botany, they can go to a park searching for specific trees, collecting samples of leaves, taking photos or notes on tree shapes, and analyzing them back in class. Thus, depending on the lesson theme, they may have to observe monuments or site details, take notes, answer questions, and take photos.

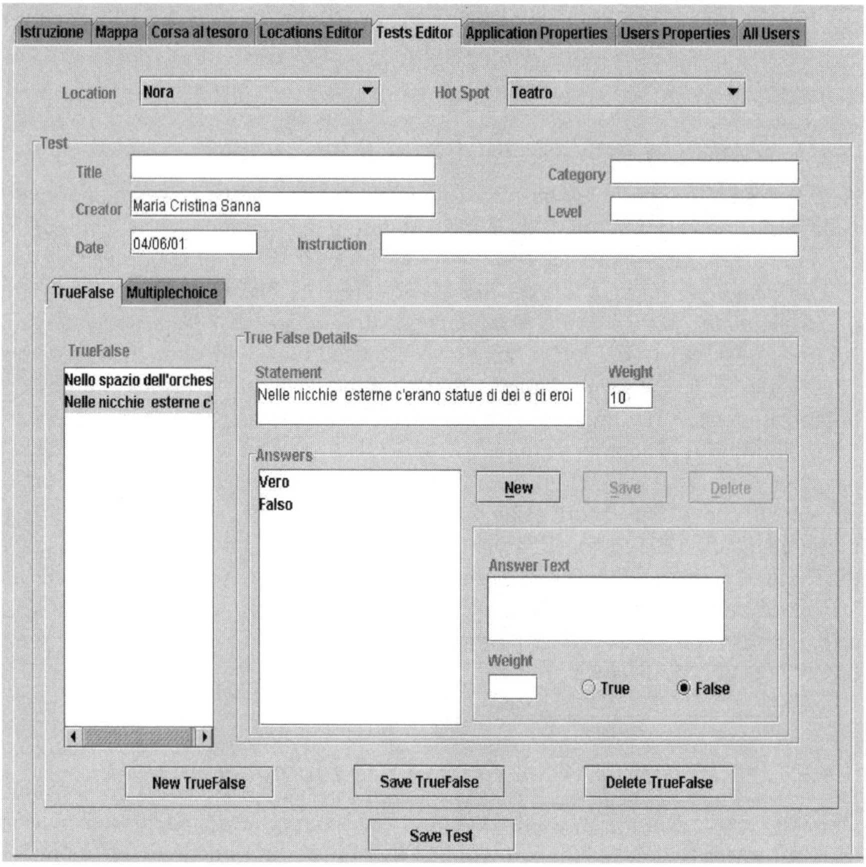

FIGURE 3.8. Questions editor.

3.4.4 Back in the Classroom: Reflecting on Content

Once back in the classroom, the lesson is not yet finished. It is time to analyze the collected data. For instance, based on their answers and observations, students can reflect on the structure of Nora, and the location of the rich quarter, the poor quarter, the marketplace, the hospital, the sea . . . They can write reports. Research on the Web can deepen their knowledge. Teachers may also provide further explanations and do a general synthesis.

3.5 Administrative Tools

Since this software has to be used by nonexperts, specific panels were provided to enter and modify basic information used by the program. The "Application Properties" panel enables specifying the location files related to users, the site name,

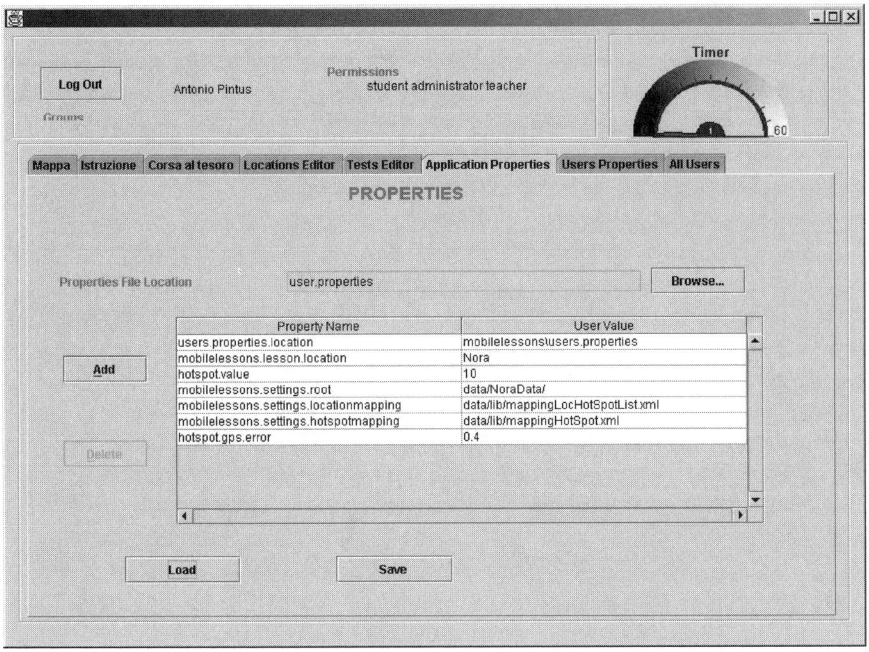

FIGURE 3.9. The "Application Properties" panel allows consulting and modifying information on user management, site geo-referenced data, and accepted discrepancy between hot-spot GPS positions recorded by teachers and student GPS locations.

the number of hot spots, the folders containing the XML files describing hot spots and questions, and the error range accepted with respect to the recorded GPS position (Fig. 3.9). Since GPS is sensitive to many factors, the last parameter enables adjusting to current conditions. For instance, precision may vary according to weather conditions. The "Users Properties" panel allows choosing authentication mechanisms and the class of instances used by the application and other related parameters, for instance the location of the users' data (Fig. 3.10). This information is particularly useful when the abstract factory design pattern is used [4]. The "User Management" panel enables managing users and editing their login name and password (Fig. 3.11).

3.6 Technology: Devices and Software

This section addresses issues related to devices and software. The experimentation in Nora described in this chapter was the starting point of the `MobileLessons` application (§3.6.1). This first release provided many interesting hints that led to the implementation of a version designed for PDA-like devices (§3.6.2), and,

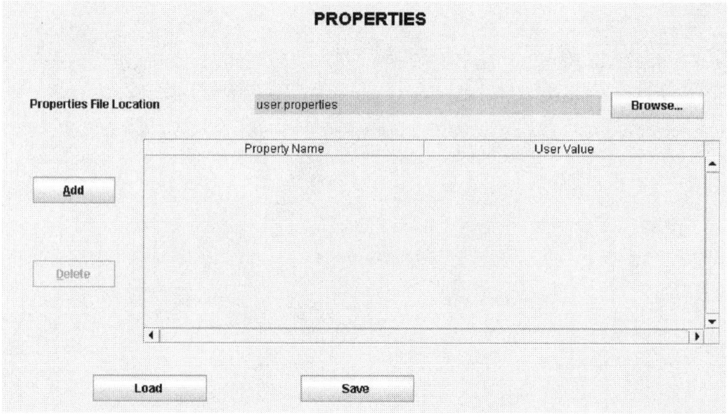

(a)

```
Authenticator.factory=mobilelessons.user.AuthenticatorFactory
user.login=guest
user.factory=mobilelessons.user.MobileLessonUserFactory
user.password=guest
users.repository=persistent\\users
```

(b)

FIGURE 3.10. Management of authentication and other implementation choices is done through the "Users Properties" panel (a) and saved in a property file (b).

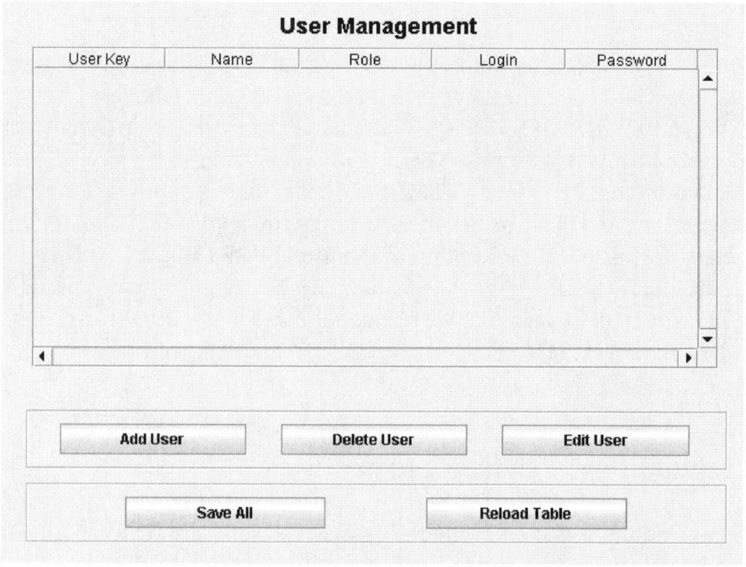

FIGURE 3.11. Information on users is accessed and modified through the "User Management" panel.

finally exploiting wireless networking and location awareness, new services were designed to make learning more interactive and collaborative (§3.6.3).

3.6.1 Mobile Lessons, Release 1.0

Release 1.0 of `MobileLessons` experimented in Nora (§3.2) is a stand-alone application. Each laptop runs a single lesson. Lesson data were also stored locally. No network connection was available. A Garmin GPS was connected to the laptop through a serial port. The implementation was in Java. The `javax.comm` Extension Package was used to read data provided by the GPS on the serial port. Data were encoded according to National Marine Electronics Association (NMEA) standards.

Inconveniences experienced by students were related to walking on a sunny site with a device that is a bit heavy, that requires caution, and on which it may be difficult to read due to the glare of the sun. Since all data were manipulated locally, one has to be careful when gathering user data coming from different laptops. Finally it was clear that a network was a necessity to implement some interesting features. For instance, the game would preferably be played simultaneously by many students to increase their emulation, which was not possible with the current setting.

3.6.2 Mobile Lessons, as Location-Based Services

The next natural step was then to transform the stand-alone version of `Mobile-Lesson` into a location-based service [7]. The aim was to provide wireless access to the network and to run the application on PDAs, cellular phones, or other similar devices. So the next release used the infrastructure provided by e-mate to deliver on-line services [2,5]. As a result, the software and devices used on the field changed while lesson content remained the same.

A mobile lesson is then defined as an e-learning distributed service that delivers adapted geo-referenced information on request. Figure 3.12 shows the architecture of the system. Only a part of the service is loaded on the terminal tier. As several PDAs are simultaneously connected, an HTTP server manages for each device the service remote tier. This server finds resources required by the service on an application server. The services portal is used for service discovery. PDAs exchange data with the HTTP server through XML documents [9,10].

3.6.3 Mobile Lessons, Toward New Services

The last release of `MobileLessons` integrates the comments of people involved in the process. We improved the data presentation, and new modules were added. Teachers can then use a laptop to monitor either all the students in the field, or just one by selecting him from the list of students (Fig. 3.13). Teachers may also chat with the students, broadcast messages, or send messages to a specific students. On their part, students may chat with or send messages to teachers and to other students.

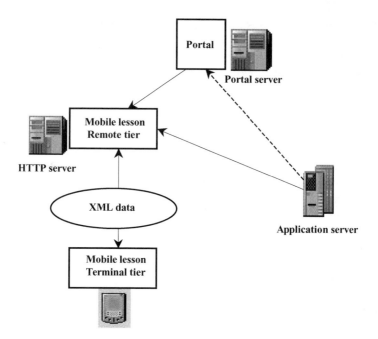

FIGURE 3.12. The architecture for the delivery of a distributed mobile lesson on a PDA.

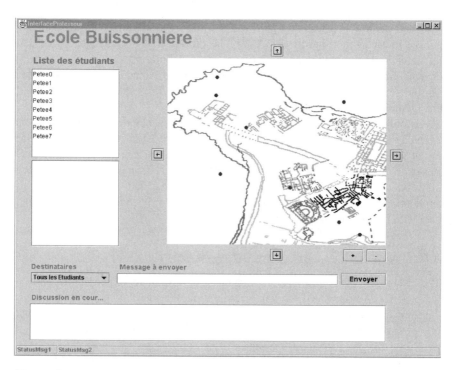

FIGURE 3.13. The teacher can monitor and interact at distance with her class on the field.

3.7 Conclusion

In this chapter, we described how technology can improve field lessons by exploiting geo-referenced information and mobile devices. Such mobile lessons are built on three complementary axes: pedagogy, content, and technology. The concept of a mobile lesson was first experimented at the Nora archaeological site for teaching the infrastructure of ancient Roman cities. Generic academic content proved quite easy to map to a geo-referenced instance. Involvement of teachers in the preparation of this lesson was decisive. The satisfaction of all students involved, their desire to repeat the experience, and the feedback of teachers indicate that the experience was a great success. In light of this experiment, it is also clear that a lesson should result from a multidisciplinary effort. Teachers are in charge of lesson structure and content. Computer scientists are responsible for software and the devices needed to support the lesson on the field.

Then we improved the structure, the features, and the implementation of `MobileLessons`. In particular, it was transformed into a location-based service. As a result, we got an implementation of a specialized toolkit for building and using "on the field" lessons based on geo-referenced information. This toolkit provides services to teachers to design a mobile lesson and to monitor and interact with their class while on the field. E-mate enables deploying such a wireless mobile lesson on the field to any devices.

As our main conclusion, we claim that a playful and motivating context that allows students to integrate various types of information, to attempt in a real setting to search for clues and information, and to try to understand why they succeeded or failed, is surely among the most enjoyable ways to acquire knowledge.

3.8 Acknowledgment

This project would not have been possible without the full support and participation of the Scuola Media Statale No. 2, Assemini, Italy. In particular, the collaboration of the teachers Maria-Cristina Sanna and Giovanna Arru was invaluable. They were so generous with their time, their experience, and their enthusiasm. All our thanks also to the students who participated in the lessons at Nora. Finally, the principal, Pier Enrico Carta, did everything needed to bring this project to reality in his school.

Our also very grateful thanks to Claude Moulin, Antonio Pintus, Raffaella Sanna, and all members of the research team of the CRS4, Sardegna, who contributed extensively to the design and implementation of `MobileLessons`.

References

1. Bunt, A., Conati, C. (2001) Modeling exploratory behaviour. In: Bauer, M., Gmytrasiewicz, P.J., Vassileva, J. (eds.), User Modeling 2001, 8th International Conference, UM 2001, Proceedings. LNCS 2109. New York: Springer, pp. 219–221.

2. Carboni, D., Giroux, S., Vargiu, E., et al. (2003) E-MATE: an open architecture to support mobility of users. In: Haav, H.M., Kalja, A. (eds.), Databases and Information Systems II: Fifth International Baltic Conference, Baltic Dbis &Is'2002 Tallinn, Estonia, June 3–6, 2002: Selected Papers. New York: Kluwer Academic Publishers, pp. 227–242.

3. Dalgarno, B. (1998) Choosing learner activities for specific learning outcomes: a tool for constructivist computer assisted learning design. In: McBeath, C., Atkinson, R. (eds.), Planning for Progress, Partnership and Profit. EdTech '98. Perth: Australian Society for Educational Technology. http://www.aset.org.au/confs/edtech98/pubs/articles/contents2.html.

4. Gamma, E., Helm, R., Johnson, R., Vlissides, J. (1995) Design Patterns. New York: Addison-Wesley.

5. Giroux, S., Moulin, C., Paddeu, G., et al. (2001) Mobilité, personnalisation, et information géo-référencée. In: Seghrouchni, A.E.F., Magnin, L. (eds.), Journées Francophones pour l'Intelligence Artificielle Distribuée et les Systèmes Multi-agents, JFIADSMA 2001, Nov. 12–14 2001, Montréal, Canada. Paris: Hermès, pp. 17–30.

6. Isola Sarda, http://www.isolasarda.com/nora-storia_e.htm, 1997–2005.

7. Rao, B., Minakakis, L. (2003) Mobile commerce opportunities and challenges: evolution of mobile location-based services. Communications of the ACM, 46(12): 61–65.

8. Vérillon, P. (2000) Revisiting Piaget and Vigotsky. In: Search of a Learning Model for Technology Education. Journal of Technology Studies, 26(1).

9. XML. (2000) Extensible Markup Language (XML) 1.0, W3C Recommendation, October 6th 2000. http://www.w3.org/TR/REC-xml.

10. Zhang, J., et al. (2000) Prototype for wrapping and visualizing geo-referenced data in a distributed environment using XML technology. In: Proceedings of the Eighth ACM Symposium on Advances in Geographic Information Systems, Washington, DC, pp. 27–32.

Part II
Building Knowledge Environments

4
TELOS: A Service-Oriented Framework to Support Learning and Knowledge Management

GILBERT PAQUETTE, IOAN ROSCA, STEFAN MIHAILA, AND ANIS MASMOUDI

Abstract. This chapter presents the basic orientations, the main use cases, and the conceptual framework of a TeleLearning Operating System. TELOS is a system under development within the LORNET research network (www.lornet.org) aiming to integrate components and services, and research results, produced by the different LORNET teams. TELOS research is at the convergence of three main trends: learning object repositories that facilitate the access to knowledge resources; learning and knowledge management support systems that use these referentials as building blocks; and the integration of these referentials and these systems in the context of the semantic Web.

4.1 Introduction

There are many specialized tools and hundreds of distance or e-learning platforms (WebCT, TopClass, LearningSpace, Ingénium, Docent, etc.), also called Learning Management Systems (LMS) or Learning Content Management Systems (LCMS), available through a Web browser. There are also a number of comparative studies of their features, and even a decision system to select an e-learning platform.[1]

Recent reviews of e-learning platforms show that there are not great differences between them. The current platforms are mostly designed for predefined actors (author, trainer, learner). They are focused on predetermined delivery models for self-training and on-line asynchronous conferencing. Most e-learning platforms look more like an extension of the former authoring tools. Their efficiency as quick authoring tools for the Web is often achieved by reducing drastically the variety of instructional strategies, every course having similar structures and components.

The advent of learning portals and Web services presents an interesting evolution toward more flexibility, presenting another vision of learning than just giving access to a predefined, preformatted and predigested content. Even though learning portals

---

[1] For this, consult www.brandon-hall.com.

also require delivery platforms, more important are the services around which the portal is organized: access learning resources, navigation in a path of learning events, training support by individuals or organizations, peer-to-peer collaboration services, access to a range of content experts, and so on. The true potential of learning portals needs to be fully exploited based on new research and development activities.

Compared to the evolution of generic software (text editors, spreadsheets, etc.), e-learning systems are now in a similar position as the integrated software of the last decade, where text, spreadsheets, and database editors could transfer data only within the integrated suite. These have been replaced by integration mechanisms at the operating system level, enabling data communication between any compliant tools through desktop operations.

The TeleLearning Operating System (TELOS) will provide similar flexibility for e-learning environments. It will allow the implementation of interactions between actors using resources dynamically related to the operations they perform in the system. Hence, within TELOS, by aggregating resources and functions differently, it is possible to build quite different distributed learning environments such as electronic performance support systems (EPSSs) integrated in a workplace activity, communities of practice, or, at the other end of the continuum, formal on-line training and technology-based classroom activities, as well as different forms of blended learning or knowledge management workflows.

A new generation of Web-based learning delivery systems is needed to integrate advanced solutions for interoperability problems, aggregation of flexible designs, adaptive agents, knowledge extraction from documents, and advanced multimedia objects processing. The actual LCMSs and portals do not provide many of these functionalities, and we are far from integrating them in a coherent integrative (instead of integrated) system. The integration of the structures or the processes can be made more flexible by sharing knowledge and ontologies referentials, by the coordination of the communication between the actors, by interoperable technical infrastructures, by standards of representation of the aggregation formulas, and by the use of aggregation editors. The TELOS system will integrate these strategies in an organic vision based on educational phenomena and on models of the aggregation process used as facilitating multi-actor interfaces.

In the last 5 years, an increasing number of organizations have recognized the importance of learning technologies and knowledge management. This has resulted in attempts to identify, formalize, organize, and sustain the use of their knowledge, through the reengineering of work and training processes and the ubiquitous use of Web-based technology [4, 15]. Knowledge management is now strongly influenced by the building of communities of practices [16] based on research in Computer Supported Collaborative Work and Learning (CSCW/CSCL). In the same time frame, an important international movement, headed by IEEE and IMS, is elaborating standards enabling users in different parts of the world to interoperate and reuse computerized resources, "learning objects", or "information resources" made available in "learning object repositories" distributed on the World Wide Web [17]. These major trends converge and integrate in another ambitious effort to construct the next Web generation, the "semantic Web" [1]. The semantic Web aims to associate knowledge with documents, and more generally to learning objects, distributed on the Web.

These major international trends form the basis of the LORNET research program and underline the need for a Web-based system like TELOS to support learning and knowledge management. Although many initiatives are blooming in this area, the TELOS is unique in its goal to integrate the major approaches and technologies that can contribute to support learning and knowledge management on the framework of the semantic Web.

This research can be situated in the context of the growing field of *service-oriented conceptual frameworks*.[2] A *framework* creates a broad vocabulary (an ontology) that is used to model recurring concepts and integration environments and is equivalent to the concept of a *pattern* in the software community. A framework supports the development by organizations of their own implementation infrastructures, using a flexible *service-oriented* approach.

Service-oriented frameworks [2, 18] are rapidly gaining popularity with the wide adoption of Web services and because of the lower costs of integration coupled with flexibility and simplification of software configurations. In a service-oriented approach, the application logic contained in the various systems across the organization, such as student record systems, library management systems, Learning Management Systems (LMSs), and so on, are exposed as services. Each service can then be utilized by other applications. For example, a student record system may expose services defining student enrollment and registration processes and related information, which can then be used by a learning management or library system.

The ultimate aim of a framework is for each identified service to be able to reference one or more open specifications or standards that can be used in the implementation of the service. A framework can support a number of organizational infrastructures that are still coherent and consistent with respect to one another. A framework does not aim to build a generic learning or knowledge management system. One of the primary goals of a framework such as the one presented here is to encourage "coherent diversity," by providing alternate service definitions that can then be used to meet the diverse goals of the organization.

In this chapter, we first define the basic orientations of TELOS as they were set at the begining in 2004. Then, we present the main use cases that have served later on to identify the services composing the system. The last section synthesizes these components in a service-oriented conceptual framework describing the organization of the system, before we conclude.

The ideas presented here are the result of work that started at the LICEF-CIRTA research center in the early 1990s based on the concept of virtual campuses [8],

---

[2] For examples of e-learning frameworks, consult [3, 6, 7].

on the Explor@ system seen as a learning portal generator [9], on the construction of a Web-based support system for instructional designers called ADISA [12], on resource aggregation [11], and on learning resource management [10]. This chapter is mainly based on recent results achieved within the LORNET[3] network by the authors [13,14].

4.2 TELOS Orientation and Vision

We first present 10 orientation principles that have guided the development of the TELOS system, a general four-level description of the system and the interaction among its main actors.

4.2.1 Orientation Principles

Here we present the main orientation principles that led to the development of the architecture and of the TELOS system.

Solving Real Learning and Knowledge Management Problems. The TELOS system aims at facilitating learning and knowledge management activities. This entails the need to examine real educational and knowledge management problems, to analyze them thoroughly, to observe future users of the system very early in the project, and to provide solutions to real user problems, not only in terms of system's tools, but also in terms of processes to use them effectively in real contexts. We must avoid being technologically driven instead of solution-driven, so the driving force is the careful definition of use cases that guides the design of the architecture and the development of the system.

Reusing and Integrating Existing and New Tools. LORNET is an oriented research project aiming to integrate technologies from different fields and to develop new ones when they are educationally significant. We reuse, as much as we can, existing editors, communication tools, interoperability protocols, and specification from norms and standards of international bodies, guided by use cases that underline the need for new tools or new ways to assemble or extend them. In these activities, we focus on specific TELOS core components that facilitate the reuse of existing tools by their users.

Concentrate on Essential Developments—Reduce Risks. The goal of the architecture is to reduce the risks by shifting the accent from tool development to careful analysis, evaluation, and well-planned specification. This will enable the TELOS team to focus on essential developments, and leave more costly development or adaptation to industrial, university or public partners in the network.

---

[3] LORNET (www.lornet.org) is a Canadian research network led by the first author and financed by the Canadian government and private companies for 5 years until 2008. The network groups six research centers and laboratories and over a hundred researchers, research professionals, and graduate students.

Flexible and Pragmatic Aggregation. Pragmatic aggregation means a convergence of technological means and human interventions or interactions to achieve certain goals. The system should have enough flexibility to be used in a variety of situations, from formal well-planned instruction, to more or less structured self-training, emerging communities of practice, or performance support systems integrated with work environments. The success of TELOS will come from its demonstrated utility in a diversity of situations.

A Society of Human and Computer Agents. Software engineering sometimes sees the "system" to be solely composed of software components separated from their users. In contrast, we adopt a multiagent view where human and computer agents are interacting components of the system, providing services to each other. Extending the "human-in-the-loop" approach we recognize that sometimes organizational adaptations, advising, documentation support, or human communication activities can be more appropriate (and less costly) than building new tools. This approach also favors maximal results with realistic efforts.

Build Technology-Independent Models. The important work involved in the TELOS system should survive the rapid updating pace of technologies in general. At the start, it enables TELOS to operate on different network, hardware, and operating system configurations, and to integrate with other learning or knowledge management systems. The architecture is built to protect the conceptual models from technological instability. The conceptual specifications are kept separate from any implementation. The TELOS system should then be able to reuse such "conceptual programs" despite different previous technology environments, and adapt to new technological implementations. Thus the conceptual models are not just prerequisite to building the TELOS system; they are part of the system, as one of its most fundamental layers.

Learning Ecosystem Models for Planning, Support, and Evaluation. Most distributed learning systems today do not have a model of the processes, the users, the operations, and the resources that they intend to support. Besides direct support for learning and knowledge management tasks, we aim to introduce tools to model the complex processes involved in a distributed learning system, before its use (to design it), during its use (to support users and observe their behavior), and after its use (to evaluate and maintain the system). These modeling components and tools are built-in features of the TELOS system. They aim to enable users to interact efficiently in preplanned as well as emerging and user-controlled events where the initial environment is transformed, thus implementing a "learning ecosystem" approach.

Modularization and Layer Independence. The very flexible system envisioned here will amount to a very small kernel at a very high level of abstraction, capable of assembling services that generally form the core of a system, for example, functions like learning object aggregations, component coordination and control, ontology-based indexation and search, function modeling, and so on. The architecture will promote modularity: horizontally between components and vertically from an abstract representation, to a concrete implementation, to a run-time version of TELOS applications.

Construct Reusable and Interchangeable Models and Components. Because TELOS is model-oriented, it then becomes possible to implement the model components in various forms and alternative tools, classified by their functionalities and grouped in interoperable classes. TELOS then appears as a flexible assembly system enabling the integration of tools, already existing or to be produced, by various groups, to support a variety of learning and knowledge management models. Even at the kernel level, the general functions could be covered by one or more alternative "kernel" modules, accessible on a service bus for selection by system configurators and designers.

An Assembly and Coordination System. TELOS will not be another huge distributed learning platform or a system to generate rigid platforms, even though it can assemble components specific to some intended set of applications. The term *TEleLearning Operating System* should be seen as a metaphor. TELOS is planned essentially as a set of coordination and synchronization services supporting the interactions of persons and computerized resources that compose a learning or knowledge management system.

4.2.2 System's Levels and Main Actors

Figure 4.1 shows a cascade of more and more specific system levels and their corresponding actors. The TELOS core is managed, adapted, and extended by system engineers. With it, technologists in different organizations produce one or more TELOS Learning and Knowledge Management System (LKMS), each generalizing the idea of an "on-line platform" adapted to an organization's particular needs. Unlike the present situation, each platform is extensible, and its components are reusable in other platforms.

With any TELOS LKMS, designers can create, produce, deliver, and maintain a number of Learning and Knowledge Management Applications (LKMAs), that is, courses, learning events, knowledge management portals, etc. The LKMS is a platform for the aggregation of resources, activities, and actors. Each LKMA, composed using a LKMS, groups one or more actor-specific aggregates called Learning and Knowledge Management Environments (LKMEs) intended for certain types of participants: learners, content experts, coaches, tutors, evaluators, managers, etc. An LKME is an aggregate of documents, tools, services, operations (activities), and actor agents.

Before delivery, an LKMA and its different LKMEs are instantiated by an actor called an application administrator to start a new session involving a group of participants. Using these instances, the participants produce results that are resources and outcomes called Learning and Knowledge Management Products (LKMP), which are stored in a database for reuse or adaptive support.

Figure 4.2 presents the five main actors on Figure 4.1 and the communication pattern between them. Learners and facilitators normally use a learning and knowledge management application (LKMA) that provides them with communication channels. This LKMA can be a structured environment built by a designer using a learning and knowledge management system (LKMS), or simply a set of general

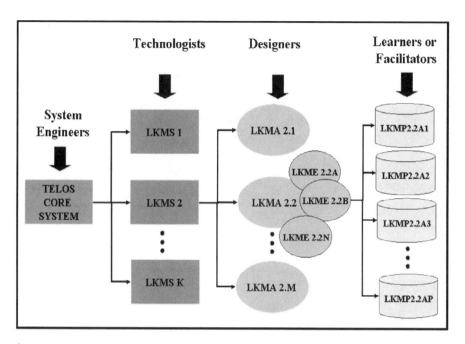

FIGURE 4.1. Four-level cascade of systems or products.

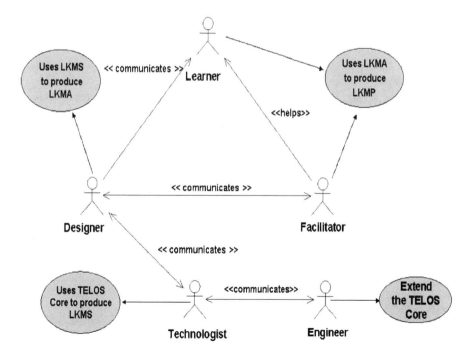

FIGURE 4.2. Interactions between the main actors.

TELOS services for emergent exploration. A LKMS is a generalization of the actual LMS, LKMS, CMS, or platforms assembled by a technologist using the TELOS system core and the libraries developed by a TELOS engineer.

Note that the roles played by a person are interchangeable. Some persons acting as learners or facilitators can also be their own designers, and their own technologists or even engineers. Conversely, persons building environment can also be their own facilitators or designers. The interchange of roles can be implemented by software role agents providing an interface between a human or system actor and the functionalities and data needed to achieve that role. Also some of the roles can be played by software agents, for example an intelligent advisor agent or a resource finder acting as a facilitator.

4.3 User Operations and Main Service Components

TELOS is a specialized operating system on top of a computer network designed to support learning and acquiring knowledge at a distance. In this section, we present the main TELOS use cases and an overview of the TELOS components needed to support these use cases.

4.3.1 Three Operational Levels

Figure 4.3 presents a conceptual view of the system by presenting its main use cases.

A TELOS user (or a team of users) possibly helped by a facilitator takes the responsibility to perform a TELOS operation. In this operation, users and facilitators use or modify resources in the TELOS core and produce new resources that sometimes are put back (embedded or referenced) in the TELOS core.

Every time a user performs an operation, his/her previous knowledge and competencies are changed to new ones. This fact is the essence of learning by doing and doing by learning. In the TELOS system, it is possible to represent explicitly knowledge and evolving competencies related to the resources (persons, operations, documents, and tools) using one or more semantic referentials. Semantic referentials can take the form of standard or specific metadata, classifications and taxonomies, thesauri, or ontologies.

In TELOS all the operations are driven (or at least initiated) by humans, always through some user interfaces and mediated by computer programs. There are three basic sorts of operations, depending on their level of granularity:

- *Basic operations on a resource* consist of asking for or delivering a service using a resource either directly or indirectly, mediated through a TELOS agent provided by the system or mediated by another resource.
- *Resource life-cycle operations* consist of a series of four sub-operations (phases) where a resource is composed, managed (prepared) for use, used in some activity, and analyzed, providing feedback to start, if necessary, a new resource life cycle.

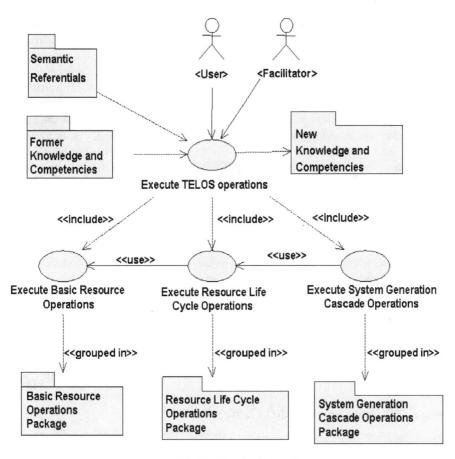

FIGURE 4.3. User levels of operations.

These operations are generally performed in sequence by a team of different actors.

- *System generation cascade operations* are even more global. They consist of extending the TELOS core with new resources, using it to produce a Learning and Knowledge Management System (a platform), designing with it one or more Learning and Knowledge Management Applications (courses, learning events, knowledge management environments), and finally, using these applications to learn and to produce results grouped in a LKMP (Learning and Knowledge Management Product). These operations are generally performed by different actors as presented in Figures 4.1 and 4.2.

The relation between the three levels of operation is represented on Figure 4.3 by "use" links. A system generation cascade is generally composed of many resource life-cycle operations. Also, a resource life-cycle is composed of many basic operations.

We can use different metaphors to describe these general processes. In a manufacturing metaphor, the resource life cycle corresponds to a process where a product passes through different productions operations. In the system generation cascade, the TELOS core is like a factory that produces machine components or complete machines; the products of this first factory are used to build machines that will be used in other factories (LKMSs); those machines are used to build cars, aircrafts, etc. (LKMAs), which are used by end users to produce an outcome. Using a biological metaphor, a simple operation corresponds to a life moment of an organism; a resource life cycle is an ontogenesis, the process of an individual organism growing from a simple to a more complex level. Finally, a system generation cascade is a phylogenesis, a process that generates new organisms from parents, similar to the evolution of life.

These images are important to understand the role of the TELOS core within an evolving TELOS system. It is similar to the genome, the code of life that composes an organic system at a moment we could call its birth, when it starts to evolve in the hands of its users toward a more and more complete and useful system. Also, as a manufacturer, the TELOS core itself starts with a complete set of components to produce LKMS factories, but it will also be open to improvement, adding new processes and operations, to produce more versatile machines.

The role of this TELOS framework is thus to identify clearly what basic components are needed in the TELOS core for this evolution process to start. To achieve this, we will represent conceptually the system at a fully operating stage, at a certain time core (t) after the system has evolved from its core (0) position.

4.3.2 Basic Operations on a Resource

We start identifying components of the TELOS core by first looking more closely at basic operations. Whatever his/her role in the system, a user needs to ask for or to deliver services by performing one or many basic operations. The simplest case is when the user interacts directly with a resource through its user interface (UI), if it has one. This resource, for example an email client or a simulation software, is referenced in a resource library within the TELOS core or obtainable from a search in external resource repositories. The user obtains the resource interface that enables him or her to interact with the service. When a separation between a resource's UI and its internal logic exists, possibly with a network distance in between, the user must obtain this resource's UI, thus enabling him or her to interact with the services it offers. For this, we need a resource distributor provided by the central part of the TELOS core called the *kernel*.

Two other situations are displayed in Figure 4.4 that require also an agent distributor component within the kernel. In these cases the user does not act directly on the resource but through an agent (mediator) provided by the central part of the TELOS core called the *kernel*. In one case, a *user agent* can represent the user in the system to mediate his or her interaction with the resource. For example, the user agent can provide filtering of the operations with the resource, or trace the user/resource interaction to prepare adapted advices. In the other case, the user

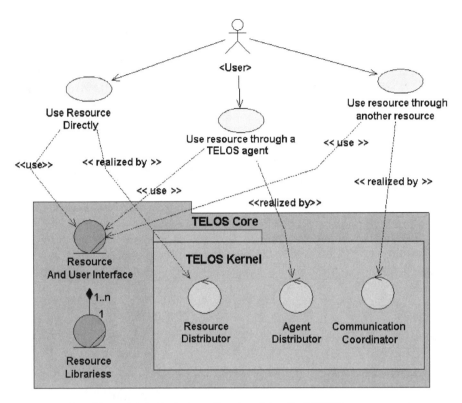

FIGURE 4.4. Basic operations involving the TELOS core.

will interact with an intermediary resource that will use a *system agent (SA)* to obtain the services of the resource. This is done through the TELOS communication hub, and a communication coordinator within the kernel will take care of the communication operations.

4.3.3 Resource Life-Cycle Operations

As shown on Figure 4.5, a resource life cycle is composed of four basic operations (or phases): compose, manage, use, and analyze. These operations form a sequence with feedback loops. They are performed by corresponding actors: composers, managers, explorers, and analysts that use corresponding tools or services.

The resource life cycle begins with the composition process in which a composer creates, edits, or composes a model or template for a class of reusable resources, using an authoring or composition tool. Depending on the type of resources, different authoring editors can be used, such as a simple text editor, a more complex learning design editor, or an LKMS aggregator. For example, with a learning design editor, a user will produce a learning scenario or a process structure that may

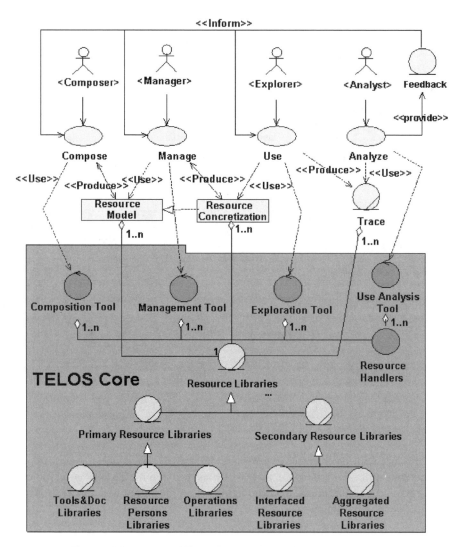

FIGURE 4.5. Resource life-cycle operation and related components.

be concretized at the next phase by associating precise documents, services, or participants with objects in the scenario model.

In the next resource life-cycle phase, a manager (a person or a team) may reference the resource model in a TELOS repository, compose a metadata description, produce a certain number of "concretizations" of the resource (versions of the resource model) obtained by parameterization, concretization, and adaptation, and finally activate the concrete resources for the use phase. For example, in this phase, a course manager will assign students and tutors to a version (instance) of a course for a certain session and prepare their communication within a forum and a videoconferencing system.

In the third phase, an explorer finds and uses an instance of the resource, producing exploration traces: annotations, logs, and other products, for example, messages exchanged in a forum, an exam, or an essay.

Finally, in the last phase, an analyst observes the exploration products (during or after the use of the resource instance) and analyzes these data to offer some useful feedback to the other resource life-cycle actors. This feedback can be made available in a simple Web page to all participants, or take the form of an advice specifically addressed to the resource explorer, manager, or composer (or to improve itself). For example, data from a forum-based learning activity can be analyzed and recommendations can be issued to the composer to modify the assignment, or to the manager to add participants or to separate the group in smaller teams, or to the explorer to interact more regularly.

All the users and the tools implied in the cycle may be equipped with agents (interfaces) connecting them to the services hub. Located within the TELOS core there are system tools that provide communication between users, resource Handlers, and resource libraries or repositories. Handlers are services provided by TELOS at different levels of the system.

The resource life cycle can be applied to all sorts of primary resources: documents that provide information to users, tools that help users to process information, persons acting as information resources, or operations descriptions that provide ways to process information. The life cycle of a primary resource may apply even to an application's (tool) software development process, where, for example, we have the developers in the role of "composers." The primary resources are referenced in the primary resource libraries, integrated in the TELOS core. Particularly for small primary resources, the distinction between "Resource Model" and "Resource Concretization" may be thin or noinexistent. For example, a primary resource like a notepad is created by a developer "as is," and is already ready to run, as an instance, not a model.

This life cycle can also be applied to secondary resources. A secondary resource is either atomic, resulting from a primary resource through a simple phase of preparation, or an aggregation from other atomic or secondary resources. Prepared resources are obtained by wrapping, filtering, scripting, or extracting parts of a primary resource for facilitating direct (possibly remote) use, or potential aggregation. Aggregates are obtained by grouping, integrating, or orchestrating some prepared resources. An aggregate may recursively contain other aggregates. Resources obtained in this way are referenced in the secondary resource libraries, also integrated in the TELOS core.

In all four basic operations of the resource life cycle, semantic referentials, integrated in the TELOS core, can be used to describe (index, reference) the knowledge, the technical properties, or the administrative context of use of any resource. Semantic referentials can take the form of standard or specific metadata, classifications and taxonomies, thesauri or ontologies. This functionality will enable TELOS to operate on the semantic Web.

4.3.4 System Generation Cascade Operations

The TELOS system is extended by a four-level cascade from the TELOS core: grandparent tools producing parent tools, which are used to compose children tools that, in turn, are used to produce results. The cascade involves four sets of operations: TELOS core extension, core use for LKMS composition, LKMS use for LKMA composition, and LKMA use for LKMP production (Fig. 4.6).

In the first step of the cascade, an engineer may extend the TELOS core, using the *core modifier*, a handler within the core, to add new resources or resource handlers, for example. He can also add components in any library, for example a system module to interact with a new non-TELOS system, a new prepared interface for an existing primary resource (application, document, operation, or resource–person), or an extension of a semantic referential. Eventually, this process may be organized as a resource aggregation life cycle as presented in the previous section. Here, the composition phase of the life cycle is the core extension by the engineer, and the use phase is the use of the core by a technologist

The second generation step is the construction, by a technologist, of a LKMS using the *LKMS Manager*, another handler tool within the core. This operation

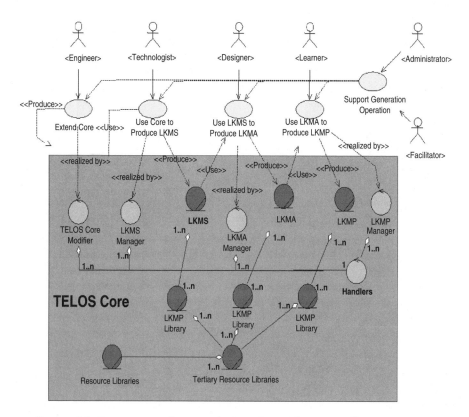

FIGURE 4.6. System generation cascade operations and corresponding components.

may be viewed as a composition part in the LKMS life cycle. The LKMS use by a designer is the use phase of the LKMS aggregation life cycle.

In the third generation step, a designer may use a LKMS instance to produce a LKMA model, for example a course scenario or community of practice environment, using an *LKMA Manager*, another handler tool within the core. The use of the LKMA by learners is the use phase for the LKMA aggregation life cycle.

The final generation step is the use of an LKMA instance to allow knowledge acquisition by a learner. Using an *LKMP Manager*, another handler within the core, the learner may produce some traceable results (activity logs, annotations, learner-produced resources, test evaluations, etc.) usable in the analysis phase. If these learner products are used for other purposes, for example to support a personal portfolio, their creation can become the composition phase for an LKMP life cycle. Any other data that an LKMA may produce internally during its execution (i.e., to preserve its internal states as a system) are private and not meaningful for external use. They do not belong to an LKMP.

At any of the four system generation steps, facilitators can provide different forms of assistance to engineers, technologists, designers, and learners, and also to other facilitators.

Each of the four steps involved in the *system generation cascade* may assume internally its own *resource life cycle*, that is, may have standard subphases. For example, an LKMA might be in the phase of composition, management (preparation for use), use (exploration), or analysis.

A shown in Table 4.1, at any of the system generation steps, except the first one where core administrators manage the core composed by engineers to produce a core instance for the technologists, administrators play two sets of roles. For example, LKMS administrators manage LKMS to produce instances for the designers, but they also analyze the core to end an LKMS life cycle, providing feedback to the engineer. Table 4.1 reconciles the resource life-cycle roles with the system generation cascade roles.

TABLE 4.1. Relation between resource life cycle roles and system generation roles

Cascade Roles:	Core		LKMS		LKMA		LKMP	
Life-Cyle Roles:	Engineer	Administrator	Technologist	Administrator	Designer	Administrator	Learner	Administrator
Composer	Core		LKMS		LKMA		LKMP	
Manager		Core		LKMS		LKMA		LKMP
Explorer			Core		LKMS		LKMA	
Analyzer				Core		LKMS		LKMA

The LKMS, LKMA, and LKMP models (classes) and activated instances resulting from the generation cascade process are *tertiary resources* that can be referenced and embedded in corresponding *tertiary resource libraries* within the TELOS core.

4.3.5 Semantic Referencing of a Resource

The semantic referencing of resources can be involved in any basic, resource life cycle or system cascade operation. Semantic referentials can be built into

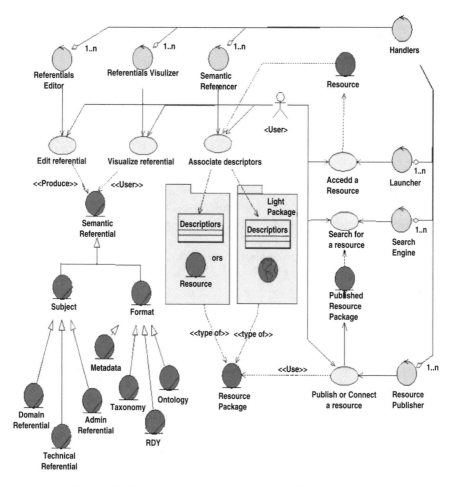

FIGURE 4.7. Semantic operations and corresponding components.

the TELOS system to represent knowledge and competencies that can be associated with a resource (Fig. 4.7). Competencies are "degrees" of knowledge, for example skills and performance that a user can perform with respect to a given unit of knowledge. They can take many forms: standardized metadata (e.g., IEEE LOM), taxonomies, thesauri, or ontology documents written using the Ontology Web Language (OWL), Resource Description Frameworks (RDF), or topic maps, [5].

Three basic handler categories are provided to process semantic referentials: *editors*, *viewers*, and *indexers*. Editors help a user construct a semantic referential. Viewers provide access to semantic referentials to help browse the knowledge and competency classes and properties. Referencers provide functionalities to associate semantic descriptors to any kind of resource. Semantic descriptors can be selected in predefined semantic referentials by a person using the indexer or by a specialized TELOS resource tool (software agent) extracting the descriptors from the resource using data mining or other forms of knowledge extraction.

TELOS-referenced resources generalize the concept of "content packages used by SCORM, content packages (CPs) group together one or more resources, their relationships and metadata describing their properties." To be shareable, CPs must be published by a handler called a *publisher*. The publisher places the referenced resource in one or more Internet-accessible resource repositories.

Another handler, a *finder*, provides one or more search methods to find a resource, displaying a list of resource names corresponding to a find request, together with their descriptors.

Then, selecting one of the resources, a *retriever* uses the resource location to perform the necessary operations to provide access to a person or a software agent, display a document or launch the resource. If needed, a special handler in the kernel, the controller, can be called by a retriever to facilitate the interaction with the resource.

4.4 TELOS Framework Organization

In this section we present the organization of the TELOS framework and the general services it provides to engineers, technologists, designers, learners, administrators and facilitators involved in the systems generation cascade.

4.4.1 TELOS Core and Kernel Structure and Extension

Figure 4.8 displays the general structure of the TELOS Core presented in previous sections. In this section, we will identify the main services used by the engineer and by the core administrator, and their facilitators to extend the TELOS core. The TELOS core comprises a kernel, a core manager that enables the evolution of the core, seven core libraries of resources, and their corresponding handlers.

The kernel contains service registries and servers, application client and agents distributor, a communication coordinator, a general resource controller, and translators between protocols and standards. The knowledge (K) library contains semantic referentials to describe application domains as well as technical and administrative metadata needed for resource management. The other libraries group resources according to their aggregation level: primary resources (documents and tools, persons or operations), secondary resources (interfaced or aggregated), and tertiary resources (LKMS, LKMA, or LKMP).

Engineering Services

The TELOS core engineers may use the services of a special handler, the *core manager*, to modify the core structure, the core handlers, or the structure and composition of the core libraries. With it, the engineers can do the following:

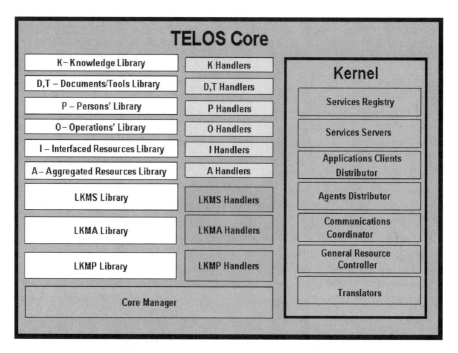

FIGURE 4.8. TELOS core and kernel main components.

- *Modify semantic handlers and semantic referential structures.* Add, suppress, or modify core knowledge handlers and library structure: ontology editors, viewers and indexers, conceptual maps editors, viewers and indexers, librarian cataloging and indexing tools, etc.
- *Add, suppress, or modify primary, secondary or tertiary resource handlers and resource library structures.* Of particular importance are the addition of modification of assistance or support tools: helpers, advisers, peer matchers, etc. may be added, respecting the conformity with their context of operation; and also the addition or modification of control tools: new floor control managers, resource sharers, security watchers, privacy verifiers.
- *Modify core structure.* These operations are delicate, involving backward compatibility problems, but add flexibility to TELOS. They include adding a new interfaced resource type to the existent ones; adding a new aggregation type to the existent ones (collection, function, fusion, project, etc.); adding a cascade fabrication type to the existent ones for LKMS, LKMA, LKMP; updating a core handler. When a new version of the TELOS core is produced, with some additional core services, it is possible that the TELOS clients have to be also modified accordingly.
- *Modify global core support and control.* The global support and control offered by the core manager can be modified. This might also involve eventual kernel modifications.

- *Note, trace, and receive support in their engineering operations.* As for any composition activity, these services can eventually be operated in a collaborative way.
- *Save, suspend, and resume core modification.* Performs these operations involved in any composition activity, operated in multiple sessions, determining the evolution of the TELOS system.

Core Administrator Services

A core administrator manages the content of some primary, secondary, or tertiary library. He may act on the request of another actor (technologist, designer, or learner), or interact with this actor to perform or delegate to him the right to add, update, or eliminate a semantic or a primary, secondary, or tertiary resource.

Core Facilitators' Services

A core facilitator supports the engineer or the core administrator in his or her task. Here, most of the time, facilitation services will be provided by the on-line TELOS technical documentation or by another senior engineer or administrator.

4.4.2 Core Use for LKMS Construction

Figure 4.8 presents the general structure of an LKMS embedded in the TELOS core or external to it. In this section, we identify the main services used by the technologist (LKMS composer), by the LKMS administrator, and by the LKMS facilitators to both of them.

The technologist constructs an LKMS model by extracting resources from the core libraries and handlers to be included in the LKMS. To achieve this, he will use a LKMS handler (editor) provided in the core. Such a handler may use a combination of aggregation principles (collections, integration, and orchestration). This variable geometry is the main purpose of constructing LKMSs instead of having only one platform or LCMS. Initially, the TELOS core may be equipped with a unique LKMS handler and therefore produce LKMS with similar structures. More diversity can be added by an engineer, adding new LKMS handlers in the TELOS core.

When the construction process is considered finished, the LKMS model is handed to the LKMS administrator to start the LKMS instance preparation phase. The administrator may begin the adaptation to the context of LKMS use. This phase may consist of a chain of sessions producing finally an LKMS active instance like the ones shown in Figure 4.9. The administrator can place the LKMS to work in the core LKMS library (embedded LKMS) or enable it to function external to the core, in an interfaced, linked, and even autonomous way. In the last case, all the necessary handlers and parts of the kernel will have to be included in the external LKMS.

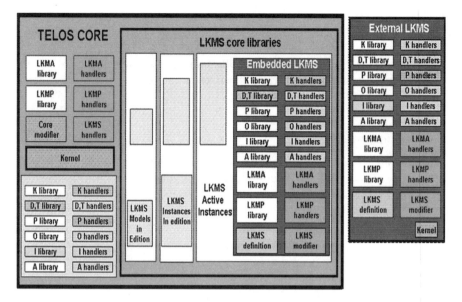

FIGURE 4.9. LKMS general aggregation structure and positions.

Technologist Services

The LKMS composition by the technologist is an aggregate composition. Therefore, he can access composition services such as finding components, making
notes, producing traces, receiving help, etc. Here we concentrate on the more
specific aspects. With an LKMS editor, the technologist can do the following:

- *Compose the LKMS knowledge referential.* If the global core referentials are not
  available or pertinent, a LKMS-specific K referential may be necessary using a
  knowledge editor.
- *Organize the LKMS structure* using an aggregation principle that will be selected,
  and choose the LKMS future destination (embedded or external: interfaced,
  linked, or autonomous).
- *Organize LKMS parts* (adding resources libraries and handlers to the LKMS
  model): knowledge handlers and documents (ontologies, metadata, etc.);
  primary resources (documents, tools, persons and operations) and their
  handlers; interfaced or aggregated resources and their handlers (editors, publishers, interpreters, structure editors, resource binders, support and control editors
  explorers, generators, data viewers, etc.; LKMA and LKMP parts, libraries, and
  handlers, or a component placed in the LKMA library.
- *Prepare the LKMS modifier* for later adaptation.
- *Organize support and control* parts of the global, depending on the destination
  (embedded, linked, autonomous).
- *Note, produce traces, and receive support* in his construction activity.

- *Save, leave, suspend, and resume LKMS construction*. An LKMS in construction may be saved in the LKMS core library. As for any other aggregate composition, the LKMS construction may be done in several sessions, the technologist suspending or resuming the composition cascade. If the composition is cooperative, we may speak about leaving a session and have it continued by another technologist.

LKMS Administrator Services

The composition and the exploration of an LKMS vary depending on the complexity of its structure. A "thin" LKMS has a simpler structure, but its execution involves remote invocation of handlers and resources. A fat LKMS has its own libraries but still needs to communicate with some core handlers. The heavy LKMS may be a cumbersome entity (with resource replication problems), but it functions autonomously. These are the main choices a LKMS administrator must make when preparing an LKMS instance for publication. We now present the main services available to him:

- *Choose a saved LKMS model and create an instance*. The LKMS models are reusable structural templates with a certain degree of flexibility in the template instantiation. The LKMS administrator begins by choosing a LKMS model, usable as an instance generation support (from the first core library).
- *Prepare the LKMS instance* (extend edition). The administrator may adapt parameterize, concretize, or extend the LKMS for insertion in the core or for external activation, deciding on the thin-fat-heavy alternative and the deployment context, and finally installing the instance in its use. This can be done in one or many LKMS instance preparation sessions.
- *Note and produce traces and receive support*. As any other meta-managed activity.
- *Save, leave, suspend, and resume*. The technologist's work may be saved in the second LKMS core library that contains LKMS instances in preparation.
- *Activate the LKMS*. The LKMS instance is activated to work in the chosen contexts: embedded in the core or published for external linked or autonomous use. It then passes to the third LKMS core library that contains LKMS active instances.
- *Core use analysis and feedback*. The LKMS administrator is, at the same time, a core analyst of the core life-cycle process. He may analyze the core use to provide some feedback propositions to engineers.

LKMS Facilitator Services

LKMS construction may involve technologists and facilitators, working synchronously or asynchronously to observe, guide, evaluate, and replace the LKMS

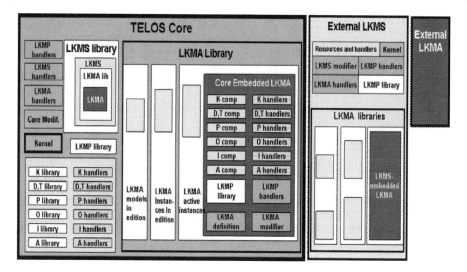

FIGURE 4.10. LKMA general aggregation structure and positions.

administrator in some of his operations, eventually by supporting also the LKMS instantiation workflow. If the LKMS composition uses an LKMS composition workflow aggregate (for example, a meta-function), the support can be treated as an execution phase of that workflow.

4.4.3 LKMS Use and LKMA Construction

Figure 4.10 presents the general structure and four positions of an LKMA, embedded in the TELOS core LKMS or LKMA library, embedded in an external LKMS, or totally external to any LKMS.

These LKMAs are composed by designers (for example an educational author) using LKMA handlers (editors) and some "raw material" (secondary resources) placed in an embedded or external LKMS. They may also use directly a LKMA handler and resources placed in the TELOS core. Designers compose a LKMA model that can be placed (and modified) in the first section of the core LKMA library, or within the LKMA library of the constructing LKMS (embedded or external).

The LKMA model is a template that may be reproduced, with some adaptations and concretizations by a LKMA administrator to produce LKMA instances. After a certain number of operations, in a single or a chain of preparation session, this administrator produces a final LKMA instance that can be activated in the core LKMA library, in the LKMA library of an embedded or external constructor LKMS, or as an autonomous LKMA.

Designer Services

- *Organize the K referential layer.* Generally, the semantic referential used in an LKMA already exists in a LKMS or in the core and can be retrieved from there. However, sometimes the designer will need to build a local semantic referential in the form of a domain ontology, conceptual maps, thesaurus, catalogues, indexing keys, etc. or a local "add-on" document, completing (adapting) a knowledge document. The most interesting case is when the LKMA is used by learners and their facilitators for an emergent modification of a semantic model.
- *Define structure.* The central part of any LKMA is its aggregate internal organization structure (in the thin case, it may be the only part). It may consist of only one aggregation layer (conforming to the collection, fusion, project, function, or other aggregation types), or in a recursive cascade of aggregate definitions. This process is also called "scenario building" or "learning design."
- *Organize an LKMA content package.* Add, suppress, or update the aggregated resources, sometimes with their handlers, and their semantic descriptors.
- *Organize actor support and the control layer*, depending on his activation type and its position.
- *Note and produce traces.* The LKMA designer may annotate his activity. These data are not included in the final aggregate, but are observable in the same way as other composition sessions. The LKMA editor used in the composition process may also intercept and save some composition activity traces.
- *Cooperate and receive support.* The LKMA composition activity (observed directly or by traces) may be collaborative and may be supported by the system (for example, using design metafunctions) or by specialized facilitators (for example, by technologists having produced the producing LKMS).
- *Save, leave, suspend, and resume.* As for any other aggregate composition, the LKMA construction may be done in several sessions, the designer suspending or resuming the composition cascade. If the composition is collaborative, the designer may leave a session and the composition can be continued by another designer.
- *Publish template.* When the construction process is finished the LKMA is published in the second section of a LKMA library, either within the core, or in the embedded or external producing LKMS used by the designer.

LKMA Administrator Services

When the LKMA model has been published for instantiation, it can move to the second section of a LKMA library, for an administrator to start the instantiation process. This can be done in one or many preparation sessions. As with other processes, collaborative LKMA instance preparation is possible, eventually driven by a LKMA workflow composed previously.

- *Choose a published LKMA model to create a new instance.* The LKMA administrator begins by choosing an LKMA model usable as an instance generation support. He declares a new LKMA instance, based on the chosen model to the second section of the LKMA library where it may be edited.

- *Prepare the LKMA instance* (extended edition). The administrator adapts the LKMA for core or external activation (parameterization, concretization, and eventually a composition extension), and decides on the deployment context: embedded thin/fat/heavy or external interfaced/linked/autonomous are the available possibilities. He then installs the instance in its future use context in the third section of the LKMA library. This concretization process may be distributed among the composing, managings, and using phases of the LKMA, applying various organization strategies or "life-cycle modes."

- *Note and produce traces and receive support.* As in any other meta-managed activity.

- *Save, leave, suspend, and resume.* As in any other management activity.

- *Activate the LKMA.* When an instantiation process is finished, the manager "closes" the instance editing chain and activates the instance for execution. The LKMA instance is integrated in the third section of the LKMA library (core, LKMS embedded, or LKMS external) or placed in an external context for LKMS-free use. In that last case, and for some types of LKMA aggregates, this step may imply a LKMA "compilation," producing an executable LKMA.

- *Analyze LKMS uses and provides feedback.* The LKMA administrator is, at the same time, a LKMS use analyst. He may analyze the LKMS used by designers for producing and managing LKMA and provide feedback to technologists.

Designer and LKMA Facilitators Services

The designer or the LKMA administrator may need synchronous or asynchronous support from technologists having composed the LKMS they use. Another possibility is to embed the LKMA life-cycle process in a design workflow or meta-functions. In that case, the meta-function acts as a system facilitator, observing, guiding, evaluating, and doing some operations for the LKMA designer or administrator, eventually supporting collaboration between teams. An example of this is given by the ADISA learning design support system [12].

4.4.4 LKMA Use and LKMP Construction

Figure 4.11 presents the general structure and eight positions of an LKMP composed using an LKMA. The learners and the facilitators who participate in LKMA instance "sessions" are the end users who will produce results to be included in these LKMPs. Some LKMA results such as annotations, learner documents, evaluations, etc., may be edited directly by the participants, while others, for example traces, may be obtained by TELOS agents placed in an autonomous LKMA, in the sustaining LKMS, in the sustaining core, or in the kernel. These results are normally placed in the data layer of the executing LKMA instance. They can be selected later for inclusion in LKMP libraries as learning or knowledge management products. They can also help compose user or group ePortfolios.

Learner Services

- *Find and access an LKMA instance.* The learner begins a session by accessing an active LKMA instance, placed in the core LKMA library, in the LKMA library of a core LKMS, in the LKMA library of an external LKMS, or in an external autonomous position. If he resumes the use of an interrupted instance exploration, he will obtain the corresponding LKMA saved data. A LKMA participant can be added to a collaborative session already opened by another participant.
- *Explore an LKMA instance.* The LKMA exploration depends on its aggregation structure and the collaborative facilities provided by LKMA handlers. In collection aggregates, it may consist of choosing and using resources grouped in a collection. In fusion aggregates, the structural relations will constrain the learner's freedom in using the components but will also reduce the "lost in space" effect. In project aggregates, every learner may dispose of special interfaces or environments, conforming to his roles in the project. In function aggregates, the learner will be guided by the model of the operational flow, for example a learning design structure.

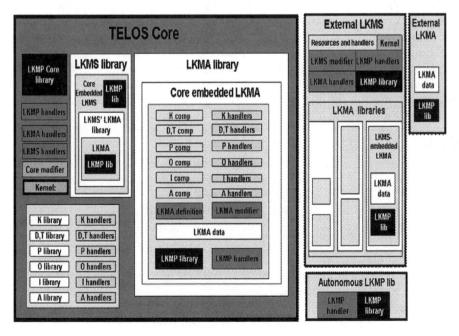

FIGURE 4.11. LKMP general aggregation structure and positions.

- *Collaborate with session partners.* If the LKMA provides synchronous and/or asynchronous collaboration, every participant may be helped in coordinating his activities with his partners, whether they act in the same, previous, or later instance sessions. Sometimes the partners are working on different operations (cooperation), sometimes they make a parallel approach to the same operation (collaboration), and sometimes they are cooperating or collaborating as proposed by the activity structure of the aggregate.
- *Receive support.* The learner may use the support integrated in the LKMA or delivered by a facilitator accessing the same instance.
- *Concretize some resources.* For example, the learning design may provide place holders for run-time learner productions. These "delivery time concretizations" may also involve a mechanism for the transmission of produced objects between instance participants.
- *Use component resources and produce new resources* (documents, tools, aggregates, etc.). The main purpose of the LKMA is to facilitate the access to its component resources. The facilitation may consist only of the organization of a selective interface allowing the opening of the resource (tool, document, service, user communication). The TELOS resource controllers may also offer resource use services: access negotiations, downloads, installation, decoding, on-the-fly dependence solving, action interception and logging, scripted events injection, inter-resources parameter propagation, concurrent use solving, quality of service (QoS) adaptations, etc. Some LKMA resources (acting as editors) may help the learner to produce results (documents, tools, etc.) usable later in another operation, or by an analyst observing the resulting data or by a LKMP administrator.
- *Produce intercepted traces.* Some LKMS sustaining a LKMA session may intercept the user actions (depending on the declared ethics policy for this LKMA instance). These "interceptions" may be used by the user observing his own advancement in the same or previous sessions, by a session or instance partner (connected simultaneously or later), by a LKMA data analyst or a LKMP administrator.
- *Mark advancement and annotate.* The learner may declare explicitly his advancement and make related annotations. These "notes" will complete the "interceptions" and the "evaluations" forming the LKMA instance "data."
- *Assess learning.* Learning is the main goal of using an LKMA. Because of its internal intellectual nature, it can only be observed and managed indirectly. The LKMA may provide some tools for the evaluation of the learning results or may make some deductions about the knowledge evolution using "the learning by doing presumption." If the learner makes some production with success, he can be assumed as possessing the associated knowledge or having attained the associated skills or competencies.
- *Add results to a LKMP.* The learner may add some of his personal results to a LKMP, a learning and knowledge management product repository that can be placed in one of eight places (as shown on Fig. 4.4): the core LKMP library, the LKMP library of an embedded LKMS, the LKMP library of an embedded

LKMA, the LKMP library of a LKMA embedded in a core LKMS, the LKMP library of an external LKMS, the LKMP library of a LKMA embedded in an external LKMS, the LKMP library of a external autonomous LKMA, or in a completely autonomous position.

- *Manage the LKMP and ePortfolios.* Whatever the LKMP's position, the learner manages its content, which can form his personal ePortfolio.

Learner Facilitator's Services

- *Observe LKMA use.* Any support activity, predefined or launched by a service request from the learner, may begin with the observation of the learner's operations. The observation can cover previous or planned activities by the learner, in the current open sessions or closed sessions of the same instance, or even in other instances of the same LKMA model. This observation depends on the awareness of the possibilities offered by the LKMA collaborative explorer: perceive the partner presence and actions, see the notes and the traces, access the resources produced by learners, and access the learner group data.
- *Guide LKMA use.* The facilitators use the communication possibilities of the LKMA explorer to guide the learner in his activities, using synchronous and asynchronous written, oral, or video messages.
- *Execute some support operations.* Some support from the facilitator may consist in actions: executing some operations, adapting some parameters, preparing some conditions, etc.
- *Make annotations and evaluations.* The facilitator may add annotations to the LKMS exploration data about the learner (and eventually his own) activities. He also may evaluate the learner competence or modify some data about the learner's knowledge and competencies, according to his mandate. He may compose some evaluation result documents. These elements may be placed in the LKMA data layer and added later to some LKMP.

LKMP Administrator Services

- *Manage LKMP.* The LKMP administrator may change the content of a LKMP, depending on the privacy policy.
- *Correlate LKMP and resources libraries.* Some products may be promoted from an LKMP to a TELOS resource library by the LKMP administrator. In this case, the LKMP products may be placed in the shared library of the producing LKMA, wherever its deployment position is; they can also be replaced in the LKMP library with pointers to these actual resources.
- *Correlate LKMP and user accounts.* Some LKMP products, for example LKMA instance exploration data, new knowledge references to the user, or new documents produced by the user, sustain an update of the user accounts.
- *Analyze LKMA data.* The data (traces, annotations, documents, products) resulting from an LKMA instance exploration (closed or not) may be accessed for analysis by a LKMP administrator. It is possible that the data analyst uses the

data view facilities of the LKMA explorer, working on a closed instance. Some other data analysis tools may be used.

- *Produce observations and propositions.* The LKMP administrator, acting as an analyst, may produce documents reflecting his recommendations to LKMA designers or users: reports, statistics, LKMA or LKMS change requests, etc.

4.4.5 Summary of TELOS Services

Figure 4.12 presents a summary of the TELOS services that we have described in the previous sections as TELOS handlers. They are grouped into five

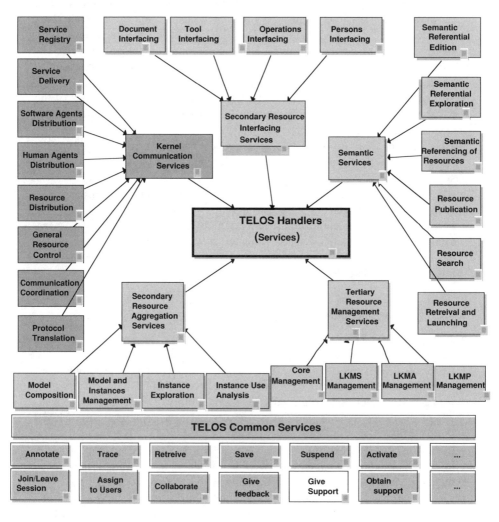

FIGURE 4.12. TELOS handlers (services) taxonomy.

categories of services: *kernel communication services*, *semantic services*, and three groups of resource management services: secondary *resource interfacing services*, *secondary resource aggregation services*, and *tertiary resource management services*.

To this TELOS system services layer, we can add the infrastructure or common services mentioned in the previous sections. These will in general be provided by the operating system but might require some adaptation for their different levels of use within the higher level handler services.

4.5 Conclusion

This chapter discussed what constitutes the strength and the originality of the proposed framework, together with some questions that need to be answered.

TELOS is based on aggregation models that fully integrate users with the resources they use, especially in the central pedagogical process from model composition, to instantiation, to exploration, and to analysis/feedback. TELOS manages this resource life cycle at all levels and in all its phases in an integrated way. But to repeat resource life cycles recursively is not enough to define the global process, so TELOS adds another level for resource generation where "grandparent" systems give birth to parents, which themselves give birth to children systems or environments. Again, TELOS manages this system generation cascade in a full integrated way.

In this global process, workflow (or function) generation is of particular importance and difficulty. Functions are workflows that are inspectable, interactive, and collaborative multiactor interfaces. The users of an instance of a function model can use the function as an interface to inform themselves, to declare or be evaluated on their progress, to obtain assistance, to access operation and coordinate with others, and to find and use material and human resources.

The knowledge/action cycle is at the center of our preoccupations. This is why TELOS combines emergent modes of operation where users organize and define their own operations (of function components) and orchestrated modes where they use predefined functions. A cybernetic loop closes when the action in a process execution is captured to produce a workflow model that can be reused. For example, a designer can use this feature to register a possible workflow in a course, and then offer it as a learning design.

With regard to knowledge representations, we have taken a pragmatic approach, looking for flexible and usable solutions. We reject one extreme of not including any representation because such a resource management system would support learning poorly. We also reject the other extreme where complex representations, theoretically more satisfactory, would exceed the capacity of most persons to use them. In many applications, simple metadata or lightweight ontologies can be used with immediate benefit, for example pairing peer users or users with appropriate resources, while at the same time supporting a facilitator to guide its interventions toward other users. We are looking for such benefits that will repay the effort made to integrate knowledge representation into the environment's design.

Our work on TELOS is continuing on two levels: the further definition of the technical architecture of the system, and the reconstruction of our actual Explor@-2 system [9,10] to bring it closer to the technical architecture proposed here. Both streams of research will be synchronized periodically as the research process unfolds. Meanwhile, other LORNET research teams work on the development of a variety of components that are taken into account in the TELOS architecture, such as new resource interoperability services, learning design and function management editors and players, adaptive learning objects editing and integration, knowledge extraction from resources, and advanced multimedia components.

References

1. Berners-Lee, T., Hendler, J., Lassila, O. (May 2001) The Semantic Web. Scientific American.
2. Blinco, K., Mason, J., McLean, N., Wilson, S. (2004) Trends and Issues in E-Learning Infrastructure Development. White Paper presented at alt-i-lab 2004.
3. CETIS-JISC. (2004) eLearning Framework Documents. http://www.elframework.org.
4. Davenport, T.H., Prusak, L. (1998) Working Knowledge: How Organizations Manage What They Know. Cambridge, MA: Harvard Business School Press.
5. Davies, J., Fensel, D., Van Harmelen, F. (2003) Towards the Semantic Web, Ontology-Driven Knowledge Management. New York: Wiley.
6. IMS Abstract Framework. (2003) http://http://www.imsglobal.org/af/index.cfm.
7. OKI Architecture Overview. (2003) Open Knowledge Initiative. http://web.mit.edu/oki/product/whtpapers/arch_overview.html.
8. Paquette, G. (1995) Modeling the virtual campus. In: Collis, B., Davies G. (eds.) Innovating Adult Learning with Innovative Technologies. Amsterdam: Elsevier Science B.V.
9. Paquette, G. (2001) Designing virtual learning centers. In: Adelsberger, H., Collis, B., Pawlowski, J. (eds.) Handbook on Information Technologies for Education and Training. International Handbook on Information Systems New York: Springer-Verlag, pp. 249–272.
10. Paquette, G., Lundgren-Cayrol, K., Miara, A., Guérette, L. (2004) The Explor@2 learning object manager. In: McGreal, R. (ed.), Online Education Using Learning Objects. London: Routledge/Falmer, pp. 254–268.
11. Paquette, G., Rosca, I. (2003) Modeling the delivery physiology of distributed learning systems. Technology, Instruction, Cognition and Learning, 1–2: 183–209.
12. Paquette, G., Rosca, I., De la Teja, I., Léonard, M., Lundgren-Cayrol, K. (2001) Web-based Support for the Instructional Engineering of E-Learning Systems, WebNet'01 Conference, Orlando.
13. Paquette, G., Rosca, I., Mihaila, S., Masmoudi, A. (2005) TELOS Conceptual Framework, version 0.8. LORNET Technical Documents.
14. Rosca, I. (2005) TELOS Conceptual Architecture, version 0.5. LORNET Technical Documents.
15. Sveiby, K.E. (2001) What is knowledge management? http://www.sveiby.konverge.com/articles/KnowledgeManagement.html.

16. Wenger, E. (1998) Communities of Practice. Learning, Meaning and Identity. Learning in Doing: Social, Cognitive, and Computational Perspectives. Cambridge, MA: Cambridge University Press.
17. Wiley, D.A. (2002) Connecting learning objects to instructional design theory: a definition, a methaphor, and a taxonomy. In: Wiley, D.A. (ed.), The Instructional Use of Learning Objects. Bloomington, IN: Agency for Instructional Technology and Association for Educational Communications of Technology.
18. Wilson, S., Blinco, K., Rehak, D. (2004) Service-Oriented Frameworks: Modelling the Infrastructure for the next generation of e-Learning Systems. White Paper presented at alt-i-lab 2004.

5
Cognitive Modeling of Personalized Software Design Styles: A Case Study in E-Learning

MAURO MARINILLI

Abstract. This chapter discusses an approach to knowledge representation and processing based on representing information at a metamodel level and adapting it to the current user at various levels of abstraction. In this way both run-time data and program code are adapted to the user. Thanks to this approach, it is possible to model sophisticated concepts in a direct and natural way, avoiding technological details. We employed this technique for developing a user-adapted system for teaching object-oriented design patterns (OODP) by leveraging on existing technologies (software generation facilities, modeling languages, specific and general standard metamodels). The design of the prototype was drawn from an ad-hoc student cognitive model. The prototype is empirically evaluated and the findings discussed.

5.1 Introduction

While a great deal of work has been devoted to conceptual frameworks and approaches to knowledge representation and processing, very little was done on the software implementation side. Nowadays most software still represents variable information using run-time data. This is somewhat surprising. Theoretically well-crafted, rich knowledge representations always boil down to run-time data structures when it comes to their implementation. The richer and more complex these representations are, the wider is the gap from the devised abstract concepts to the implementation and the run-time processes. This approach creates a number of practical and cognitive shortcomings.

The assumption of this work is that explicitly representing and processing knowledge at a metamodel level [technically by means of adopting a model-driven engineering (MDE) approach] can provide an effective approach to represent and process knowledge-intensive domains (such as, for example, those needed in rich educational environments). In order to test this assumption, a prototype e-learning system was developed.

The chapter is structured as follows. Section 5.2 introduces the problem outlined above, presenting a general solution that draws from various state-of-the-art software engineering (SE) approaches. Section 5.3 discusses a prototype developed with the proposed approach. Section 5.4 reports its empirical evaluation. Section 5.5 discusses some related work. Section 5.6 concludes the chapter.

5.2 The Limits of Current Modeling Approaches

Current knowledge representation techniques typically represent dynamic information with run-time data. Also complex information handling (such as adaptation and knowledge processing) is mostly performed on run-time data. This approach is limiting for a number of reasons:

- Data structures are implemented at a low level of abstraction, and often the chosen technology dictates unnatural characteristics to the information being represented. See, for instance, a common scenario where complex knowledge representation is built with couples of string values, representing attribute-value pairs.
- Behavior is represented differently than data. When there is a need to represent and manipulate explicitly behavior knowledge, such a behavior is often unnaturally treated as a different form of run-time data.
- The overall domain representation is tightly bounded with the underlying computing run-time environment. Ephemeral or overly abstract concepts need to be bounded to the life cycle of a software application or even within the horizon of a single application session.
- Domain experts seldom can interact naturally with rich knowledge representation systems. They need skilled personnel or some sort of advanced computer skills (such as programming or knowledge of an application's implementation details).

These are all well-known shortcomings of current software engineering methods for representing knowledge effectively in software environments. Despite the wealth of approaches that have been proposed in the literature over the last decades, the way knowledge is engineered in software artifacts (i.e., relying on software as run-time data plus some form of behavior) did not substantially change since the early days of computing.

Despite the introduction of interesting approaches such as MDE or domain-specific languages that (re)introduce the concept of an abstract model as a cornerstone of software design and development, this has not substantially changed the way knowledge is engineered. The main reason is that power of MDE approaches has been so far applied to software design and construction only. Models at various levels of abstraction can indeed play an important and innovative role in knowledge representation when applied consistently to the whole software life cycle.

The next subsection discusses the foundational approach to knowledge representation that is suited for overcoming the problems discussed above.

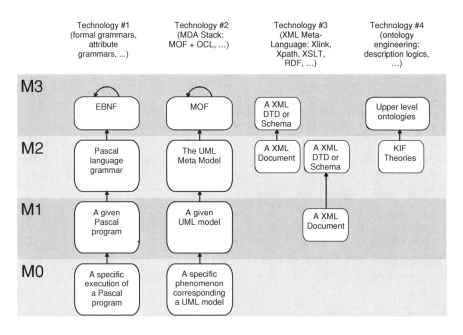

FIGURE 5.1. Levels of abstraction for some example technologies.[1]

5.2.1 Representing Knowledge with Abstraction Layers

Following MDE approaches [6, 12, 13, 19], our generic models are organized in abstraction layers placed on top of each other. One level (except the lowest level) can be seen as a model, and some of the elements in the level below are instances of this model. Figure 5.1 shows how the proposed representation applies to some example technologies.

The abstraction levels in Figure 5.1 are as follows:

- Level 0 represents the instance level, i.e., the execution of a give program in a given time in a given context (user, underlying hardware and OS, etc.). For uniformity we call (inexactly) models also the items in level 0, which are not models but rather real-world "runs," particular executions of a given program in a given real-world context.
- Level 1 represents the abstraction model common to most programming languages. We will make the assumption that object-oriented (OO) code and UML diagrams are equivalent and represented at this level of abstraction. A source code (or an equivalent level 1 model M_1) can be thought of as an abstraction over a set of executions (i.e., M_0 instances).

---

[1] From Jèzèquel, J.-M. Model-Driven Engineering: Core Principles and Challenges (2004). Available at: http://www.irisa.fr/triskell/publis/2003/Jezequel03e.pdf.

- Level 2 represents a model for expressing level-1 models, i.e., a metamodel. The UML modeling language can be thought of as a general metamodel representing a vast set of models (OO models). More specific metamodels can be defined for specific domains. For example, the JCP26 specification could be seen as a partial metamodel that describes the technical details of Enterprise Java Beans (EJB) technology [15]. Also metamodels not explicitly designed for code generation can be ascribed to this layer, such as EML and its successor IMS Learning Design[2] [16].
- Level 3 is yet another level of abstraction upon level 2 and it is a model representing metamodels (or, alternatively, a meta-metamodel). An example is the Meta Object Facility (MOF) for Model Driven Architectures (MDA) [10].
- Theoretically, more abstraction layers can be thought on top of M_3 [19]. Even though, for simplicity, we will deal at most with only level-2 models.

The layering structure discussed above applies to current software approaches as well. In object-oriented programming a class describes a set of objects; in a meta-modeling context the objects constitutes the lowest level and the classes the next lowest level. Traditionally EBNF notation has been used to describe a programming language; this would be the next level. The top level would be a definition of EBNF done with EBNF. These levels correspond to the four levels of the four-layer metamodel architecture of object management group (OMG), but here visual UML models are used instead of EBNF. This architecture is based on strict meta-modeling, which means that all elements on one level are instantiated from the level directly above. The instantiation logic is typically operating with three levels and instantiation over two of them; as an example: we have a description of what a class is (M_2), then we have a class (e.g., class Person), and finally we have an object (M_0).

As of Figure 5.1, MOF and UML both offer support for object-oriented concepts (the core of MOF and UML are structurally equivalent). Since MOF is an instance of itself, the level above MOF (M_4) can be seen as MOF once more. One can imagine an infinite number of MOF levels, having a form of infinite regression (the same applies to EBNF).

5.2.2 A Class of Adaptive Systems

This subsection introduces a class of adaptive systems that adopts the knowledge representation structure introduced in the previous subsection. Such a class of systems is proposed in order to solve some of the problems discussed in Section 5.2.

User-adapted recombining systems (UARS) are defined in terms of models at various abstraction layers where some of these models are modified following the user's domain-specific needs. Recombination is defined as a particular model transformation that preserves run-time session consistency even though it alters

---

[2] Such metamodels describe the design of learning units from a pedagogical perspective. IMS LD is available at http://www.imsglobal.org/learningdesign/ldv1p0/imsld_infov1p0. html.

(recombines) the system from a generic level i to level 0 (from M_i down to M_0). Run-time session consistency is defined as the ability to maintain a substantial part of the run-time application's state from one transformation to the next.

The UARS recombine themselves based upon particular representations of the user called recombining user models (RUM). These models drive the transformations from higher level models down to executable code. Other forms of domain-dependent user models (statically defined at level 1) are called system user models (SUM).

Note that traditional MDE transformations occur only at software build time. The UARS instead perform run-time, user-adapted (and model-driven) transformations. This requires additional run-time support, as we will see in subsection 5.3.4.1.

Recombination can be thought of in several ways. For instance, RUM could be thought of as models of the user as a software designer. When manufacturing traditional software, designers and developers go through cycles of application, tuning and testing before releasing the product to end users. By distilling this knowledge in very specialized models (both for technology and domain logic), it is possible to automate part of this process for some limited domains and technologies. Through recombination cycles UARS evolve accordingly to (system-perceived) user needs.

From a software life-cycle point of view, UARS can be seen as systems where the design and execution phase (habitually two distinct phases in traditional software manufacturing) collapse into a unique augmented run-time phase, where the system converges on the (model-represented) user's needs through recombination cycles. Of course, in order to enable this architecture a number of complex models and model transformations need to be built up front. Figure 5.2 shows the basic run-time cycle of this class of interactive systems.

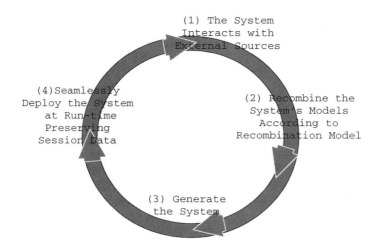

FIGURE 5.2. Basic recombination cycle (taken from [17]). MDE techniques are applied in a user-centered way during run-time interaction with end users. Usually only small portions of the system are generated.

The next section introduces a prototype tutoring system that employs the approaches introduced here. In particular, we will show how this approach provides a high-level, natural, and technology-independent framework to model and process highly user-dependent knowledge. In fact, the software will be designed directly from some high-level cognitive modeling assumptions in a technology-independent manner.

5.3 A Tutoring System for OODP

To validate the assumptions discussed in the previous section, a prototype system was developed. The prototype implemented a user-adapted, computer-based learning system for training students on OO design patterns (OODPs). Several factors influenced the application domain choice:

- Computer-based learning and the related fields are domains with an already relatively large number of standard metamodel initiatives and specifications that speeded up the design of the metamodel and also provided a perfect test bed for practical metamodel reuse (and its related expensive-to-gather domain knowledge).
- User adaptation has been studied and applied extensively in this and related fields providing an important research background for the work.
- Finally, knowledge of the domain by the author helped the design and development.

The proposed computer-based tutoring (CBT) prototype supports students in learning OODP. The tool is embedded in a well-known software development platform, IBM's Eclipse.[3] While drawing their OO class diagrams (OOCDs), students can ask the proposed prototype for suggestions on how to use OODP. The system provides learners with the structural class diagrams that most closely match the current learner's software design style for a selected portion of OOCD. Suggestions are retrieved from a predefined library of recurring designs drawn from standard software design patterns.[4]

The tool was designed to be nonintrusive and seamlessly integrated with a visual OO class diagram editor, promoting self-paced learning (the user activates the tool for requesting design suggestions by means of invoking a pop-up menu). The tutoring support provides the closest OO design available in a solution library for the current user's design. The system was instantiated for the OODP domain (the system was implemented as a CBR engine, it represented 33 OO design patterns variants, and the library stored 49 real cases taken from the Java APIs and other OO designs). A screenshot of the prototype is provided in Figure 5.3.

---

[3] http://www.eclipse.org/.
[4] A list of the OODP used can be found at: http://home.earthlink.net/~huston2/dp/patterns.html.

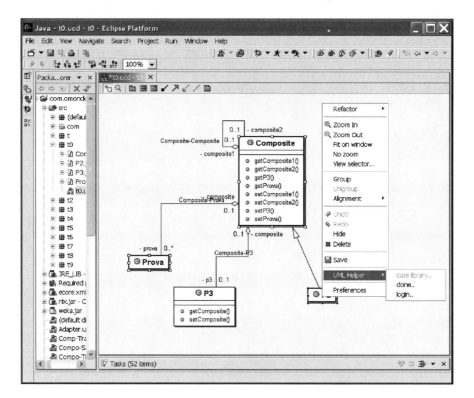

FIGURE 5.3. A screenshot of the prototype. The user interacts with a graphical UML editor and can invoke the support tool by selecting portions of the edited class diagram and invoking the contextual menu item.

The graphical editor of choice for drawing OOCD was Omondo 1.2.1,[5] freely available for Eclipse 2.1.1. Other editors could be used interchangeably as long as they are available as Eclipse plug-ins and they support in-memory exporting to an EMF representation.

Our objective was to assess the benefits of the user-adapted support provided by the OODP classifier module. Consequently, we avoided any spurious support for the tutoring process (such as additional teaching heuristics, classic ITS pedagogical support, and the like).

5.3.1 An Example Session

The session starts with the user logging in. For first-time users the system proposes a Wizard dialogue where all relevant data can be inserted. The user is not able to proceed before all mandatory fields are correctly filled in, as shown in Figure 5.4.

---

[5] http://www.omondo.com/.

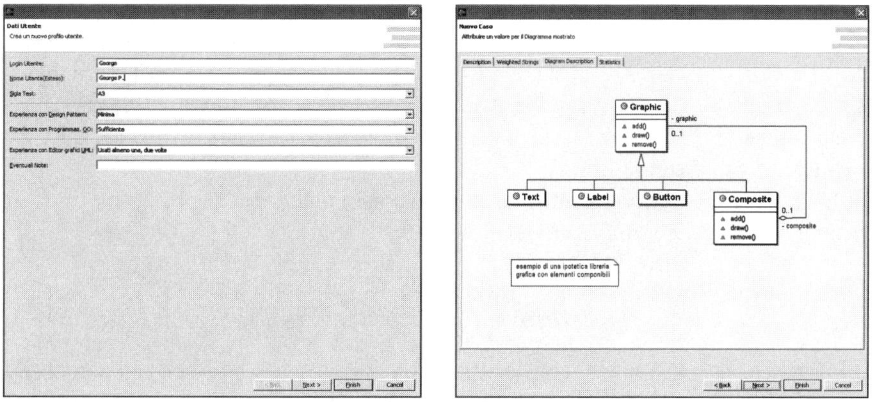

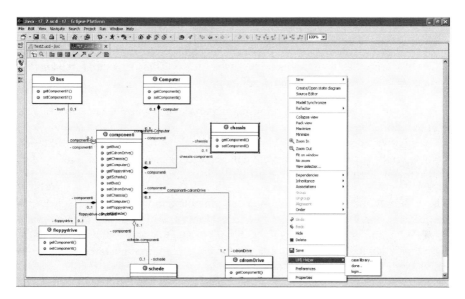

FIGURE 5.4. The first login Wizard. The figure on the left shows the first page of the Wizard (personal data), and the figure on the right shows optional feedback on some randomly extracted cases from the library.

After the preliminary login dialogue has been closed and startup data collected for an initial startup of the user model, the user can start editing class diagrams with the editor. Users will request system suggestion by means of selecting a portion of the OOCD and invoking the contextual menu commands, as shown in Figure 5.5.

FIGURE 5.5. A prototype screenshot showing the user while requesting suggestions for an OOCD.

The prototype then suggests to the user the OOPD variants that most closely resemble user's design style, as extracted from the current design[6] and the overall user model. The user is left free to adopt the proposed suggestions or ignore them. The user can also provide feedback to the system in order to refine the model of the design style. The user assesses the (user-perceived) similarity of some designs extracted from the case library.

In the next subsection we introduce the design of the proposed prototype, derived from a high-level cognitive model.

5.3.2 Perceived Affordances and Software Design

We present here a concept derived from psychology that will be the base of the conceptual cognitive modeling approach in the proposed prototype. We introduce the concept of learner's perceived affordance for a given design. As we will see, the application of the UARS approach to perceived affordances will provide a highly flexible, user-adapted, software representation of students' software design styles.

5.3.2.1 Perceived Affordances

The term *affordance* was originally introduced by the perceptual psychologist J.J. Gibson [13] to refer to the actionable properties (often implicit) between the world and an actor (a person or animal). Norman [18] introduced the term *perceived affordance* (related to product design) where affordances are actionable properties of some objects as perceived from the product user. These are the properties that determine how the product could possibly be used. For example, certain doors afford pulling, while buttons in a graphical user interface afford pushing, etc. For more details on the concept of perceived affordances, see, for example, [14].

In our prototype the concept of perceived affordance was applied to the design of OOP software, rather than to general product artifacts. This focus shift is reasonable for a number of reasons, the main ones being:

- Programming (and OOP programming in particular) can be seen as an instance of the more generic task of product design.
- OOP classes, designs, and object interactions allow for perceived affordances, not from the software end users but from developers who use them. This applies also to the same developers that build these artifacts.

The assumption that developers (or more exactly anybody who has to deal with source code and its more abstract structures) interact with code representations in a way very similar to how users interact with product designs seems reasonable.

In the following subsection we apply the concepts introduced here to the cognitive modeling of the practice of software design.

---

[6] Clearly, no suggestion would be given if the user didn't attempt to apply any form of OODP in her/his design.

5.3.2.2 A Simple Cognitive Model for Software Design

On a wider perspective, the modeling of the learner's cognitive processes has been extensively studied in the past decades and a number of theories have emerged, such as ACT [4].[7] We are not interested in a low-level, generic theory like classic cognitive psychology's theories (see [3]). Instead, we focus on a practical, even if approximate, model of learning that can represent a satisfying mix between automatic tractability and representation power for the domain at hand.

On a more particular, domain-specific perspective one could see the learning of software design skills as the iterative refinement of a (possibly contradictory) set of perceived affordances upon the various entities involved in software development (general programming and OOP concepts, software tools, and reusable assets like existing libraries) as perceived by developers.

Although this approach could be applied to software development in general, we focus here for brevity on OOP only. Given this (apparently) simple viewpoint, perceived affordances gain the status of primary actors in the modeling of high-level cognitive processes involved in learning and mastering OOP.

Recapping, learning software design skills can be seen as an iterative refinement process of a designer's implicit set of perceived affordances. This set of (constantly evolving) perceived affordances form an approximate and simplified, but still rich and useful, representation of the cumulative design experience of a software designer. Perhaps the most interesting aspect of this approach lies in its trade-off between representation complexity and expressive power, as we will see in the following and we will evaluate empirically in Section 5.4.

Having introduced the well-grounded concept of perceived affordances for a given design, we now focus on representing them explicitly for automatic representation and manipulation. This is not a trivial task, given the abstractness of the concept itself.

5.3.3 Representing Perceived Affordances for OOP Design

The UARS modeling approach introduced in subsection 5.2.1 seems a perfect candidate for representing designer's perceived affordances in that:

- It allows for high-level, platform- and technology-independent representations of complex information.
- It provides simple, high-level manipulations of the represented information, supplying a simple yet powerful knowledge processing means.
- User personalization is automatically built into the approach.

A model suited to be used in our prototype is depicted in Figure 5.6. The model is represented using the UML OOCD formalism.

Existing metamodels will be indicated with UML profiles, as in Figure 5.6. In such a figure a UML class diagram shows the main properties occurring in our model:

---

[7] ACT is a theory of cognition developed by O. Anderson and others

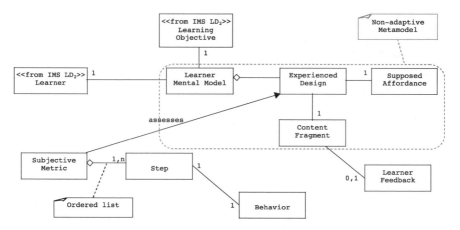

FIGURE 5.6. The SUM$_2$ used in the prototype. Stereotypes indicate concepts drawn from external metamodels.[7] (hence the *"from IMS LD"* stereotype in Learner indicates that this is taken from the IMS LD specification).

- A learner mental model is composed of a design style that in turn is represented by a number of perceived affordance instances.
- Learners implicitly have a learning objective that drives their interaction with the CBT tool. Such a learning objective has been modeled from IMS LD.
- Each learner has a particular learner model and a given learning objective.

Our cognitive hypothesis is that designers maintain an (often implicit) conceptual representation of the possible (perceived) uses of a given software design while crafting or employing it.

The role of subjectivity in OOP design-perceived affordances is twofold. Clearly, software design is a subjective process that draws from a designer's skills and past experience. Apart from the designer, then, the software design activity itself allows for many viable solutions to the same problem. These representations are subjective. Design in general (and OO software design in particular) is a rather subjective process, and there may not exist the right design for a given situation. There could be instead a set of equally valid alternatives for the adoption of a given OODP. We assumed that learners develop their own subjective design style by evolving an implicit set of affordances for designs.

One could alternatively see this knowledge representation approach as an attempt to model a designer's perceived affordances through models at various levels of abstraction. The resulting representation of a given perceived affordance is a somewhat blurred entity shared between a given set of run-time instances and their level 1 code (i.e., software design). This provides a powerful and expressive

---

[8] The SUM$_2$ metamodel was designed as a test bed of complex modeling situations for testing the UARS approach rather than as a reusable asset.

paradigm both for knowledge representation and processing, as we will see in the following sections.

5.3.4 Recombination Aspects

We call relevance function (RF) the software implementation of a perceived affordance in our prototype. Following standard GP techniques,[9] RF is created by composing families of algorithms (which will be discussed in subsection 5.3.7) using a generative approach. This subsection discusses the main details of technological aspects related to code generation in the proposed prototype.

We explicitly represented OOP design styles in our system by means of user-perceived relevance functions between different designs. Given a user u, we indicate with r_u the related RF. The function $r_u(d_1, d_2) \rightarrow [0,1]$ represents the distance between two designs d_1, d_2 as perceived by the user u. Two designs that afford similar uses have a small distance r_u.

As for the suggestion phase, given the user design d_u the system provides another design d_R with

$$d_R \mid r_u(d_u, d_R) \leq r_u(d_u, d_x) \ \forall \ d_x \in \ \texttt{Library}.$$

Our prototype's user model contains a set of software implementations of relevance functions $\{R_u^i\}$ evolved by means of user feedback f_u. These $\{R_u^i\}$ are algorithms (represented as executable Java classes) generated through the UARS cycle exposed before, returning a value $\in [0, 1]$ and a confidence measure $c_u^i \in [0, 1]$.

We assumed that during their learning process learners continuously refine r_u adapting it to new scenarios and solutions. The final value R_u (prototype's supposedly best representation of r_u) is obtained as

$$R_u \mid \max(c_u^i) \ \ \forall R_u^i \in \{Ru\}$$

If no RF has a confidence value higher than a minimum, then a new recombination phase is launched, and the result value obtained from the new RF is provided to the learner. Recombination comes into play in those situations where no $\{R_u^i\}$ returns a confidence value higher than a minimum $c_u^i > minThreshold$.[10] In these cases our prototype resorts to obtain a new R_u^j that will be inserted in $\{R_u\}$ as discussed in subsection 5.3.4.2.

As already mentioned, the UML stereotype <<from IMS LD2>> represents the IMS learning design metamodel (in order to allow for metamodel reuse, a number of decompositions have been performed on the metamodels that are not reported here for brevity). For brevity we also don't show other parts of the external metamodels related to the imported concepts. Figure 5.7 shows the structure of the RUM_1.

---

[9] Generative programming is an approach to software engineering aiming at designing and implementing software modules which can be combined to generate complex systems.
[10] It has been set empirically minThreshold $= 0.35$.

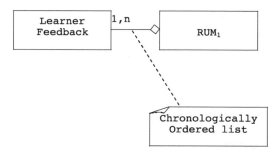

FIGURE 5.7. RUM_1 represented as class diagram. This model (the sequence of user feed-backs) drives the recombination process in the prototype.

From Figure 5.7 we can see that the recombination process is adapted to the current user by means of learner feedback information. In the next subsection we focus in the details of the prototype implementation.

5.3.4.1 Target Platform for the Prototype

Within generative and model-driven approaches, programs are generated against a so-called *target software platform* by combining together reusable parts of a family of programs. Such a platform for the proposed prototype is shown in Figure 5.8.

Figure 5.8 shows the target platform as decomposed in a number of functional layers. Recombined code substitutes are added on the generated application code base. Note that the application can have a small portion of its code base that is subject to recombination (the grayed area are represented as the product of the recombination transformations).

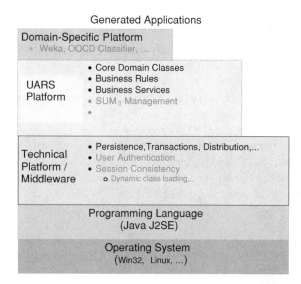

FIGURE 5.8. The rich target platform for the proposed prototype.

The target platform built for the prototype is composed of standard facilities (such as persistence, user authentication, and the like) provided by the various layers underneath our application (i.e., the Eclipse framework, the Java platform, and the underlying operating system). The so-called domain platform is composed of all UARS-specific code such as basic facilities for achieving recombination (i.e., code generation and compilation, run-time loading of newly generated classes, and state switch from one generation to the next).

By providing a rich target platform (with complex high-level services), the code generation phase can be greatly simplified. Obtaining a simple and fast recombination phase is essential in UARS implementation because recombination takes place at run time during user interaction.

In the case of the proposed prototype, memory and run-time constraints were not trivial. A generic session of the application running in experimentation mode (i.e., with many machine learning (ML) algorithms in execution at the same time) consisted of a memory allocation of few hundreds megabytes (a single run-time session comprised the JVM, the Eclipse IDE, various accessory plug-ins such as the OOCD editor and the experimenter plug-in, the various machine learning algorithms, and the OOCD classifier with its case library).

Special attention was devoted to the implementation of the target platform, which needed to be built using rather low-level code generation facilities (such as the JET library[11]) given the need of high customization and user adaptability not provided by other third-party code generators.

5.3.4.2 Recombination Cycle for the Prototype

Having discussed the technological aspects of the UARS architecture for the proposed prototype, we now focus on the conceptual phases involved in recombination cycle as realized in our system. Figure 5.9 details the general recombination cycle in Figure 5.2 for our prototype. Such a sequence occurs at every recombination cycle.

As already said, the first time the user registers with the prototype, an optional, preliminary cold-start setup takes place. The user is proposed a dialogue with 10 feedbacks in order to tune a default startup RF with the initial student's skills. This phase can be skipped by dismissing the dialogue (even if this will possibly provide a poorer initial performance).

After the startup phase (which occurs only once at user model (UM) creation) the following transformations occur at every recombination cycle:

1. The user provides feedback to the system. The feedback is added to the run-time instance recombining user model (RUM_0) and to the system user model (SUM_0).
2. RUM_0 is used for seeding the adaptation of the level 1 model generation (see discussion above).
3. After the level 1 models have been generated, they are assembled together to provide executable code. In our prototype we generate only a new class representing a new R_u^i.

---

[11] JET is a Java library for generating source code.

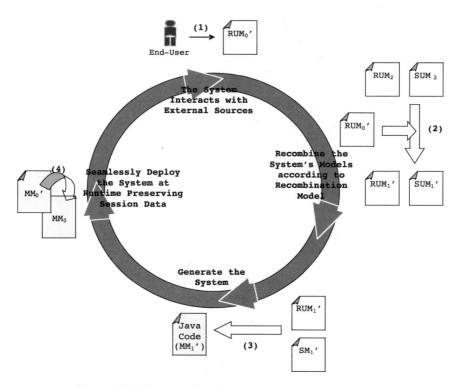

FIGURE 5.9. The recombination cycle in the proposed prototype.

4. The newly generated executable code is deployed and dynamically loaded into the previous running session, in a seamless fashion (from the end user's point of view). In the proposed prototype a new RF class is added to SUM_0.

The same user feedback thus performs a twofold purpose: as a part of SUM_0 it is provided to past generated RF for fine parameter tuning, while as part of RUM_0 it is used to drive the recombination process and create a new RF.

In our prototype the recombination cycle is performed locally on the client machine. In order to curb complexity and boost performance, a special "focused" generation technique was adopted. Such a generation technique concentrates recombination and adaptation on only some model (and then code) areas.

Run-time deployment of the newly generated code is performed using custom Java class loaders. Run-time context (i.e., level 0 data) is passed from one generation to the next through object serialization.

5.3.5 Overall Software Architecture

In this section we discuss the software architecture of the proposed CBT prototype (see Figure 5.10). The main modules of the system are:

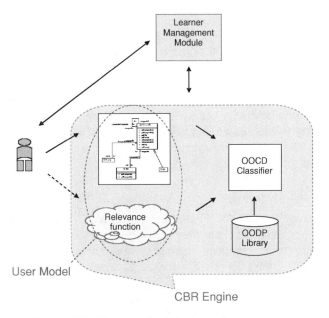

FIGURE 5.10. The overall architecture of our prototype.

- A user model, containing the various run-time data structures discussed before plus the source code (and, more importantly the related executables) of the user-adapted RF.
- The OOCD classifier, implemented as a CBR engine that uses a case library containing all classic OODP plus their main variations, as we will discuss later. The classifier provides the most similar OODP available in the library for the current input OOCD given the set of RF currently maintained in the UM.
- A Learner Management Module handles all the other modules of the system and interacts with the user. It encapsulates pedagogical behavior and the various actions that the prototype provides to the user.

Note that Eclipse was employed both as the application domain technology—the prototype was packaged as an Eclipse plug-in—and as the technology for implementing code generation (thanks to technologies like EMF and JET).

In the next section we introduce the OODP classifier module.

5.3.6 OODP Classifier

The classifier has been designed to be used also outside the prototype, as a stand-alone classification tool, and as such it is evaluated in section 5.4. It was designed following a CBR (case-based reasoning) architecture.[12]

---

[12] For an introduction to CBR see the classic [1].

The CBR engine used for the OOCD classifier in our prototype currently encompasses only the retrieve and revise phases, while the reuse phase is merely the visualization of the OODP found by the user. In turn, the learner provides feedback about the (perceived) retrieval goodness, thus implementing a simple revise phase. Concluding, the OOCD classifier implements a simple CBR engine, where the case library is (run-time) read-only. The case library is modified only by the administrator for adding/updating existing OODP diagrams during a preliminary knowledge base definition. Such a phase is performed once for all installations. The next subsection describes how the case library was built during this preliminary configuration phase.

5.3.6.1 OODP Case Library

The OODP case library was built as follows. For each OODP (as presented in [11]), a number of practical real cases were stored for each known valid variant of the pattern, together with a standard "template" variant that describes abstractly the OODP, as in [11]. Whenever possible, the real cases were taken from Java libraries in order to keep the representation homogeneous, with one common OOP language.

For convenience, cases were tagged as belonging to one macro-category, corresponding to one of the classic OODP listed in [11] plus the "Not Available" category. This simple arrangement allowed for both coarse-grained classification (where the result is obtained by returning the macro-category corresponding to the matched case) and fine-grained classification (where the single variant of the given OODP is considered).

Figure 5.11 shows the structure of the case library.

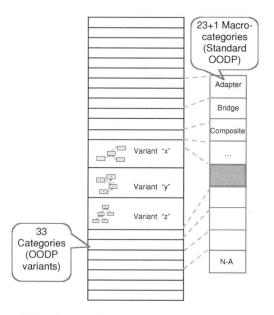

FIGURE 5.11. The case library structure for the OODP classifier.

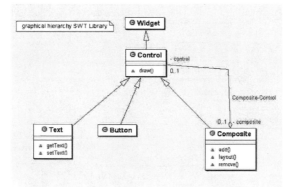

FIGURE 5.12. Composite OODP: "safe" variant.

The OODP variants were taken from well-established sources such as [11] and other reference Web sites.

Figures 5.12, 5.14 show some examples of cases stored in the library. Cases were entered into the system in the same way students draw their class diagrams (in fact, OODPs are stored and managed by the prototype as specializations of OOCD). Figure 5.12 shows the composite OODP in its "safe" variant, as instantiated in the Java simple widget toolkit: A JAVA user interface library (SWT) graphical user interface (GUI) toolkit.

Figure 5.13 shows an example of application of the composite OODP in its "compact" variant as employed in the modeling of the JTree widget part of the Swing library.

Figure 5.14 illustrates the "transparent" variant of the composite OODP as used in the Apache Struts Web presentation library.

Figure 5.15 shows the "transparent" variant of the composite OODP in its template (abstract) form, as presented in [11].

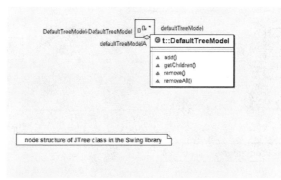

FIGURE 5.13. Composite OODP: "compact" variant.

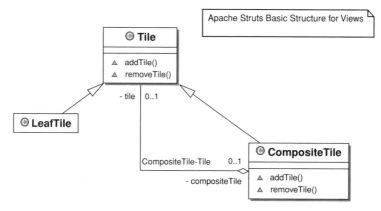

FIGURE 5.14. Composite OODP: "transparent" variant.

The UML comments were not processed by the matching algorithm. Their presence is useful for pedagogical reasons, when cases in the library are presented directly to students.

5.3.7 Algorithm Families

Each family of algorithms has the following common behaviors:

- Input representation. Each algorithm extracted a suitable representation of the current OOCD. For instance, Weka algorithms represented the current OOCD as

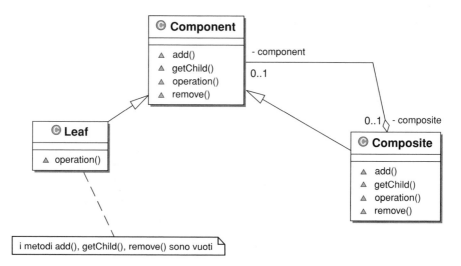

FIGURE 5.15. Composite OODP: "transparent template" variant.

a Boolean vector, while keyword-based algorithms created a semantic network representation.

- Algorithm feedback. Every family of algorithms performs a custom feedback process and maintains its own user model data structures.
- Matching procedure. The CBR engine uses RF for assessing the distance between two cases (i.e., two OOCD, one the current case and another one taken from the library).

In the following subsection we discuss briefly the main points of each of the families of algorithms employed in the proposed prototype.

5.3.7.1 Weka Algorithms

Weka [23] is an open-source Java library that implements many state-of-the-art machine learning (ML) algorithms. Weka algorithms can be parameterized, and the public availability of source code makes it easier to understand their implementation and to customize their features.

In order to use Weka ML algorithms in our prototype, we need to represent an OOCD as a Boolean vector of features (called attributes in Weka terminology) using the extraction procedures discussed in the following subsection.

5.3.7.1.1 Extracting Boolean Features from OOCD

Common to all Weka algorithms, there are a set of attributes describing the domain of interest. Instances of such attributes (what we represented as cases in our CBR approach) are used as a representation of both the learner's OOCD and for all the cases in the library (i.e., real applications of OODP). In order to create a suitable Boolean vector, representing the input OOCD graph to the CBR engine, an extraction algorithm has been defined, based on the work of various schema matching systems, discussed in subsection 5.3.

The basic procedure is to look for particular graph patterns (which we informally called constellations) within the input OOCD (either drawn by the user or extracted by the case library). Such patterns were represented by nodes (in an OOCD they could be classes or interfaces) and arcs (references such as use, aggregation, etc.).

For experimentation purposes, two different set of constellations were created:

- A simple type of patterns, where only one node (class) was expressed with all ingoing/outgoing references.
- An "extended" set where two nodes, their mutual references, and possibly the arcs with other nodes were represented.

For concreteness, we show in Figure 5.16 an example of a simple constellation (matching the composite, "basic" variant OODP), while in Figure 5.17 is shown an example of extended constellation (matching the flyweight OODP, in its "template" variant).

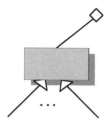

FIGURE 5.16. An example of simple constellation. This kind of pattern defines all ingoing/
outgoing references (and their type) for only one node (class).

Clearly, representing an OOCD with extended constellations is much more expensive than using simple constellations. One of the objectives of our experimentation in section 5.4 was to understand if there was any significant difference (and eventually how much this was) in classification performance when using one representation or the other. In particular, our aim was to understand how useful was the much less expensive simple constellation approach instead of the extended representation.

The extraction algorithm was rather simplistic: in case of simple constellations, every node in the OOCD was checked to match with any of the recorded patterns. Each positive matching resulted in turning on true the corresponding Boolean value in the vector. For extended patterns instead, the Cartesian product of all possible nodes was calculated (excluding a node with itself and symmetric combinations) and every pattern was checked against the pair of nodes.

5.3.7.1.2 Weka Subsystem Architecture

Before getting into the details of the algorithms employed in our prototype from the Weka library, it is useful to recap the overall architecture for Weka-based RF implementations. Figure 5.18 shows graphically the Weka module architecture within the proposed prototype.

As already mentioned in the previous subsection, a key role is played by the extraction phase, which builds the feature vector out of an OOCD instance. The ML algorithms used from Weka [23] are:

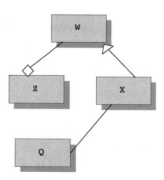

FIGURE 5.17. An example of extended constellation. This kind of pattern describes all the mutual occurring, and ingoing/outgoing links between two nodes (classes).

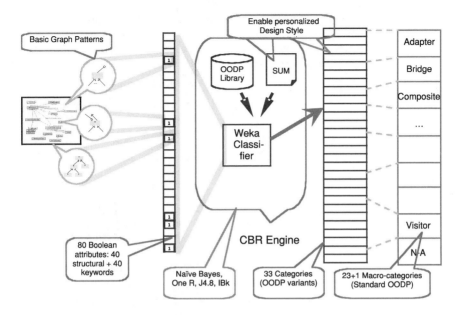

FIGURE 5.18. The Weka module architecture. Patterns are matched in the input OOCD in order to create a Boolean vector that will be fed to the Weka classifier. Optionally results may be mapped to more general categories (the macro-categories shown on the right side).

- Naïve Bayes. This algorithm implements the probabilistic naïve Bayesian classifier.
- One R. This algorithm learns a one-level decision tree (generates a set of rules that test on one particular attribute).
- J4.8. This is an implementation of the C4.5 decision tree, an extension of the basic ID3 algorithm.
- IBk. An implementation of the k-nearest-neighbors classifier that employs a custom distance metric discussed in [23].

Next subsection describes the keyword-based family of algorithms.

5.3.7.2 Keyword-Based Algorithms

Besides the Weka family of algorithms, we wanted to explore the algorithms based on keywords, whose effectiveness is reported in [25]. In order to do so, we developed from scratch a family of algorithms based on matching the text available in OOCD.

Our keyword-based family of algorithms is based on a set of four predefined steps, each with a number of possible implementations, in order to provide a wide range of combinations, as shown in Table 5.1. Such an organization is able to generate $6 \times 6 \times 8 \times 8$ combinations (all legal), thus providing 2304 different

TABLE 5.1. Keyword-based family of algorithms; every generated RF of this family was composed by one step of extraction, followed by one enumeration processing, a pair-wise matching of the enumerated elements, and a final aggregation step that provides a unique value out of the results of the previous pair-wise match.

Step	Available Implementations
Extract	Basic
	Random
	Adaptive
	Coarse
	Delta
	Random adaptive
Enumerate	Cartesian product
	Random Cartesian product
	Threshold Cartesian product
	Constant permutation
	Threshold + constant permutation
	Random constant permutation
Pair-wise match	Boolean
	Exact
	Random Boolean
	Threshold weights
	Weights product
	Pseudo-fuzzy
	Simple
	Adaptive constant
Aggregation	Absolute maximum
	Average
	Productory
	Summatory aggregation
	Simple sigma
	Adaptive sigma
	Nonlinear average
	Simple

members of the keyword-based family of algorithms. Table 5.1 shows some details related to the keyword-based family of algorithms.

Each of the substeps in Table 5.1 was tested together with the other substeps to verify that its use was meaningful as a part of a compound algorithm instance. Furthermore, some of the substeps have their own feedback algorithm to adjust their behavior to user feedback.

5.4 Empirical Evaluation

In this section we present a preliminary evaluation of the proposed prototype, concluding with a discussion of the results obtained.

5.4.1 Evaluation Process

In the design of the experiment we followed the advice given in [7]. We made two groups (group A of 16 users and group B of two expert users) for our empirical evaluation. The main difference in the two groups was in the number of proposed problems. Group A users had to solve four problems while group B users had to solve six problems (the first four being the same as of group A). Problems were always paired. They were chosen from the literature and recognized Web sites with the following characteristics: they belonged to different application domains while being solved by using the same OODP (i.e., first and second designs were different cases of the same DP, while the third and fourth focused on a different DP). Between the first and the second problem of the same pair the user was asked to invoke our prototype on her/his design D_i. The system provided five suggested designs, and users were asked to assess whether or not these suggestions, abstracted from their application domain, would solve the proposed problem.

The proposed suggestions were organized in a GUI in a sequence of OOCD and an input field, where users had to tell whether or not, in their opinion, the design was able to solve the given problem. The importance of such input was carefully highlighted to users, because it served two important purposes: (1) it forced the user to reason about the proposed OODP, so to fully understand it; and (2) served as a form of feedback for the adaptive machine learning algorithms employed for the given user. Feedback was provided as follows: if the user acknowledged the fitness of the suggested OODP for the current problem, the given design was classified to belong to the corresponding OODP that solved the problem. No action was taken in the opposite case (the user decided that that case suggested that OODC was not suitable to solve the given problem).

The OOCD suggested by the system were created in two ways: nonadaptively and user-adapted. The nonadaptive mode extracts randomly four designs from the case library and then adds the correct design pattern in its "template" version. A template version of an OODP is the standard version, abstracted by any real application context, as defined in [11]. Usually template versions are the learning objective of classic OODP tutoring systems as in [24]. The user-adapted version instead uses the classifier to select the closest design pattern variant to the user design. In this way the system proposes the OOCDs available in the case library that are closer to the actual user's design style. In all the pairs of problems proposed to students, there was always a user-adapted suggestion and a nonadaptive one, only the order changed (see Figure 5.20).

Users didn't know the purpose of the experiment, or how the suggested designs were chosen. Users were told the reason for the experiment was to gather statistics about OOCD design. They were recommended to carefully evaluate the designs proposed by the prototype.

To study the usefulness of the system, we chose a heterogeneous user population ranging from new college graduates to experienced software designers (with less than 10 years of experience in the industry). Two expert designers (>10 years of experience) were managed separately in group B and additional tests were used for them.

5.4.2 Experimentation Prototype

We used a special version of the prototype for the experiments in that it also traced user behavior (application's screenshots were taken automatically every 15 seconds) and four standard RF realized with Weka [23] implementations[13] were always generated at first with the following variations:

- Adaptive vs. nonadaptive. The nonadaptive RFs weren't given any user feedback.
- Extended vs. simple matching graph patterns. The input Boolean vectors for classification were composed using two different sets of graph patterns. Simple graph patterns involved only one node and its associations (and generalizations), while extended graph patterns were properties defined on two nodes. Our objective was to assess the difference in final performances for these two types of pattern.

Overall the prototype for experimentations handled 16 RFs extra than the standard prototype. These extra RFs were only used for experimental purposes (data recording); their output was not used in the system. The overall recorded data from the whole experimentation set amounted to more than 195 MB.

5.4.3 Results

The first issue we were interested in was the pedagogical usefulness of the prototype. Users' designs were automatically recorded by the prototype as pictorial images and stored (with scrambled filenames) in a common directory. An expert (not being part of the experiment or involved with its setup) judged all 76 designs, providing a score $V(D_i) \in [0,1]$ with preset standard criteria (fitness to the purpose, good use of OODP, and engineering qualities of the solution). After that, the system manager associated the judged scores with the user Ids.

To evaluate the benefit of the system, we proceeded as follows:

1. Differences between scores of paired designs were calculated (e.g., $\Delta_{21} = V(D_2) - V(D_1)$. When $\Delta_{21} < 0$, we assumed that the design done after suggestions was (judged) worse than the design done before the system's suggestions (whether it was adaptive or not), while a $\Delta_{21} > 0$ implies that the user was able to provide a better design after the system's suggestions.
2. For each user in group A we obtained two delta values, while for group B users we considered only the first two values, discarding the third. We then separated the delta values obtained adaptively from those obtained with nonadapted suggestions.
3. We obtained the raw data in shown Table 5.2.

---

[13] The Weka algorithms were C4.5 decision tree, naïve Bayes, 1R rule-based classifier, and IBk k-nearest-neighbors classifier.

TABLE 5.2. Some of the final results data for variants of Weka algorithms. For every design (A$_{1-16}$), 4 different algorithm variants with various combinations were tested, besides the usual, user-adapted algorithms generated by the prototype.

The table is organized into three blocks (ending in columns **D1**, **D2**, **D3**). Each block contains a *simple constellations* group and an *extended constellations* group; each group contains an *adaptive* and a *non-adapt* sub-group with the four algorithm columns NB, J48, 1R, Bk.

Block D1

	simple constellations								extended constellations								D1
	adaptive				non-adapt				adaptive				non-adapt				
	NB	J48	1R	Bk	NB	J48	1R	Bk	NB	J48	1R	Bk	NB	J48	1R	Bk	
A1	8	1	8	26	8	1	8	26	8	1	8	26	8	1	8	26	26
A2	26	26	26	26	26	26	26	26	26	26	26	26	26	26	26	26	26
A3	26	26	26	26	26	26	26	26	26	26	26	26	26	26	26	26	26
A4	26	26	26	26	26	26	26	26	26	26	26	26	26	26	26	26	26
A5	26	26	26	26	26	26	26	26	26	26	26	26	26	26	26	26	26
A6	26	26	26	26	26	26	26	26	26	26	26	26	26	26	26	26	26
A7	26	26	26	26	26	26	26	26	26	26	26	26	26	26	26	26	26
A8	26	26	26	26	26	26	26	26	26	26	26	26	26	26	26	26	26
A9	8	10	8	8	8	10	8	8	8	10	8	8	8	10	8	8	10
A10	10	10	10	26	10	10	10	26	10	10	10	26	10	10	10	26	8
A11	8	10	8	8	8	10	8	8	8	10	8	8	8	10	8	8	8
A12	26	26	26	26	26	26	26	26	26	26	26	26	26	26	26	26	26
A13	10	10	10	26	10	10	10	26	10	10	10	26	10	10	10	26	10
A14	26	26	26	26	26	26	26	26	26	26	26	26	26	26	26	26	26
A15	26	26	26	26	26	26	26	26	26	26	26	26	26	26	26	26	26
A16	26	26	26	26	26	26	26	26	26	26	26	26	26	26	26	26	26

Block D2

	simple constellations								extended constellations								D2
	adaptive				non-adapt				adaptive				non-adapt				
	NB	J48	1R	Bk	NB	J48	1R	Bk	NB	J48	1R	Bk	NB	J48	1R	Bk	
A1	26	26	26	26	26	26	26	26	26	26	26	26	26	26	26	26	26
A2	26	26	26	26	26	26	26	26	26	26	26	26	26	26	26	26	26
A3	26	8	8	26	26	8	8	26	2	26	26	26	2	26	26	26	26
A4	26	26	26	26	26	26	26	26	26	26	26	26	26	26	26	26	26
A5	8	8	10	8	8	8	10	8	8	8	10	8	8	8	10	8	8
A6	26	26	26	26	26	26	26	26	26	26	26	26	26	26	26	26	26
A7	8	8	8	8	8	8	8	8	8	8	8	8	8	8	8	8	8
A8	26	26	26	26	26	26	26	26	26	26	26	26	26	26	26	26	26
A9	8	8	10	8	8	8	10	8	8	8	10	8	8	8	10	8	8
A10	8	8	10	8	8	8	10	8	8	8	10	8	8	8	10	8	8
A11	8	8	10	8	8	8	10	8	8	8	10	8	8	8	10	8	8
A12	26	26	26	26	26	26	26	26	26	26	26	26	26	26	26	26	26
A13	8	8	10	8	8	8	10	8	8	8	10	8	8	8	10	8	8
A14	8	8	10	8	8	8	10	8	8	8	10	8	8	8	10	8	8
A15	10	10	10	10	10	10	10	10	10	10	10	10	10	10	10	10	10
A16	8	8	10	8	8	8	10	8	8	8	10	8	8	8	10	8	8

Block D3

	simple constellations								extended constellations								D3
	adaptive				non-adapt				adaptive				non-adapt				
	NB	J48	1R	Bk	NB	J48	1R	Bk	NB	J48	1R	Bk	NB	J48	1R	Bk	
A1	5	26	5	26	5	26	5	26	5	26	5	26	5	26	5	26	26
A2	5	26	5	26	5	26	5	26	5	26	5	26	5	26	5	26	26
A3	5	26	5	26	5	26	5	26	5	26	5	26	5	26	5	26	26
A4	5	26	5	26	5	26	5	26	5	26	5	26	5	26	5	26	26
A5	5	26	5	26	5	26	5	26	5	26	5	26	5	26	5	26	26
A6	5	26	5	26	5	26	5	26	5	26	5	26	5	26	5	26	26
A7	5	26	5	26	5	26	5	26	5	26	5	26	5	26	5	26	26
A8	5	26	5	26	5	26	5	26	5	26	5	26	5	26	5	26	26
A9	5	26	5	26	5	26	5	26	5	26	5	26	5	26	5	26	26
A10	5	26	5	26	5	26	5	26	5	26	5	26	5	26	5	26	26
A11	5	26	5	26	5	26	5	26	5	26	5	26	5	26	5	26	22
A12	5	26	5	26	5	26	5	26	5	26	5	26	5	26	5	26	26
A13	5	26	5	26	5	26	5	26	5	26	5	26	5	26	5	26	26
A14	5	26	5	26	5	26	5	26	5	26	5	26	5	26	5	26	26
A15	5	26	5	26	5	26	5	26	5	26	5	26	5	26	5	26	26
A16	5	26	5	26	5	26	5	26	5	26	5	26	5	26	5	26	26

TABLE 5.3. Evaluation results for design scores. Columns D_1–D_4 show the score for each of the four designs. Deltas are calculated as follows: $\Delta_1 = V(D_2) - V(D_1)$. $\Delta_2 = V(D_4) - V(D_3)$. Shaded delta values indicate an adaptive suggestion from the prototype. The last two columns report the adaptive delta values (higher than the nonadaptive ones) and nonadaptive ones.

Name	D1	D2	D3	D4	??	??	adaptive	nonadapt
A1	0,60	0,40	0,30	0,00	-0,20	-0,30	-0,20	-0,30
A2	0,40	0,10	0,40	0,80	-0,30	0,40	0,40	-0,30
A3	0,60	0,40	0,40	0,50	-0,20	0,10	-0,20	0,10
A4	0,60	0,40	0,40	0,80	-0,20	0,40	0,40	-0,20
A5	0,40	0,60	0,50	0,60	0,20	0,10	0,20	0,10
A6	0,20	0,50	0,20	0,70	0,30	0,50	0,50	0,30
A7	0,40	0,60	0,50	0,60	0,20	0,10	0,20	0,10
A8	0,40	0,10	0,40	0,80	-0,30	0,40	0,40	-0,30
A9	0,40	0,90	0,60	0,70	0,50	0,10	0,50	0,10
A10	0,70	0,80	0,50	0,90	0,10	0,40	0,40	0,10
A11	0,60	0,90	0,70	0,90	0,30	0,20	0,30	0,20
A12	0,60	0,70	0,50	0,90	0,10	0,40	0,40	0,10
A13	0,50	1,00	0,70	0,80	0,50	0,10	0,50	0,10
A14	0,70	0,80	0,40	0,90	0,10	0,50	0,50	0,10
A15	0,60	1,00	0,60	0,60	0,40	0,00	0,40	0,00
A16	0,50	0,60	0,50	1,00	0,10	0,50	0,50	0,10
A17	1,00	1,00	1,00	1,00	0,00	0,00	0,00	0,00
A18	1,00	1,00	1,00	1,00	0,00	0,00	0,00	0,00

In the next section we discuss the effectiveness of the proposed prototype as regards the pedagogical aspect.

5.4.3.1 Pedagogical Effectiveness

To evaluate the usefulness of the prototype as regards its added value to the student learning process, we compared the differences in OODP skills (measured with the scores given to the designs) before and after the suggestions. Scores for the user-adapted suggestions compared with the nonadapted ones clearly reveal a better performance for user-adapted suggestions. We then used a non-parametric statistical test to ensure that our findings were not due to chance.

Table 5.3 reports the data obtained from the empirical evaluation. The higher values in the adaptive column with respect to the nonadaptive column show the benefit of the user-adapted suggestion.

The last two columns in Table 5.3 report the adaptive delta values and the non-adaptive ones. We ran a Wilcoxon signed-rank test for paired data [22] on the adapted–nonadapted pairs for each user. As in Table 5.3 we obtained

$$\texttt{pValue} = 8.4104\text{E} - 4 \ll 0.01 \text{ (significance value)},$$

showing that the null H_0 hypothesis ("there is no difference in performance between the adaptive and the nonadaptive system") can be rejected and the H_1 hypothesis

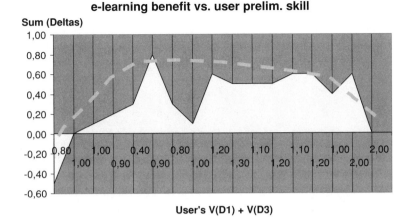

FIGURE 5.19. Overall empirical evaluation results compared with user's preliminary skills. A1-16 and B1-2 are reported on the x axis.

("The differences observed between the two distributions are not due to chance but are due to the difference between the populations they belong to") can be accepted.

This is an important positive result, which shows that the prototype (as used in the experiment) is effectively supporting the learning experience of students being taught OODP.

We also compared the benefit of the system (summing $\Delta_{21} + \Delta_{43}$) against the pre-existing user skills. These were measured as the sum of the scores of first two designs V(D1) + V(D3) created by users using only their own previous knowledge. The result is somehow expected: the prototype is not so effective for too expert users (they don't need tutoring) and for not-enough skilled ones (they don't have a clear enough comprehension of OODP and/or OOCD).

The supposed preexisting level of proficiency with the subject was measured as the sum of scores obtained on the first and the third experiment (new experiments on different topics), while the overall mastery was calculated by summing together all obtained scores for all the experiments.

A possible interpretation of the provided results can be seen in Figure 5.19, where we made the assumption that range ends don't have any substantial benefit from using the prototype, either because students are already proficient with the topic and won't gain any extra insight from teaching (right side in Fig. 5.19) or because students don't even have knowledge of basic skills (such as, for example, OOCD formalism), thus making any teaching effort useless.

The next section discusses the results obtained for the classifier module.

5.4.3.2 Classifiers Results

For brevity's sake, we report here only one diagram about the evaluations we performed on the empirical data found for the OOCD classifier only. Figure 5.20 shows how the various algorithms performed in terms of precision, recall, and

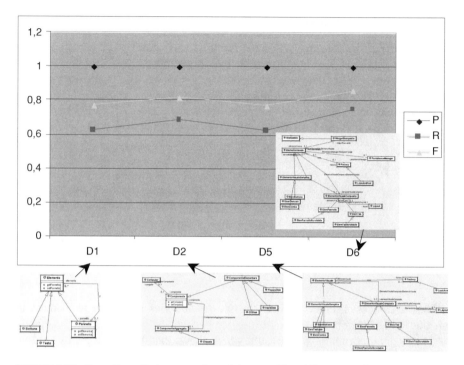

FIGURE 5.20. Overall results in terms of precision, recall, and F-measure for a concrete test in group B. The figure also shows the designs the student did while interacting with the system.

F-measure[14] in an aggregate (i.e., averaging all the results, from all the available classifiers) for a concrete test, showing also the designs created by the user while interacting with the system. The user belonged to group B (with six designs), showing only adaptive RF performance. One can see the evolution of the RF as the user was providing feedbacks to the system.

The next section discusses the related work available in literature.

5.5 Related Work

The design and development of the proposed prototype draws from a number of diverse research fields (such as psychology, schema matching, software engineering, and e-learning). Such multidisciplinary work requires the additional discussion of a number of fields and contributions of interest available in the literature.

---

[14] For an introduction to these measures see http://galahad.plg.inf.uc3m.es/~docweb/ad/transparencias/tutorialTM.pdf

5.5.1 Metamodel Reuse

Reuse of metamodels has been addressed in a number of ways and within several representation frameworks and software engineering approaches (see, for example, [8, 12, and 19]). In this section we briefly discuss the rationale behind metamodel reuse, as applied in the proposed CBT prototype. In such a system we reused the following two metamodels:

- IMS Learning Design.[15]
- SCORM Metadata.[16]

Of course, both these metamodels were originally designed without having in mind the kind of reuse we are discussing here. Nevertheless, this unorthodox use of such standards makes sense, for a number of reasons:

- The mentioned metamodels describe aspects of the e-learning application domain that apply also in our situation.
- Such metamodels encapsulate wide and complex knowledge (built in many years by a wide community of experts) about the domain of interest that hardly would have been achieved in an independent modeling effort.
- From an engineering viewpoint there would be little incentive in replicating already defined and widely accepted solutions to well-known modeling problems.

Reuse is performed at a conceptual level by "adopting" the entire conceptual framework in the reused metamodels (as in the case of the pedagogical domain in IMS LD) and on a practical level by using the concepts into our models (see Fig.5.6).

5.5.2 Object Oriented Design Patterns

Christopher Alexander, a building architect and urban planner, coined the term *design pattern* in, the mid-1970s to refer to recurring designs in building architecture [2]. He observed:

Each pattern describes a problem that occurs over and over again in our environment and then describes the core of the solution to that problem in such a way that you can use this solution a million times over without ever doing it the same way twice.

The concept resurfaced unexpectedly in the late 1980s applied to software design. In those years, almost contemporaneously and independently, a number of practitioners and researchers started to observe certain "regularities" within the OOP software designs they were building. It proved to be a valuable idea. Nowadays, design patterns are widespread well beyond OOP. Also, outside computer

---

[15] IMS Learning Design Best Practice and Implementation Guide. IMS Global Learning Consortium. (2003). Available at http://www.imsglobal.org/profiles/lipbest01.html.
[16] Official Web page at http://www.adlnet.org/scorm/index.cfm.

science patterns are investigated for analysis, user interface design, and in many other fields.

5.5.2.1 Teaching Object Oriented Design Patterns

As discussed in [5] and [21], OODPs are learned effectively only with a learning-by-doing approach rather than with theoretical courses (or similar computer-based courseware). According to [20], the variety of OODP applications that students get exposed to plays an important role in the effective learning of OODP. Furthermore, OODPs are not learned by solving small exercises. As observed in [21], in small exercises it becomes apparent which OODPs apply in order to solve the problem.

These few considerations make clear that building effective OODP CBT systems is a very complex task. It is not by surprise that most tutoring systems for OODP (including intelligent tutoring system (ITS)) are based on limited interactions where exercises are (expensively) corrected by human experts or where the didactic material is limited to some clever form of courseware [24].

Matters are complicated even more by the abstract nature of OODP that can be validly instantiated in many different variants [11, 21] and where the creativity of the designer plays an important role [5]. On the other hand, all these considerations tend to favor our prototype and its hands-on, practical interaction style. Indeed, the prototype was designed with these pedagogical observations in mind. In the following subsection we discuss some of the issues related to representing knowledge in such a domain.

5.5.3 Schema Matching Algorithms

The task of matching schema or diagram instances (like, for example, tree-like structures such as XML data, or generic graph-like as entity-relationship diagrams) has been extensively studied in literature as part of the wider problem of schema matching.

Schema matching is the task of finding semantic correspondences between elements of two input schemas providing as output a map indicating which elements of the input schemas correspond to each other (that is, match each other) [24, 25]. This is a recurring problem in many application domains, like data integration, E-business, or XML data mapping. Examples of schema matching algorithms and systems presented in literature are Clio [26], TransSCM [25], or the similarity flooding [27] algorithm.

Classifying OOCD against other class diagrams (representing categories, i.e., OODP in our case) can be seen as a special case of schema matching. Some systems were instantiated and tested on OOP diagrams. This proves the affinity of schema matching to our problem when compared to other research fields such as graph matching. The most important point in choosing a schema matching approach to address the problem of classifying OOCD is that both problems involve a strong semantic bias. Schemas (and OOCD schemas as well) are not mere data structures but they obey complex semantic relationships that cannot be solved only with plain structural comparisons.

The classifier used in our prototype was built by taking advantage of successful schema matching systems and approaches presented in literature. The main ideas that inspired the design of our OOCD classifier are:

- Successful matching can be achieved cost-effectively by examining simple node-wise patterns (that is, performing a type of node-to-node comparison between schemas represented as graphs) [25].
- Labels and other text available in schema instances can be used for performing a similarity assessment [26, 27].
- Given the semantic nature of the data representation involved and the strong dependency on users, some form of feedback is needed to adapt matching criteria to user-intended semantic.

We conclude this section by comparing the proposed prototype with an existing system also targeted at OODP tutoring.

5.5.4 Comparison with an Existing ITS System

In this section we compare the proposed prototype with the ITS for design pattern (ITS DP) [24]. Both applications targeted the same domain (OODP teaching). This comparison will be useful both to better understand the differences between "classic" programs and UARS, and as a concrete discussion about the advantages of our proposed approach for high-level knowledge representation and processing against traditional, state-of-the-art approaches.

Thanks to the UARS approach, the data structures used in our prototype allow for a much higher level of abstraction. This in turn creates a number of conceptual mismatches when attempting a detailed comparison of the two applications, especially for knowledge representation. For a fair comparison of a UARS application with a non-UARS one, we should focus only on level 1 models (i.e., programs). Even this approach makes a comparison difficult, because UARSs have a somewhat "fuzzy" level 1 structure, and a particular instance of an UARS application at a given time would depend too much on context data (past user behavior, etc.).

Luckily, in this current case we can use the particular domain-specific abstractions for an attempt at a rough yet useful comparison. By using the concept of relevance function (r_u) to describe the "cloud" of level 1 models of our UARS application, we could compare level 1 structures between the two applications.

The SUM_1 model in ITS DP is composed of pairs of attributes-values. In our UARS prototype the SUM_1 model can be roughly represented as a set of RF (whose exact nature depends on past user behavior and the external context). Figure 5.21 shows the main differences between the proposed UARS prototype and ITS DP.

A direct, exact comparison focused on measuring the effectiveness of the two systems is not possible, mainly because it would need a homogeneous student set and the related evaluation procedures.

One thing we can observe, though, is the impact of the UARS approach on model representation. While there could be a certain degree of overlap between the set of concepts represented with the two different approaches (after all, both systems model students for OODP teaching), what is radically different is the degree of

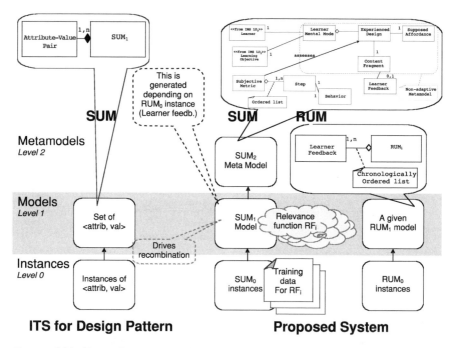

FIGURE 5.21. Comparing user models between the proposed prototype and the ITS for DP system [24].

representational power allowed by UARS when compared with traditional (non-UARS) applications.

In ITS DP the student model stores details about students' current problem-solving state and long-term knowledge progresses. Student characteristics are modeled as attributes. Three categories of student's characteristics are considered [24]:

- Personal data—the student's personal characteristics (name, ID, e-mail etc.).
- Performance data—the student's cognitive and individual characteristics, as well as other general long-term characteristics.
- Overlay data—the current level of mastery of design patterns and attributes related to the corresponding elements in the domain model.

Focusing on design styles, the main subject of user modeling within the prototype UARS, we can observe how RFs are represented by the metamodel at the next level of abstraction (namely SUM_2). Even if this concept would have been represented in the UM of ITS DP, it would have been implemented with pairs of attributes and values, thus providing a much lower level of expressivity and quality of representation.

Furthermore, UARS have a much finer degree of adaptation, because adaptation is achieved not only during recombination (by means of RUM models) but also at lower abstraction levels, where several UMs can be adapting SUM data as in traditional user-adapted applications.

5.5.5 The Proposed Approach and the Existing Literature

User-adapted generative technologies are increasingly being studied in user-tailored ubiquitous software[17] for computing devices with limited resources where user-adapted code generation can be performed on remote servers at deployment time. Despite some research in the convergence area of generative programming (GP) and user modeling (reference [2] introduces an architecture for personalizing applications based on a model-driven, user-centered approach), the adoption of GP techniques together with "strong" user adaptation for general systems is still missing.

Some work focused on investigating the adoption of software engineering techniques and approaches to adaptive hypermedia (AH) systems. The Munich reference model,[18] aimed at providing a formal reference model for AH systems, using UML (with OCL) and providing a user and adaptation metamodels together with a comprehensive design method and development process for AH applications. These initiatives focused on engineering AH applications development by adapting state-of-the-art techniques and methodologies, providing a comprehensive framework that lacks enough flexibility and expressive power to handle powerful adaptation models and nonstandard situations (quite the norm in intelligent adaptive applications).

Our proposed approach is different in several ways from the previous contributions in that it embodies a somehow visionary yet general SE approach that still needs to be fully explored. Far from being limited to technological aspects only (model-based knowledge representation and GP techniques), the proposed approach allows the definition of technology-independent, powerful user models at several abstraction layers, allowing for sophisticated knowledge representation and processing. Moreover, the introduction in the field of user adaptation of rich metamodels suitable for code generation can foster standardization and reuse both in vertical domains (as is happening on the software technology front) and as a general modeling foundation for an infrastructure for a rich set of user modeling services.

5.6 Conclusion

In this section we discuss both the proposed prototype and its underlying SE approach. As regards the former, the encouraging results from the evaluation discussed in section 5.4 prompted a number of extensions of the CBT prototype (such as a better pedagogical heuristic, the reuse and enhancement of the classifier as a stand-alone module, etc.).

---

[17] See for instance: Bonnet, S. Model Driven Software Personalization. In: Proceedings of Smart Objects Conference, Grenoble France (2003). available at http://www.grenoble-soc.com/proceedings03/Pdf/50-Bonnet.pdf.

[18] Parcus de Koch, N. Software Engineering for Adaptive Hypermedia Systems—Reference Model, Modeling Techniques and Development Process. PhD Dissertation (2001). Available at: http://www.pst.informatik.uni-muenchen.de/personen/kochn/PhDThesisNoraKoch.pdf.

We focus now on the findings related to the general approach introduced in section 5.2.2. We found that UARSs have a number of advantages over more traditional adaptive systems, even if they are much more labor-intensive to set up (at least with current technology):

- UARSs represent adaptive and system functional models at a high level of abstraction, isolated from implementation and other nonmeaningful details. Clear and more maintainable representations are thus encouraged;
- they may take advantage of existing standard metamodels, ontologies, and other modeling facilities (which are growing in many application domains), thus reusing knowledge representations;
- by taking advantage of generative technologies they provide a very powerful and general adaptation mechanism that includes as a particular case classic adaptation techniques;
- such systems are particularly useful for generating user-tailored software for devices where computing resources don't allow for sophisticated client-side user adaptation;
- UARSs fit nicely in special application niches such as dedicated user-adapted systems, prototypes where tuning is extremely important and depends on the current users, etc.

Furthermore, UARSs embody the interesting paradigm of self-designing software, based on the user adaptation approach.

The main drawbacks we found in the proposed approach could be summarized as follows:

- The creation of an effective recombination abstract model (which describes the theoretical domain-specific rationale behind the adoption of the UARS approach) requires many interdisciplinary skills[19]:
  - Domain knowledge, in order to define the domain-specific details of the recombination process.
  - Technical knowledge for building effectively the UARS RTP (rich target platform) based on reusable software assets (such as third-party libraries, open source code, etc.)
  - Knowledge related to user-centered design and usability, needed for packaging an effective product out of such a large base of diverse specification. UARSs are interactive systems that must be focused on end users.
- Software support for generative software and software families is still in its early stages, and advanced facilities such as run-time configurable platforms are still far from reality. This issue is perhaps the easiest to cope with, for example by providing a general rich target platform (RTP) that can accommodate a large number of scenarios. In general, though, given the wide array of technologies and domain scenarios, it is clear that these are partial solutions and that only the support of a wide community can really enable a development cost-savvy, mass diffusion of UARS.

---

[19] These issues apply to other knowledge-intensive application as well.

- Another hurdle we have found in our work is related to the novelty the approach brings to the software design and development mindset. Apart from well-understood domain and model-based development environments, a really challenging situation is caused by the presence of the recombination abstraction. This forces designers to deal with a powerful, novel, and demanding application model.

Recapping, there are two main hurdles to the effective, large-scale development of UARS applications: a conceptual one, given the sheer power of such a class of systems. It may be hard to come to a practical recombination model for a given application domain in a cost-effective way. The other one is technical. As of the time of writing, there are no standard supports (among the various tools and platforms related to MDE and GP) that can be employed to build cost-effectively a UARS run-time platform.

As regards the comparison of the UARS approach with non-UARS systems, we discussed also the impact of the UARS approach on model representation. In addition, we found UARSs exhibiting a much finer degree of adaptation. This is achieved not only during recombination (by means of RUM models) but also at lower abstraction levels, where several UMs (in the case of the proposed prototype one model for each RF in the current SUM) can be adapting to the user as in traditional (i.e., non-UARS) user-adapted applications.

This chapter introduced a class of self-design software systems based on MDE techniques. A prototype UARS for teaching OODP was introduced and evaluated empirically, with encouraging results. The evaluation also showed concretely the complexities and the related power of this class of user-adapted systems.

References

1. Aamodt, A., Plaza, E. (1994) Case-Based Reasoning: Foundational Issues, Methodological Variations, and System Approaches. Amsterdam, NL: Artificial Intelligence Communications.
2. Alexander, C., et al. (1977) A Pattern Language: Towns, Buildings, Construction. New York: Oxford University Press.
3. Anderson, J.R. (2002) Spanning seven orders of magnitude: a challenge for cognitive modeling. Cognitive Science, 26.
4. Anderson, J.R. (1983) The Architecture of Cognition. Cambridge, MA: Harvard University Press.
5. Beck, K., et al. (1996) Industrial experience with design patterns. In: Proceedings of the 18th International Conference on Software Engineering, ICSE'96.
6. Bézivin, J. (2001) From object composition to model transformation with the MDA. In Proceedings of TOOLS USA, Vol. IEEE TOOLS-39, Santa Barbara, CA.
7. Chin, D. (2001) Empirical evaluation of user models and user-adapted systems. Journal of User Modeling and User-Adapted Interaction, 11: 181–194.
8. Clark, T., Evans, A., Sammut, P., Willans, J. (2004) Applied Metamodelling. A Foundation for Language Driven Development. Version 0.1. Xactium Technical Report.

9. Do, H.-H., Melnik, S., Rahm, E. (2002) Comparison of Schema Matching Evaluations. http://www.old.netobjectdays.org/pdf/02/papers/ws-webdb/02-Do.pdf.

10. Frankel, D. (2003) Model Driven Architecture: Applying MDA to Enterprise Computing. New York: J. Wiley.

11. Gamma, E., Helm, R., Johnson, R., Vlissldes, J. (1993) Design patterns: abstraction and reuse of object-oriented design. In: Proceedings of European Conference on Object-Oriented Programming (ECOOP). Kaiserslautern, Germany: Springer-Verlag.

12. Gavras, A., Belaunde, M, Ferreira Pires, F., Almeida J.P.A. (2003) Towards an MDA-based development methodology for distributed applications.

13. Gibson, J.J. (1977) The theory of affordances. In: Shaw, R.E., Bransford, J., (eds.), Perceiving, Acting, and Knowing. Hillsdale, NJ: Lawrence Erlbaum Associates.

14. Hartson, H.R. (1999) Cognitive, Physical, and Perceptual Affordances in Interaction Design. Technical Report. Department of Computer Science, Virginia Tech. http://courses.cs.vt.edu/~cs5714/fall2004/Templates/Affordances,%20as%20appeared.pdf.

15. JCP26 specification. http://www.jcp.org/en/jsr/detail?id=26.

16. Koper, R. (2001) Modeling Units of Study from a Pedagogical Perspective—The Pedagogical Meta-Model Behind EML. Heerlen, NL: Open University of the Netherlands.

17. Marinilli, M., Micarelli, A. (2005) Generative programming driven by user models. In: Proceedings of Tenth International Conference on User Modeling UM05, Edinburgh, UK.

18. Norman, D.A. (1988) The Psychology of Everyday Things. New York: Basic Books.

19. Nytun, J.P., Prinz, (2004) A Metalevel Representation and Philosophical Ontology. In: ECOOP 2004 Workshop: Philosophy, Ontology, and Information Systems, Oslo, Norway.

20. Schmidt, D. (1995) Using Design Patterns to Develop Reusable Object-Oriented Communication Software. Communication of ACM, 38(10).

21. Stuurman, S., Florijn, G. (2004) Experiences with Teaching Design Patterns. In: Proceedings of ITICSE'04, Leeds, United Kingdom.

22. Wilcoxon, F. (1945) Individual comparisons by ranking methods. Biometrica Bulletin, 1: 80–83.

23. Witten, H.I., Eibe F. (1999) Data Mining: Practical Machine Learning Tools and Techniques with Java implementation. Morgan Kaufmann.

24. Jeremic, Z., Devedzic, V., Gasevic, D. (2004) An Intelligent Tutoring System for Learning Design Patterns, ICALT Joensuu, Finland.

25. Milo, T., Zohar, S. (1998) Using Schema Matching to Simplify Heterogeneous Data Translation. VLDB, New York, USA.

26. Yan, L.L., Miller, R.J., Haas, L.M., Fagin, R. (2001) Data-Driven Understanding and Refinement of Schema Mappings. SIGMOD, Santa Barbara, CA, USA.

27. Melnik, S., Garcia-Molina, H., Rahm, E. (2001) Similarity Flooding: A Versatile Graph Matching Algorithm and Its Application to Schema Matching, Stanford, CA, USA.

6
Skills SuperStore: Online Interactive Study Skills Environment

CAITRIONA BERMINGHAM AND ABDULHUSSAIN MAHDI

Abstract. An online interactive environment for provision of flexible student-centered study and interpersonal skills training is described, and preliminary results of its evaluation are reported. The system has been designed to assist higher education students develop study skills via formulating effective strategies that help them learn, retain, and apply new knowledge during their university education and beyond. The system's features, functionality, and architecture were developed based on the findings of a viability study conducted at our institution and facilitated by (a) evaluation of various approaches for the provision of study skills training employed by higher education institutions worldwide, and (b) surveying students from various departments and disciplines. The system comprises a number of interactive modules used as flexible learning aids in conjunction with existing learning skills materials and resources. The interactivity of the system is achieved by users making choices, answering questions, and completing activities related to their own experiences.

6.1 Introduction

6.1.1 Background and Rationale

The importance and need for education to play an essential role in society has always been recognized. Without a high-quality education infrastructure, people with a high level of skills and expertise, who are crucial to sustain and build any modern civilization, would not be adequately trained and qualified. Consequently, educational authorities worldwide place considerable time and funds into developing their education policies. In no place is this more evident than in third-level institutions, i.e., university and college education. In Ireland, higher education institutions have seen an enormous increase in the number of students entering third-level education in the last 40 years. This confirms the increasing role of third-level education institutions in producing a ". . . high-skilled, knowledge and innovation-based economy that will underpin ongoing and sustainable prosperity" [7].

One of the most significant roles of any higher education institution is the pursuit of excellence and quality in teaching and research. However, in fulfilling such a mission it should always be ensured that it is conditioned by relevance to the times and changing students' needs. In a rapidly changing world of business and technology, higher education institutions must ensure that their study programs provide students with the relevant skills they need during their studies, after graduation and beyond.

Students entering third-level education face a number of significant changes to their daily lives. For the vast majority, they are moving away from home and away from their parents for the first time. This new lease of freedom means that they must now accept complete responsibility for themselves and their actions. All decisions, right or wrong, must now be made by the student. The most notable of these changes is in terms of education and the responsibility they must accept for their own learning. They are no longer told by teachers what to do, how to do it, and when to do it. They must take complete responsibility for their education.

Due to lack of effective study and learning skills, such as note taking, preparing for exams, time management, etc., most students who enroll in third-level courses in Ireland find it difficult to adapt to the higher education study and learning system. As they proceed through their years of study, they will likely find themselves under increasing pressure in terms of what is expected of them in their courses. Students find that study strategies employed in high school don't work at the university level, that reading lists in upper-level courses are more rigorous, and that the research process for an academic paper is a learning experience in itself. Tutors and student counselors often hear student statements such as:

- "I have put a lot of effort into my studies but I don't seem to be able to improve my results."
- "I'm not sure what skills I am going to need to succeed in my studies ... to embark on a sound career."
- "I'm looking for new ideas to develop my skills, such as essay writing, reading, learning from lectures, preparing for exams, researching an assignment ... "

For students to be successful in third-level education and effective as graduates it is acknowledged that they need to acquire efficient and effective study, learning, and other transferable skills [17, 18]. In college, students must become independent learners. They must learn to examine past experiences and make any changes to their practices essential to surmount new challenges. Research has also shown that recent graduates do not possess the necessary skills required for full-time employment. In fact, it is often communication skills, problem-solving abilities, and interpersonal skills that highlight those who are preferred for employment [2, 6].

Educators in higher education institutions should encourage students, particularly first-year students, to aim toward developing a deeper and more strategic approach to their learning, moving away from surface approaches. Such a process will need considerable resources that support both educators and students. It is the responsibility of all modern higher education institutions to make available such resources, tools, and mechanisms that facilitate effective development of students various skills. There is now an inexorable drive by universities all over the world to take advantage of information and communication technology (ICT) technology-based learning systems, commonly referred to as virtual learning environments (VLEs), as a means of exploiting new markets, easing resource issues, and widening access. In most cases, it has been proven that such technology coupled with multimedia techniques can provide flexible and cost-effective complementary learning and study tools.

Web-based learning environments are becoming progressively more common as a support tool to assist teachers in creating material that is both stimulating and engaging [6]. Taking this into consideration, our approach to the above issues has been to provide an engaging and interactive study skills training system that is facilitated by an online Web-based learning environment [10].

6.1.2 Skills SuperStore: Project Aim and Objectives

The objective of the project was to research, design, and develop a screen-delivered interactive computer-based learning system for developing students' study, learning, and other transferable skills. The system was designed for use as a flexible learning aid in conjunction with existing learning skills materials and programs offered by third-level institutions for the facilitation of study skills training. The content of the system was designed to help users explore and evaluate their own approaches to learning and to encourage them to become active self-learners. The interactivity mechanisms of the system will be facilitated by users answering questions, completing activities, and selecting options according to their own experiences, communicating with each other via a discussion forum, etc.

It is envisaged that the developed "Skills SuperStore" learning environment will have the following specific outcomes:

- Improving students' academic performance via developing their abilities to learn.
- Improving students' transferable/professional skills and enhancing graduates' employability.
- Development of more responsible, independent, self-learners and lifelong learners.
- Raising students' awareness of information sources and how to search for them in a higher education environment and beyond.
- Promoting appropriate use of technology in teaching and learning approaches in the higher education system.
- A commercial potential and possible marketable product.

6.1.3 Chapter Organization

This chapter discusses in detail a study skills on-line training environment termed the "Skills SuperStore." It presents the need for and benefit of such a system and concludes with an in-debt account of the development process of the target system. A brief description of each of the sections in the chapter is supplied here:

- *6.2. Need for Study Skills*: Presents an overview of the importance of study skills and why students need to acquire them in order to succeed in third-level education. It also examines why it is felt that current study skills training approaches are not always relevant and why a different approach is required.

- *6.3. The Way Forward and a Solution*: A brief summary of the current training approaches discussed in the previous section is provided again here. Following this, a detailed description of the viability study conducted at the University of Limerick is presented. Analysis of the results of this study along with the system requirements and initial design are also discussed.
- *6.4. System Design and Development*: This section presents the iterative process involved in the design and development of the target system. It provides insight into each of the stages of development: requirements gathering, analysis, design, implementation, and testing.
- *6.5. Conclusion*: This final section provides a brief conclusion to the chapter.

6.2 Need for Study Skills

6.2.1 Retention Issues in Third-Level Institutions

Noncompletion is a significant issue in all higher education institutions worldwide. Each year a considerable percentage of students, for one reason or another, fail to complete their third-level courses in which they are enrolled. Though a number of these students may have simply made the choice to leave third-level education in order to move onto what they perceive to be a better alternative, it remains that the majority of students fail to complete third-level education without a conscious decision to leave. This is a very worrying issue, and it is important to discover the many reasons behind noncompletion so that adequate steps can be taken to combat the problem.

International statistics show that on average, approximately a third of all students who enroll in a third-level course fail to complete their studies and leave university without graduating. Ireland is positioned toward the lower end of the scale, with 23% of third-level students failing to complete their higher education [12].

There are countless causes behind noncompletion at third-level institutions. However, it has been identified that at a macro-level the causes for non-completion include, for example, choosing unsuitable courses, the influence of financial security, and other personal circumstances. In some instances the attraction of the buoyant labor market may encourage students to leave before completing their courses and securing accreditation [12].

Another cause of noncompletion that was acknowledged was the issue of poor study skills. The view was expressed that secondary school did not prepare students for independent learning, required for third-level education. In second-level education students studied because they were given homework, which on a regular basis was assessed. Now, on entering third-level education, they failed to understand that they should attend lectures and study for their own benefit and that there would be nobody responsible to ensure that they worked consistently and efficiently. The example was given of students demanding to know exactly what chapter of a book to read, or if a particular topic was going to be on the exam. Many students were considered too nervous to speak up and contribute their opinions in a discussion group. Also it was identified that while some students did not know how to study outside of class, others did not have discipline. Some students had difficulty taking notes, and since lecturing was a completely different method of information delivery for them, they needed support and help in setting up a study plan and developing techniques of learning [8].

The key purpose of higher education institutions is to facilitate learning, i.e., to deliver knowledge, which is to be learned by students. Learning, which can be defined as the art and science of acquiring knowledge, is one of the most important and unrecognized life skills in today's society [15]. By recalling and applying knowledge, acquired through learning, any demand or situation can be confronted and many exciting opportunities created. Learning effectively is a skill that we need to know throughout our lives, but it is rarely properly taught.

It is well recognized that students in higher education need to acquire and develop effective study and interpersonal skills in order to be successful in their study courses and after graduation [17, 18]. The greater need is when students first arrive at university. At this stage, the majority are adjusting to their new lifestyle as university students and to the freedom that is afforded by it. They are suddenly faced with a radically different educational environment in terms of the way in which knowledge is delivered and the amount of independent learning that is required. They often have little awareness of the way in which they learn and tackle problems. To be successful in higher education, students must develop the ability to examine their behavior and become more independent self-learners [13]. On the other hand, it has been observed that many of the skills needed by new students are the same as the transferable skills often missing in graduates, such as communication skills [2, 6]. In fact, employers often prefer graduates who show abilities to communicate with other people and to manage time and work [2]. Therefore, the solution is to provide students with appropriately delivered training in these skills at the very beginning of their university education.

6.2.2 Study and Transferable Skills Needed

The importance and need for traditional study skills, which can be defined as an assortment of skills specific to aiding students to successfully complete their education, such as note taking, researching and conducting a project, and revising and completing exams, can too frequently be underestimated by students, particularly those who may benefit most from them. Also transferable skills, which to some degree can be defined as life skills, that is, skills that can be applied outside of the education sector in most or all professions, such as time management and writing reports, are habitually unrecognized as skills that could be of great benefit to students both during and beyond their third-level education. The following subsections discuss in further detail the most common skills required by third-level students to assist them in their studies.

Note Taking

Adequate notes are a necessary adjunct to efficient study and learning in college [27]. Many students in higher education lack the ability to take well-organized and appropriate notes. They don't realize that by taking clear, concise, and personal notes they are concentrating on what must be learned. Notes help understanding, as ideas are put into the student's own words and diagrams.

Reading Effectively

In third-level education reading effectively is a skill that is essential in aiding students to succeed in their studies. However, it is unfortunate that not every student can read in the most effective way to understand a selected piece. It is essential for students to acquire the ability to identify the purpose for reading a particular piece and then choose the appropriate strategy to meet that purpose.

Writing Essays

Aside from exams, papers are probably the most popular means in third-level education for evaluating students abilities and skills [25]. Given that fact, it is important for students to be able to write well-researched and well-written essays. However, many students find that they are unable to start essays, and others make a start but find themselves unable to finish. Students simply don't know how to divide an essay into more manageable and less daunting components.

Researching and Conducting a Project

In third-level education students may be required to complete an extended piece of coursework, project, dissertation, or thesis. No matter how successful the results of the project, it will be evident that the completed project is lacking unless the student can write up the research, analysis, and findings effectively [15]. A universal difficulty for students when completing a project is that there appears to be no end to the project. It is essential for students to develop the ability to judge where to end their project so that it includes no loose ends, while ensuring that the project isn't too extensive.

Revising

Throughout a students educational life, testing will be an inevitable reality. The key to exam preparation is that of revision. Revision can be separated into two subcategories: concurrent revision and rapid revision.

Concurrent revision is that which occurs continuously throughout the college year and is composed of four key sources:

- Lecture notes
- Questions and answers to past exam papers
- Background reading
- The students own understanding of the subject

Rapid revision is carried out in the 24 hours before the exam and will ensure the maximum use of short-term memory so that the student will peak on the day of the exam. Rapid revision can be divided into three interrelated skills:

- Read over the revision notes created as a result of the concurrent revision.
- Engage and harmonize as many senses as possible during the review, that is, see the notes, read the notes, hear the notes, etc.
- Use a shorthand writing technique.

Through good effective revision the student will be more confident of their knowledge of the subject, and better prepared for the examination.

Preparing for Exams and Assessments

Along with the various written and oral assignments students are required to complete during their course, they are also assessed by quizzes, tests, and examinations. Many exams are as much a measure of the way the student studies—the student's ability to organize a mountain of material—as they are a measure of the student's knowledge of the material itself [9]. There are a number of ways in which a student can better prepare for an exam:

- Begin revision early.
- Have all the equipment required for the exam packed and accounted for the night before.
- Know the type of examination: multiple-choice, essay type, short answer type, etc.

Time Management

Effective planning and time management is an essential skill required for students completing third-level education. Using the time management skill correctly and effectively enables students to function efficiently even in times of intense pressure. Students are often inundated with essays, projects, lab assignments, and various other assessments that can be very time-consuming, which, in addition to constant course revision, can be very overwhelming for students and instill a feeling of panic and anxiety, which is counterproductive. In higher education institutions many students don't know how to manage their workloads in the time available to them so that they may achieve their highest potential in their studies.

6.2.3 Importance of Study and Transferable Skills

Students at third-level institutions need to learn study skills. This is most important when students are in their first year of higher-level education. It is at this stage that the students will acquire methods that will be used to complete their study right throughout their college experience. But students also have the added pressure of adjusting to a new and exciting lifestyle. For the first time in their lives they must become familiar with a freedom associated with living away from home and away from parental supervision. They are also faced with a radically different educational system from what they were used to in their previous five or six years in secondary education. Suddenly all the responsibility for their education is shifted from secondary school teachers and parents to themselves. They are no longer told what to do and when to do it. All decisions, right or wrong, now must be made by themselves. These two factors, freedom and educational responsibility, often result in students adopting inefficient methods of study, which unfortunately become a pattern adopted right throughout their university education.

For this reason it is very important to bring to the attention of third-level students, particularly when they first enter higher education, the need for and importance of acquiring and developing various study and other transferable skills. If these skills are introduced at this stage, then it may help them to acquire better study habits that will enable them to study more effectively in less time.

College is a life experience and is as much about students discovering who they are as it is about learning and acquiring knowledge. It is hoped that by helping students to become more independent and effective self-learners that they may be able to enjoy their college experience while getting the results that reflect not only their effort but also their ability.

6.2.4 Approaches Currently Employed in Higher Education to Train Study Skills

Higher education institutions have three central approaches for the development of study and transferable skills of the students: (1) the inclusion of special modules as part of the course curriculum, (2) optional extracurricular classes/workshops made available to students, and (3) the provision of written and other multimedia materials that are usually made available by university information centers [2]. Each of these study skills training approaches is discussed in further detail in the following subsections.

Special Modules as Part of the Course Curriculum

This method of delivering study skills and other transferable skills training entails creating a module dedicated to the teaching of the various skills considered of great importance to the students in their university education and beyond. It is preferable that these modules be included as part of the students' first-year curriculum, but this may not always be the case. The study skills module is a typical lecture scenario in which students attend lectures on various topics such as time management, note taking, effective reading, etc. from one or more lecturers. Students are also required to complete assignments and most often a final exam in order to receive credit for the module.

Unfortunately, this method has one major limitation. These modules are generally unrelated to the students' main discipline of study and for this reason it may have the effect of reducing students' motivation to attend and complete the module satisfactorily.

Extracurricular Classes/Workshops

Extracurricular classes/workshops are another approach for the delivery of study skills training used in higher education institutions. This method is somewhat comparable to the previous method discussed—special modules incorporated as part of the course curriculum—in that the classes/workshops are presented in lectures on the various subjects that comprise the field of study and transferable skills. Conversely, the difference is that these classes/workshops are voluntary; therefore, it is up to the students' discretion whether to attend.

Unfortunately, a few limitations to this method can also be identified. Often these training methods are viewed by many students as being remedial and hence if voluntary are not attended, particularly by those who could benefit from them. Also, as there is no recognition for the completion of these classes/workshops, there is little or no motivation for students to sacrifice their personal time in order to attend. Finally, the lack of flexibility and the poor scheduling of these additional courses often contribute to their poor attendance [2].

The Provision of Written and Other Multimedia Materials

The last skills delivery approach used in third-level education institutions is the provision of written and other multimedia materials. Many colleges and universities produce booklets, create various multimedia material such as audiocassettes and videos, and develop Web sites in order to make available to their students study skills training resources. It is then up to the students' discretion if they have a problem with some area of study to find the information from one of these resources to aid them in acquiring and developing the study skills they lack.

As with the proceeding approaches discussed, there are a number of shortcomings associated with this study skills training method. If a detailed booklet or any other similar resource were to be compiled, it would contain a mountain of information, all of which would be relevant. But many of the resources produced are mere summaries of each of the skills, omitting a great deal of the detail. Another shortcoming encountered with this method is the generalization of the material. When acquiring and developing their study skills, students must adopt and personalize their own methods, which is very difficult to achieve when faced with very general information.

6.2.5 Study Skills Training: Limitations of Current Approaches

As is evident from the preceding discussion, some type of a study skills development resource is necessary to aid students in acquiring and developing these skills. The various approaches for study skills training adopted by colleges and universities worldwide were discussed. Although these methods fit the requirement of delivering study and transferable skills training, they have a number of limitations that needed to be addressed.

Four major limitations were identified from the above methods:

1. The training modules are viewed by some students as remedial and hence, if voluntary, not attended by those who may benefit from them [2].
2. As the courses/materials are seen as being unrelated to the student's main discipline of study, it may have the effect of reducing the student's motivation.
3. The lack of flexibility and the poor scheduling of these additional courses often contribute to their poor attendance.
4. Research has shown that effective skills training is difficult to achieve because students must adopt and personalize their own study skills and methods. Study skills cannot be taught to students by conventional teaching using a set of established procedures, which can be reproduced for examination purposes.

To overcome the above issues it was proposed to provide a flexible study skills training system that is facilitated by a technology-based learning environment [10]. The system described in this report, called the "Skills SuperStore," has been designed and developed to be used as an interactive self-learning tool to aid students in acquiring and developing study and other transferable skills in conjunction with existing skills learning resources.

6.3 The Way Forward and a Solution

To determine how to achieve study skills training, what it should entail and the requirements of the target system, a viability study was conducted at the University of Limerick. The aim of this study was to gather as much information as possible to assist in determining the appropriate features of the system, such as required architecture, functionality, services, and means of delivery. The study was effected by two means:

1. Investigating and evaluating a number of approaches employed by various higher education institutions to facilitate study skills training.
2. Conducting voluntary surveys of students and academic staff from various departments, courses, and disciplines. The purpose of these surveys is to identify problems, needs, and potential solutions regarding students' personal study habits and requirements.

6.3.1 Investigation of Current Approaches

The first part of the viability study was an investigation and evaluation of the various methods employed by higher education institutions worldwide for the provision of study and other transferable skills training. These approaches have already been discussed in detail in section 6.2.4.

6.3.2 Surveys and Analysis

The second element, which affected the viability study, was the survey of students and academic staff from various departments, courses, and disciplines.

The Student Survey

A voluntary survey of 150 students—86 males and 64 females—from various departments, courses, and disciplines was conducted in our institution. The majority of the surveyed students were in their first year of studies, but second-, third-, and fourth-year students were also included. The survey consisted of a questionnaire with the purpose of highlighting problems, needs, and potential solutions regarding study skills, personal habits, and requirements. The questionnaire contained 30 multichoice questions categorized according to the following three areas:

• Lack of certain study/learning skill(s)
• Personal study habits
• Potential solutions and preferred training means

Analysis of the Student Survey

The responses on the student survey gave a good indication of the many problems faced by students when they study and also highlighted a number of methods employed to successfully aid them in overcoming these problems.

For the first category, the questions were designed to evaluate which study skills students find difficult to acquire and develop. Using the format of "Do you have problems with . . . ," the questions highlighted nine different study skills ranging from note taking to planning and time management. Our findings regarding this category are summarized in Table 6.1, where the percentages of students who specified difficulty with the various study skills are given. The table shows that 48% of the surveyed students indicated that they experience problems with effective planning and time management. Conversely, only 8% feel they have difficulty with taking notes in lectures.

TABLE 6.1. Study requirements survey—areas of difficulty

Area of difficulty	Percentage
Effective planning and time management	48
Reading effectively	18
Learning blockages	12
Note taking	8
Writing reports and essays	18
Researching and conducting a project	26
Understanding course material	24
Revising	32
Preparing for exams	24

From the analysis of the students' feedback concerning the second category of questions, personal study habits, it was possible to identify some of the causes behind the problems faced by students with various study skills. For example, it was discovered that 50% of the surveyed students usually study in environments that lack adequate resources and are prone to distractions. Another question concerning amount of time spent studying showed that the majority of students (64%) think that 5 or fewer hours per week on average is adequate. Also, when asked whether students prefer to study individually or in groups, the majority preferred individual study.

The last category of questions were designed to gather information on the most effective way of helping students in developing their study skills. One question asked about preferred methods to receive adequate training in study skills, with choices such as workshops, modules included within the curriculum, an on-line system, audio/video material, etc. From this it was discovered that 60% of the students surveyed preferred the on-line system. The audio/video option proved to be the least popular.

The Academic Staff Survey

The second of the two surveys conducted at the University of Limerick as part of the viability study was the academic staff survey. This voluntary survey was composed of approximately 20 questions with the purpose of acquiring some of the information obtained by academic staff from years of lecturing experience about third-level student study habits and some advice on how students can optimize these study skills.

Approximately 50 lecturers from various departments, courses, and disciplines were surveyed.

Analysis of the Academic Survey

From responses to questions such as: *For each contact hour, how many hours a week of self-study do you advise your students to complete?* and *What solution would you suggest to help students avoid cramming?* etc., it was possible to achieve two functions: first, to make a comparison to responses from the students' survey to determine the differences between the typical student and the ideal student, and second, to guide the content and the structure of the study skills module to be created for the target system.

6.3.3 Pedagogical Underpinning of the Skills SuperStore System

Based on the findings of our viability study and numerous other research projects worldwide into learning and study skills training, it was decided to adopt and integrate the following educational concepts in the target on-line study skills training system:

- Student-centered learning/reflective learning
- Interactive delivery
- Accommodation of learning styles
- Personalization of content delivery to meet individual students' needs and experiences
- Collaborative peer-assisted learning

The facilitation by the Skills SuperStore of each of the above educational concepts is discussed in the subsequent sections.

Student-Centered Learning/Reflective Learning

Students need to become independent and lifelong learners. In fact from research, it has been found that employers want graduates who accept responsibility for their own learning and their own personal and professional development [16].

The role of developing independent lifelong learners has become one of the main missions of third-level education institutions. To achieve this mission, however, it is essential to shift learning from the traditional teacher-centered approach to a more student-centered learning approach. By definition, student-centered learning is where students are given more control over the subject matter to be learned, how they learn the material, and the pace of their study.

In keeping with this desired outcome, the Skills SuperStore system accommodates student-centered learning through the delivery of interactive study skills modules that encourage students to reflect on past experiences, thus becoming active participants in their learning and taking more responsibility for their learning outcomes (Fig. 6.1). These study skills modules offered by the system enable the student to direct the delivery of the module content based on their selection to the interactive activities. Following a section that presents information on a specific topic, an interactive page is encountered that asks a question related to the previous section of the module. This question encourages students to reflect on their own personal experiences in relation to the topic presented and make the appropriate selection according to their experience, which in turn determines the material content to be presented next.

Taking as an example the time management study skills module, the student encounters a section on motivation. This section first presents some general information on motivation and the different categories motivation falls under, for example, intrinsic motivation and extrinsic motivation. Following these information pages, students encounter a multiple-choice interactive page inquiring into what motivated them to choose their course of study. This question encourages them to think back to when they selected their degree course. Their selection determines whether their choice was motivated by intrinsic factors or extrinsic factors and

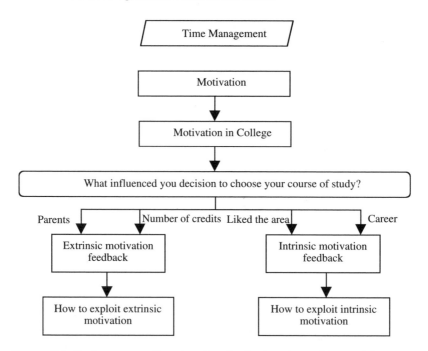

FIGURE 6.1. Student-centered learning via reflective learning and interactivity pages.

provides the appropriate feedback. This methodology continues throughout the module.

This approach enables students to direct the module material, making it more specific to their desired learning outcomes, and also as no one is setting the pace (as in the case of the teacher-centered approach), they can go as quickly or as slowly as they desire in order to complete the module.

Learning Styles

A vast amount of research has been carried out into learning psychology: how students learn, how to facilitate learning more effectively, etc. New and interesting information is being continually uncovered. Many of the results found underlie the content delivery approaches employed by various learning environments to deliver content to be learned more efficiently and more effectively.

One such research study identified that students of third-level education are characterized by different learning styles. Students have a prodivity for a preferred method of receiving information, and they tend to achieve understanding of this information at different rates. The research found that students whose learning styles match the teaching styles of their lecturers achieve better results than those whose learning styles are mismatched with the lecturers' teaching style [19].

This teaching style/learning style mismatch has some serious consequences for students. It has been found that students whose learning style is mismatched with their lecturers teaching style generally feel as if the information is delivered in a foreign language, receive lower grades than their counterparts whose learning styles are a better match with the lecturers' teaching styles, and generally fail to develop an interest in the course content.

In our everyday lives we use our senses to gather information about the environment around us. However, some of us employ one sense more than others. The main senses employed to gather and absorb information are as follows:

- Visual
- Auditory
- Reading/writing
- Kinesthetic

To assist third-level students in identifying their preferred learning style so that they will be more aware of how they acquire knowledge and information, it was decided to include some form of learning style assessment. To achieve this the visual, aural, reading/writing, kinesthetic (VARK) system, created by Neil Flemming, was incorporated into the "Skills SuperStore" study skills training environment.

This assessment, by asking a series of questions, will determine from the users' input the learning style they employ in their everyday lives, thus highlighting their preferred learning style. Once students have completed the VARK questionnaire, they are then provided with further information on their preferred learning style and how they can employ it more effectively in their study and learning.

In addition to the learning styles assessment, the study skills modules offered by the Skills SuperStore system includes video and audio files so that students who have identified their preferred learning style as visual or auditory can use these files instead of, or in conjunction with, the typical method of completing the study skills modules, that is, reading. This is to assist them to acquire and retain the information being presented more effectively and efficiently. An added advantage of this system's functionality is that it encourages the student to break away from the traditional methods of study and learning and to use whatever methods and approaches are necessary to succeed in college and as practicing graduates.

Personalization of the Module Material to Meet Each
Students' Problems and Needs

This educational approach, which underlies the Skills SuperStore system, is included to overcome the problem found in other study skills training approaches, that is, that study skills cannot be taught using conventional methods. Each student needs to personalize the material so as to address one's own personal problems and needs. To illustrate how the system achieves the above goal, a run-through of the system operation for the student will now be presented, highlighting in particular the content delivery of the study skills modules.

On commencing a session of the Skills SuperStore system, students are first asked whether they are a new or returning user of the system. If they are new to the system, they are required to register such information as name, ID, password, etc. to be stored in the system user database table, by selecting the register option. This facilitates the user personalization of the system; that is, the system will know who is using the system at any given time, what modules they have completed, their preferred learning style if they completed the VARK questionnaire, etc. If previously registered users are commencing a session with the system, they will be requested to log onto the system. This facilitates a customized and authorized access to the system based on the category of user as identified by their ID.

Once students have successfully registered or logged onto the system, they will be directed to the student menu page. This page provides students with four different options that they can select from:

- The "Introduction to Learning Skills" tutorial
- The "How to Use" tutorial
- The module index
- The resource center

On the first use of the system the student is asked to first complete the "Introduction to Learning Skills" tutorial and the "How to Use" tutorial to obtain the optimum use of the system. The "Introduction to Learning Skills" tutorial is a short introductory tutorial that provides a brief overview of the importance and benefits of acquiring various study and other transferable skills. The "How to Use" tutorial goes through the structure of the system, all the features and facilities that the system offers to students to ensure that they are able to use the system to its optimum potential.

Once students have completed both tutorials, they can then select the module index option. A page that lists all the modules offered to the users by the system is displayed. Students select the module they wish to complete.

The purpose of these modules is to encourage students to examine their own approaches to study and apply the methods suggested by the modules to build on and develop their existing skills. Each of the modules offered by the "Skills SuperStore" system to students will have one skill for the student to acquire and develop. As each student's study approach is different, that is, no two students have the same style of learning, a module that simply provides general information about the study skill is not sufficient. For this reason the modules were required to be customizable for each individual user. Student are guided through the module in response to their personal needs and habits. This is achieved via the interactivity pages incorporated into the module.

Students select a module they wish to complete in order to acquire and develop a specific skill they feel they lack proficiency with. As with all the available modules, they will initially encounter a number of general overview pages that provide a brief description of the study skill they wish to acquire or develop. However, at some point the module needs to branch off to enable students customize the module to accommodate their own personal problems and needs. This is achieved through interactive pages. There are four types of interactive pages included in the Skills SuperStore study skills modules:

- Matching
- Picture selection
- Multiple choice
- True or false

The answers or selections made by students in an interactive page determine in what direction they will be directed through the module.

By way of example, consider the study skills module "Time Management." When students select to complete this module, they are first presented with a number of general overview pages providing information such as an introduction into the importance and need for good time management, why it is necessary to manage your time, studying smarter and not harder, etc. However, there comes a point when the module content needs to be customized to deal specifically with the student's personal problems and needs. This is where interactive activities are essential. As an example in the time management module, following the general introduction pages, students are asked if they are genuinely interested in the majority of the modules that comprise their study course. The selection of the student user will determine what comes next in the module. Continuing on from the given example, if students selected the "No" option, they would encounter another interactive activity page inquiring as to what influenced their decision to enroll in their study course, and so on. The more interactive pages encountered one after another, the more specific the information becomes in relation to the student's personal situation. The module will then continue on through the module requiring the student to make various choices along the way so as to direct the module on a personal level (Fig. 6.2).

It should also be noted here that following successful commencement of a Skills SuperStore session, students have access to a number of other features, such as a search feature, a discussion forum, etc. that will assist them to use the system and in particular to acquire and develop required study skills more effectively and efficiently.

Collaborative Peer-Assisted Learning

Many of the problems faced by third-level students in relation to study skills have already been encountered and overcome by other students. Accordingly, as an alternative to students with a specific study or transferable skills problem searching through masses of somewhat relevant material, it would save them time and needless effort if they could just ask their peers for help. These other students could then supply solutions and suggestions that can be read through and employed as required. It was decided to include a collaborative peer-assisted learning function

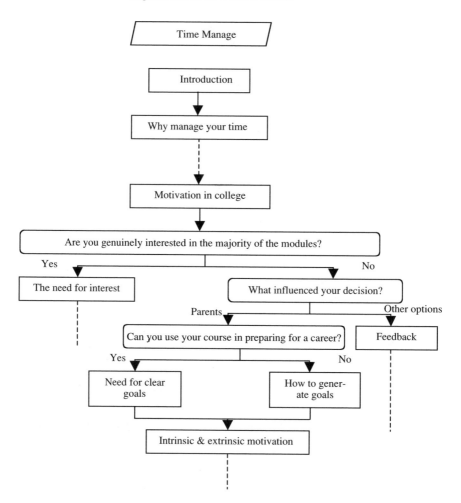

FIGURE 6.2. Example of Study Skills modules and their interactivity.

in the Skills SuperStore system in the form of a discussion forum to facilitate the above requirement.

Underlying the discussion forum feature is the idea of collaborative peer-assisted learning. One of the great advantages of this theory is that it works in two ways. Contributing students who are explaining a method, concept, approach, etc. are reinforcing their knowledge and deepening their understanding of the material being presented. On the other hand, those who are recipient students, receiving information from their peers, are benefiting from reviewing important material that they couldn't fully comprehend in a very simple way, which their peers adopted in order for them to understand the material in the first place.

The purpose of the discussion forum is to enable students to post (anonymously) any problems or solutions to problems they may have experienced in terms of

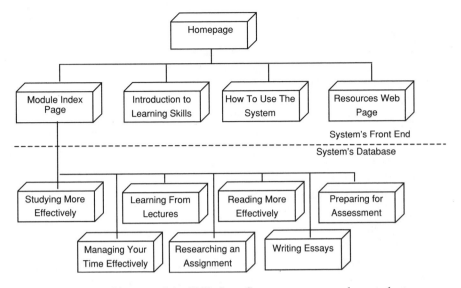

FIGURE 6.3. Architecture of the Skills SuperStore system as seen by a student user.

study skills. It also enables them to look at the various problems other students have encountered and subsequently posted, and as a result critically assess their personal approaches to various study situations and possibly share any ideas they feel might assist others in overcoming their posted problems.

6.3.4 System Requirements and Initial Architecture

Based on the findings of the viability study, it was decided that an on-line computer-based interactive study skills training system would best serve the collective students' needs and preferences.

To facilitate future expansion and developments of the system, a design-for-scalability approach has been adopted in the design and development of the Skills SuperStore system. Based on this approach, the system has been divided into two layers, (Fig. 6.3).

a. A front-end layer consisting of a number of static and dynamic pages to provide the following:
   - A registration and log-on page, which facilitates a customized and authorized access to the system based on the category of user as identified by ID.
   - The Skills SuperStore user customized main page, which contains links to the main section of the system.

   The front-end layer of the system also provides access to other complementary services and features offered by the system to different users. For the student user this includes a discussion forum, a search feature, and a feedback feature.

To the administrator users, access to authoring tools is made available via this layer.

b. A system database: the purpose of the database is to store the material, which assembles the various Skills SuperStore modules. This enables the customization of the module content to suit each student's requirements of the specified module. It also enables easy maintenance, and retrieval and updating of material associated with current and future study skills modules. In line with the scalability approach of the systems configuration, the system provides a set of templates for creating and adding new modules. Currently, the system offers the following interactive study skills modules:

- Time Management
- Learning from Lectures
- Reading More Effectively
- Preparing for Assessment
- Researching an Assignment

Modules' material has been adapted from a number of specialized references and Web-sites. Each module in the system provides students with an opportunity to evaluate their study habits and develop a particular study skill in a way that would improve their learning, retaining, and application of knowledge.

The database also holds and facilitates the user-controlled access mechanism and all administrative resources (Fig. 6.4). The purpose of the administrative resources is to enable the maintenance, updating, and creation of modules.

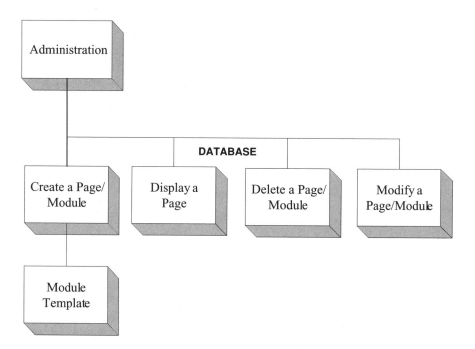

FIGURE 6.4. Architecture of the Skills SuperStore system as seen by an administrator user.

6.4 System Design and Development

The development process for Web applications is the same as that used for software development (Fig. 6.5). It is an iterative process composed of six stages:

1. *Requirements gathering.* Determines what the system should do, any input that may be required, and what output would be expected.
2. *Analysis.* Creates a model of the various components that comprise the system by examining the requirements of the system.
3. *Design.* Refines the results of the analysis phase until a model is generated that is realizable in software.
4. *Implementation.* The process of writing code and thus realizing the target system.
5. *Test and evaluation.* Evaluates the operation of each prototype, returning to analysis and design if more work is required.
6. *Deployment.* Delivering the system.

Web applications, like other software intensive systems are typically represented by a set of models: use case model, implementation model, deployment model, security model, and so forth. An additional model that is used exclusively by Web systems is the site map, an abstraction of the Web pages and navigation rates throughout the system [4].

Therefore, to create a model of the target environment, it was decided to employ the Unified Modeling Language (UML). The UML provides a visual modeling language that enables system builders to create blueprints that capture their visions in a standard, easy-to-understand way, and provides a mechanism to effectively share and communicate these designs with others [1]. The UML is not sufficient to represent the components that comprise a Web application. Fortunately, an

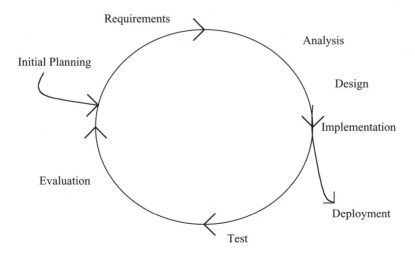

FIGURE 6.5. Iterative Process [4].

extension mechanism was created in order to correctly demonstrate the relevant semantics of a Web application using UML.

The remainder of this chapter discusses in detail each of the phases of the iterative process used in the development of the Skills SuperStore system.

6.4.1 Requirements Gathering

The first stage in the development of the Web application is that of requirements gathering. The purpose of this process is to break the target system into smaller, more manageable components by determining what functions the target system will facilitate. Adopting the role of potential system users and envisioning what tasks they would complete when using the system and what steps are involved in implementing these tasks achieves this. The results of this stage will be a series of clear and concise definitions of the requirements of the system. In carrying out this stage, it is important to bear in mind the following three issues [14]:

- Each requirement should be clear and concise.
- A requirement statement should focus on one point.
- Every requirement must be verifiable.

Based on the above, the first step in the requirements gathering stage of the Skills SuperStore system development was to identify the potential stakeholders of the system. Two different categories were identified, as indicated in Fig. 6.6:

- The student user
- The administrator user

Services to each category of user were also identified. For example, a student user needs to be able to register and log onto the system, view selected modules, and use the various facilities offered by the system to interact with any of the available skills modules. On the other hand, administrator users were given privileges of being able to log onto the system and have access to the maintenance features in order to maintain both the user information and study skills modules.

Documenting clear and concise requirements of the system that are agreed to by developers and the potential end users of the system ensures that there is a focus, preventing any discrepancies of the end product between what has been developed and what is expected by the system users.

6.4.2 Analysis

The analysis phase is the process of looking at the requirements, which were determined from the viability study discussed in the previous section, and determining the classes and the class relations, which are required in order to build a model of the system. The analysis phase identifies the classes needed by the program and works out how objects of these classes send each other messages in order to perform the tasks identified by the requirements, which is termed the dynamic behavior.

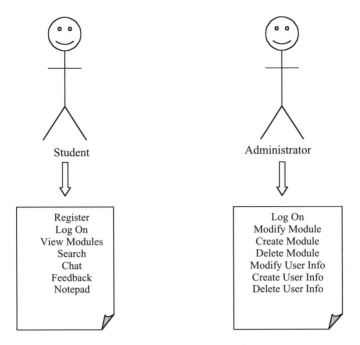

FIGURE 6.6. System users and requirements.

The goal of the analysis stage is to illustrate the functionality of the system requirements so that they may be realized in software, without yet taking into consideration the architecture of the system. The result of the analysis stage is a preliminary mapping of the required behavior onto the structural elements—classes and collaborations—in the system [14].

When completing the analysis stage of the Skills SuperStore Web application development a three-step process was employed:

- Use-case modeling: demonstrates the relationship between the actors (i.e., system users) and the use cases (i.e., system requirements).
- Class modeling: demonstrates the classes of the system, their interrelationships, and the operation and attributes of each of the classes.
- Dynamic modeling: demonstrates the actions performed by or to each class to facilitate system requirements.

The process of the analysis stage is iterative. On each iteration the resulting models are refined, inserting additional detail to demonstrate more accurate system functionality.

Use-Case Modeling

The purpose of the use-case-diagram is to illustrate how the system should function from the perspective of the system's users. It has the benefit of assisting the system

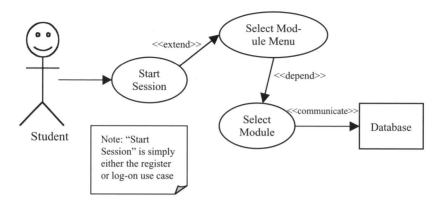

FIGURE 6.7. View module use case.

analyst in developing an understanding of how the system should operate ideally without needing to know how it achieved it technically.

Within the framework of UML styles [1], the use-case modeling is often used to:

• Provide an overview of all or part of the usage requirements for a system or organization in the form of an essential model or a business model,
• Communicate the scope of a development project, and
• Model the analysis of the usage requirements in the form of a system use-case model.

A use-case diagram consists of two main components: actors, which symbolize the roles the users can play, and the use cases, which symbolize what the users should be able to do with the system. Each system requirement identified from the requirements gathering stage of the system development maps onto a use-case diagram. These use-case diagrams depict the steps involved in fulfilling a system requirement. As way of illustrating this point, Figure 6.7 depicts the View Module system requirement. This use-case diagram depicts the steps involved in accomplishing the specified requirement and how these individual steps relate to each other.

The complete collection of use cases, actors, and diagrams form a use-case model, see Fig. 6.8.

The use-case model illustrates the basic design of the Web application without showing the dynamic behavior required to facilitate each system requirement. To illustrate the dynamic behavior of the system, interaction diagrams are required (sequence, collaboration, and activity diagrams).

On the initial iteration of the analysis phase and in particular the requirements, gathering stage, a general use-case model was rendered. Following this and on each subsequent iteration the use-case model was refined and further divided into smaller, more manageable components.

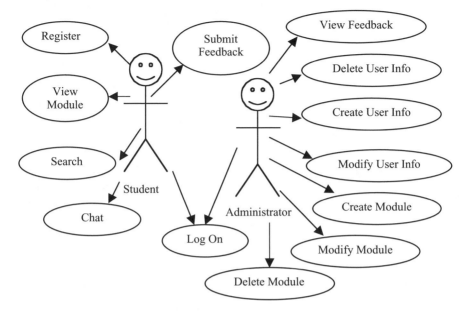

FIGURE 6.8. Use-case model.

Class Modeling

Class modeling is another activity that is done when the use cases near completion. Class diagrams identify the class structure of a system, indicating the properties and methods of each class. Also depicted are the various relationships that can exist between classes, such as an inheritance relationship. The class diagram is the main diagram in any UML model. It is used throughout the project from first-cut object analysis through to implementation. It provides the main reference point for discussion, review, and communication of the static structure of the system.

Class diagrams are used to [1]:

- Explore domain concepts in the form of a domain model,
- Analyze requirements in the form of a conceptual/analysis model, and
- Depict the detailed design of object-oriented or object-based software.

For class modeling, which is the generation of the class diagram, the classes and their attributes must first be extracted. Once this has been achieved they must then be represented using an entity relationship diagram, see Fig. 6.9. To determine the classes and their attributes and functions, they must be determined from the use cases and their scenarios. There are two approaches to class modeling: noun extraction and CRC classes. For the purpose of the development of the Skills SuperStore system, it was decided to employ the noun extraction method. This method has three stages:

- Stage one: Concise problem definition
  - Define the product in a single sentence.
    - *Provide study and transferable skills modules along with various complementary services to assist in the acquisition of these skills; also provided are administrative features to maintain the system and its users profiles.*
- Stage two: Informal strategy
  - Incorporate constraints; express results in a single paragraph.
    - *User logs into the Skills SuperStore system. This authenticates the user as a specific user type: student or administrator. Based on the type of user, a main menu will be displayed; for example, if a student user logs on, then the student main menu will be displayed. From the main menu the student user can select one of the following: "How to Use the System" module, "Introduction to Skills SuperStore" module, resource page, or the module index page, which provides a list of skills modules available to the student user. Students can also select one of the complementary services available to them to assist them in completing the skills modules: Discussion forum, Search service, and the Feedback service. The administrative user can maintain both the modules and the system user profiles.*
- Stage three: Formalize the strategy
  - Identify nouns in the informal strategy.
    - *Database, Feedback service, Search service, Discussion forum, menus, modules, and administrative services.*

Classes identified from the analysis stage of the Skills SuperStore Web application development can be divided into three types:

- *Boundary objects*: the interface between the actor and the system. Instances of these objects are typically entry screens or special user-interface controls. In Web applications these may represent whole Web pages.
- *Entry objects*: things described in the use case but that will outlast it.
- *Control objects*: system activities that can often be named. Control objects direct the activities of the entity and interface object [4, 5].

Dynamic Modeling

Following on from the use-case modeling and class modeling, the next step in the analysis phase of the target system is to demonstrate the dynamic behavior of the user requirements. This is achieved by illustrating the use-case scenarios with sequence diagrams and collaboration diagrams.

UML sequence diagrams are a dynamic modeling technique. They document the interaction between classes to achieve a result, such as a use case. These diagrams express the interaction behavior between the actor and the system, with a special emphasis on the time line [4]. The sequence diagram lists objects horizontally and

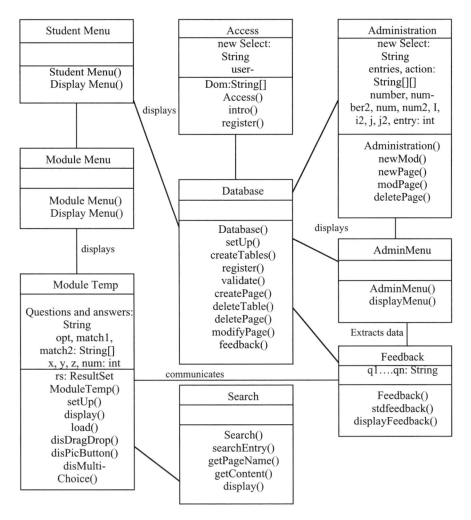

FIGURE 6.9. Class diagram for Skills SuperStore system. () represents methods/operations of the object. [] indicates that the attribute is an array.

the time vertically, and models the communications between objects, known as messages, over time. Sequence diagrams are typically used to [1]:

- Validate and flesh out the logic of use cases and their scenarios.
- Explore the design of the system as they enable the analyst to visually step through invocation of the operations defined by the classes.
- Detect bottlenecks within an object-oriented design, by looking at what messages are being sent to an object, and by looking at evidence where changes need to be made to the design of the system in order to distribute the load within the system.
- Indicate which classes in the application are going to be complex.

On the first iteration of the analysis process, the sequence diagrams will only depict the dynamic behavior of a use case (i.e., a system requirement) between the two principal players involved in the use case, namely the system user and the target system. The system user is represented as a stick figure placed at the top left corner of the diagram, and the system object is represented as a rectangle placed at the top right corner of the diagram. Extending downward from both the system user and the target system representations is a line that represents the object time line. The top of this line is the beginning of the scenario and the bottom is the end. Once all this is depicted, the next step is to place the scenario in the diagram. Each individual step that comprises the scenario is entered separately, beginning with the first step entered at the top of the lifeline and ending with the last step entered at the bottom of the lifeline. A message sent from one object to another (i.e., from the system user to the target system and vice versa) is represented with an arrow moving from the calling object to the responding object. For example, if the system user inputted some data to the system, an arrow being drawn from the system user's lifeline to the target system lifeline would represent this. The messages are ordered sequentially from top to bottom and numbered for clarity as well. (See Figure 6.10 for an example of a sequence diagram in the analysis phase.)

UML collaboration diagrams, like UML sequence diagrams, are used to explore the dynamic nature of the software. Collaboration diagrams show the message flow between objects in a Web application and imply the basic association (relationships) between classes. Collaboration diagrams are often used to [1]:

- Provide a bird's-eye view of a collection of collaborating objects, particularly within a real-time environment.
- Allocate functionality to classes by exploring the behavioral aspects of a system.
- Model the logic of the implementation of a complex operation, particularly one that interacts with a large number of other objects.
- Explore the roles that objects take within a system, as well as the different relationships they are involved with in those roles.

As already mentioned on the first iteration of the analysis phase of the Skills SuperStore Web application development, the sequence and collaboration diagrams depicted interaction of just the principal players of the use-case scenario, that is, the system user and the target system. On each subsequent iteration of the analysis phase, these interaction diagrams are elaborated by adding other structural elements determined from the class model.

From the class model various different classes were identified that can be placed into one of three categories [4, 5]:

- Boundary objects
- Entry objects
- Control objects

For the design and development of the Skills SuperStore Web application, only boundary objects and control objects are of interest. During the design phase

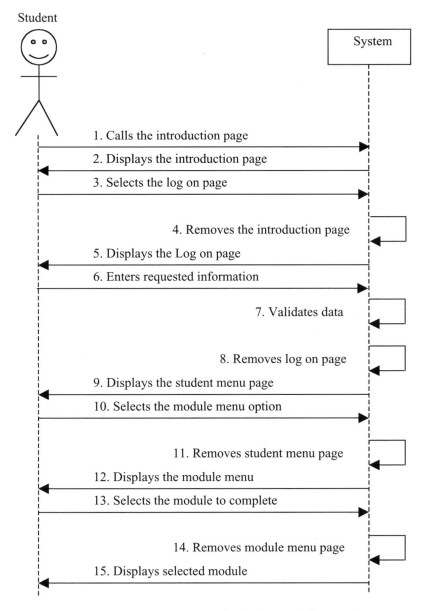

FIGURE 6.10. Sequence diagram for the view module scenario.

boundary objects generally map to HTML pages, while control objects map to the server-side activities of the dynamic Web pages. Each of these objects should focus on a singular functionality. If an object has more than one functionality, it can become overloaded and difficult to build and perhaps even unreadable by basic client browsers.

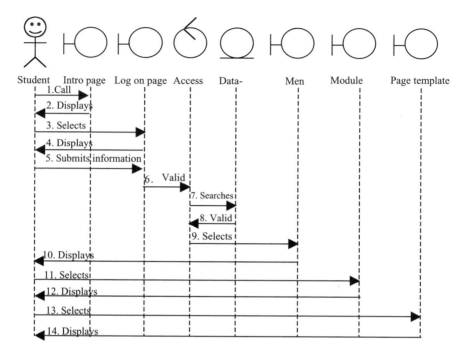

FIGURE 6.11. Refined sequence diagram for the view module scenario (analysis).

The sequence and collaboration diagrams that result from these iterations of the analysis phase will depict the interaction between the various objects required to realize a use-case scenario. Figure 6.11 provides an example of a sequence diagram created at this stage of the analysis phase, and Figure 6.12 is an example of a collaboration diagram.

6.4.3 Design

The major inputs of the design phase in the development of the Skills SuperStore system is the analysis model, which resulted from the analysis phase, and the architecture of the target system. The purpose of this phase is to refine the results of the analysis phase to the point where code can be written.

In addition to elaborating the classes and collaborations, design activities include [4]:

- Partitioning objects into tiers, such as client, server, and so on.
- Separating and defining user interfaces, or Web pages.

As with any Web application, one of the main components of the Skills Super-Store system is Web pages. The purpose of Web pages is twofold. First, it is via Web pages that the user interface of the system, that is, the study skills module, search engine, discussion forum, etc., is displayed to the users, and second, they

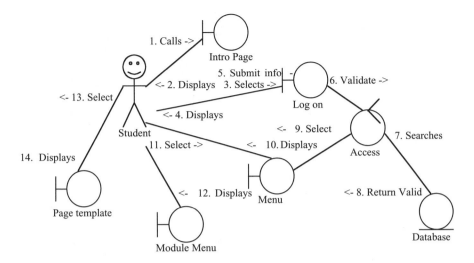

FIGURE 6.12. Collaboration diagram for the view module scenario (analysis).

contain the functionality that make possible these services offered by the system. For this reason it is of great importance to accurately represent Web pages in the design model alongside the other components that comprise the rest of the model

However, due to the nature of dynamic Web pages, it is difficult to represent Web pages accurately with UML in the design model. The problem occurs when a Web page is encountered that has dual functionality, that is, it contains code that interacts with resources on a server and then when sent to the client as a completed interface contains additional code that is executed on the client. For example, in the Skills SuperStore system, when a module is selected by a student to be completed, a page is called that first interacts with the database to request the data required to display the module, and then determines what type of page template is necessary for the first page of the module. It then concludes by building the required page to be displayed on the client browser. This page contains both server-side script, that is, interacting with the database and determining the template to be displayed, and client-side script, that is, the actual building of the page template to be displayed on the client Web browser.

To model these Web pages more accurately, an extension to UML is expressed in terms of stereotypes, tagged values, and constraints. A brief definition of each of these elements is as follows:

- *Stereotype*: an extension of the vocabulary of the language. A stereotype allows us to attach a new semantic meaning to a model element.
- *Tagged value*: an extension of a property of a model element. A tagged value is the definition of a new property that can be associated with a model element.
- *Constraints*: an extension of the semantics of the language. A constraint is a rule that defines how the model can be put together [4].

When an extension to the UML is included in a model, it must begin with a description followed by a list and description of all the stereotypes, tagged values, and constraints of the extension. The rules used to determine whether a model is semantically consistent with itself must also be included.

In the Skills SuperStore Web application, objects can reside exclusively on the server, e.g., container objects, the client, input validation objects, and specialized user interface widgets. It is complex behaviors such as these that make modeling truly invaluable.

Another role of the design phase is to define each of the individual Web pages that comprise the Web application. This activity was achieved by determining Web pages and what relationships exist between them and with objects of the system. In this activity, the system objects in the sequence diagrams created during analysis evolved into objects and Web pages [4].

Once the functionality of each Web page was identified and its relationship with other components of the Web application had been uncovered, the next step was to commence designing the individual Web pages themselves. This was achieved by identifying the operations and attributes of each of the server pages.

6.4.4 Implementation

Following the analysis and design phases of the iterative prototyping comes the implementation phase. The implementation phase is the process of writing the code that realizes the target system. The steps involved in the implementation phase include:

- Mapping the design into code and components
- Unit testing
- Reverse engineering

The principal goal of the implementation phase is to convert the results of the design phase into executable code. As each individual Web page component is completed, it is tested to ensure that it executes as specified by its requirements. Finally, it is necessary to reverse engineer any code changes that affect components in the model. This is important as once the actual system and the model get out of synch, the model's ability to answer questions about the system is limited. At this stage reverse engineering may be the simple act of manually updating the model [4].

The first stage in the implementation phase, even before the coding commenced, is to decide what programming languages to use in order to build the target system. In making this decision it is important to consider each potential programming language, for example, active server pages (asp), JSP, servlets, hypertext preprocessor (php), etc., in relation to [21]:

- Browser/platform compatibility
- Speed of execution/delivery
- Development time

- Features
  - ◦ Is there a need for enterprise interface widgets and functionality?
  - ◦ Does it require multithreading?
  - ◦ Does it require network programming like manipulation of sockets?
- Maintainability

Taking into consideration the above guidelines it was decided that the JavaServer Pages (JSP) technology would be employed to program the code for the Skills SuperStore Web application [23].

JavaServer Pages are a third-generation solution that enables quite easy integration with some second-generation solutions, such as CGI and servlets, enabling the creation of dynamic content and easing the creation of Web applications that work with a variety of other technologies: Web servers, Web browsers, etc. [22].

JavaServer Page technology is the integration of HTML, XML, and small pieces of Java code to enable the creation of dynamic Web pages. This is achieved in such a way that the dynamic code, such as business logic (middle and back-end tiers), is kept separate from front-end presentation code. When compiled, the JSP page is converted to a servlet, which is executed on the Web server and results in the creation of a modified Web page to be displayed on the requesting client Web browser. This application logic may involve JavaBeans, Java Database Connectivity (JDBC) objects, Enterprise JavaBeans (EJB), and Remote Method Invocation (RMI) objects, all of which can be easily accessed from a JSP page. It is a great rapid application development (RAD) approach to Web applications [20]. JSP technology is being used everywhere on the Web including on-line airline reservation systems, banking systems, and shopping [3].

When a JSP page is called, it is compiled (by the JSP engine) into a Java servlet. At this point the servlet is handled by the servlet engine just like any other servlet. The servlet engine then loads the servlet class (using a class loader) and executes it to create dynamic HTML to be sent to the browser as shown in Figure 6.13.

In terms of the Skills SuperStore Web application, there are two components that are of great importance for the operation of the system:

- Forms
- Databases

Forms are necessary to enable the users of the system to interact with the system itself. In the Skills SuperStore system it is through forms that students customize the module to suit their own personal problems and needs. The JSP code takes the user input data, performs manipulations on this input, determines what material will be presented next, and delivers this required material to be displayed by the client browser.

The second of the two components, which facilitate the dynamic aspect of the Skills SuperStore system, is the use of a rational database. Again this is very important for the target system as it enables the easy customization of the module content to suit each student's personal requirements. The data stored in the rational

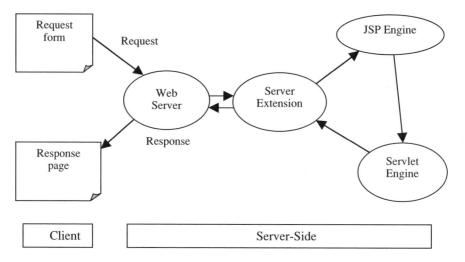

FIGURE 6.13. Request/response flow when calling a JSP [3].

database are accessed by the system via Java Database Connectivity (JDBC). JDBC is an Application Program Interface (API) that facilitates the retrieval, storage, and manipulation of data in virtually any data source. However, to specifically manipulate data on a opensource relational database management system (MySQL) database, a driver is required to obtain a connection to the database. Fortunately, drivers are readily available for most databases, including MySQL.* As long as the JDBC driver is available for the database server, the database can be accessed from Java code. The steps required to access data in a database are as follows:

1. Load the JDBC database driver.
2. Create a connection.
3. Create a statement.
4. Create a result set, if you expect the database server to send back some data.

A final point to note for the implementation of the Skills SuperStore system is the use of JavaBeans. In the Skills SuperStore system, JavaBeans were used to facilitate the administration functionality. As there was a lot of execution code required to realize this functionality, it was advisable to separate it from the presentation code by placing it in a JavaBean. JavaBeans technology is a portable, platform-independent component model that allows developers to write components and reuse them everywhere. There are several benefits to using JavaBeans to augment JSP pages:

• Reusable components: different applications will be able to reuse the components.
• Separation of business logic and presentation logic: you can change the way data are displayed without affecting business logic.
• Protecting your intellectual property: by keeping source code secure [22].

---

* MySQL is an open source relational database management system.

6.4.5 Testing and Evaluation

Given that the main goal of the Skills SuperStore system is to deliver study skills training to students in third-level education in such a way that it responds to input entered by the user and as a result tailors the study skills modules to suit each individual's personal problems and needs, it is essential that the completed system will be bug free, operating as expected, responding to user interaction in a timely fashion etc. Unfortunately, Web applications, as with any network deployments, can suffer from a number of undesirable issues, causing an unpredictable and unsatisfactory application. A destabilized Web application directly affects the experience that a user has with the site, and the impressions that result range from minor annoyance to outright anger with the state of the site [11].

As a consequence, it was of great importance to thoroughly test the Skills SuperStore learning environment to ensure that it meets the quality expected by the users of the site. Testing of the application involved a number of different aspects, including ensuring that it performs the functions correctly and securely, that it is compatible with different browsers and operating system configurations, and that it can handle a large amount of concurrent users (Fig. 6.14). The remainder of this section discusses in detail the various steps involved in testing the Skills SuperStore system.

To avoid any problems that may have occurred during the development of the Skills SuperStore system, and as a result reduce the amount of testing required to ensure the system is deemed good enough to deploy, a detailed plan was created.

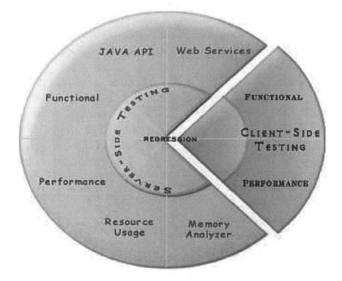

FIGURE 6.14. Redefining software quality (source www.adventnet.com).

Planning increases understanding of what is required from the application, meaning less ambiguity of system features and functionality and in how they should communicate and operate together. Early testing helps find issues and design flaws, resolve performance problems, locate bottlenecks and failures, and ultimately deliver a final system that is more reliable and has fewer unexpected problems [26]. The testing should include [24]:

- Unit testing
- Integration testing
- Stress testing
- Compatibility testing
- Functional testing

The purpose of unit testing is to test each individual component of the Web application to ensure that it operates as expected. For example, the discussion forum Submit Posting page would be tested first, separately, to ensure that it operates as expected before it is added to the rest of the discussion forum and tested as a whole. This test is done early in the development of the target system. It is an iterative process, that is, the Web unit is developed and tested; if any errors are uncovered it goes back into development to be fixed again; if no errors are uncovered, it is passed on to the next step in the development process, which is the integration of the individual components. This then leads to the next test that is required to be implemented: integration testing.

When two units have being completed and tested individually, the next step is to combine these units together and employ integration testing to ensure that they operate as would be expected. As each individual unit is completed and tested, it is added to the other units, which comprise a system process, and integration testing is employed to ensure ideal operation. The purpose of integration testing is to ensure that no problems occurred when two or more units were combined. Due to each individual unit being tested separately (unit testing), if any error occurs during integration testing, it can be deduced that the problems lie in the interface between the two individual units [20].

The purpose of stress testing is to test the application to ensure that it will function normally even under an environment more demanding than what it would normally operate under. To achieve the stress test, a significant number of concurrent users were employed to use the system. This figure was slightly more than what would normally be expected to use the system at any given time. This was to test whether, under an increased load, the system operation would degrade. Stress testing reveals Web applications behavior under extreme circumstances, causing it to run out of resources.

With every Web browser comes variations and differences in the way a Web page is displayed and works. That is why there was a need to test the Web application on not only all the major brand of browsers, but also the major versions and on different platforms to ensure that the application is presented as specified. To achieve compatibility testing of the target system, it was executed on all the main browser brands, with different versions of each brand, different operating systems, and different screen resolutions to ensure that the user interface of the system was not altered significantly from one environment to another [28].

Functional testing checks to ensure that the Web application operates as specified from its mission statement and goals. The best way to achieve this test is to simulate the real environment that the Web application is expected to operate in. To facilitate this test for the Skills SuperStore system, a simulation of the various different types of users and their behaviors (including Web application usage patterns, browser versions, page think times, and user abandonment), predicting how various input and expected output would be carried out. Also the Web application was tested to see how it operates on the network, testing it against all possible network issues, such as end-to-end latencies, link speeds, packet loss, IP fragmentation, jitter, and bursty traffic patterns [11].

The main purpose of system testing is to induce system failure so that you can ensure under normal operating conditions that these failures are dealt with without hindering user functionality of the system. Results from the testing phase were satisfactory, indicating that the system would operate as expected.

Also, to assess the achievement of the objective of the system, that is, to provide a flexible learning environment for higher-education students to help them evaluate and develop their study, learning, and other interpersonal skills, and monitor the performance of the system, an ongoing evaluation process is currently being implemented. As part of this process, a comparison with currently available e-learning platforms for on-line training and course delivery has been conducted in terms of available functionalities and ease of use. Table 6.2 gives a summary of the functions provided by the Skills SuperStore. Our comparison showed that the Skills SuperStore provides about 80% of the most common functions usually available in e-learning platforms.

Regarding the degree of user-friendliness, feedback data are being continuously collected from users, particularly students, via both the on-line feedback facility of the system and written and oral surveys conducted by lecturers, tutors, and support staff from the Teaching and Learning Center at the university. In addition, an access counter has recently been added to the system to monitor the frequency of its use. To date, the feedback has been very positive, indicating a good level of satisfaction with the system, its contents, and its user-friendliness. Also, a number of lecturers, tutors, and other associated academics are currently being surveyed. The survey involves completing a questionnaire based on the current status of the Skills SuperStore system and ways/suggestions for improvements.

TABLE 6.2. Functions provided by the Skills SuperStore

Administration	Yes	Learning Preferences	No
Course material development	Yes	Interaction	Yes
Behavior	No	Learning content	Yes
Assessment	Yes	Multimedia	Yes
Learner info	Yes	Course configuration	Yes

6.5 Conclusion

The facilitation of a new interactive study-skills training environment using a Web-based system has been presented and its various development stages discussed. The system has been designed to be used in conjunction with existing study skills learning material and resources in third-level institutions. The functionality and contents of the Skills SuperStore system were designed and developed such that they enable students to formulate their own learning strategies, and provide positive guidance and direction on how to develop study skills. An on-going evaluation process is currently being implemented and feedback data are being continuously collected and analyzed. The main objectives of the Skills SuperStore system are to provide a flexible learning environment for higher education students—University of Limerick students in particular—to help them evaluate and develop their study, learning, and other interpersonal skills. It is envisaged that by providing a system such as the Skills SuperStore, both the students and staff of higher-level institutions will benefit in the following ways:

- Students' academic performance will be improved via developing their study and learning skills.
- Improved professional skills will enhance graduates' employability.
- Students will be motivated to become more responsible, independent, and life-long learners.
- Students' awareness of the importance and benefits of information resources within their institution and beyond, and how to search for them, will be increased.
- The appropriate use of technology in teaching and learning approaches at the University of Limerick and other higher-education institutions in Ireland will be promoted.

References

1. Ambler, S.W. (2003) The Elements of UML Style. Cambridge: Cambridge University Press.
2. Blair, G.M., Robinson, C.M. (1995) Professional skills for first-year engineering students. Engin. & Sci. Educational J, 4:23–28.
3. COAST Web Quality Management. (2002) Web Quality Testing and the Rational Unified Process. White paper.
4. Conallen, J. (1999) Modelling Web applications architectures with UML. Communications of the ACM, 42: 63–70.
5. Conallen, J. (2000) Building Web Applications with UML. New York: Addison-Wesley.
6. Connelly, J.D., Middleton, J.C. (1995) Personal and professional skills for engineers: one industry's perspective. Engin. & Sci. Educational J, 5:139–144.
7. Department of Education and Science. (2004) A Brief Description of the Irish Education System. Communications Unit. http://www.education.lc/servlet/bbbservlet/dept_education_system04.pdf?language=EN.
8. Eiverd, E., Flanagan, R., Morgan, M. (2002) Non-Completion in Institutes of Technology: An Investigation of Preparation, Attitudes and Behaviors Among

First Year Students. Educational Research Center. http://www.erc.le/erc_reports_and_
publications/Non-completionIt02.pdf.

9. Fry, R. (1997) How to Study. London: Kogan Page Ltd, p. 157.

10. Hartley, J.R. (1999) Effective pedagogies for managing collaborative learning in online
learning environments. Educational Techn & Society 2:12–19.

11. Joung, P. (2004) Bulletproof Web Application Deployments: Best Practices in Testing.
Find Articles, Web Services Journal. http://webservices.sys-con.com/read/39949.htm

12. Morgan, M., Flanagan, R., Kellaghan, T. (2001) A Study of Non-Completion in
Undergraduate University Courses. Higher Education Authority. http://www.hec.le/
index.cfm/page/publications/category/143/section/details/id/378

13. Ritzen, M.M.J. (1996) Study skills, multimedia and business economics. IEEE International Conference on Multimedia in Engineering Education, Melbourne: Australia,
pp. 65–70.

14. Schmuller, J. (2002) Teach Yourself UML in 24 Hours. Indiana: Sams Publishing. pp. 5.

15. Shah, P. (1998) Successful Study—The Essential Skills. London: Letts Educational.

16. Stefani, L.A.J., Clarke, J., Littlejohn, A.H. (2000) Developing a Student-Centred Approach to Reflective Learning. Invocations in Education and Training International,
37(2):163–171.

17. Tinto, V. (1993) Leaving College: Rethinking the Causes and Cures of Student Attrition.
Chicago: The University of Chicago Press.

18. Upcraft, M.L., Gardner, J.N. (1989) The Freshman Year Experience: Helping Students
Survive and Succeed in College. New York: Jossey-Bass, Inc.

19. Watson, S.A. (2003) Implementing learning styles into the design classroom.
Journal of Design Communication 5. http://scholar.lib.vt.edu/ejournals/JDC/spring-
2003/learningstyles.html.

20. http://agiletesting.blogspot.com/2005/02/performance-vs-load-vs-stress-testing.html.

21. http://javaboutique.internet.com/articles/ITJ/quanda/q11.html.

22. http://java.sun.com/developer/technicalArticles/javaserverpages/JSP20/.

23. http://java.sun.com/developer/technicalArticles/xml/WebAppDev/.

24. http://msdn.microsoft.com/library/default.asp?url=/library/en-us/vsent7/html/
vxconintegrationtesting.asp.

25. http://www.coun.uvic.ca/learn/essay.html.

26. http://www.macronimous.com/resources/web_development_life_cycle.asp.

27. http://www.ucc.vt.edu/stdysk/notetake.html.

28. http://www.wduk.co.uk/services/cross_browser_compatibility.php.

7
E-MEMORAe: A Content-Oriented Environment for E-Learning

Marie-Hélène Abel, Ahcene Benayache, Dominique Lenne, and Claude Moulin

Abstract. Many documents and resources can be provided to students in the context of e-learning. They can be stored in learning objects repositories and then reused, combined, and adapted in different contexts. They can also be selected and organized in learning memories that are directly accessed by the learners. In the MEMORAe project, we adopted this second approach, by considering a course unit as a learning organizational memory. This memory stores not only selected resources, but also concepts representing notions to learn. The resources are indexed by the concepts that are part of two ontologies. These ontologies are also used to ease the navigation through the memory. In this chapter, we present this memory, the associated E-MEMORAe environment, and the results of an evaluation with students in the framework of the B31.1 applied mathematics course at the University of Picardy in France.

7.1 Introduction

At the present time, the term *e-learning* is used to designate various types of situations such as administrative course management, Web-based learning, or video-conferences. Beyond this diversity, e-learning, focuses more on learning (and consequently on the student) than on teaching.

In accordance, within the MEMORAe project,[1] our approach is to let the users be largely autonomous and to allow them to find by themselves the resources needed to learn about a notion or to reinforce their knowledge. This approach differs from more classical expositive approaches where learning is more guided by the teacher's viewpoint.

More and more documents and resources may be used in an e-learning application. Some are created by the actors involved in the e-learning. Others are available on the Web: on-line courses, course supports, slides, bibliographies, frequently

---

[1] MEMORAe stands for Organizational Memory dedicated to e-learning (in French: MEMoire ORganisationnelle Appliquée au e-learning).

asked questions, lecture notes, etc. This increasing number of available resources is a real problem in content management systems.

Different approaches may be adopted to exploit them. They can be stored in learning objects repositories and then reused, combined and adapted in different contexts. They can also be selected and organized in learning memories that are directly accessed by learners.

In the MEMORAe project, we adopted this second approach. We consider a course or a training unit as being an organization. Indeed, it is based on actors (learners, trainers, course designers, administrators, etc.), on resources of different types (definitions, exercises, case studies, etc.), on different forms (reports, books, Web sites, etc.), and on the knowledge and skills that it should provide. We propose to manage the resources and knowledge of this organization by means of a "learning organizational memory" based on ontologies [1]. Learners as well as teachers have access to this memory, which is different from a classical organizational memory because its goal is to provide users with content and, more precisely, learning content. This content is the result of the capitalization of knowledge, information, and resources relating to the training or course unit during its building and life.

To organize and to index resources in the memory, we made the choice of using ontologies to model metadata, and to represent them with the Topic Maps formalism. The environment we designed put the emphasis on learning by exploration. Our goal is to allow the user to explore the memory thanks to an ontology and to access the resources it indexes by this means. We used two pilot applications to evaluate our propositions: the first was NF01, a course on algorithms and programming at the University of Technology of Compiègne, and the second was B31.1, a course on applied mathematics at the University of Picardy (France).

In this chapter we first situate our approach among content management projects for e-learning. Then we show how we modeled the memory (the choice of ontologies and Topic Maps), and we present the E-MEMORAe environment, which is based on this model. Finally we present the results of a first experimentation of the B31.1 memory at the University of Picardy.

7.2 Content Management for E-Learning

Content management for e-learning is often based on the use and sharing of large sets of learning objects. A set of learning objects can be a "repository" shared by a network of actors whose goal is to reuse and adapt pedagogical material. It can also be a "learning memory" where resources are structured and organized in order to support distance learning [2]. In this section, we briefly describe the main characteristics of the SCORM model for training content management, then we present the distinction we make between learning objects repositories and thematic resources bases.

7.2.1 Content Sharing

The SCORM (Sharable Content Object Reference Model)[2] has been developed by Advanced Distributed Learning (ADL) Co-Laboratory, the University of Wisconsin, and the Wisconsin Technical College System (WTCS). It defines the rules governing the introduction of a training management model by use of the Web. This model includes a course structure format, which facilitates the transfer of contents by defining the elements, the structure, and the external references. This model aims at addressing three problems:

- The transfer of contents from a training platform to another
- The creation of granular materials[3] that can be used in various modules
- The computerized search for training materials

The means are the standardization of the resource descriptions and the functionalities for exchanging these materials on the networks. SCORM has thus mainly defined the specifications used to represent the structure of a course and the metadata intended for documentary description.

7.2.2 Learning Objects Repositories and Thematic Resources Bases

Many projects aiming at building bases of learning resources, in order to share and reuse them, have been launched. These projects often rely on a network of contributors who feed the base with collaboratively controlled resources. Conversely, each contributor can benefit from resources brought by other contributors.

We make a distinction between learning objects repositories, which usually group many subjects, and what we call "thematic resources bases," which contain resources related to only one domain. Then we situate our approach in relation to these two categories.

7.2.2.1 Learning Object Repositories

Learning object repositories usually group all subjects. Their scope can be restricted to one or several universities or to a country and it can also be international. If their expected scope is wide, they are grounded in a network of contributors or in a consortium of institutions.

An example of this kind of repository is MERLOT (Multimedia Educational Resource for Learning and Online Teaching) [3]. MERLOT gives access to many resources in all subjects. These resources are evaluated and selected by an editorial committee. There is also a peer review evaluation that helps the users (learners and teachers) find resources adapted to their needs. But the selection of resources is not easy, because they are not explicitly associated with the knowledge and competencies they facilitate acquiring. Furthermore, resources are not stored on

---

[2] http://www.altrc.org/specification.asp.
[3] granular materials = learning contact.

the MERLOT site. They are accessed through links without a guarantee on the effectiveness of these links, even if some controls are periodically made. Also, the resources are not built to be directly used. Authoring tools help to integrate them in on-line courses.

In Europe, ARIADNE [4] focuses on the share and reuse of hypermedia pedagogical documents. These resources are stored in a "knowledge pool system" and are indexed by metadata based on the LOM (Learning Object Metadata) [5] standard. These resources can be reuse by

- creating new materials from pieces of course material to which the author can add new elements,
- making a new presentation of existing course material obtained by a rearrangement of its semantic components.

This implies that each author involved in the knowledge pool experience allows, under citation restrictions, the use and modification of the components he brings into it. Conversely, he can do the same thing with other components.

ARIADNE thus has an interesting selection and access features, but instructional design work remains necessary to reuse the resources.

7.2.2.2 *Thematic Resources Bases*

The restriction on resources related to a particular domain brings more homogeneity and facilitates more precisely managing the resources and associated knowledge. Thus, relying on knowledge engineering techniques, Paquette et al. [6] designed a knowledge and resources base on tele-learning. To this end they relied on a task ontology, based on use cases, and on a domain ontology, which allows them to better index the resources.

As in the case of repositories, the idea is also to share and reuse resources. These resources are not ready to be used by learners, as instructional design work is usually needed beforehand.

7.2.2.3 *The MEMORAe Approach*

In contrast, in the MEMORAe project our goal is to let learners directly access the resources of a course memory. Following a knowledge engineering approach, we organize the resources in an organizational memory. In fact, it is in a course memory where a course is seen as an organization (see section 7.3). A course memory is different from a learning memory [7] because its goal is not to help learners to remember what they previously studied. Rather, it is a memory of concepts and resources that teachers or designers find useful in the framework of a particular course.

To give learners direct access to the memory, a part of the instructional design work has to be done earlier. The advantage is that the memory is ready to be used by learners, provided that the pedagogical choices that were made earlier are acceptable. This can therefore lead to a loss of flexibility, but we make the assumption that these choices can at least shared by the teachers' community, which could act as a "community of practice" [8].

7.3 A Course Memory : the MEMORAe Model

In firms or organizations, knowledge management is a necessity. Related processes often rely on an "organizational memory" [9]. In the same way, the environment around a given course or training can be seen as an organization. Hence, different actors (teachers, learners, administrative staff, etc.) are involved in this environment. They produce, use, and exchange documents and knowledge. These actors have to access the resources and adapt them to their needs. That is why, in the MEMORAe project, we propose to manage resources, information, and knowledge of this kind of organization by relying on a "course memory." This memory can be accessed by teachers when they want to reuse resources, as in a thematic resources base (see 7.2.2). Let us note, however, that these resources cannot be seen as "knowledge grains" [10] to be composed to build a course unit.

But our main goal is to allow learners to directly use the memory. We now describe the contents of the memory and why we chose the Topics Map formalism to model it. We will see later how learners can enhance their knowledge by using this memory.

7.3.1 Contents of the Memory

The course memory contains the resources and the topics regarded as pertinent by the teaching team for the given course. It relies on two ontologies that facilitate organizing and indexing the resources.

7.3.1.1 Resources

Resources can be very different from one another. They vary according to their size (Web page or book, for example), their nature (course, exercises, definitions, case studies, etc.), their form (book, report, Web site, etc.), and their medium (paper, video, audio, etc.). A resource can be present in the memory, if it is digital, but it can also only be referenced, in cases of nondigital or external resources.

7.3.1.2 Topics

Topics are not only chosen because they are related to the course theme. They are selected on the basis of a pedagogical work. For example, in the context of a course on algorithms and programming, why and how do we decide to establish a link between the topics of "array" and "loop" ?

Resources are selected and indexed relying on this work. Indexing is not done automatically. The course manager, with the help of an editing committee if needed, is responsible for the pertinence of this link. It is not because a document addresses a topic that it will automatically be indexed by this topic. This is the result of a choice, that is to say that the document must have been judged suited for the learning of this topic. These decisions result from the pedagogical goal the course manager wants to achieve.

7.3.1.3 Ontologies

We chose to model our course memory with the help of ontologies. By using ontologies, our goal is, on the one hand, to define a vocabulary that can be shared by all the actors in order to characterize the topics to be learned, and on the other hand, to organize the access to the resources (see section 7.4). To be more precise, we distinguish two ontologies [11]: the first concerns the domain of the training organization in a general way, and the second concerns what is specific to a given course or training. But before presenting these two ontologies, let us briefly describe how they were built.

7.3.1.3.1 Building the Ontologies

Building an ontology is quite a complex task, which is made easier by using a method. In the MEMORAe project, we used the OntoSpec [12] method. OntoSpec is a method of semi-informal specification of ontologies. It supposes that a conceptualization is made up of a set of concepts (or conceptual entities) and relations. The concepts in OntoSpec are organized in a taxonomy. Subconcepts inherit all the properties of their superconcept. The relations make it possible to connect various concepts.

A conceptual entity owns a definition and denotes a set of objects having properties. The entity definition structure is based on a classification of these properties. An ontology is a differential set of concepts: the concepts are positioned according to their differences. In fact, the set of concepts are structured hierarchically and the properties are bound by conceptual properties. The conceptual property that structures a hierarchy of concepts is the subsumption that binds two concepts: the concept C1 subsumes another concept C2 (respectively the relation R1 subsumes another relation R2, if and only if all instances of C2 are necessarily instance of C1). The subconcept is more specific than the superconcept and denotes fewer objects (smaller extension). Sibling concepts are organized in semantic axes according to their similarities.

7.3.1.3.2 Application Ontology

The application ontology describes the topics associated with a specific course. Figure 7.1 shows an excerpt of the B31.1 ontology. An ontology is not only a taxonomy, it also includes a definition for each of the concepts, conditions on these concepts, and relations between them.

Concepts can be specialized according to "semantic axes." For example, the *set* concept is specialized according to three axes: finite/infinite, countable/uncountable, and subset/superset (see Fig. 7.1).

Let us stress that an ontology is always constructed in connection with the application it will be used for. In the case we consider here, the concepts corresponds to topics to teach and to learn. There are relations between these topics, for example the "prerequisite of" relation, which can reveal different angles on the learning domain. Therefore, the ontology we have constructed is not an ontology of applied mathematics; it is an ontology of a specific course in applied mathematics.

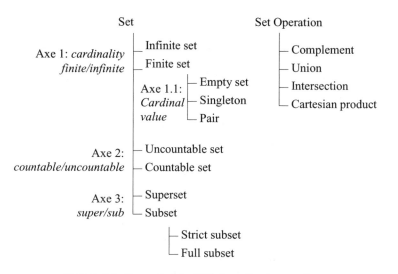

FIGURE 7.1. Excerpt of the B31.1 application ontology.

However, we think that this ontology could be reused by teachers who share the same vision of applied mathematics learning. Moreover, the head of the course B31.1, who was in charge of the ontology, changed schools before we could assess the ontology's memory with her students. Meanwhile, the teacher who replaced her validated without greater modifications the existing ontology. Moreover, he accepted the experiment with the students taking his course (see 7.6).

7.3.1.3.3 Domain Ontology

The domain ontology describes the concepts of the training organization, which includes persons (student, teacher, administrative staff, etc.), documents (books, slides, Web pages, etc.), resource access (digital, solid), pedagogical features (e.g., activity type), or means to express a point of view (e.g., annotation).

For this first ontology (Fig. 7.2), it was tempting to partially or totally try to reuse existing ontologies. But reusing is often not easy because an ontology is never completely independent of the application it has been constructed for. We considered some of these ontologies, for example the one of Paquette et al. [6] on telelearning. Examining these ontologies has been useful for us, but the reusing rate was low.

Some concepts of this ontology are part of Dublin Core [13] and Learning Object Metadata (LOM) [5] standards. But we do not use the categories of these standards; we define some of their elements by means of ontologies. Thus we define concepts, subconcepts, and relations.

For example, to build the document ontology, we use elements from Dublin Core and LOM. These elements take the shape of a concept, attribute or relation. Thus to represent the document author, we created the relation *author* between the two concepts *document* and *person*. The title of a document is represented by

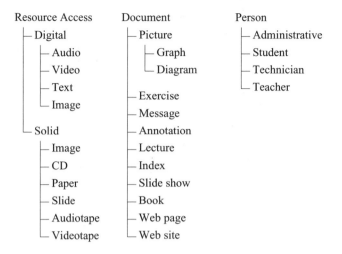

FIGURE 7.2. Excerpt of the domain ontology.

an attribute of the document concept. The element *type* of Dublin Core becomes the specialization axis of the sub-ontology document. The element *subject and keywords* is not a part of the domain ontology in our memory but represents the root of the application ontology (the ontology of the topics to be learned). The application ontology enables to define the notions to learn. These notions may play the role of subject and keywords to index resources. Thus, concerning the course B31.1, we find these concepts: finite set, cardinal, etc.

7.3.1.3.4 Linking the Two Ontologies

These two ontologies, application and domain, are not independent. The second one is necessarily linked to the first. For example, to express that a document is an introduction to finite sets, the concepts of "introduction" and "finite set," which are not part of the same ontology, have to be linked. Moreover, pedagogical relations such as "pre-requisite of" and "uses" are defined in the domain ontology, while other that are more specific are part of the application ontology (e.g., "has cardinal number" in the B31.1 ontology).

7.3.2 The Choice of the Formalism: Topic Maps [14]

The modeling of a training memory that is presented here contains three elements: two ontological parts and an index.
   The modeling must allow three operations:

- The union of two ontologies: the generic one and the application one
- The substitution of an application ontology by another one coming from another domain
- The attachment of the document indexing on the reunion of two ontologies
   The modeling must also facilitate answering queries on the memory, such as:

- What are the documents (books, presentations, Web pages) that talk about, introduce, and develop a topic that appears in the training?
- What are the topics associated (prerequisite, studied at the same time ...) with a given subject?

The choice of the formalism(s) for representing the memory is very decisive. It must go beyond the hybrid aspect of the modeling (ontology and indexing), and favor the interoperability between various tools that have to deal with the memory (edition, updater, consultation, navigation, etc.).

Two paths can be followed: either to choose the languages better adapted to the specific nature of each element of the modeling, or to choose a unique language. The first choice requires a system to easily integrate data coming from the two formalisms. The advantage of the second choice is that it unifies the description of data. It can be valid only if this formalism allows describing some features that it is not appropriate for.

The second choice can be split into two parts: we can choose a formalism adapted to ontology features representation, or a formalism adapted to document indexing. The main aspect of the memory and its main use influence the choice of the formalism.

Even if the indexing of the pedagogical documents is the main aspect of the memory, it is necessary to use a formalism allowing representing ontological elements. Several formalisms can be envisaged, but we recommend the Topic Maps (TM) formalism [15].

This formalism is useful to define and manipulate the information attached to resources. It provides a logical organization to a large quantity of resources, keeping them accessible and facilitating the navigation between them. Since 2001, it is possible to write a TM using the norm XTM 1.0 [16], which can be considered as a particular XML language.

The building of a TM is based on an organization of topics. Each resource is directly attached to one or more topics by an occurrence link. The association concept facilitates defining roles between topics. Moreover, the TM standard allows reifying some associations in order to place them in a particular "scope." Some resources can also be reified as a topic when it is necessary to attach other resources or data on them. In this manner, we can add annotations to resources. Annotations are resources that express a point of view on other resources.

Overall, we chose the TM formalism because it keeps a semantic level close enough to the model of our memory. With an ontology-oriented point of view, also developed in [17], this formalism facilitates envisaging the following important characteristics:

- It is possible to consider some topics as generic concepts and other as concept instances.
- It is possible to consider associations, scopes, and occurrences as roles between concept topics.
- Associations have no limitation in their number of members.

- The occurrence relation facilitates directly attaching resources to concepts (the same resource can appear in several occurrence relations and be accessible from more than one concepts).
- Relations (associations, occurrence) and concept labels can be defined inside scopes. This facilitates simply implementing annotations (or points of view in the memory).

To adopt this formalism, we verified it was possible to take into account ontological features and mainly the relation superclass–subclass for building hierarchies of concepts.

7.3.3 Memory Modeling: An Example

In this subsection, we illustrate several points we talked about above with examples using the XTM language syntax. We do not indicate the definition of all topics, but it is easy to imagine the undefined items. The following excerpts illustrate the way to query the memory: how to find the objectives of the course, and how to find an introductory document about the array notion.

7.3.3.1 Ontologies

The following excerpt shows the nf01 topic declaration, of type *course* (declared elsewhere). It uses an occurrence of type *site* (declared elsewhere), to which the precise resource is linked.

```
<topic id="t-nf01" >
  <instanceOf>
    <topicRef xlink:href= "#tt-course"/>
  </instanceOf>
  <baseName>
    <baseNameString>Algorithms and Pascal programming
    </baseNameString>
  </baseName>
  <occurrence>
    <instanceOf>
      <topicRef xlink:href="#tt-site" />
    </instanceOf>
    <resourceRef xlink:href=
      "http://www.hds.utc.fr/~ ptrigano/nf01/"/>
  </occurrence>
</topic>
```

The following excerpt shows the declaration of the topic *nf01-head* of type *person* (declared elsewhere).

```
<topic id="t-nf01-head">
  <instanceOf>
    <topicRef xlink:href= "#tt-person"/>
  </instanceOf>
```

```
<baseName>
  <baseNameString>head</baseNameString>
</baseName>
</topic>
```

The following excerpt shows the relation (of type association) *in charge of* between the course nf01 and its head.

```
<association id="in-charge-of" >
  <instanceOf>
    <topicRef xlink:href= "#at-in-charge-of-course"/>
  </instanceOf>
  <member>
    <roleSpec>
      <topicRef xlink:href="#tt-person"/>
    </roleSpec>
    <topicRef xlink:href="t-nf01-head" />
  </member>
  <member>
    <roleSpec>
      <topicRef xlink:href= "#tt-course"/>
    </roleSpec>
    <topicRef xlink:href="#t-nf01"/>
  </member>
</association>
```

In the previous examples, relations facilitate finding the person who is in charge of a given course.

7.3.3.2 Course Objectives

The following excerpt shows the relation between the course *nf01* and its objectives with the help of the topic *nf01-obj*. This relation is declared elsewhere and is linked to an internal resource of the TM where the objectives are clearly declared.

```
<association id= "nf01-obj" >
  <instanceOf>
    <topicRef xlink:href= "#at-course-objectives"/>
  </instanceOf>
  <member>
    <roleSpec>
      <topicRef xlink:href="#tt-objectives"/>
    </roleSpec>
    <topicRef xlink:href="t-nf01-obj"/>[3]
  </member>
  <member>
    <roleSpec>
      <topicRef xlink:href= "#tt-course"/>
    </roleSpec>
    <topicRef xlink:href="#t-nf01"/>
  </member>
</association>
```

The previous examples and relations facilitate finding the objectives of a given course.

7.3.3.3 An Array Introduction

The following excerpt shows the declaration of the topic *array* of type *data-struct* (declared elsewhere) and its link with a resource of type *site-page*, which is an introduction to the topic *array*.

```
<topic id = "t-array" >
  <instanceOf>
    <topicRef xlink:href= "#tt-data-struct"/>
  </instanceOf>
  <baseName>
    <baseNameString>Array</baseNameString>
  </baseName>
  <occurrence>
    <instanceOf>
      <topicRef xlink:href="#tt-site-page"/>
    </instanceOf>
    <resourceRef xlink:href=
        ''http://www.hds.utc.fr/~ webtrig/webnf01/cou
        rs/chap09/cours.htm" />
  </occurrence>
  <occurrence>
    <instanceOf>
      <topicRef xlink:href="#tt-introduction"/>
    </instanceOf>
    <resourceRef xlink:href=
        "http://www.hds.utc.fr/~ webtrig/webnf01/cou
        rs/chap09/cours.htm" />
  </occurrence>
</topic>
```

The type of declaration facilitates finding all the resources having a given pedagogical objective (here introduction) and having a given form (here Web page).

Obviously, users do not need to know the Topic Maps formalism to use the memory. We developed the E-MEMORAe environment to this end.

7.4 The E-MEMORAe Environment

The E-MEMORAe environment is an e-learning environment that enables access to resources by navigating through a graphical display of the ontologies on which it relies. Thus it facilitates autonomous learning.

---

[3] The topic t-nf01-obj is linked elsewhere by way of an occurrence to a document describing it.

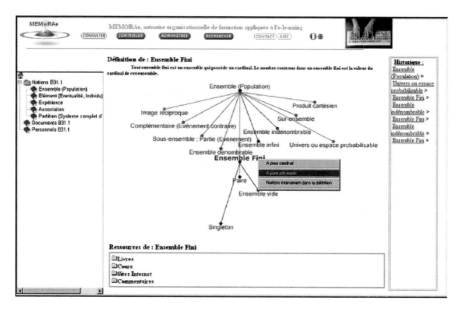

FIGURE 7.3. Vertical navigation in the memory.

We present this environment by using examples from the B31.1 application.

7.4.1 The User Interface

E-MEMORAe helps the users of the memory to acquire the topics of a given course. To this end, the users have to navigate through the application ontology that is related to the course, and to access the indexed resources of this ontology.

The general principle is to give the learner, at each step, either precise information on what he is searching for or graphically displayed links that allow him to continue navigating through the memory. He has no need to use the keyboard in order to formulate a request, even if the environment permits it.

To be more precise, the user interface (Figure 7.3) proposes:

• Entry points (left of the screen) allowing navigation with a given concept: an entry point provides a direct access to a concept of the memory and consequently to the part of the memory dedicated to notions. The person who is in charge of the course has to define the notions that (s)he considers essential.

• Resources (bottom of the screen) whose contents are related to the current concept: they are ordered by type (books, course notes, sites, examples, comments,[4] etc.). Starting from a topic, an entry point or a topic reached by the means of

---

[4] The comments are the only elements of the memory that the user can modify. An a posteriori control is made by the editorial committee in order to keep the comments or not.

the ontology, the user can directly access associated resources. Descriptions of
these resources help the user choose among them.

- A short definition of the current topic allows the learner to get a preview of the
  topic and to decide if he has to use it or not.
- A history of the navigation: it allows the learner to recall the path he followed
  before. Of course, he can get back to a previously studied topic if he wants to.
- The part of the ontology describing the current resource is displayed at the center
  of the screen.

If the learner wants access a topic that is not an entry point, he has to choose
the entry point that he thinks is the closest point to the searched topic.

7.4.2 Learning by Exploration in the Memory

Vertical navigation facilitates exploring subsumption relations and reaching related
concepts. For example, if the user wants to discover the Finite Set notion, the best
entry point is Set (population). By choosing this entry point, (s)he has access to the
local taxonomy associated with the notion of Set. Among the subconcepts of Set,
the user can find Finite Set. By clicking on this concept, a local taxonomy centered
on this new concept is displayed (Figure 7.3). The iteration of this process allows
the learner to browse the ontology using its taxonomic form.

Some presentation rules are used to allow the user to visually explore this
hierarchical organization: the current concept C is at the center of the screen; all
the subconcepts of C that represent more specific topics are presented; at last,
the superconcept of C, which represents a more general notion, is also presented.
We did not find it useful to extend this representation. Our goal was to keep it
understandable.

To end with the hierarchical navigation, let us finally note that the representation
uses semantic axes. To visualize them, we used different colors for each of these
axes (Fig. 7.3). At this stage, their meaning is not explicit.

Let us suppose now that the learner decides to temporarily stop the navigation
and to focus on a particular concept. This concept is at first described by a short
definition. If the user wants to learn more on the selected topic, (s)he has access
to a list of resources ordered by type. For example, Figure 7.3 shows that if the
user wants to deepen the topic of Finite Set, (s)he can select among the associated
resources, for example a book entitled *Mathematics for Computer Science*, by
left-clicking on the name of this resource. A description text is then displayed in a
new window (Fig. 7.4). Other bibliographic information such as the ISBN number,
authors, publisher, etc., is also available. When the resource is digital, it can be
displayed or sent to someone by email.

A concept can refer to concepts other than those that are displayed in the taxonomy. Access to these concepts is sometimes needed in order to understand
some topics. Proximity relations (other than subsumption) are useful for that. Examples of these relations are prerequisite-of, in-the-definition-of, suggests, etc.
Other application-specific relations such as subset-of, has-cardinal, etc., can also

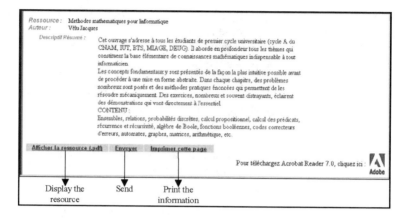

FIGURE 7.4. A book resource.

be considered. We call this kind of navigation "horizontal navigation," in comparison with the "vertical navigation" that we considered before. These relations are accessed by right-clicking on the source concept C: a pop-up menu contextually displays the available relations starting from C. Let us consider one more time the case of the Finite Set concept (Fig. 7.3). Among the available horizontal relations, the learner can choose, for example, "prerequisite-of" and learn more about prerequisite notions such as "Countable Set" or "Cardinal" (Fig. 7.5).

Choosing the "Countable Set" concept in the list of the prerequisite concepts of "Finite Set" allows one to switch back to a vertical navigation centered on this new concept of "Countable Set." Finally, one can see that the navigation through

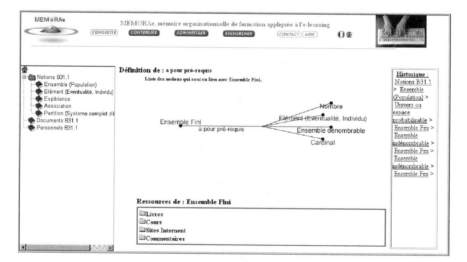

FIGURE 7.5. Horizontal navigation.

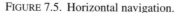

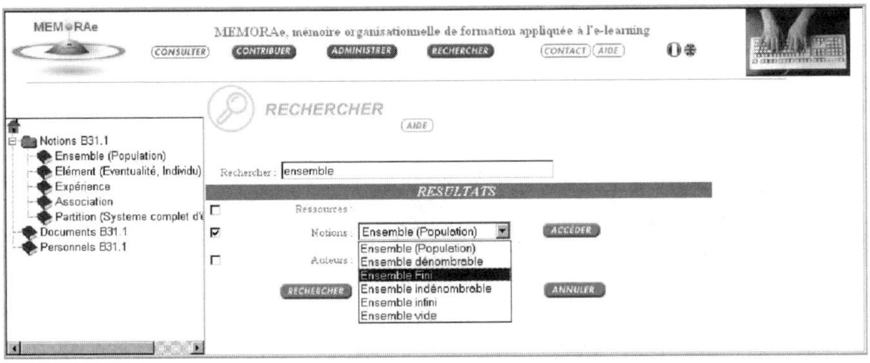

FIGURE 7.6. Searching the Finite Set topic.

the application ontology is made very easy by combining vertical (left-click) and horizontal (right-click) moves.

After each exploration action made by the learner, the history (Fig. 7.3, right frame) is actualized. This history keeps track of the path followed by the user during the exploration. Of course it is possible to go back to a previously visited topic by clicking on it in the history.

7.4.3 Learning by Querying the Memory

We have seen in the previous section how to access to the contents of the memory by navigation ("Consult menu"). It is also possible to directly access a topic by querying the memory ("Search menu"). This interface allows searching for a word in the textual data contained in the memory. The word can be all or a part of an author, topic or resource name, and it can be included in the textual description of the topic, etc.

For example, Figure 7.6 shows the search results for the "set" word.

When choosing a topic in the search results, the user has access to the part of the taxonomy related to this topic. He can continue to explore the memory horizontally or vertically (see 7.4.2).

7.5 Architecture

The E-MEMORAe environment is a three-tier architecture: MySQL/PHP, Appach, and JavaScript/HTML+SVG. This type of architecture separates the application into three levels of distinct services: presentation, treatment, and storage.

Figure 7.7 shows the functional architecture of the E-MEMORAe environment: one can indeed find a storage part (MySql database), a treatment part (Topic Maps modeling, etc.), and an information presentation part.

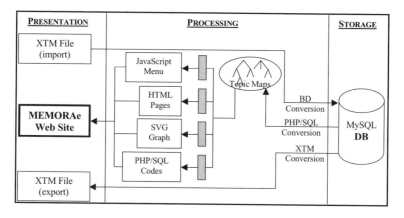

FIGURE 7.7. Functional architecture of the E-MEMORAe environment.

The MEMORAe Web site is accessible at http://www.hds.utc.fr/~abenayac/
Site-MEMORAe

7.6 Experiments

In this section, we present the conditions and the results of our first experiment,
with 15 students attending the B31.1 course at the University of Picardy.

7.6.1 Conditions of the Experiment

We defined a usability test[5] to see how students could use the E-MEMORAe environment. Such a test facilitates measuring the learning and memorizing facilities,
and the usability of the environment. It also facilitates measuring the efficiency of
the system and the satisfaction of the user.

Our objective was to see how E-MEMORAe could allow learners to discover
by themselves new topics to learn. To assess the understanding of these topics the
learners have to solve some problems related to them.

More precisely, our goal was to verify if it was relevant to:

- Index and structure the content of a training session by an ontology.
- Propose a tree representation of the ontology for facilitating the navigation
  through the resources.
- Offer a list of entry points for giving quick access to the main topics of the course.

The experiment took place at the University of Picardy and concerned the students enrolled in the course of applied mathematics B31.1. We describe now the
conditions of the experiment.

---

[5] http://www.usabilis.com/gb/whatis/usability.htm.

First, a presentation of the environment was made to all the students. It was followed by a real use case showing how to solve an exercise. The Web site URL was given to the students, and some of them found it useful to discover the site by themselves.

They worked in the same room and had access to workstations (computer and Internet connection). They had to solve a problem requiring some topics that they had not studied before. They could learn them by using the E-MEMORAe environment.

For each student, the history of the navigation was stored in the memory. We could analyze the way to reach important topics and the resources employed.

A questionnaire was distributed at the end of the session. Some questions concerned the tool itself. For example, "Is it easy to use, and to find the functionalities?" We could also verify with these questions whether the students had manipulated the environment before the session or not. Other questions concerned the presentation of the information on the site pages (tree structure of the notions, entry points).

The students could give their assessment of the site and add some suggestions in order to improve the tool.

7.6.2 First Results

The first results concern the experiment with a set of 15 students attending the B31.1 course. Globally, 10 students attended the knowledge presentation. We call this set of 10 students FOR and the others AGAINST. In the following, we describe the results concerning the essential choices we made to design E-MEMORAe and the results of the problem to solve before making a synthesis of the whole analysis.

- The FOR students were not embarrassed by the use of an ontology structure to index resources. The majority of AGAINST students were embarrassed. We can suppose that the general opinion of E-MEMORAe is linked to the use of an ontology. It will be interesting to study why the AGAINST students were embarrassed (their profile, ...).
- The AGAINST students were embarrassed with the tree presentation. In fact, 60% of students had no difficulty and 85% of them had little or no embarrassment with this approach.
- The use of colors to represent the semantic axes has not reached the expected objective. Some students noticed the different colors but did not understand their utility (semantic regrouping).
- The right click was very little used. We can suppose that this practice is not often used among Web users. Another explanation is the familiarity with E-MEMORAe. It is a first utilization, and users are not familiar with this kind of navigation.
- The entry points were used by 80% of FOR students and 60% of AGAINST students. Among these users, 80% appreciated this functionality.

The marks obtained by the two groups of students for the assessment were very similar. Thus, the assessment of E-MEMORAe is not related to these marks. To understand these results, we studied the history of navigation. We noticed that a majority of students tried different ways to access a topic: entry point, navigation (left click), search engine, history (right frame).

The navigation histories of AGAINST students are on average longer than those of FOR students. AGAINST is a little more dispersed than FOR regarding the amount of access (the time was limited to two hours and there was no extra time to explore unneeded topics). The FOR students had more difficulties in finding the searched knowledge.

Topics required to solve the problem were visited somehow or other. Some students were curious and studied several topics thoroughly; they visited more specific topics.

After this first experiment, we can conclude that using an ontology to index and structure the content of a training is a good choice: a majority of students appreciated it. The results obtained by the students from the assessment show that a majority of them were able to find the knowledge required to solve the problem in time. Suggestions about E-MEMORAe were mainly related to practical aspects: improving the search engine, use of scrollbars to visualize the tree, and use of inner links to have direct access to a part of the resource.

To go further in the evaluation of E-MEMORAe, another experiment is planned with students attending the NF01 course at the University of Compiègne (France).

7.7 Conclusion

We presented in this chapter the course memory we designed in the framework of the MEMORAe project and the E-MEMORAe environment that we developed. In contrast to the approach that is generally adopted with learning object repositories or thematic resource bases, this course memory is bound to be directly used by learners. This involves earlier instructional design work. Let us note, however, that this approach is only feasible with learners having self-regulating abilities.

The E-MEMORAe environment we developed is based on the use of two formalisms: ontologies and Topic Maps. It is used as a support for e-learning. The objective is to help the users understand the topics starting from documents selected by the teachers. The indexing of the documents is supplemented by pedagogical criteria that allow the learner to appreciate their pertinence. We think that using such a memory enhances the activity and the autonomy of the learner.

The first evaluation of E-MEMORAe with students in the framework of the B31.1 mathematics training at the University of Picardy in France gave us encouraging results. Another evaluation is planned with students attending the NF01 course at the University of Compiègne.

References

1. Abel, M.-H., Barry, C., Benayache, A., Chaput, B., Lenne, D., Moulin, C. (2004) Ontology-based organizational memory for e-learning. Educational Technology & Society. Journal, October issue, Volume 7, Issue 4, pp. 98–111.

2. Paquette, G., Bourdeau, J., Henri, F., Basque, J., Leaonard, M., Maina Cirta, M. (2003) Construction d'une base de connaissance et d'une base de ressources pour le domaine du téléapprentissage. Sciences el technologies de l'information el de la communication pour l'education el la formation (STICEF), Institut National de Recherche Pédagogique (INRP) 29–56.

3. MERLOT. (2004) Multimedia Educational Resource for Learning and Online Teaching. http://www.merlot.org/Home.po .

4. ARIADNE. (2004) Alliance of Remote Instructional and Distribution Networks for Europe. http://www.ariadne.eu.org.

5. LOM. (2002) LOM standard, document 2002; 1484.12.1. http://ltsc.ieee.org/wg12/files/LOM_1484_12_1_v1_Final_Draft.pdf.

6. Paquette, G. (2001) Telelearning systems engineering—towards a new ISD model. Journal of Structural Learning and Intelligent Systems 14(4):43–54.

7. Azouaou, F., Desmoulins, C., Mille, D. (2003) Formalismes pour une Mémoire à Base d'Annotations : Articuler Sémantique Implicite et Explicite. Strasbourg, France: EIAH.

8. Wenger, E. (1998) Communities of Practice. Learning, Meaning and Identity. Learning in Doing: Social, Cognitive, Computational Perspectives. Cambridge, MA: Cambridge University Press.

9. Dieng-Kuntz, R., Corby, O., Gandon, F., et al. Méthodes et Outils pour la Gestion des Connaissances, 2nd ed. Paris: Dunod.

10. Boullier, D. (2001) Les choix techniques sont des choix pédagogiques: les dimensions multiples d'une expérience de formation à distance. Sciences et Techniques Educatives, 8:275–299.

11. Breuker, J., Muntjewerff, A. (1999) Ontological modeling for designing educational systems. Workshop on Ontologies for Intelligent Educational Systems, Ninth International Conference on Artificial Intelligence in Education, AI-ED'99, Le Mans, France.

12. Integration of the DOLCE top-level ontology into the OntoSpec methodology https://hal.ccsd-cnrs.fr/cccsd-00012203

13. Dublin Core. http://www.schemas-forum.org/workshops/ws2/ws2-presentations/DC-Ed/.

14. Moulin, C., Abel, M.-H., Lenne, D. (2004) Indexing of resources in e-learning context. Proceedings of the Workshop on Knowledge Management and Semantic Web, EKAW 2004, Whittlebury Hall, England, pp. 40–53.

15. International Organisation for Standardization (ISO). International Electronical Commission (IEC). (1999) Topic Map, International Standard ISO/IEC 13250, 19 April.

16. XTM. (2001) TopicMaps.org XTM Authoring Group, XML Topic Maps (XTM) 1.0: TopicMaps.org Specification, 3 March. http://www.topicmaps.org/xtm.

17. Park, J. (2002) XML Topic Maps, Creating and Using Topic Maps for the Web, by Jack Park (ed), Addison-Wesley.

Part III
Building Knowledge Networks

8
Designing and Testing an Open-Source Learning Management System for Small-Scale Users

KEVIN JOHNSON AND TIMOTHY HALL

Abstract. The vision of reusable learning resources or objects, made accessible through coordinated repository architectures and metadata structures, has gained considerable attention within education and training communities. A proliferation of standards, architectures, Web technologies, and functionality abound to help realize this promise. This chapter outlines the issues associated with designing solutions for small-scale users such as small to medium-sized enterprises (SMEs). It describes the requirements and architecture for the development of an open-source small-scale learning object (LO) management system that supports the full management of learning objects, by bringing together the most promising advances in this field to attain a learning system for use by small-scale users to leverage the power of learning objects for improved training at an individual and organisational level.

8.1 Introduction

This chapter focuses on a solution to the problem of the diverse and changing information, training, and learning needs associated with small-scale systems that are needed by small to medium-sized enterprises (SME) and the mismatch between current e-learning systems and content-generation techniques, and the needs of their customers and employees. We can extrapolate the solution that matches this SME need to the promised more personalized e-learning resources of the future.

E-learning initiatives are frequently driven by an awareness of knowledge as an important source of wealth creation and a need to respond to the quickening pace of environmental change and the rapid development of information technologies. However, various criticisms have been raised about the marginal benefits that arise from using technology in education. Whether or not there are advantages to taking this route still remains to be seen. Despite these concerns, learning technology is continually advancing, and new initiatives are underway to standardize e-learning tools, technologies, and content [1].

Attempting to take advantage of developments in learning technologies, companies have purchased off-the-shelf e-learning courses, only to find them a less than satisfactory solution to their training needs. These courses are too generic and cannot economically be tailored for a better match to specific company needs. However, recent advances in learning standards (such as SCORM [2], IEEE LOM [3], and IMS [4]) and in using XML (eXtensible Markup Language) to classify content now make it possible to create learning content management systems (LCMSs), that can handle the required diversity and specificity efficiently. An LCMS is an environment where developers can create, store, reuse, manage, and deliver learning content, based on a learning object model, from a central object repository (database), with good search capabilities to find the text or other media needed to build training content quickly. LCMS strives to achieve a separation of content, tagged in XML, from a Web browser–based presentation framework; this facilitates publishing a wide range of formats, platforms, or devices, all from the same source content material.

These content fragments have become known as learning objects. A learning object, for all practical purposes, is an object or set of resources that can be used for facilitating intended learning outcomes and can be extracted and reused in other learning environments. The term has been recently associated with electronic learning resources that can be shared in multiple learning environments. The value of a learning object lies in its object-oriented nature, which lends itself to reuse; however, therein lies its complexity. Two major issues that affect the pedagogical validity of a learning object are granularity and combination. Stated succinctly, combination relates to how the learning objects are amalgamated, whereas granularity refers to the size of the learning object itself.

Current-generation commercial LCMSs for the education market—WebCT [5], Blackboard [6], TopClass [7]—and for the corporate training market—Docent [8] and TrainerSoft [9]—offer a "corporate solution" and include functions such as mail services, authentication services, intranets, or the Internet. These are services that many users already have, so duplication would be a waste of resources. Small companies are additionally limited by the capital required for purchasing such expensive proprietary systems. From the system engineer's point of view, these products are not easily modified to include tailored features. Commercial LCMSs, such as WebCT and Blackboard, however, have valuable features that are not easy to duplicate, for example, tools to support the creation of instructionally sound learning content that normally would require the services of a trained instructional designer.

Our task was to create a small-scale LCMS environment that met the needs of SMEs (as representative of a class of similar small-scale users), countering their neglect in the current drive toward the use of e-learning. The proposed solution would have to develop a methodology and technology that would address the inhibiting issues of cost and complexity, and allow SMEs to take advantage of e-learning for skills development and for use in training/educating its clients, representatives, field support personnel, etc., and incorporating elements of sound instructional design for use by those without training design experience. By basing the system on reusable learning objects, the customization of modules of learning tailored to suit the individual SMEs learning requirements was possible, and a flexible dynamic delivery system provided a "just-in-time" and "just-enough" learning approach.

By following our development path, we explore the associated issues and problems and illustrate the system design process in a time of shifting and developing standards.

8.2 Learning Management Systems to Learning Content Management Systems

Although it is easy enough to provide access to a piece of learning content directly from a Web page, many organizations and educational institutions want to control access to the courseware and track data such as the user ID, the level of usage, and the outcome. A learning management system (LMS) is a Web server–based software application that provides the administrative and data-tracking functions necessary to achieve this. The LMS also relieves the teacher of a burdensome administrative effort. The specific features and functions of an LMS vary considerably from one system to another, but generally they offer the following:

- Administrative functions: these include course setup, learner registration, course assignment and reporting of the learner's progress by tracking data such as scores on tests or quizzes, the time spent in courses, and the completion status of each course.
- Learner interface: permitting learners to log in to the LMS using a personal ID with or without a password and receive access to the e-learning content via a personalized menu of their assigned courses. Usually they can also monitor their own progress by viewing test scores, completion status on courses and topics, and so on.
- Sequencing: LMSs are also responsible for sequencing learner access to lessons within courses, such as allowing learners access lessons in any order or forcing them to access the lessons in a predetermined sequence.

An LMS enables organizations to collect data about the level of usage and effectiveness of courses. Usage data includes the number of learners registered for a course, the average amount of time spent on a course, and the number of learners completing a course.

Learning content management systems (LCMSs) are a more recent development that exploits the wider use of standards-compliant learning objects to add a further level of functionality to LMSs. However, a natural result of the adoption of learning objects is that there is a much larger number of content pieces to deal with; thus LCMSs, need more advanced content management, organization, and search capabilities. The systems are designed to meet the following requirements [10]:

- Generate unique descriptions for each learning object.
- Discover (search for and locate) the required learning object.

- Provide multiple hierarchies for storing and organizing learning objects.
- Facilitate the assembly of complex course structures.

A typical LCMS includes the following components:

- Content tagging and assembly functions for creating learning objects from lower-level content objects and for grouping learning objects to form larger learning content structures such as topics, lessons, and courses.
- A content repository for storing assets, learning objects, content aggregations and other content structure.
- A delivery interface including functions for searching and organizing learning objects to provide individualized learning experiences.
- Authoring tools for producing content objects.
- Some form of collaboration tool that allows the end users to talk among themselves as well as post questions and queries to someone who administers the course. This tool can be in the form of a chat room or instant message system (synchronous) or a forum or bulletin board area (asynchronous).

The international research consultants at IDC (2002), in their paper "Learning Content Management Systems: A New E-Learning Market Segment Emerges," identify the components of an LCMS as consisting of an authoring application, a data repository, a delivery interface, and administration tools. Many other vendors such as Click2Learn and Avaltus [11] also concur with this architectural structure. The authoring tools provide templates and storyboarding capabilities, and can be used to convert existing content. The data repository uses metadata to store and manage individual learning objects. The delivery interface dynamically delivers content that can be modified to reflect the required look or feel.

Most LCMSs additionally contain LMS functionality with administration functions to manage learner profiles, assessment, and course catalogues, and provide a learner interface.

8.3 Reusability and Interoperability

Ultimately, the usefulness of these environments from a teaching and learning point of view is their ability to assemble and deliver lessons and courses from granular pieces of instruction based on learning objects, and their ability to take an object and reuse it in a different lesson (reusability) or modify it for a different definition of repurpose; from a technical point of view, a learning object should be deliverable through a different LCMS than that in which it authored (interoperability). This is a very different concept than the majority of existing e-learning, where courses are one indivisible unit delivered only through the original system.

8.3.1 Reusability

Reusability has more than one meaning when associated with e-learning and learning content management systems. For now we'll focus on content reusability, that is, the reusability of the material delivered to the learner to achieve a learning goal.

- ICT-based delivery has several advantageous features that made its adoption as a means of industrial training, that is computer-based training (CBT) attractive.
- Media-rich interactive CBT was a far more effective training tool that printed manuals.
- The addition of assessment and data tracking meant that management could be assured that its personnel met the required standards.
- CBT was available to personnel 24 hours per day, 7 days per week (24/7).
- Personnel could access the training material on a just-in-time basis, so that they could carry out a particular task immediately after reviewing the latest information [10].

The CBT was delivered stand-alone, on CD-ROMs, or across a local area network for multiple user access. However, authoring this rich content is time-consuming, 100 times the delivery time not being uncommon. CBT systems had delivery programs designed for specific end users, and reuse of the content for other purposes was not seen as an important factor [12]. Early e-learning content followed this path, with significant resources being devoted to authoring locked-in content.

With the spread of e-learning to other less well resourced areas of education and training, much of the research into the creation of learning content has focused on authoring resource economy, and the notion of reusable rich media content components and learning objects becomes attractive. The driving force is that reuse of such components can lead to important savings in time and money, whereas richer media enhances the quality of the learning experience. The end result is faster, cheaper, more effective learning.

Reuse of learning content is not simple. It comes in a number of conceptually or technically different guises, for example:

- Multiple output (distribution) formats, or media
- Multiple purposes: training, performance support, reference documentation, marketing information, etc.
- Multiple delivery: the same material over and over
- Multiple "disciplines" or market segments

Reuse does not involve any change in the learning content, but if we extend the principle of resource conservation to allow a reuse that involves a degree of modification or reauthoring of learning objects (LOs), we arrive at the concept of repurposing, which can be thought of as the ability to use, without any (significant) changes, the same piece of content for a purpose significantly different from what it was originally intended for when created [13]. We do not pursue this topic further here.

Again extending the meaning of reuse along a technical route, we must consider enabling content to be delivered through other systems than that in which it originated; this is termed interoperability.

8.3.2 Interoperability

Interoperability is defined as "enabling information that originates in one context to be used in another in ways that are as highly automated as possible" [14]. More specifically: the ability of objects from different, multiple, potentially unknown or unplanned sources to "work" or operate when put together with other objects. Examples include:

- Content objects from different original creation/authoring tools working together when assembled into a learning object.
- Learning objects and content objects being able to work properly when moved from one infrastructure (operating system, LCMS, etc.) to another

This requires standardization of common protocols, formats, etc. The vision of an open, large-scale learning object infrastructure is conditional on the achievement of interoperability.

Interoperability can exist at different scales:

- Between learning objects
- Between learning objects and learning management systems
- Between learning object repositories
- Between metadata schemas

The more general notion of interoperability is that it enables crossing cultural or linguistic boundaries. Interoperability requires full exchange of data between the systems' heterogeneous data models. For an exchange to take place, a consistent set of interpretations must be provided for the information. Ensuring this consistency requires semantic interoperability, in other words, agreement on the meaning of the exchanged information [15]. Accordingly, "the achievement of interoperability should be viewed as an enabling condition for interoperation between application systems and semantic integration of information from diverse sources" [16]. Thus, interoperability relies heavily upon communication of information between systems, applications, and databases wherein formal language and model representations of complex information have been resolved.

Efforts to create standards for the interchange of information or metadata over the past 10 to 15 years have produced a number of national and international standards. The prevalent approach has been to develop interfaces that allow translation of data from one proprietary format to a standard or "neutral" format, from which the information can again be translated into a second proprietary format. Much effort has been directed at formalizing general aspects of storing and retrieving properties and entities, most notably by the IMS [4], IEEE [17], AICC [18], and ARIADNE [19].

Metadata comprise a key component of any interoperability schema. As the format of metadata evolves toward machine readability, improved reliability and consistency in the interchange of information occurs. Further work is needed in storing and representing metadata, specifying metadata requirements for different domains, and building tools that are able to find commonalties between interchanged data from different agencies [20].

8.4 Metadata

Metadata are often defined as "data about data" [21] and are understood to represent descriptive information (element names, definitions, lengths, etc.) about populated data fields. Benefits of implementing a metadata model are seen in:

- Locating information: metadata associate information with objects that otherwise would not exist or are not easily accessible. This in turn benefits searching for a specific object and returns a higher percentage of accurate results.
- Interpreting information: metadata fields associated with objects offer a clearer description of an object and better define what the object is about [22].

Metadata support the search for information by providing data definitions, transformation logic, and lists of valid values, business rules, and more. The main components within a metadata system are the repository that holds all of the information, the user interface, and the interface to other software and publishing, both electronic and paper [23].

The repository captures the metadata, usually in a relational database. All repositories hold the basics: length, definition, data type, etc., and additionally, source and target mappings, the relationship between elements, and much more.

The user interface allows the metadata administrator to enter and maintain records, though most entries come to the system through data uploads or interface with other software. Metadata maintenance can be surprisingly complex, so an intuitive and powerful user interface is important.

The software interfaces both receive and send information about the data to any applications that may touch or define data, such as a data modeling tool, business modeling tool, RDBMS (Relational DataBase Management System), change management tools, and testing support tools. At the moment, this is a strong developmental area of metadata systems [24].

Publishing makes metadata available to the business and technical user community. Usually published metadata are viewable via an Internet browser window and on hardcopy reports such as mapping specifications or a data dictionary. Not all information captured in the repository is publishable, and the amount of control over the user interface and report designs varies among metadata tools.

In order for the positive potential of learning objects to be realized, they need to be labeled, described, investigated, and understood in ways that make the simplicity, compatibility, and advantages claimed for them readily apparent to teachers, trainers, and other practitioners [22]. The information to enable this must be stored in the associated metadata.

Standards—whether they are for data collection, data transfer, documentation (metadata), or software—are all designed to facilitate the dissemination, communication, and use of information by multiple producers and users. (Almost all standards rely on or incorporate metadata in order to accomplish their purpose.)

Recent trends in education are also highlighting the importance of metadata, as the vast amount of educational material on the Web needs to be cataloged and organized in a standardized way so that it can be utilized interoperably for different educational environments [4].

We have established a framework for e-learning content to be assembled for delivery dynamically from a repository, where the pieces are located and sequenced according to the metadata, but what about the pieces of learning themselves, the learning objects?

8.5 Learning Objects (LOs)

Technology is an agent of change, and major technological innovations can result in entire paradigm shifts. The computer network known as the Internet is one such innovation. After effecting sweeping changes in the way people communicate and do business, the Internet has begun to bring about a paradigm shift in the way people learn. Consequently, a major change may also be coming in the way educational materials are designed, developed, and delivered to those who wish to learn. An instructional technology called "learning objects" [25] currently leads other candidates for the position of technology of choice in the next generation of instructional design, development, and delivery, due to its potential for reusability, generativity, adaptability, and scalability [26,27].

Learning objects, as discussed in Chapter 1, are elements of computer-based instruction grounded in the object-oriented concept. Object-orientation highly values the creation of components (called "objects") that can be reused [28] in multiple contexts. This is the fundamental idea behind learning objects; instructional designers can build small (relative to the size of an entire course) instructional components that can be reused in different learning contexts. Learning objects are generally understood to be digital entities deliverable over the Internet. Any number of people can access and use them simultaneously (as opposed to traditional instructional media, a book, or video tape, which can only exist in one place at a time).

Supporting the notion of small, reusable pieces of instructional media, Reigeluth and Nelson [29] suggest that when teachers first gain access to new material, they often break it down into constituent parts. They then reassemble these parts in ways that support their individual instructional goals. This suggests one reason why reusable instructional components—learning objects—may provide significant benefits. If instructors had access resources as components in the first place, the initial step of decomposition could be bypassed, increasing the speed and efficiency of instructional development.

The IEEE Learning Technology Standards Committee chose the term *learning objects* to describe these small instructional components, established a working group, and provided a working definition.

Various other terms are in use including *content object, knowledge object, reusable information object*, and *reusable learning object*. Although no universal definition exists, a learning object generally refers to a "reusable unit of learning." An initial definition for a learning object could be any entity, digital or nondigital, that can be used, reused, or referenced during technology-supported learning. Examples of technology-supported learning include computer-based training systems, interactive learning environments, intelligent computer-aided instruction systems, distance learning systems, and collaborative learning environments. Examples of learning objects include multimedia content, instructional content, learning objectives, instructional software and software tools, and persons, organisations, or events referenced during technology-supported learning [30].

This definition is extremely broad—too broad. It failed to exclude any person, place, thing, or idea that had existed at anytime, ever, since any of these could be "referenced during technology supported learning." Different groups have attempted to narrow the scope of this canonical definition to something more specific. Other groups had refined the definition but continued to use the term *learning object*. Confusingly, these additional terms and differently defined learning objects are all Learning Technology Standards Committee learning objects in the strictest sense. The proliferation of definitions for the term *learning object* has made communication confusing and difficult.

The Learning Technology Standards Committee definition seems too broad to be useful, since most instructional technologists would not consider the historical event the First World War or the historical figure Billy the Kid to be learning objects. At the same time, the creation of yet another term only seemed to add to the confusion, so in the context of this chapter, a learning object is defined as "any digital resource that can be reused to support learning." This definition includes anything that can be delivered across the network on demand, be it large or small. Examples of smaller reusable digital resources include digital images or photos, live data feeds, live or prerecorded video or audio snippets, bits of text, animations, and smaller Web-delivered applications, such as a Java calculator. Examples of larger reusable digital resources include entire Web pages that combine text, images, and other media or applications to deliver complete experiences, such as a complete instructional event. This definition of learning object, "any digital resource that can be reused to support learning," is used for two reasons. First, it is sufficiently narrow to define a reasonably homogeneous set of things: reusable digital resources. At the same time, the definition is broad enough to include the estimated 15 terabytes of information available on the publicly accessible Internet [31]. Second, it is based on the LTSC definition (and defines a proper subset of learning objects as defined by the LTSC), making issues of compatibility of learning object and learning object as defined by the LTSC explicit. It captures the critical attributes of a learning object, "reusable," "digital," "resource," and "learning," but rejects aspects of the LTSC that include nondigital and nonlearning focused.

A learning object is thus, for all practical purposes, an object or set of resources that can be used to facilitate intended learning outcomes and can be extracted and reused in other learning environments, "reusable learning objects" (RLOs). Learning objects become the building blocks of e-learning content and can be used to construct any desired type of learning experience—Legos for e-learning [32,33].

Many educators see learning objects as a viable alternative to the traditional yet not very flexible and difficult-to-adapt instructor-led course format that has been the foundation of education and training for the last two centuries. Learning objects stored in a database and properly tagged for easy search are designed specifically for flexibility and reuse and are easily aggregated into lessons and courses.

The value of a learning object lies in its object-orientated nature, which lends itself to reuse. However, therein lies its complexity. Two major issues that affect the pedagogic validity of a learning object are granularity and combination—combination relating to how the learning objects are amalgamated, and granularity referring to the size of the learning object.

8.5.1 Combination

While groups like the Learning Technology Standards Committee exist to promote international discussion about the standards necessary to support learning object–based instruction, apparently no one had considered the role of instructional design in composing and personalizing lessons [34]. Metadata, descriptive information about a resource such as title, author, version, format, etc., facilitate finding objects by searching, as opposed to browsing. Problems arose when consideration was given to what it means for a computer to automatically and dynamically assemble a lesson, by taking individual learning objects and combining them in a way that makes sense: in instructional design terms, "sequencing" the learning objects. In order for a computer to make sequencing or any other instructional design decisions, it must have access to instructional design information to support the decision-making process. However, no such information was included in the metadata specified by the version of the Learning Objects Metadata Working Group standard in use at the time. An IEEE LOM working group is considering this problem [21].

8.5.2 Granularity

Sequencing cannot be discussed without mentioning "granularity" [35]. How big should a learning object be? The Learning Technology Standards Committee's definition leaves room for an entire curriculum to be viewed as a learning object, but objects so large preclude notions of reuse that lies at the core of learning object features, as generativity, adaptivity, and other-ivities are all facilitated by the property of reuse. Clearly LOs should be smaller and from a reuse point of view as small as possible. Unfortunately, it's not so straightforward. Learning objects must be tagged with metadata (with more than 20 fields with names like "Semantic Density"), very small objects become prohibitively expensive to tag, a trade-off between flexibility of reuse and the cost of tagging has to be made, and an intermediate size for LOs chosen. Alternatively, the decision between how much or how little to include in learning objects can be viewed as a problem of "scope." Reality dictates that cost must be considered, but only after decisions regarding the scope of learning objects have be made in an instructionally grounded, principled manner.

To facilitate the ability to find and share learning object's, various standards groups have worked together to define a consistent set of metadata to be provided for each learning object. The metadata is not part of the learning object itself; rather, it is held in a separate document designed to travel with the learning object, and this document is accessed without opening or displaying the actual LO content.

As described earlier, LOs can be considered the building blocks of e-learning content. Building blocks are not particularly useful unless they are assembled into larger structures. Most learning content, regardless of how it is delivered, uses some sort of hierarchical structure. A course may be divided into lessons, for example, and the lessons further divided into topics, and so on. A major requirement for e-learning specifications is the provision of a simple but flexible method for representing a wide variety of content structures or taxonomies.

8.6 Standards

National and international committees, consortia, and other organizations have been busy developing standards and specifications for e-learning technologies at least since the late 1990s. They have been doing so with the understanding that the benefits of this standardization work will be manifold and various:

Not only would the development and use of international standards (in e-learning) produce a direct cost savings, but the information technology systems could be used in a wider range of applications, and used more efficiently. Better, more efficient and interoperable systems, content, and components will produce better learning, education, and training—which has a positive effect upon all societies [36].

Organizations actively developing these standards and specifications include the IMS Global E-Learning Consortium, the IEEE Learning Technologies Standards Committee, and the ISO Subcommittee on "Information Technology for Learning Education and Training." The development of technical standards in e-learning can be understood as a part of the maturation of this sector or industry. Before, and especially since, the popular emergence of the Internet and the World Wide Web, ICT has been used widely in education, both distance and classroom based, and in off-line and online training. However, the technology has been applied in ad hoc and diverse forms, innumerable courses, course components; and systems for managing and delivering these courses have been developed independently of one another. Moreover, the content and management systems are often created in a manner that makes it very difficult if not impossible to enable content sharing or successful interoperation. Standards in e-learning seek to address these shortcomings by ensuring the interoperability, portability, and reusability of content and compatibility of systems. Until the emergence of standards in the e-learning industry, organizations were often constrained to buying all their e-learning from one vendor. Courses came with their complete software already integrated, and although data flowed freely between the LMS and the courseware, there was no way that courses or LMS could interoperate with another vendor's system. Customers were effectively locked into one vendor.

The observation that "the nice thing about standards is that there are so many to choose from" [22] has been circulating in e-learning standards circles for some time. Although no one involved in standards development would claim to be seeking a situation in which standards and specifications compete, overlap, or develop in parallel, this statement certainly reflects the varied and complex nature of standards organizations and standards development processes.

Standards can be defined as "documented agreements containing technical specifications or other precise criteria to be used consistently as rules, guidelines, or definitions of characteristics, to ensure that materials, products, processes and services are fit for their purpose" [36]. In e-learning the standards that are in use today are a result of the work of several standards bodies, principally the Institute of Electrical and Electronic Engineers Learning Technology Standards Committee (IEEE LTSC) [25], the IMS Global Consortium [17], Advanced Distributed Learning Networks (ADL Net) [37], and the Aviation Industry Computer Based Training Committee (AICC) [18], and they ultimately define the metadata to be used in tagging LOs. Eventually the international organization will advance most of the standards developed by the IEEE/LTSC as International Standards for Standardization (ISO).

8.6.1 Standards Evolution

The IMS project was founded as part of the National Learning Infrastructure Initiative of EDUCAUSE (then Educom) as a fee-based consortium of learning-technology vendors, publishers, and users. Its members included many U.S. universities, and its original focus was on higher education. It produced specifications covering multiple areas of e-learning—metadata, content, administrative systems, and learner information—each developed by its own working group. IMS later relaunched as a nonprofit organization with a more international outlook, the IMS (Instructional Management System) Global Learning Consortium [38].

IMS produces open specifications for locating and using e-learning content, tracking learner progress, reporting learner performance, and exchanging student records between administrative systems such as LMSs. Two of these specifications have been adapted for use within the ADL framework:

- The IMS Learning Resources Metadata Specification defines a method for describing learning resources so that they can be located using metadata search software.
- The IMS Content and Packaging Specification defines how to create reusable learning objects that can be accessed by a variety of administration systems such as LMSs and LCMSs.

The Open University of the Netherlands (OUNL) was the creator of EML (Educational Modeling Language) over a 3-year R&D program and was closely involved in the development of the learning design specification in IMS [39]. Currently they are collaborating with the dotLRN community to integrate their learning platform with instructional design defined according to the current standards.

The ADL (Advanced Distributed Learning) common technical framework is referred to as SCORM—the Sharable Content Object Reference Model (SCORM^{TM}). SCORM defines a Web-based learning Content Aggregation Model and Run-time Environment for learning objects [37]. At its simplest, it is a model that references a set of interrelated technical specifications and guidelines designed to meet the Department of Defense's high-level requirements for Web-based learning content. The SCORM applies current technology developments—from groups such as the IMS Global Learning Consortium, Inc., the Aviation Industry CBT Committee, the Alliance of Remote Instructional Authoring and Distribution Networks for Europe (ARIADNE) [19], and the IEEE LTSC—to a specific content model to produce recommendations for consistent implementations by the vendor community.

SCORM is being developed through active collaboration among private industry, education, and the U.S. federal government with the goal of producing guidelines that meet the common needs of all sectors. To facilitate this collaboration, the ADL established the ADL Co-Laboratory Network, which provides an open collaborative environment for sharing and testing learning technology research, development, and assessments [40]. Rather than reinventing the wheel, the SCORM leverages the work of the standards bodies by bringing together their disparate specifications and adapting them to form an integrated and cohesive implementation model.

SCORM documents are constantly evolving as further specifications are refined and added to the base model. Figure 8.1 gives an overview of the SCORM structure in its book format bases on the SCORM 2004 documentation.

The AICC develops technical guidelines known as AICC Guidelines and Recommendations (AGRs). An AGR is a short document that references a detailed specification document. AGR 010 is the AICC's guidelines for interoperability between Web-based courseware and LMSs. It references another document, CMI001—"CMI Guidelines for Interoperability"—which is commonly referred to in the e-learning industry as the AICC CMI specification.

The AICC offers certification testing for the AGR 010 CMI interoperability guidelines as well as for the AGR 006 guidelines, which apply to LAN-based management systems. To achieve AICC certification, products are put through a testing process by an independent third-party testing organization. Vendors are also able to self-test their products using the AICC test suite. This enables them to claim AICC conformance for their products.

The ARIADNE European Projects (phases I and II) were formed to develop a set of e-learning tools and methodologies. The ARIADNE began research and technology development projects in January 1996. These projects pertain to the Telematics for Education and Training sector of the 4th Framework Program for R&D of the European Union. The projects focus on the development of tools and

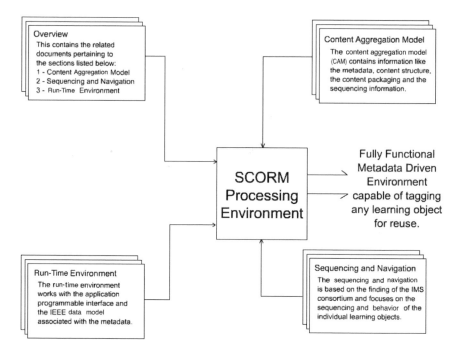

FIGURE 8.1. SCORM "books" outlook.

methodologies for producing, managing, and reusing computer-based pedagogical elements and telematics supported training curricula. The project, which was largely funded by the European Union and the Swiss government, ended in June 2000. Subsequently, the ARIADNE Foundation formed to promote the widespread adoption of state-of-the-art and platform-independent education in Europe [41].

The International Standards Organization (ISO) is a worldwide federation of national standards bodies from some 140 countries [42]. It has created a Joint Technical Committee in cooperation with the International Electrotechnical Commission (IEC), which is the international standards and conformity assessment body for all fields of electrotechnology [43]. This technical committee, known as JTC1, includes a subcommittee known as SC36 (subcommittee 36), which is responsible for work on information technology for learning, education, and training [44].

The bodies and organizations listed previously have been working together to create a specification or standard that would allow all users of learning object-based content to define interoperable metadata for learning objects, a standard known as the Learning Object Metadata standard.

To facilitate the widespread adoption of the learning object approach, the IEEE LTSC formed in 1996 to develop and promote instructional technology standards [25]. Without such standards, universities, corporations, and other organizations around the world would have no way of ensuring the interoperability of their instructional technologies, specifically their learning objects. Multiple organizations (ADL, AICC, IMS, ARIADNE) began developing technical standards to support the broad deployment of learning objects. Many of these local standards efforts have representatives on the LTSC group.

8.6.2 Learning Object Metadata Standards

An emerging standard is developing for learning objects metadata. The IEEE is the main accredited standards body (Fig. 8.2). The approved IEEE Learning Object Metadata standard is created with the cooperation of a variety of specification consortia and laboratory test beds and markets. Technical specifications are developed by the AICC, IMS, and ARIADNE, and feed into reference models for ADL [2] and ALIC [45]. These reference models, in turn, aid the standard bodies in developing approved standards. Each of these organizations and their role are outlined below.

The IMS gathers functional requirements, technical capabilities and deployment priorities from end users, vendor, purchasers, and managers. These requirements are consolidated into one or more specifications. These specifications have become a draft for the Learning Objects Metadata specification of the IEEE standards body. The active groups with IMS follow an open process to develop a specification package consisting not only of content metadata but also information models, XML

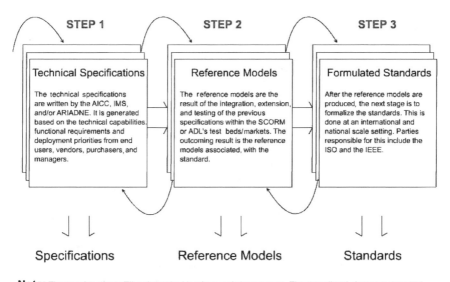

Note: The creation of an affiliated standard is a long and slow process. The steps listed above are repeated over and over until a satisfactory outcome is achieved. The specifications stage is iterated until all contributing bodies are happy with the proposed outcome. This is, in turn, passed on to the reference model test beds. Here it will be tested and retested based on features such as implementation guidelines, requirements etc. When it has sucessfully passed this stage, the ISO and IEEE formally standardize it.

FIGURE 8.2. Standards development process.

binding, and best practice guides. Similar efforts started in the ARIADNE project groups on metadata definitions, and these groups are now closely collaborating with IMS.

In addition, the AICC has been working to provide interoperability standards for computer-managed instruction systems, now more widely known as Learning Management Systems or Course Management Systems (CMS). AICC primarily caters to the CMI systems developed for the aviation industry and related vendors. It provides AICC guidelines and recommendations. The contribution of AICC is particularly important in the CMI database schema and the interoperability of the database objects extending to several computer-based training course management and assessment systems. AICC is working closely with the IEEE LTSC in several areas of mutual interest. It also provides test suites for AICC certification.

Following on from the technical specifications produced, reference models are extrapolated. One organization involved in efforts toward that end is the ADL. The activities of ADL co-labs focus on the development of the Sharable Content Object Reference Model specifications, including metadata standards from IEEE LTSC P1484 (as submitted by IMS) and CMI database schema (submitted to IEEE by AICC).

The intent of ADL co-labs in the development of standards is to make SCORM an integrated model reliant on extended specifications from other groups. ADL participates with other organizations, such as AICC and IMS, in the development of specifications, and when the specifications become stable, it incorporates them into a SCORM release.

The ADL Co-Labs are collaborating closely with ARIADNE, IMS, AICC, and IEEE. At present, SCORM 2004 is distributed and includes the content packaging and sequencing recommendations proposed by IMS. The specific goal for SCORM is to create learning technology standards for the creation of durable, reusable, interoperable, and accessible courses for defense and industry training.

Partners such as ARIADNE, IMS, and AICC have recognized that it would be inappropriate to develop competing metadata systems. They therefore have agreed to cooperate under the auspices of the IEEE LTSC. It is hoped that this will lead to a joint adoption of the metadata standards while retaining the option of producing extensions to these standards that address the particular needs of the respective projects. All four organizations have participated in the development of the IEEE LTSC standards. The procedure for this development of standards is as follows:

- Technical specifications are written within AICC, IMS, or ARIADNE.
- They are integrated, extended, and tested in SCORM/ADL generating reference models.
- They are formalized nationally and internationally in ISO/IEEE.

From this a formal ISO standard is created. The Learning Object Model (LOM), standard was approved by the IEEE in July 2002. It represents the first standard for learning content to be released by an accredited standards organization. The official designation of the LOM standard is IEEE 1484.12.1-2002 [25]. According to the LOM,

The purpose of this standard is to facilitate search, evaluation, acquisition, and use of learning objects, for instance by learners or instructors. The purpose is also to facilitate the sharing and exchange of learning objects, by enabling the development of catalogues and inventories while taking into account the diversity of cultural and lingual contexts in which the learning objects and their metadata will be exploited [25].

Currently, the IEEE LTSC learning object metadata standard specifies the syntax and semantics of learning object metadata, to fully/adequately describe a learning object. It focuses on the minimal set of attributes needed to allow learning objects to be managed, located, and evaluated. The standards accommodate the ability of locally extending the basic fields and entity types, and the fields can have a status of obligatory (must be present) or optional (may be absent). Relevant attributes of learning objects that can be described include type of object, author, owner, terms of distribution, and format. Where applicable, learning object metadata may also include pedagogical attributes such as teaching or interaction style, grade level, mastery level, and prerequisites. It is possible for any given learning object to have more than one set of learning object metadata. The standard does not concern itself with how these features are implemented.

The IEEE LTSC LOM model has nine categories, and each category is broken down into constituent parts that further describe a learning object. The categories are:

- General—information describing the LO as a whole
- Life cycle—contains information about the life cycle and status of the LO
- Meta-metadata—information about the metadata that describes the LO
- Technical—technical requirements and characteristics of the LO
- Educational—information about the interactivity type and selected difficulty of the LO and any pedagogical details
- Rights—information about the copyright issues associated with the LO
- Relation—relative LOs in a similar area
- Annotation—history of who created the LO and when
- Classification—where the LO falls within a particular classification system

8.7 Learning Object Metadata (LOM)

The simplest definition of metadata is structured "data about data." Metadata is defined as "something that describes an information resource, or helps provide access to an information resource" [34]. Metadata are descriptive information about an object or resource whether it is physical or electronic.

While metadata itself is relatively new, the underlying concepts have been in use for as long as collections of information have been organized. Inherent is the concept of an association between the metadata and the information resource that it describes. For example, library card catalogues represent a well-established type of metadata that have served as collection management and resource discovery tools for decades. Metadata can be generated either "by hand" or derived automatically using software.

Metadata standards are applied by using a "template" that, upon completion, holds sufficient information about the object or learning material for a search of the metadata to retrieve it. Using metadata to tag a resources allows users to search at a more refined level, and hence more accurately.

There are three principal reasons for using a metadata system:

- Sufficiency: Can a resource be adequately described by the resource itself? For example, an image may contain a picture of a particular geologic structure, but it would be hard to search for this. Words are needed. Although some resources may contain text, they need further information to describe or use them. Not all materials contain inherently adequate self-descriptions.
- Scalability: It is possible to do full text analysis on a single repository with thousands of resources, but it is impractical for large multiple repositories with resources. Metadata provide a highly targeted, rapid search and recovery option at a low cost and greater flexibility.
- Interoperability: The ability for different systems to interchange information, processes and resources is called "interoperability." If different systems can agree to create a mapping between their metadata, then it is possible for each to search one another's metadata. It is also possible for systems to accomplish wide-area searches among many systems if they all have created common mappings. Metadata, as a descriptive system, should allow descriptive mappings among systems—hence, interoperability. Interoperability is important for systems that expect to access resources from a variety of sources [22].

Metadata stored in a system require a schema to structure them. A schema describes what one or more XML documents can look like, and it defines:

- The elements the document contains, and the order in which they appear
- The element content and element attributes, if any

The purpose of schemas is to allow machine validation of document structure. Instead of using the syntax of XML 1.0 DTD declarations, schema definitions use XML element syntax. A correct XML schema definition, therefore, is a well-formed XML document [46].

Research commenced with the study of the work carried out by the organizational bodies associated with generating standards for metadata. The IEEE, ADL, IMS, and AICC all contribute to the LOM standard and Dublin Core (DC) work with the Dublin Core Metadata element set. The extension of the LOM v1.0 metadata schema is covered stating the reason for the necessary extensions to appropriately accommodate the tagging requirements of the metadata repository. The problems that arose from extending the LOM v1.0, namely an ambiguous ontology and methodology, resulted in the base schema being discarded and a new subset schema being drafted.

8.7.1 Dublin Core Metadata Initiative

The Dublin Core Metadata Initiative (DCMI) is an open forum engaged in the development of interoperable on-line metadata standards that support a broad range of purposes and business models. The DCMIs activities include consensus-driven working groups, global workshops, conferences, standards liaison, and educational efforts to promote widespread acceptance of metadata standards and practices. The Dublin Core Metadata Element Set (DCMES) was the first metadata standard developed out of the DCMI as an IETF—Internet Engineering Task Force—standard. The DCMES provides a semantic vocabulary for describing "core" information properties, such as "Description" and "Creator" and "Date" [47].

Dublin Core metadata are used to supplement existing methods for searching and indexing Web-based metadata. Most DCMI participants are involved in large-scale archiving or cataloging projects that require the use of Dublin Core metadata to enable large collections of object "resources" to be grouped, named, classified, and indexed in a useful fashion.

There are 15 elements in the DC metadata set, and each of these elements has 10 attributes associated with it. Of all of the groups that are creating standards for metadata, this is the largest number of attributes associated with any one set.

The Dublin Core metadata set was the original metadata set from which all other metadata sets stemmed. Groups like the IEEE, AICC, IMS, ADL, ARIADNE, ALIC, and many more based their metadata sets on work carried out by the Dublin Core. At the time of the research, work conducted by the aforementioned groups has progressed significantly, and metadata standards from each of these individual groups were developed or at some stage of development. These metadata sets were better equipped to handle the fast evolution of the standard creation process. From a working point of view, no advantage was apparent from taking the Dublin Core metadata set and implementing it within the scope of the SME Learning Management System.

The Dublin Core metadata set did not sufficiently describe a learning object within the scope of the SME repository. Options for extending the metadata set were not apparent, and altering the set would make it un-interoperable. Another metadata standard was required, leading to the IEEE LOM.

8.7.2 Modifying the IEEE Learning Object Metadata (LOM)

The LOM standard is meant to provide a semantic model for describing properties of the learning objects themselves, rather than detailing ways in which these learning objects may be used to support learning. The LOM indicates the legal values and informal semantics of the metadata elements, their dependencies on each other, and how they are assembled into a larger structure. LOM has specifically been designed to be extendable to accommodate future growth or individual adaptation. The LOM information structures are support metadata exchange, and are neither specifications of an implementation nor specifications of a user interface. The

LOM does not define recommendations concerning bindings or implementations of metadata in representations or notations.

The LOM data model is a hierarchy of data elements, including aggregate data elements and simple data elements (leaf nodes of the hierarchy). In the LOMv1.0 base schema [3], only leaf nodes have individual values defined through their associated value space and data type. Aggregates in the LOMv1.0 base schema do not have individual values. Consequently, they have no value space or data type.

An outline of the LOM metadata mapping is shown in Figure 8.3. The LOM structure is composed of nine elements, which in turn break down into a series of subelements, making up the complete model. Initially in our implementation we

1 General
- 1.1 Identifier
  - 1.1.1 Catalog
  - 1.1.2 Entry
- 1.2 Title
- 1.3 Language
- 1.4 Description
- 1.5 Keyword
- 1.6 Coverage
- 1.7 Structure
- 1.8 Aggregation Level

2 Life Cycle
- 2.1 Version
- 2.2 Status
- 2.3 Contribute
  - 2.3.1 Role
  - 2.3.2 Entity
  - 2.3.3 Date

3 Meta-Metadata
- 3.1 Identifier
  - 3.1.1 Catalog
  - 3.1.2 Entry
- 3.2 Contribute
  - 3.2.1 Role
  - 3.2.2 Entity
  - 3.2.3 Date
- 3.3 Metadata Schema
- 3.4 Language

4 Technical
- 4.1 Format
- 4.2 Size
- 4.3 Location
- 4.4 Requirements
  - 4.4.1 OrComposite
    - 4.4.1.1 Type
    - 4.4.1.2 Name
    - 4.4.1.3 Minimum Version
    - 4.4.1.4 Maximum Version
- 4.5 Installation Remarks
- 4.6 Other Platform Requirements
- 4.7 Duration

5 Educational
- 5.1 Interactivity Type
- 5.2 Learning Resource Type
- 5.3 Interactivity Level
- 5.4 Semantic Density
- 5.5 Intended and user role
- 5.6 Context
- 5.7 Typical Age Range
- 5.8 Difficulty
- 5.9 Typical Learning Time
- 5.10 Description
- 5.11 Language

6 Rights
- 6.1 Cost
- 6.2 Copyright and Other Restrictions
- 6.3 Description

7 Relation
- 7.1 Kind
- 7.2 Resource
  - 7.2.1 Identifier
    - 7.2.1.1 Catalog
    - 7.2.1.2 Entry
  - 7.2.2 Description

8 Annotation
- 8.1 Entity
- 8.2 Date
- 8.3 Description

9 Classification
- 9.1 Purpose
- 9.2 TexonPath
  - 9.2.1 Source
  - 9.2.2 Taxon
    - 9.2.2.1 Id
    - 9.2.2.2 Entry
- 9.3 Description
- 9.4 Keyword

FIGURE 8.3. LOM version 1.0 overview model.

proposed extending the LOM to meet the special needs of the SME environment, building from the base scheme defined in the released version of the standard IEEE 1484.12.1 in July 2002.

Our metadata were designed to be an application profile of the LOM standard. Some extensions were made where LOM was insufficient for the specific purposes of an SME-based repository. The original LOM metadata elements were not replaced or changed; they were taken as they were defined in the standard. Not all of the LOM metadata elements had significance for the goals of SME training, and so some were not used. Those that were used were not changed to maintain conformance to the standard. According to LOM, there can be extension elements, but none of the LOM elements or subelements can be replaced or transformed in any way, so the LOM metadata allow for extensions, but only if the original LOM elements are retained as they were originally defined. The only exception is the possibility to use other values in the Value space than the values defined in the Vocabulary of the Data type of that metadata element.

Originally it was felt that the LOM model did not provide a sufficient level of granularity in identifying learning objects within an SME context, so an extension of the LOM was pursued. There are essentially three ways of extending the metadata schema to suit the particular needs of the system:

1. Creating extensions to the metadata schema that do not overwrite the original schema.
2. Modifying or changing the vocabulary used in the LOM elements.
3. Using classification systems in Category 9 Classification.

Our initial base scheme for the SMEs proposed a number of such extensions, driven primarily by the requirement of increased granularity, and also a specific domain orientation toward SME education and training. Category 1, Category 4, and Category 5 saw the most significant changes based on the original outline (Fig. 8.4 highlighted entries).

Changes in Category 1, General, were primarily focused on more precise definition of the area of application of the learning object. Additional elements, modeled from ARIADNE metadata version 3.0 [48], such as 1.9: Discipline; 1.10: Subdiscipline; 1.11: MainConcept; 1.12: MainConceptSyn; and 1.13: OtherConcepts, were added. Changes in Category 4, Technical, referred to providing a better technical definition of the requirements of the learning object, with extensions in 4.4: Requirement, and several subelements of 4.4, and with 4.8: Material Description being added. The most significant change was in Category 5, Education, with the proposed addition of 5.12: TrainingActivity; 5.12.1: DeliveryMethod; 5.12.2: Time dependence; 5.12.3: Loc dependence; 5.13: Evaluation; 5.13.1: Assessment; 5.13.2: Method; 5.13.3: Number; 5.14: Registration; 5.15: Pre-requisite; 5.16: Qualification; 5.17: Pedagogy; and 5.18: Course-Level—in order to better classify the educational or pedagogic characteristics of the learning object. Much of the change in Category 5, Education, was modeled on proposed changes to metadata schema by both the CUBER [49] and GEMSTONES [50] metadata projects.

1 General
    1.1 Identifier
        1.1.1   Catalog
        1.1.2   Entry
    1.2 Title
    1.3 Language
    1.4 Description
    1.5 Keyword
    1.6 Coverage
    1.7 Structure
    1.8 Aggregation Level
    1.9 Discipline
    1.10 SubDiscipline
    1.11 MainConcept
    1.12 MainConceptSyn
    1.13 OtherConcepts

2 LifeCycle
    2.1 Version
    2.2 Status
    2.3 Contribute
        2.3.1 Role
        2.3.2 Entity
        2.3.3 Date
    2.4 ValidPeriod
        2.4.1 Begin
        2.4.2 End
        2.4.3 Action

3 Meta-Metadata
    3.1 Identifier
        3.1.1 Catalog
        3.1.2 Entry
    3.2 Contribute
        3.2.1 Role
        3.2.2 Entity
        3.2.3 Date
    3.3 Metadata Schema
    3.4 Language

4 Technical
    4.1 Format
    4.2 Size
    4.3 Location
    4.4 Requirements
        4.4.1 OrComposite
            4.4.1.1 Type
            4.4.1.2 Name
            4.4.1.3 Minimum Version
            4.4.1.4 Maximum Version
    4.5 Installation Remarks
    4.6 Other Platform Requirements
    4.7 Duration
    4.8 Material_Description

5 Educational
    5.1 Interactivity Type
    5.2 Learning Resource Type
    5.3 Interactivity Level
    5.4 Semantic Density
    5.5 Intended and user role
    5.6 Context
    5.7 Typical Age Range
    5.8 Difficulty
    5.9 Typical Learning Time
    5.10 Description
    5.11 Language
    5.12 TrainingActivity
        5.12.1 DeliveryMethod
        5.12.2 Time_dependance
        5.12.3 Loc_dependance
    5.13 Evaluation
    5.14 Registration
    5.15 Prerequisites
    5.16 Qualification
    5.17 Pedagogy

6 Rights
    6.1 Cost
    6.2 Copyright and Other Restrictions
    6.3 Description

7 Relation
    7.1 Kind
    7.2 Resource
        7.2.1 Identifier
            7.2.1.1 Catalog
            7.2.1.2 Entry
        7.2.2 Description
    7.3 Concatenation
        7.3.1 Position
        7.3.2 Associations

8 Annotation
    8.1 Entity
    8.2 Date
    8.3 Description

9 Classification
    9.1 Purpose
    9.2 TexonPath
        9.2.1 Source
        9.2.2 Taxon
            9.2.2.1 Id
            9.2.2.2 Entry
    9.3 Description
    9.4 Keyword

FIGURE 8.4. Extended LOM metadata overview model.

Next there were also a number of proposed variations in classification, or ontology, from that described in the LOM draft standard. To accommodate increased granularity six aggregation levels were defined, as compared to four in LOM version 1.0. The proposed levels were level 0, Fragment; level 1, Topic; level 2, Lesson; level 3, Module; level 4, Course; and level 5, Curriculum. The aggregation levels were used to describe the differences between study elements within an SME learning environment. There were a number of further proposed changes in ontology and vocabulary from that in LOM v1.0, in order that the semantics of the SME environment more accurately reflect the delivery objectives of the SME learning management program.

8.7.3 Taxonomy Models and Ontology

The LOM did not offer an adequate level of metadata coverage for the population of the SME repository. The LOM was lacking in its definition of aggregation levels, or granularity. The associated level of the LOM did not sufficiently define a SME learning object. The educational requirements of the learning objects were not met. There was a need for finer detail in relation to the training activity of the learning object, as well as the evaluation and prerequisites associated with any given learning object. The overall general information related to the learning object was unclear with regard to discipline and concepts tied to a learning object. The solution was to extend the LOM to meet the needs of the SMEs. All the metadata categories, metadata data elements, and subelements adopted from LOM were used as such; they were not changed because of the notes of conformance in LOM.

The IEEE LOM definition of a learning object allows for an extremely wide variety of granularities. This means that a learning object could be a picture of the Mona Lisa, a document on the Mona Lisa (that includes the picture), a course module on da Vinci, a complete course on art history, or even a 4-year master curriculum on Western culture.

In one sense, this is appropriate, as there are a number of common themes to content learning objects of all sizes. In another sense, though, this vagueness is problematic, as it is clear that authoring, deploying and repurposing are affected by the granularity of the learning object.

To address this problem, a learning object taxonomy was developed to identify the different kinds of learning objects and their constituent parts (Fig. 8.5):

- Fragments are the smallest level in this model. These elements reside at a pure data level. Examples include a single sentence or paragraph, illustration, animation, etc.
- Topics are the next level of granularity. This refers to a single learning objective and constitutes 10 to 15 minutes of learning. Fragments are grouped together to form topics.
- Lessons are next in the taxonomy. Lessons consist of topics grouped together with additional tests or assessments areas included, as well as objectives, overviews, summary, prerequisites, etc. [51]. This other content is not seen as reusable in the

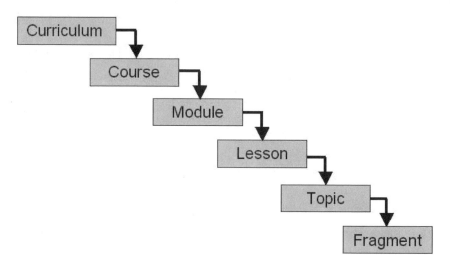

FIGURE 8.5. SME taxonomy model.

strictest sense as it was viewed as being focused on a specific thread or learning concept.

- Modules are a set of lessons that were focused on one study or subject area.
- Courses consist of coherent modules aggregated together.
- Curriculum was a number of courses to provide competence at a designated level in an occupation or profession.

Topics contain fragments. Lessons contain topics. Modules consist of lessons, and courses are made up of separate modules. Curriculum contains courses. The smaller level of granularity in this taxonomy is essential, as research showed that repurposing can only be accommodated by explicitly identifying the information objects and the fragments they contain [13].

CISCO [52] and IMS [17] used tried-and-tested ideas from Open and Distance Learning [53] to determine how to package or collect learning objects together. The smallest unit is a reusable information object (RIO) [54]. It develops a single objective only. CISCO defines each RIO as either being a concept, fact, process, principle, or procedure [52]. Content items and practices (learning activities) are presented to the learner to support that objective. The smallest stand-alone unit is a reusable learning object (RLO), a collection of seven plus-or-minus two RIOs grouped together to teach a common job/task based on a single learning objective. To make the collection of RIOs into a complete learning experience or "lesson," an overview, summary, and assessment are added to the package. The overview is used to introduce the RLO and act as an advanced organizer for the learner by listing the objective, outline, and job-based scenario for this "lesson." The summary is used to conclude the RLO and tie the scenario and objectives covered in each RIO together. It also offers a suggested course of action for learners to broaden their knowledge and skills in this area. Finally, the summary is a transition between the RIOs and the final assessment. This structure is drawn directly from ODL.

Comparing the CISCO concept with our SME model in Figure 8.5, the aggregation-level "topic" is equivalent to RIO, and "lesson" is equivalent to the RLO. Any of the higher levels of learning content are seen as a combination of lower material. Additional fields were required to store the summary, outline, aims, objectives, prerequisites, and other fields relating to courses and curricula, but this information was not seen as reusable in the strictest sense as it documented a focus on a specific area only.

A number of issues needed to be better understood if large-scale LO (re)use was to become a reality isues such as aggregation and the notion of design for reuse.

Traditionally, authoring tools mainly support the process of authoring from three points of departure:

- A blank document that needs to be "filled" with content, where the structure of the LO is defined during the elaboration of that content;
- A template that needs to be instantiated, where the structure of the LO is defined a priority;
- An existing LO that is edited and modified in the process of authoring, and then typically saved as a new LO.

The main idea, however, was that learning objects were created by selecting fragments from a repository, usually with the significant assistance of metadata and profiles to do so. These learning objects were then assembled into a new learning object. This was referred to as authoring by aggregation [13].

This new learning object, as it provided new context for the learning, may need to provide "glue" that takes the learner from one learning object to another. A simple example of this kind of facility is the way that presentation authoring tools (like Microsoft Powerpoint, SliTeX, etc.) allow for existing slides to be included in new presentations and then add automatically "next" and "previous" transitions between those slides. More sophisticated "glue" would enable the author of the aggregated learning objects to include transitional material (for example, "In this section, the content will show the concept of inertia that was introduced in Chapter X"), so as to give guidance to the learner on how the components fit together in the aggregate. This kind of "glue" is dealt with by "sequencing" specifications that enable the definition of learning paths. These learning paths are themselves discrete learning objects and as such can be stored separately, modified independenly of the content, reused, AND of course also have their own associated metadata to aid with discovery, search, and retrieval.

Some issues that needed to be taken into consideration when "designing for reuse":

- Ease of modification: The fragments used often depended on the context, and they should be consistent within a given context. The content should be designed in such a way that it becomes easy to alter the information in one fragment, thus producing a new fragment, accessible to all.

- Easily replaced labels: A related issue is that of textual labels in visual material; it should be simple to replace such labels with alternatives, for instance in a different language, or using an alternative vocabulary.
- Adaptive look and feel: Methods need to be developed for adapting the look and feel of content. When different learning objects are aggregated together, the result should not look like a collection of learning objects from different origins. One could think of aggregation tools that allow the author to apply a "design template" to impose a specific look and feel on the resulting aggregate.
- Fragment integration: Fragments within the current repository need to integrate with other fragments with little trouble. This integration can be viewed in the form of a sequential listing of fragments, or within a higher level of granularity. A sequential listing produces a sequence of fragments that form a detailed piece of learning. The higher level of granularity, at a topic level, requires fragments to integrate together to form a more substantial piece of learning content.

It was necessary to have a greater level of granularity that that specified in the LOM. An increase in the level of granularity increased the chance of reusability of learning objects, or pieces of learning objects, and also permitted easier structuring of the learning content. The reusable learning material is below the LO level, and these fragments have little to no context, no formatting, and no specific style. Style and context are added to a learning object via combinations of the design, the learning paths, and/or the presentation layers with typical style sheets [13].

In recent years the development of ontologies—explicit formal specifications of the terms in the domain and relations among them [55]—has been moving from the realm of artificial intelligence laboratories to the desktops of domain experts. An ontology defines a common vocabulary for researchers who need to share information in a domain. It includes machine-interpretable definitions of basic concepts in the domain and relations among them [56].

An ontology development process consists of seven steps [57]:

1. Specification: What is the goal of the ontology? What is relevant to fulfill the goal? What needs to be modeled, and what types of granularity are useful?
2. Knowledge acquisition: Collect the information based on the available documents in different data sources. Put this information into a hierarchy structure with respect to the ontology scope. This step occurs in parallel with the specification step.
3. Conceptualization: Concepts in the ontology should be close to objects (physical or logical) and relationships in the related domain. Try to get definition for your ontology from other ontologies.
4. Integration: Integrate the ontology with another ontology if applicable.
5. Implementation: Define the ontology components through an ontology definition language in two stages:
   - Informal stage: sketch the ontology using either natural language descriptions or some diagram techniques.
   - Formal stage: ontology is encoded in a formal knowledge representation language, that is machine computable.

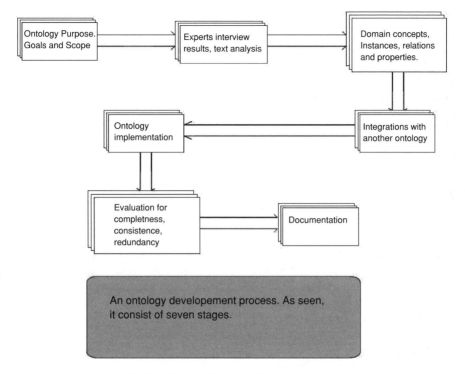

FIGURE 8.6. Ontology development process.

6. Evaluation: Consists of checking for completeness and consistence and avoiding redundancy.
7. Documentation: Produce clear informal and formal documentation. Make the ontology understandable by everyone. An ontology that cannot be understood will not be used.

A number of ontology development tools currently exist; notable among these are Protégé [58], Oiled [59], OntoEdit [60], OntoLingua [61], and WebODE [62].

Most of the tools provide an integrated environment to build and edit ontologies, check for errors and inconsistencies, browse multiple ontologies, and share and reuse existing data by establishing mappings among different ontological entities. However, these tools are influenced by traditional knowledge repository–based ontology engineering methodologies, with steep learning curves, making it cumbersome to use for casual Web ontology development.

The process of ontology development was seen to be an iterative one. Any data elements or subdata elements that were altered or introduced to extend the existing LOMv1.0 metadata schema required an ontology. The ontology defined the terms associated with each data element in the schema. Following from this, cataloging of learning objects within the repository was easier and automated in places. Beyond that, the requirement for greater granularity, and the definition of learning objects

in an SME context required that a revised ontology be implemented for existing
LOM elements.

Therefore, a new or extended ontology was required for the additional elements
added to the schema, as shown in Figure 8.4. Problems arose within the ontology
definitions. Redefining the ontology to cater to the additional new elements and
expanding existing data element ontology proved difficult. Achieving an unam-
biguous ontology was not feasible, and therefore automatic metadata generation
was impossible. The fast-paced evolution of the e-learning standards made extension of the LOMv1.0 difficult, as changes in the draft version meant upgrading the
SME schema to the latest release and starting again. It was decided to work from
the opposite end of the scale and approach this problem with a cut-down version
of the LOM as opposed to an extended version of the LOM.

8.7.4 Final Schema of Our System

The initial base schema resulted in additional fields being added to the metadata
categories. The drawback of this was that the user, upon uploading content to the
repository, was required to insert a lot of information about the learning object.
We strongly believed that the users should not have to do this—it should be an
automated process or as automated as is humanly possible [63]. Being unable to
produce an automated form-filling process for the schema was one of its failings.
An ambiguous ontology restricted this automation and resulted in the rejection of
this schema as a final version.

An alternative schema, based on the LOMv1.0, was required. The goal was to
have the minimal number of fields necessary to adequately describe all learning
objects within the central repository. The ADL net [40] listed tables with a variation
of the LOM metadata content, and SCORM listed their categories and elements and
weighted them with regard to the different levels of granularity. SCORM uses three
levels of granularity to define its learning objects: assets, sharable content objects
(SCOs), and content aggregation models. Assets within the SCORM represented
fragments from a SMEs point of view. SCOs mapped to topics within the levels
of aggregation, and everything else was seen as a form of content aggregation.

Initially separate schemas were drafted to accommodate the metadata associated
with fragment level and topic level content, as draft no-naming conventions were
associated with them. Then an aggregation level data element was inserted into
the schema, allowing for the combination of schema to result in a final schema
version for the SME metadata. This allowed for the storage of all metadata under the one schema. The elements chosen from the original LOM are shown in
Figure 8.7.

The final schema was still standards compliant, and other management systems
could access the repositories and search for content based on the metadata information. Figure 8.7 shows the final schema in relation to the LOM v1.0. The
required data elements are highlighted in red. This solution permitted an 80 percent
automated-tagging process, thus alleviating authors from the necessity of entering
known information into the meta-tagging form. The metadata schema allowed for

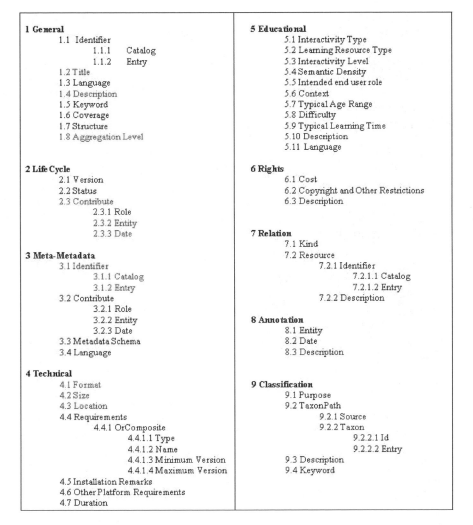

1 General	5 Educational
1.1 Identifier	5.1 Interactivity Type
1.1.1 Catalog	5.2 Learning Resource Type
1.1.2 Entry	5.3 Interactivity Level
1.2 Title	5.4 Semantic Density
1.3 Language	5.5 Intended end user role
1.4 Description	5.6 Context
1.5 Keyword	5.7 Typical Age Range
1.6 Coverage	5.8 Difficulty
1.7 Structure	5.9 Typical Learning Time
1.8 Aggregation Level	5.10 Description
	5.11 Language
2 Life Cycle	**6 Rights**
2.1 Version	6.1 Cost
2.2 Status	6.2 Copyright and Other Restrictions
2.3 Contribute	6.3 Description
2.3.1 Role	
2.3.2 Entity	**7 Relation**
2.3.3 Date	7.1 Kind
	7.2 Resource
3 Meta-Metadata	7.2.1 Identifier
3.1 Identifier	7.2.1.1 Catalog
3.1.1 Catalog	7.2.1.2 Entry
3.1.2 Entry	7.2.2 Description
3.2 Contribute	
3.2.1 Role	**8 Annotation**
3.2.2 Entity	8.1 Entity
3.2.3 Date	8.2 Date
3.3 Metadata Schema	8.3 Description
3.4 Language	
	9 Classification
4 Technical	9.1 Purpose
4.1 Format	9.2 TaxonPath
4.2 Size	9.2.1 Source
4.3 Location	9.2.2 Taxon
4.4 Requirements	9.2.2.1 Id
4.4.1 OrComposite	9.2.2.2 Entry
4.4.1.1 Type	9.3 Description
4.4.1.2 Name	9.4 Keyword
4.4.1.3 Minimum Version	
4.4.1.4 Maximum Version	
4.5 Installation Remarks	
4.6 Other Platform Requirements	
4.7 Duration	

FIGURE 8.7. Final schema version for SME based on LOM v1.0.

the population of the SME database and central repository with learning content and objects.

8.8 The Phoenix System

The system that was designed built and tested was called Phoenix, an approximate acronym for PHp Enabled Environment Integrated with XML. It comprised a set of intuitive graphic user interfaces that permitted nontechnical experts to convert electronic content into learning objects and sequence these learning objects into an instructionally sound piece of learning. The objectives of the system were:

- To provide the standard features of any learning content management system
- To facilitate the decomposition of electronic material into smaller pieces of learning termed learning objects
- To dynamically display this content to the end user upon request
- To sequence the learning objects into instructionally sound learning content.

The standard features of any learning management systems exist in Phoenix and aid in the overall functionality of the tool [64,65]. These standard features are necessary for Phoenix to operate properly. For example, in order for the sequence process to work, the search function is required to locate the learning objects that will be utilized in the sequencing procedure.

Standard features include:

1. Access-related features like login and logout, and registration for a new course.
2. Administrative features like modifying user details on the system and maintaining databases.
3. Taking a course and continuing an existing course are basic student requirements.
4. Search capabilities were necessary for the learner, as well as the author, to perform well.

In more detail:

- Users: A definition of the users of the system was required in order to determine what functionality was needed to support them. The users were the learner, the author, and the administrator.
- Login: The users on the system were required to login before accessing any of the material on the Web site. Once users logged in successfully, the functionality of the system was available to them, depending on their access level.
- Logout: If the user closed the browser window, the session was automatically closed and the user was logged out. The session could time-out from inactivity, and the user was prompted to log in again. This was added as a security feature of the tool.
- Search: This function was divided into two sections. The first section was a browse scenario. Authors could browse the content in the repository and select individual fragments. The other option was to search for a specific piece of content. This functionality was to support authors in the finding of learning objects.
- Registration: Learners on the system could register for a new course and, once accepted, could commence taking the course.
- Take a course: After learners logged in, they were presented with the option to continue with an existing course that was partially completed or register for a new course.

- Maintain databases: The administrator on the system maintained the databases and provided support for the authors and learners using the system.

8.8.1 Implementing Phoenix

The best implementation option for possible future extensions or modification was an open-source one. To create a system that was adaptable and extendable, the source code needed to be available so that source code editing could include new system features. Open-source software (OSS), also offered significant cost, reliability, and support advantages that are attractive to SMEs. The Phoenix system consists of several layers that work together to form the overall system. These layers include the base layer, the search layer, the dynamic delivery layer, and the management layer. A base layer requires the following features:

- An operating system capable of running the server and handling at least a database server, a Web server, and a mail server.
- A stable Web server that was capable of handling multiple requests for numerous users.
- A database server to handle the metadata, and store the information pertaining to the users accessing the system. Content stored locally on dynamically created folders based on the users accounts.
- A scripting language that was capable of interacting easily with the Web server as well as the database server and operating system. It should be robust and have fast access times based on execution of code and be easily portable to other systems (for backing up systems or mirroring sites to disperse the server load).

Our final system was based on the established LAMP technology: Linux (operating system), Apache (Web server), MySQL (database server) and PHP (scripting language) [66].

The search layer of Phoenix divides into a browsing process and a searching process. The browse permits an author to browse through the content in the repository; published files in the repository are displayed for the author to see. Anything suitable can be selected and aggregated by the LO being authored.

Alternatively, authors may search the metadata for a specific learning object under headings determined by the metadata schema design and select relevant pieces of learning for use within a learning object. This search accesses all levels of granularity.

The administrative layer, accessed through a Web interface, allows administrators to perform two main tasks: authorize new users and change the user access levels. Administrators may also activate and deactivate accounts.

Dynamic delivery is an important feature of any learning management system. E-learning is designed with just-in-time or just-enough learning in mind. Users take courses at their own speed or access material on-line for a specific answer or piece of information. Metadata and standards influence the dynamic delivery of content. The tagging process and storage of the learning objects in a central repository permit the reusability of the content. Reuse of the learning objects assists in the dynamic delivery process.

8.9 Phoenix System Architecture and Functionality

Phoenix was required to facilitate the creation, storage, and publishing of content by nontechnical users, to include LO sequencing into topics and courses and the dynamic delivery of learning content. The technical layers, that is, the Web server, the database server, the operating system, etc., needed to integrate with current IT environments, without requiring the purchase of additional hardware and software. Finally the system needed to support the administration of all users [67].

Each element of the LAMP acronym provided an essential layer of functionality (Fig. 8.8):

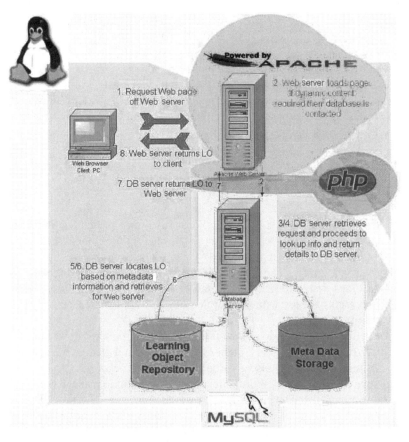

FIGURE 8.8. Phoenix overall structure based on LAMP technology.

- Linux is the operating system. Linux has grown into a reliable operating system that now gets corporate support from start-ups like Red Hat and big companies like IBM.
- Apache is the Web server, the world's most-used Web server. It is controlled by a group called the Apache Software Foundation and has also been embedded in commercial products like IBM WebSphere.
- MySQL is the DBMS (database management system). The MySQL database server is the world's most popular open-source database. With more than five million active installations, MySQL has quickly become the core of many high-volume, business-critical applications. Customers such as Yahoo!, Google, Cisco, Sabre Holdings, HP, and NASA are realizing significant cost savings by using MySQL's high-performance, reliable database management software to power large Web sites, business-critical enterprise applications, and packaged software applications [68];
- PHP is an object-oriented web scripting language. It's similar to Java Server Pages (JSP) and Microsoft Active Server Pages (ASP). PHP is another Web-scripting technology that mixes HyperText Markup Language display code with programming instructions.

8.9.1 Unique Features for the SMEs

Several unique elements were coded and implemented in Phoenix specifically for SMEs. They respond to the recognition that in SMEs and other small-scale users, content authoring and aggregation are likely to be carried out by people who are not trained educators These elements included an upload tool, an authoring section, and an aggregation environment. Learning material can be uploaded as either a fragment or a topic. A fragment, the lowest level of granularity, consists of raw data elements, images, text, movie clips, etc. Fragments are selected from elsewhere on the PC or network and submitted to Phoenix. The system determines if the material is valid: the file size is not zero bytes, the file has an acceptable format, and the file name is not already used or exists already in the database.

If all is OK, the file is stored in the repository and the author is asked to fill in the metadata form (Fig. 8.9). Meeting our requirement for minimum form filling, 80% of the fields are automatically completed. The author only needs to supply the remaining 20%. The author is shown a preview to verify that the correct material is being uploaded.

Assembling fragments into topics is done by building a composite knowledge object (CKO) (Fig. 8.10). Again a user-friendly form-filling format is used. The form permits the insertion of content, text, audio, images, etc., between or around fragments. It also allows existing topics to be edited to form new ones—a very useful reuse feature for authors.

The CKO tool interrogates the metadata database and displays any fragments that the author calls up. The necessary additional metadata fields are part of the form. The CKO creation process uses an open-source what-you-see-is-what-you-get

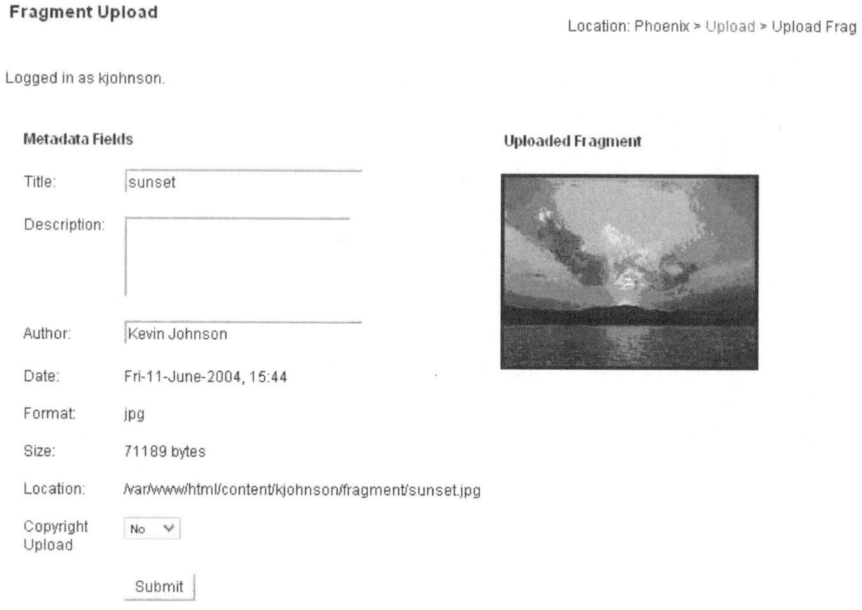

Fragment Upload

Logged in as kjohnson.

Metadata Fields   **Uploaded Fragment**

Title: sunset

Description:

Author: Kevin Johnson

Date: Fri-11-June-2004, 15:44

Format: jpg

Size: 71189 bytes

Location: /var/www/html/content/kjohnson/fragment/sunset.jpg

Copyright   No ∨
Upload

                Submit

FIGURE 8.9. Upload fragment screenshot.

(WYSIWYG) on-line HTML editor called, solmetra PHP asp.net wysiwyg (SPAW)[1] [69]. Through SPAW authors can edit and reedit a topic until satisfied it is ready for publishing.

This aggregation tool permits the sequencing of fragments to form topics, topics to form courses, and so on. Adding a new topic to the system requires the execution of five steps. The first step creates the topic name, and description, the author, creation date, size, and aggregation level are autogenerated. The author determined the copyright issue. Next, fragments are chosen from the central repository. The author must hold the copyright or the fragments must be copyright free and they must be fragments (not some higher level of aggregation). The author has an option to view fragments in a pop-up window (Fig. 8.11).

Step 3 involves the ordering of the selected fragments, the author chooses the first fragment to be displayed followed by the second fragment and so on. Error checking ensures the sequence's uniqueness.

Step 4 verifies step 3 and enables returning to previous steps for re-authoring again. Error checking verifies uniqueness.

Step 5 creates an XML file and its storage in the central repository. The XML holds the ID of all the fragments used within a given topic and the sequencing. This approach enables dynamic delivery to learners. When a learner requests a given topic, the XML is interrogated and the content dynamically gathered and delivered.

The XML file is created in accordance with the IMS simple sequencing specification [38] and is termed a manifest file (Fig. 8.12). A manifest also enables

---

[1] S=solmetra, P=PHP, A=ASP.NET, W=WYSIWYG

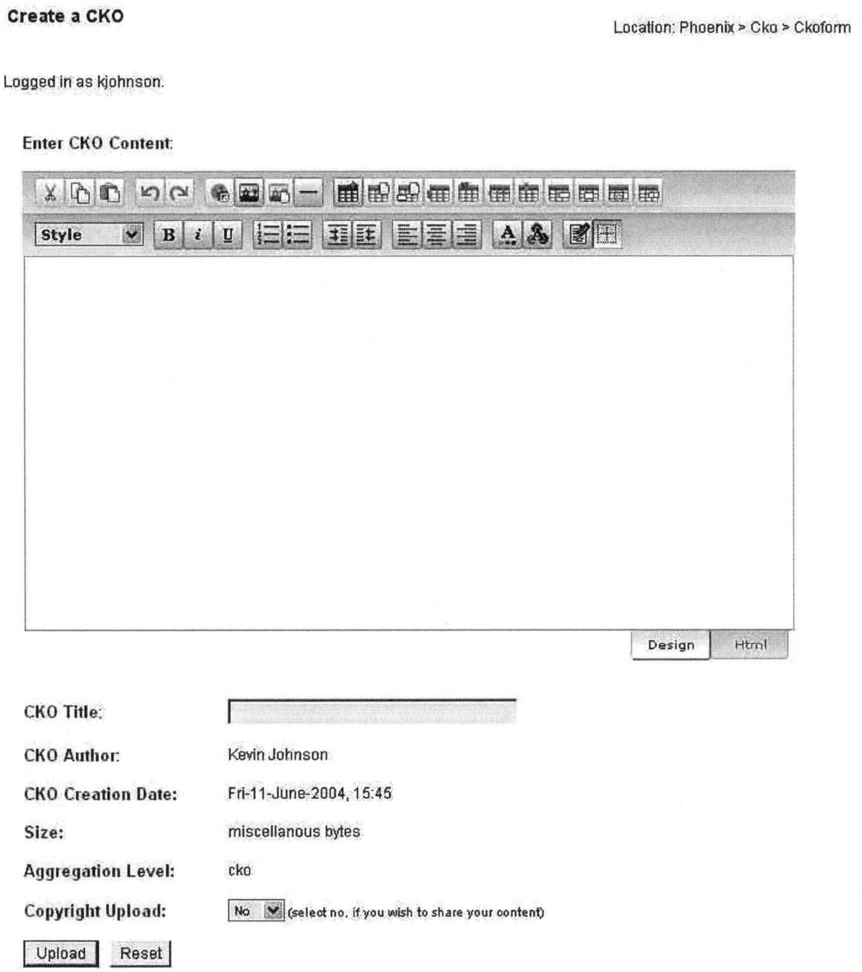
Create a CKO
Location: Phoenix > Cko > Ckoform
Logged in as kjohnson.
Enter CKO Content:
Style
Design
Html
CKO Title:
CKO Author:
Kevin Johnson
CKO Creation Date:
Fri-11-June-2004, 15:45
Size:
miscellanous bytes
Aggregation Level:
cko
Copyright Upload:
No
(select no, if you wish to share your content)
Upload
Reset

FIGURE 8.10. Composite knowledge object (CKO) editor within Phoenix.

interoperability. If a topic is to be exported, its XML file is scanned and the fragments referenced are collected, packaged, and compressed into a single file ready for transport, in conformance with the IMS content packaging specification [17, 70]. Interoperability of standards permits this process to execute successfully.

8.10 Delivery, Evaluation, and Results

The Phoenix tool was designed to be rapidly adaptable to the needs of any specific learning environment. Its open-source nature enables this. Some might say that the dotLRN [71] system is very similar to the Phoenix system, but it was necessary to create our own system for several reasons. Foremost of these included being able to

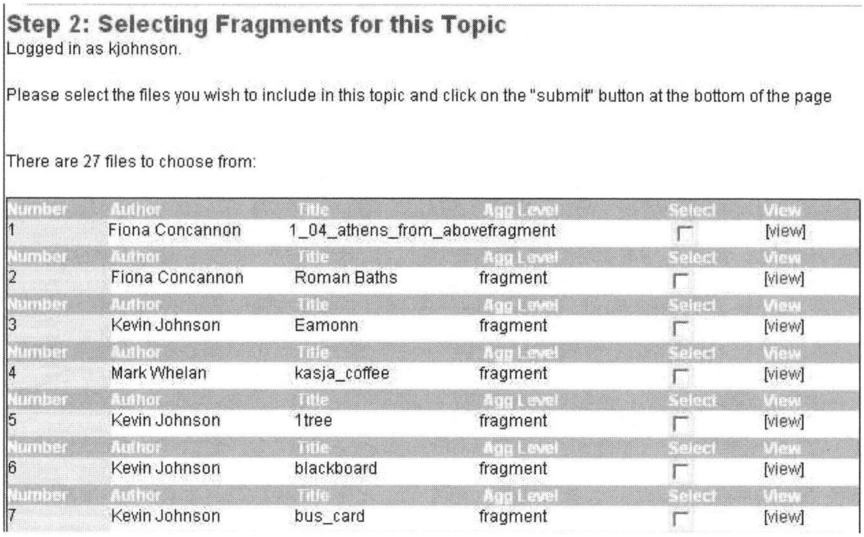

Step 2: Selecting Fragments for this Topic
Logged in as kjohnson.

Please select the files you wish to include in this topic and click on the "submit" button at the bottom of the page

There are 27 files to choose from:

Number	Author	Title	Agg Level	Select	View
1	Fiona Concannon	1_04_athens_from_abovefragment		☐	[view]
Number	Author	Title	Agg Level	Select	View
2	Fiona Concannon	Roman Baths	fragment	☐	[view]
Number	Author	Title	Agg Level	Select	View
3	Kevin Johnson	Eamonn	fragment	☐	[view]
Number	Author	Title	Agg Level	Select	View
4	Mark Whelan	kasja_coffee	fragment	☐	[view]
Number	Author	Title	Agg Level	Select	View
5	Kevin Johnson	1tree	fragment	☐	[view]
Number	Author	Title	Agg Level	Select	View
6	Kevin Johnson	blackboard	fragment	☐	[view]
Number	Author	Title	Agg Level	Select	View
7	Kevin Johnson	bus_card	fragment	☐	[view]

FIGURE 8.11. Selection process within the Phoenix environment.

implement the above schema that resulted from the study of the needs of the SMEs. While the dotLRN is built on open-source technology also, the level of understand and technology savvy required to operate and maintain the system is higher than that of a standard LAMP build. The code associated with dotLRN is also harder to manipulate and understand as opposed to PHP and MySQL. Our initial testing of the open-source concept was carried out in an on-campus university environment, as opposed to within an SME, so as to enable better monitoring and control.

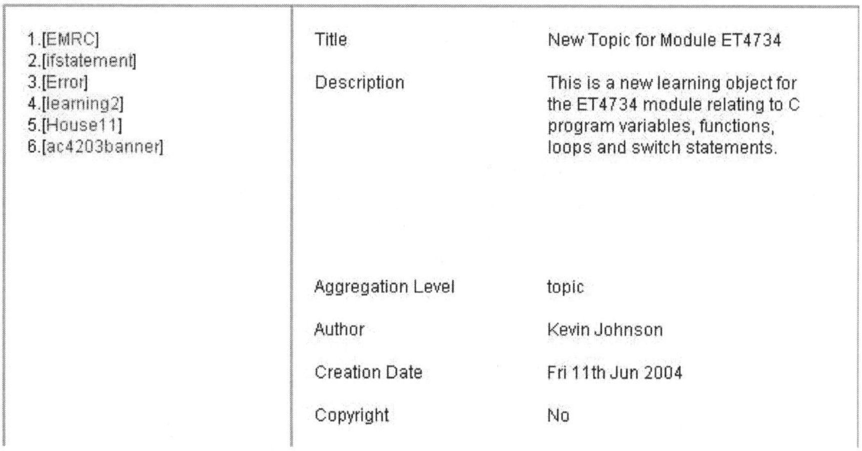

1.[EMRC] 2.[ifstatement] 3.[Error] 4.[learning2] 5.[House11] 6.[ac4203banner]	Title	New Topic for Module ET4734
	Description	This is a new learning object for the ET4734 module relating to C program variables, functions, loops and switch statements.
	Aggregation Level	topic
	Author	Kevin Johnson
	Creation Date	Fri 11th Jun 2004
	Copyright	No

FIGURE 8.12. XML-based output from the Phoenix system.

We chose a course based on the constructivist cognitive apprenticeship model with learners who were new to e-learning. In the cognitive apprenticeship model, parallels are made with the teaching tradition of apprenticeship and schooling. Alan Collins, John Seely Brown, and Ann Holum [73] propose that students learn best when the thinking is made visible. Traditional apprenticeship focuses on the combination of observation, coaching, and scaffolding. Our aim was to imitate this successful form of learning in the more controllable university environment. The design used the apprenticeship model through adaptive learning guides posing as superheroes. The superhero related his/her power or weakness to a creative writing technique and thus serves, as both a guide and a mnemonic device.

Two student groups were phased sequentially. The Phoenix-based system was adapted to meet specific course needs in each of these phases. Adaptations were carried out by code modification of the base system, access to the source code being enabled by the open-source nature of Phoenix.

The student group in Phase One consisted of 17 students studying a course in electronic production over one semester. Their comments and reactions were solicited by email and by on-line questionnaires (Fig. 8.13).

In phase one most students were satisfied with the LMS and the on-line course. They suggested the following:

- Increased file size for uploading assignments
- More sample assignments and links to relevant Web sites
- More comments on corrected assignments
- Email notification to lecturer/TA when assignments have been uploaded
- Better access to information on the assignment titles

The exact nature of these suggestions is not of direct importance, but they illustrate areas for adaptation or improvement in the system to better meet the

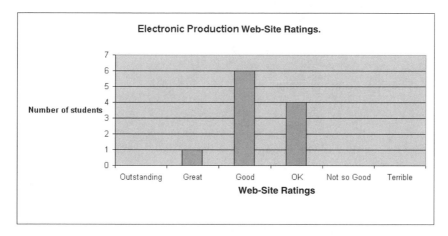

FIGURE 8.13. Phase one feedback information.

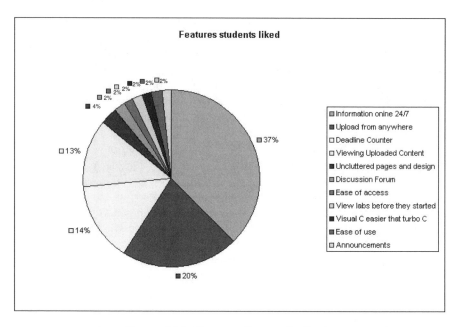

Features students liked

- Information onine 24/7
- Upload from anywhere
- Deadline Counter
- Viewing Uploaded Content
- Uncluttered pages and design
- Discussion Forum
- Ease of access
- View labs before they started
- Visual C easier that turbo C
- Ease of use
- Announcements

37%
20%
14%
13%
4%
2%
2%
2%
2%
2%
2%

FIGURE 8.14. Phase two features feedback.

needs of the learners. The information gathered provided a means to create further evolution of the code and extend the functionality of the tool to better suit the requirements of the learners and the author [72]. For example, a deadline counter was added to let students know by when assignments must be uploaded.

In phase two, 50 students following a different course, again over a semester, in general approved of this style of learning and the delivery approach. They liked having access to the notes on-line anytime, anywhere, liked that labs could be uploaded from anywhere, liked the new deadline counter feature, and liked the upload viewer (a feature that was added partway through the semester, again illustrating the power of the use of open source code) (Fig. 8.14).

The students in phase two had many more suggestions for additional or improved features (Fig. 8.15).

Although much of the student feedback in both phases related to their impressions of this style of learning and would apply to almost any LMS/LCMS, we found the rapid adaptability afforded by direct access to the code of Phoenix a uniquely advantageous feature. It enabled us to add desired new functionality rapidly and accurately, and indicated that tailoring to the needs of specific SMEs would be practical. We set out to create a system that was adaptable, flexible, extensible, and inexpensive that met the needs of the learners. Our test confirmed we have achieved this. Access to the source code permitted the numerous updates to the system, resulting in improved variants of the Phoenix tool. The open-source choice justified itself. Phoenix proved rapidly adaptable to different learning scenarios and was responsive to the needs of both novice and the more experienced users—both teachers and learners. The basic system was robust and responsive.

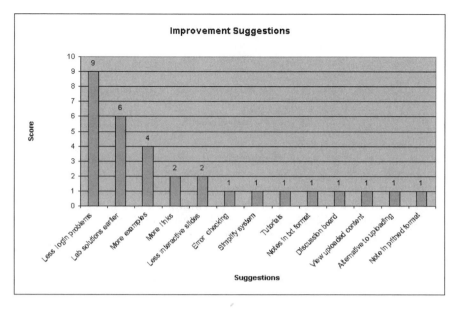

FIGURE 8.15. Phase two improvement suggestions.

8.11 Conclusion

The main task we undertook was to make an LCMS with an embedded e-learning content creation tool for use by nonexpert authors and suitable for use in SME or other small-scale situations. The resulting Phoenix system was based on a novel metadata schema with clearly defined ontology focused on an implementation using reusable and interoperable e-learning learning objects. It supports the creation of instructionally sound e-learning content, and provides the functionality to aggregate and sequence this content into larger learning structures. The tool's attributes included being flexible, adaptable, customisable, standards compliant, using reusable learning objects, and inexpensive.

The main achievements include:

1. A successful standards-based interoperable compliant metadata set permitting the search and retrieval of any learning objects within the repository
2. An operational open source–based implementation successfully tested for functionality and robustness on two separate groups of learners over a one-year period
3. An adaptable learning system open to future modifications. These separate testing stages highlight the extensibility and adaptability of the system to meet the users' requirements and cater to their needs.

Phoenix encompasses the following attributes: flexible, adaptive, customizable, standards compliant, uses re-usable LOs, and low cost, making it ideal for its intended use in small companies or other small-scale users. Additional tools have subsequently been added to include a training or learning needs analysis phase.

References

1. Hokanson, B., Hooper, S. (2000) *Computers as cognitive media: the potential of computers in educations.* Computers in Human Behaviour, 16(5):537–552.
2. SCORM. http://www.adlnet.org/.
3. IEEE. (2002) IEEE LOM Version 1, final draft. http://ltsc.ieee.org/wg12/files/LOM_1484_12_1_v1_Final_Draft.pdf.
4. IMS. (2001) http://www.imsproject.org.
5. WebCT. (1997) WebCT—e-learning solutions for higher education. http://www.webct.com.
6. Blackboard. (1997) Blackboard Software Company. http://www.blackboard.com.
7. TopClass. (1995) TopClass Computer Systems. http://www.wbtsystems.com.
8. Docent Docent Software Company. http://www.docent.com.
9. TrainerSoft TrainerSoft Company. http://www.trainersoft.com.
10. Fallon, C., Brown, S. (2003) *e-Learning Standards: A Guide to Purchasing, Developing and Deploying Standards—Conformant e-Learning.* Boca Raton, Florida: St. Lucie Press.
11. Avaltus. (2000) http://www.avaltus.com/.
12. Brahler, C.J., Peterson, N.S., Johnson, E.C. (1999) *Developing on-line learning materials for higher education: An overview of current issues.* Educational Technology and Society, 2(2):42–54.
13. Duval, E., Hodgins, W. (2003) *A LOM research agenda.* In: *WWW2003.* Budapest, Hungary.
14. Rust, G., Bide, M. (2000) The "indecs" metadata framework: principles, model and data dictionary. http://www.indecs.org/pdf/framework.pdf. Indecs Framework Ltd in 2000.
15. Sciore, E., Siegel, M., Rosenthal, A. (1994) *Using semantic values to facilitate interoperability among heterogeneous information systems.* ACM Transactions on Database Systems (TODS), 19(2):254–290.
16. Drew, P., et al. (1993) *Report of the workshop on semantic heterogeneity and interoperation in multidatabase systems.* ACM Sigmod Record, 22(3):47–56.
17. IEEE. (1999) Institute of Electrical and Electronic Engineers. http://www.ieee.org/portal/index.jsp?pageID=corp_level1&path=about/whatis&file=index.xml&xsl=generic.xsl.
18. AICC. (1988) http://www.aicc.org/.
19. ARIADNE. (2001) European ARIADNE Project. http://www.ariadne-eu.org.
20. UCGIS. (1998) University Consortium for Geographic Information Science (UCGIS) Research Priority White Papers—Paper 5: Interoperability of Geographic Information. http://www.ncgia.ucsb.edu/other/ucgis/research_priorities/paper5.html.
21. Wiley, D.A. (2000) *Learning object design and sequencing theory.* In: *Instructional Psychology and Technology Department.* Provo City, UT: Brigham Young University, p. 142.
22. Tannenbaum, A. (1991) *Computer Networks*, 2nd ed. New York: Prentice-Hall.
23. Padrick, N. (2003) *Information you can use: A Data Mart Primer.* Solutions Journal, 9(2):23–27.
24. Dushay, N. (2002) *Localising experience of digital content via structural metadata.* In: *International Conference on Digital Libraries. Proceedings of the second ACM/IEEE-CS joint conference on Digital libraries*, Portland, Oregan. New York: ACM Press.
25. LTSC. (2002) IEEE *Learning Technology Standards Committee Mission.* http://grouper.ieee.org/groups/ltsc/index.html.

26. Gibbons, A.S., Nelson, J., Richards, R. (2000) *The nature and origin of instructional objects*. In: *The Instructional Use of Learning Objects: Online Version.*, Wiley, D.A., ed., Agency for Instructional Technology. available at http://www.reusability.org/read/chapters/gibbsons.doc

27. Hodgins, W. (2000) Into the future. http://www.learnativity.com/download/MP7.PDF.

28. Dahl, O.J., Nygaard, K. (1966) *SIMULA—an algol based simulation language*. Communications of the ACM, 9(9):671–678.

29. Reigeluth, C.M., Nelson, L.M. (1997) *A new paradigm of ISD?* Educational Media and Technology Yearbook, 22:24–35.

30. LOM. (2002) IEEE LTSC WG12—Learning object metadata. http://ltsc.ieee.org/wg12/.

31. Newsroom. (1999) Internet growing too fast for search engines. http://www.editors-service.com/articlearchive/search99.html.

32. Cisco. (2000) Reusable learning object strategy: definition, creation process, and guidelines for building. http://www.cisco.com/.

33. Hodgins, W. (2000) Everything you ever wanted to know about learning standards but were afraid to ask. http://www.linezine.com/2.1/features/wheyewtkls.htm.

34. Wagner, E.D. (2002) The new frontier of learning object design. http://www.elearningguild.com.

35. Wiley, D.A. (2000) Connecting learning objects to instructional design theory: a definition, a metaphor, and a taxonomy. http://reusability.org/read/chapters/wiley.doc.

36. ISO. (2002) Information technology: learning by IT. http://jtc1sc36.org/doc/36N0264.pdf.

37. Friesen, N., McGreal, R. (2002) International Review of Research in Open and Distance Learning. http://www.irrodl.org/content/v3.2/tech11.html.

38. IMS. (2001) IMS content packaging (CP). http://www.imsproject.org/content/packaging/index.cfm.

39. UNFOLD. (2003) The UNFOLD Project. http://www.unfold-project.net/.

40. ADLNet. (2000) Advanced Distributed Learning Network (ADL Net) *Advanced Distributed Learning, SCORM Past.* http://www.adlnet.org/index.cfm?fuseaction=scormhist.

41. IMS. (2001) IMS simple sequencing (SS). http://www.imsproject.org/simplesequencing/index.cfm.

42. ADL. (2003) Advanced distributed learning network (ADL Net). *ADL Co-Labs: overview.* http://www.adlnet.org/index.cfm?fuseaction=colabovr.

43. Ariadne. (2002) ARIADNE Foundation Presentation 1.1 http://www.ariadne-eu.org/en/about/general/benefits/index.html.

44. ISO. (2004) About ISO, introduction. http://www.iso.org/iso/en/aboutiso/introduction/index.html.

45. IEC/CEI. (2004) International Electrotechnical Commission. http://www.iec.ch/.

46. ISO/IEC. (2004) International Organisation for Standardisation/ International Electrotechnical Commission JTC1 SC36. http://jtc1sc36.org/.

47. ALIC. (2001) Advanced Learning Infrastructure Consortium. http://www.alic.gr.jp/eng/.

48. XMLSPY. (2000) http://www.xmlspy.com/.

49. DublinCore. (1998) Dublin Core metadata element set, version 1.1—reference description. http://dublincore.org/documents/1999/07/02/dces/.

50. Ariadne. (1999) ARIADNE metadata recommendation version 3.0. http://ariadne.unil.ch/Metadata/ariadne_metadata_v3final1.htm.

51. CUBER. (1999) EU 5th Framework IST Programme, Personalised Curriculum Builder in the Federated Virtual University of the Europe of Regions, final version of metadata specification.http://www.cuber.net/web-v1/publications/cuber-d9-1.pdf.

52. GEMSTONES GESTALT, ACTS (Advanced Communications Technologies and Services) project, courseware metadata design V3 (GEMSTONES). http://www.fdgroup.com/gestalt/D0401_3.pdf.

53. Moodle Moodle Web site. http://moodle.org.

54. Gruber, T.R. (1993) *A translation approach to portable ontology specification*. Knowledge Acquisition, **5**:199–220.

55. Noy, N.F., McGuinness, D.L. (1999) Ontology developement 101: a guide to creating your first ontology. http://www.standford.edu/.

56. Poggi, A., Bergenti, F. (2000) *Multi-agent systems: ontology*. In: *ESAW Workshop at ECAI 2000*, London, England.

57. Protege. (2000) Technical report: using Protégé-2000 to edit RDF. http://www.smi.Stanford.edu/projects/protege/protegerdf/protege-rdf.html.

58. Bechhofer, S., et al. (2001) *OilEd: a reasonable ontology editor for the semantic Web*. In: *KI2001, Joint German/Austrian conference on artificial intelligence*, Vienna, Austria.

59. Sure, Y., et al. (2002) *OntoEdit: collaborative ontology development for the semantic Web*. In: *International Semantic Web Conference (ISWC02)*, Sardinia, Italy.

60. Farquhar, A., Fikes, R., Rice, J. (1996) *The Ontolingua server: a tool for collaborative ontology construction*. In: *10th Knowledge Acquisition for Knowledge-Based Systems Workshop*, Banff, Canada.

61. Arpírez, J.C., et al. (2001) *WebODE: a scalable ontological engineering workbench*. In: *First International Conference on Knowledge Capture (K-CAP 2001)*, Victoria, Canada.

62. Duval, E., et al. (2002) Metadata principles and practicalities. http://dlib.org/dlib/april02/weibel/04weibel.html.

63. Brennan, M., Funke, S., Anderson, C. (2001) Learning Content Management Systems: a new e-learning market segment emerges. http://www.idc.com.

64. Concannon, F., Johnson. K. (2002) *Learning through learning content management systems*. In: *Human Computer Interaction, HCI*, Brighton, England.

65. Cross, J., Hamilton, I. (2002) The DNA of E-learning. http://www.austrainer.com/elearning/dna-of-elearning.htm.

66. Kearns, D. (2004) Open Source all stars. http://www.nwfusion.com/newsletters/nt/2004/0322nt1.html.

67. O'Droma, M., Ganchev, I., McDonnell, F. (2003) *Architectural and functional desgin and evaluation of e-learning VUIS based on the proposed IEEE LTSA reference model*. The Internet and Higher Education, 6(3):263–276.

68. Cisco. (1999) Cisco Systems—reusable information object strategy. http://www.cisco.com/warp/public/779/ibs/solutions/learning/whitepapers/el_cisco_rio.pdf.

69. MySQL. (1995) http://www.mysql.com.

70. SPAW. (2002) http://www.solmetra.com/spaw/.

71. dotLRN. (2001) http://dotlrn.org/.

72. IMS. (2001) IMS Global Consortium, Inc *IMS Background*. http://www.imsproject.org/aboutims.cfm.

73. Collins, A., Brown, J.S., et al. (1991) Cognitive Apprenticeship: Making Thinking Visible. American Educator: The American Federation of Teachers, 15(3):6–11, 38–46.

9
Reinforcement Agents for E-Learning Applications

HAMID R. TIZHOOSH, MARYAM SHOKRI, AND MOHAMED KAMEL

Abstract. Advanced computer systems have become pivotal components for learning. However, we are still faced with many challenges in e-learning environments when developing reliable tools to assist users and facilitate and enhance the learning process. For instance, the problem of creating a user-friendly system that can learn from interaction with dynamic learning requirements and deal with large-scale information is still widely unsolved. We need systems that have the ability to communicate and cooperate with the users, learn their preferences and increase the learning efficiency of individual users. Reinforcement learning (RL) is an intelligent technique with the ability to learn from interaction with the environment. It learns from trial and error and generally does not need any training data or a user model. At the beginning of the learning process, the RL agent does not have any knowledge about the actions it should take. After a while, the agent learns which actions yield the maximum reward. The ability of learning from interaction with a dynamic environment and using reward and punishment independent of any training data set makes reinforcement learning a suitable tool for e-learning situations, where subjective user feedback can easily be translated into a reinforcement signal.

9.1 Introduction

This chapter focuses on the investigation of the user-machine interface and the complexity of a dynamic environment like an e-learning application based on reinforcement learning. In e-learning applications the user needs access to the most suitable sources of information. Reinforcement learning has the ability to autonomously lead the search engines to adapt themselves based on monitoring the user's queries, reactions to messages, and even actions that the user takes (e.g., deleting a file or searching again for the same object category). As a consequence, an intelligent search engine could improve its behavior in order to personalize search tools, save the user's time, and avoid confusion and fatigue by providing the shortest path to the optimal learning object.

We present the techniques for developing user-oriented RL agents, and discuss design requirements and limitations. The techniques for presenting the states and actions and defining the objective and subjective reward are introduced as well. Some hybrid systems using reinforcement learning techniques are provided.

In image-based applications (image as a learning object), defining states, actions, and reward is usually a difficult task. The high- and low-level image processing techniques must be applied to extract features, patterns, and clues from an image set or a single image. We present an example of the application of RL in image processing, and collaboration of the expert (user) with the agent to deal with images. Typical problems of user interaction with the agent for acquisition of reward and punishment are discussed.

The chapter is organized as follows: Section 9.2 gives an overview of different aspects of a multiagent system in interaction with users. In section 9.3, reinforcement learning techniques and their components are described. A brief discussion of some hybrid techniques is also presented. In section 9.4 we present the outlines of RL agents for personalized search engines and multiagent issues. Our discussions in section 9.5 include partial observable Markov decision processes, hidden Markov models, and semi-Markov decision processes. Section 9.6 concludes the chapter.

9.2 Multiagent Systems and Interaction with Users

In the framework of e-learning, we are interested in the design of an artificial intelligent system to provide services for the user (learner) through the Web or other interfaces. Intelligent (software) agents should act rationally to perform a task for the user and reduce human error or fatigue [25]. Reinforcement learning (RL) agents can be employed to design a personalized system to adapt to human intention, intuition, needs, and requests. We especially need to consider that the user may not be able or willing to provide detailed information as feedback to the system. To design an adaptive personalized mechanism, the artificial intelligent system must communicate with the user through a graphical user interface (GUI). Users can provide their requests, responses, and reactions for the computer by using the intelligent GUI. This yields the most efficient system that can perform challenging tasks, save the user's time, and prevent user fatigue and confusion. To accomplish this, we need a link between artificial intelligence (AI) and a graphical user interface [11]. Mixed-initiative interaction represents a link between AI and human–computer interaction, and refers to a flexible interaction strategy in which each agent (user or computer) contributes what it is best suited for at the most appropriate time [11].

The concept of *agent* must be considered here as it is referred to in the definition of mixed-initiative interaction. By general definition, an agent is "something that acts" or "something that perceives and acts in an environment" [25]. More specifically by *intelligent agent* we mean intelligent software that performs a task for a human user. A rational agent attempts in a way to maximize the expected value of a performance/quality measure, given the percept sequence it has seen so far [25]. Agents should have the ability to manage themselves, optimize task performance, and increase the level of security. Agents can operate in dynamic and uncertain environments, plan appropriate actions, and perform individually or in coordination with other agents.

Based on the user's needs, an e-learning agent can perform different actions such as:

- Searching for information
- Gathering information
- Providing services like tutoring and scheduling
- Updating the user's information
- Providing on-line tests or examinations
- Providing Web-based communication with teachers and students

A system with several agents that work with each other toward their goals is called a *multiagent* system. For Web-based systems with a large number of users and time/resource constraints, it is necessary to use multiagent systems for task coordination and sharing resources such as databases.

An intelligent e-learning system can be achieved by monitoring the users actions, such as searching the Web using keywords, deleting a file, closing a help window, researching for different object categories, typing a search query, selecting or saving documents or images, choosing a specific picture or text from a set of pictures or text documents, and asking for help or selecting help options. In a more advanced intelligent system, an agent can talk/listen to or monitor the user in order to gather information and provide the most suitable service. This advanced system can provide a variety of options for the user, especially for people with disabilities or communication difficulties.

In e-learning applications the agent must provide different levels of information resources and services based on the user's level of knowledge and understanding. The level of knowledge can be evaluated based on queries that the agent receives from the user [33]. It also can be determined by the user's reaction or search queries. The agent must improve its performance by considering the user's (learner's) satisfaction. For this reason a measure of user satisfaction must be defined for the agent. In the following section, we discuss this issue in the framework of reinforcement learning by defining reward and punishment.

9.3 Reinforcement Learning

The motivation behind using reinforcement learning is designing an effective goal-directed intelligent agent to learn from interaction with a dynamic environment that relies on reward and punishment, and prediction of rewards. Learning is the core characteristic of any intelligent system. Learning can be described as the "process of acquiring an internal representation for the persistent constraints in the world," "as well as assembling the computational facilities by which predictions and explanations are produced" [21]. In the RL model, an agent is an autonomous learner or decision maker. What is outside the agent is the environment (user, learning objects, search algorithms, etc.). Reinforcement leaning is *on-line* learning, meaning that the RL agent improves its behavior in real time. The RL agents design is based on the characteristics of the problem at hand. RL agents learn from their own experience without relying on teachers or training data (in contrast to neural networks that need a large set of training samples). This makes RL agents more suitable for e-learning since on-line interaction, as the learning mechanism for RL agents, can always be assumed.

The history of RL has two major parts: the study of animal learning, and the solution of optimal control problems using value functions and dynamic programming [31]. Value functions are functions of states or functions of state-action pairs that estimate how good it is to perform a given action in a given state [31]. Watkins [35,36] developed the Q-learning algorithm in 1989 in such a way that the agent maintains a value for both state and action, which represents a prediction of the worth of taking that action from the state.

Reinforcement learning agents are autonomous [23]. The behavior of an autonomous agent is determined by its own experience. The RL agent maps the states of the environment to appropriate actions and tries to maximize the reward or minimize the punishment [1,7,31]. The reward function represents the goal of the reinforcement learning problem. The reward values could be objective or subjective. In the subjective case, the agent receives reward and punishment directly from the interactive user. In the objective case, the reward is defined based on some optimality measure or desired properties of the results [25,28,31]. Reinforcement learning is based on trial and error. Actions could affect the next situation and subsequent rewards. The agent must be aware of the states by interacting with the environment. The states are parameters (features) describing the environment, and actions must have the ability to optimize the environment's state [16,31].

For an RL agent, the learning process has two components: exploration and exploitation. Exploration means that the agent tries to discover which actions yield the maximum reward by taking different actions repeatedly and in a random manner. Exploitation, on the other hand, means taking the most rewarding actions. The agent does not have any previous background knowledge about taking the correct actions. This kind of learning is *not supervised*, but since we use a reward function, weak supervision can be assumed. The agent does not need a set of training examples. Instead, it learns on-line and can continuously learn and adapt while performing the required task. This behavior is useful for all user-dependent cases where sufficiently large training data are difficult or impossible to obtain.

Figure 9.1 illustrates the components that constitute the general idea behind reinforcement learning. The RL agent, which is the decision-maker in the process, takes an action that influences the environment. The agent acquires knowledge of the actions that generate rewards and punishments, and it eventually learns to perform the actions that are the most rewarding in order to attain a certain goal. In the RL model presented in Figure 9.1, the process is as follows [23,31]:

- Agent observes the states from environment
- Agent takes an action and observes reward and punishment
- Agent observes the new state

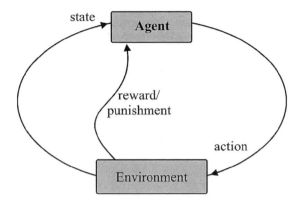

FIGURE 9.1. Basic structure of a reinforcement learning problem.

Another element of reinforcement learning is the *action policy* that defines the agent's behavior at a given time and is a core component of reinforcement learning. It maps the perceived states to the actions to be taken [31]. There are three common policies: softmax policy, ϵ-greedy policy, and greedy policy. The Boltzmann policy is the most common softmax method, and uses a Gibbs, or Boltzmann distribution. The ϵ-greedy policy explores the state space with probability ϵ and exploits the rewarding actions with a probability of $1 - \epsilon$.

Reinforcement learning is learning from interaction of the agent with the environment to achieve the goal, that is maximizing the accumulated rewards over the long run. If the reinforcement learning task satisfies the *Markov property*, it is called a finite Markov decision process [31]. In a particular case the Markov property is used to predict the probability of the possible next state as follows [31]:

$$P_{ss'}^a = Pr\{s_{t+1}|s_t = s, a_t = a\}, \tag{9.1}$$

where s is the current state, a is the action, s' is the next state, and $P_{ss'}^a$ is the probability of possible next state s' given any state s and action a [31]. The solution of the reinforcement learning problem is the policy that maximizes the reward over several learning episodes. There are three elementary classes of techniques for solving reinforcement learning problems: dynamic programming, Monte Carlo algorithm, and temporal-difference (TD) learning [31]. There are also "eligibility traces" that can be considered as a bridge between TD methods and Monte Carlo techniques [31]. Here, we focus on TD approaches as described elsewhere [31].

9.3.1 Temporal-Difference Learning

Temporal-difference learning is a combination of Monte Carlo and dynamic programming ideas. If at time t a nonterminal state s_t is visited, TD methods estimate the value of that state, $V(s_t)$, based on what happens after that visit [31]. TD methods wait until the next step ($t + 1$) to determine the increment to $V(s_t)$ as opposed to Monte Carlo that must wait until the end of the learning episode. The simplest

TABLE 9.1. Tabular TD(0) for estimating V^{π} [31]

Initialize $V(s)$ arbitrary, π the policy to be evaluated
Repeat (for each episode):
    Initialize s
    Repeat (for each step of episode):
        $a \leftarrow$ action given by π for s
        Take action a: observe reward, r, and next state, s'
        $V(s) \leftarrow V(s) + \alpha[r + \gamma V(s') - V(s)]$
        $s \leftarrow s'$
    until s is terminal

TD method, called TD(0), is presented in relation 9.2 where α is a constant and $r_{t+1} + \gamma V_t(s_{t+1})$ is the target [31].

$$V(s_t) \leftarrow V(s_t) + \alpha[r_{t+1} + \gamma V(s_{t+1}) - V(s_t)]. \tag{9.2}$$

The tabular TD(0) for estimating V^{π} is presented in Table 9.1.

Sarsa

Sarsa is on-policy TD control. For an on-policy method the state-action value $Q^{\pi}(s, a)$ must be estimated for the current policy π, and all states s and actions a. The transition from state-action pair to state-action pair must be considered and the value of state-action pair must be learned. The general algorithm for Sarsa method is presented in Table 9.2.

Q-Learning

Q-learning is off-policy TD control and is one of the most popular methods in reinforcement learning. In an off-policy technique the learned action-value function, $Q(s, a)$, directly approximates the optimal action-value function Q^*, independent of the policy being followed [31]. The agent learns to act optimally in Markovian domains by experiencing sequences of actions. The agent takes an action at a particular state and using immediate reward and punishment and estimating the

TABLE 9.2. Sarsa: an on-policy TD control algorithm [31]

Initialize $Q(s, a)$ arbitrary
Repeat (for each episode):
    Initialize s
    Choose a from s using policy derived from Q (e.g., ϵ-greedy)
    Repeat (for each step of episode):
        Take action a, observe r, s'
        Choose a' from s' using policy derived from Q (e.g., ϵ-greedy)
        $Q(s, a) \leftarrow Q(s, a) + \alpha[r + \gamma Q(s', a') - Q(s, a)]$
        $s \leftarrow s', a \leftarrow a'$
    until s is terminal

TABLE 9.3. Q-learning: an off-policy TD control algorithm [31]

Initialize $Q(s, a)$ arbitrary
Repeat (for each episode):
    Initialize s
    Repeat (for each step of episode):
    Choose a from s using policy derived from Q (e.g., ϵ-greedy)
        Take action a, observe r, s'
        $Q(s, a) \leftarrow Q(s, a) + \alpha[r + \gamma \max_{a'} Q(s', a') - Q(s, a)]$
        $s \leftarrow s'$;
    until s is terminal

---

state value, it evaluates the consequences of taking different actions. By trying all actions in all states multiple times, the agent learns which action is best overall for each visited state [36]. The agent must determine an optimal policy and maximize the total discounted expected reward. Using the policy π, the value of state s is presented in equation 9.3 [36].

$$V^\pi(s) \equiv R_s(\pi(s)) + \gamma \sum_y P_{sy}[\pi(s)]V^\pi(y). \qquad (9.3)$$

The task of Q-learning is determining an optimal policy, π^*. The values of the matrix Q are the expected discounted reward for executing action a at state s, taking policy π [36]. The (theoretical) condition for convergence of the Q-algorithm is that the sequence of episodes that forms the basis of learning must visit all states infinitely. The Q-learning algorithm is presented in Table 9.3. where s is state, a is action, and s' is next state.

9.3.2 Hybrid Techniques

Reinforcement learning algorithms have been combined with other techniques to improve learning efficiency. For instance, the problem of balancing exploration of untried actions with exploitation of rewarding actions is discussed by Dearden et al. [6]. They use value information to estimate the improvement of learning that results from exploration. The uncertainty about the current value must be also evaluated. The Bayesian approach is used to capture the uncertainty. The probability distribution over Q-values is applied to extend Watkins's Q-learning. Based on conducted experiments, it is concluded that improvement can be achieved over some well-known model-free exploration strategies. The reward distribution is calculated using the Bayesian approach.

Dearden et al. [6] provide brief and valuable information about Q-learning, semi-uniform random exploration, Boltzmann exploration, and directed and undirected exploration to discuss the balance between exploration and exploitation. The Bayesian approach is applied for Q-learning to use a probability distribution to deal with uncertainty in estimating Q-values. In the case of undirected explorations the actions are based on local Q-values, but the distributions over Q are stored and propagated to make better decisions that yield global exploration without explicit exploration bonus.

The Bayesian approach for modeling multiagent reinforcement learning problems (MARL) is presented by Chalkiadakis and Boutilier [4] to allow reasoning under uncertainty. The optimal exploration techniques for the proposed model are introduced and several computational approximations for Bayesian exploration in MARL are presented.

Many different variations of fuzzy Q-Learning have also been proposed [2,9,10,14]. Walker and Marilyn [34] propose an application of the reinforcement learning method in dialogue strategy selection in a spoken dialogue system for email. Zhang and Dieterich [39] also discuss job-shop scheduling with RL techniques. Another application of reinforcement learning could be image segmentation [28,29,30].

9.4 RL Perspectives for E-Learning

In this section we discuss RL design issues in the framework of e-learning applications. We also propose algorithms to personalize search engines, and provide a general scheme for learning object identification (LOID) to facilitate the design of RL agents. The details of the RL design for e-learning applications are discussed here to illuminate the challenges and establish accessible procedures to overcome them. As well, an example of the implementation of an RL agent interacting with a human operator is provided to verify the step-by-step analysis and design procedure. Reinforcement learning reliability and adjustable autonomy are discussed at the end of this section.

9.4.1 Design Requirements

The design of a reinforcement learning agent is generally based on the problem at hand. First we have to clearly define and analyze the problem. We need to decide the purpose of designing the RL agent. There could be a variety of applications and tools for e-learning that specifies our purpose of design (partly discussed in section 9.2).

In daily activities, learners (users) search the Internet and local (private) databases to access the information they need. The result of these searches are learning objects (pages, links, images, text files, etc.) that may or may not be what the learner needs. The goal is designing a personalized search engine that can be adapted based on the learner's feedback in order to increase learning efficiency.

The general framework of an RL-based search engine is presented in Figure 9.2.

The RL-based personalized search engine works as follows:

- Learners can send requests to their (personal) RL agent.
- A database of learning objects is available to the agent, containing text documents, images, audio and video files, etc.

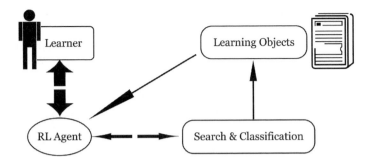

FIGURE 9.2. Framework of an RL-based personalized search engine.

- A set of searching, sorting, and classification algorithms can be accessed by the RL agent.
- The RL agent can activate searching and classification in order to receive a sorted list of learning objects corresponding to the learner's request.
- The RL agent provides the most suitable learning object(s) to the learner.
- Learners (directly or indirectly) provide feedback to the RL agent indicating their satisfaction level.
- The RL agent collects the learner's feedback (rewards and punishments) to use in refining its search and classification strategy.

To completely design and implement the personalized RL agent, the following questions should be answered:

1. What are the *states*? → The parameters, factors, or features that describe the learning situation.
2. What are the *actions*? → The changes that the RL agent can make in order to optimize the learning situation.
3. How to receive *reward* and *punishment*? → Explicit (direct) or implicit (indirect) learner's feedback to let RL agent know whether the learning object is suitable.

These questions, as has been mentioned before, can only be answered for a given learning environment; general valid solutions are not possible. We now concentrate on one specific example to demonstrate how an RL approach can be embedded into an e-learning framework.

9.4.2 Reinforced Learner-Oriented Search Engines

Local and global search engines are an integral part of every e-learning environment. Learners search for learning objects in order to deepen their knowledge or clarify questions. Assuming that the learner has access to a database containing a large number of learning objects (probably shared with other learners), standard search strategies, blind to individual needs of different learners, offer only limited help.

The following general parameters can be assumed in order to completely design a personalized (learner-oriented) search engine:

Learning object: $LO_1, LO_2, \ldots, LO_n$
Learning object IDs: $ID_1, ID_2, \ldots, ID_n$
Learning object subclasses: $C_1, C_2, \ldots, C_m$
Most recent learner's request: L_R (infinite variations)
Request mapping: L'_R (finite predetermined keywords)
Sorting weights for all learning objects: $w_1, w_2, \ldots, w_n$
Search/classification parameters: $P_1, P_2, \ldots, P_k$ ($k \ll n$)
State vector (private): $[L'_R, C_i, w_1, w_2, \ldots, w_n]$
State vector (global): $[L'_R, C_i, p_1, p_2, \ldots, p_n]$
Action (private): $w_i \pm \Delta_w$
Action (global): $P_i \pm \Delta_P$

Learning Objects

Images, text documents, URLs, and video and audio files can be regarded as learning objects.

Learning Object Subclasses

Within each learning object class, there are subclasses that can help the RL agent to optimize the learning process. For instance, images as learning objects can be divided into subclasses with respect to domain category (e.g., technical, medical, natural, etc.) and/or content descriptions (e.g., *"road, trees, sky"*).

Learning Object ID

The learning object identification (LOID) is in the form of metadata describing the nature of the learning object. LOIDs are necessary to avoid on-line recognition tasks, which are a challenge even for off-line algorithms. Recognizing what the learning object represents is a highly complex pattern recognition problem regardless of whether the learning object is text, image, or speech (see section 9.4.3).

Learner's Request

The learner can request a new learning object via a search phrase. Any possible combination of relevant search phrases should be anticipated. This is a first obstacle for RL agents since an unlimited number of states cannot be handled.

Request Mapping

To reduce the *request space*, the original learner's request should be mapped to a limited number of keywords such that the overall state space remains tractable.

For instance, the search inquiry *"Einstein relativity black holes"* could be mapped to the keyword *"Physics."*

Sorting Weights

The relevancy or suitability of learning objects for a given request (generally in [0, 100%]) can be delivered by diverse classification and ranking algorithms. The RL agent should be able to modify the sorting weights in order to match the learner's expectation.

Search and Classification Parameters

For a global design the parameters of the classification and search algorithms can be adjusted in order to change the sorting weights of learning objects.

State Vector

The state (learning situation) can be defined either at a private or a global level. If the RL agent changes the sorting weights w_1, w_2, ..., w_n, only the corresponding learner will be affected. However, if the RL agent modifies the parameters P_1, P_2, ..., P_n of the search and classification algorithms, this will not only be a more difficult task but also will affect all other learners whose agents use the same algorithms. A global modification is more challenging because it needs agent coordination at a more complex level, and because the parameters of adjusting algorithms used to generate the desired results are generally not straightforward.

Actions

For *private* implementation the actions modify the sorting weights of learning objects, whereas for the *global* case the parameters of the classification and search are modified by proper actions. It should be emphasized that the latter case bears a more challenging design level.

Reward and Punishment

The agent takes an action (e.g., chooses a picture from a database) and presents it to the learner. The learner can provide subjective reward to the agent directly or indirectly. In the direct case, the learner must click one of the icons, *accept* or *reject*. The *accept* option is a reward for the agent and the *reject* option is a punishment. If the learner does not provide a direct reward for the agent, then the agent must observe the learner's reaction to the search result (image or any other learning object). The learner may click on the image or save the image, which can be considered as a reward by the agent. The learner may close the window or request another search procedure, which can be considered as a punishment by the agent. After a while, the agent learns the proper sorting weights for learning objects in which the learner is interested. The training process is complete at this point and the search engine is personalized.

9.4.3 Learning Object ID (LOID)

Reinforcement learning agents can be employed to manage information. By managing information we mean producing a personalized digital library containing learning objects with descriptive IDs (LOIDs). When learners search for a learning object (document, image etc.), they save learning objects by different names in different files. When they need to access the stored information, they do not know exactly the content of the files or location of the information. Reinforcement learning can help the learner build a personalized digital library by producing LOIDs for each learning object. The LOID represents the main features of the learning objects by providing a tag or *metadata* for them. Moreover, by using LOID, defining the states becomes easier in the design of personalized agents. Information can be extracted from the metadata and used to define the state space. An example is provided in Figure 9.3 to present metadata for an image. The metadata consists of link, category, content, color, format, type, and size of the image.

Example 1: In this example we consider two general solutions of producing ID, the *manual* and the *automated* techniques. In the manual technique the user directly provides the LOID for each learning object. In the automated case the agent must learn it based on extracting information from the learning object such as name, caption, and feature information. If a learning object is an image, then low- and high-level image processing can be applied. For example, if the image is binarized, then the number of pixels represents the area of the object of interest.

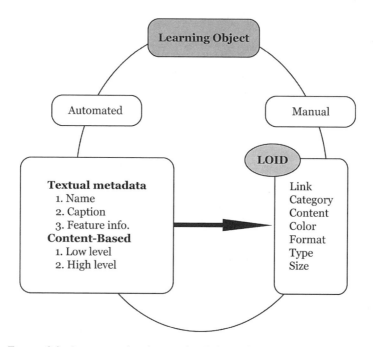

FIGURE 9.3. Automatated and manual techniques for producing image IDs.

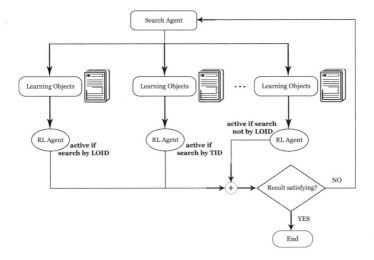

FIGURE 9.4. General architecture for producing IDs for learning objects.

If the learning object has the associated metadata representing its LOID, then it can be provided to the learner to be added to the personalized digital library if necessary, or to be used for future search requests. If the learner knows the LOID (completely or partly), then the search process can be performed faster and the result more accurately matches the learner's request. For any advanced intelligent search engine like the example proposed in Figure 9.4, the learning object can be provided by its associated LOID for the user. There are several agents providing services to the users in this example. Based on the search query, different agents can be activated. If the user knows the LOID and uses it as a search query, then one of the agents can be activated to search the databases based on that query.

If some information in metadata associated with the LOID is not accurate or is missing, then in order to distinguish the complete metadata from incomplete one, a temporary ID (TID) can be generated. Users can conduct the search by using the TID. Another agent with the responsibility of completing or correcting metadata attached to TID will automatically be activated. The learner can also perform this task manually. In the manual case the user has interaction with the agent to provide the required information and complete or correct the TID. In the automatic case the agent extracts information from the learning object to complete or correct the TID. The architecture of the process is presented in Figure 9.4.

9.4.4 Learning Speed Considerations

Reinforcement learning can be regarded as a stochastic learn and optimization methodology. It does not need a model or training data to learn from, and starts, so to speak, from scratch. The interaction with the environment (learner, database, other algorithms) is the only mechanism, which the RL agents employ to steer the environment into an optimal state. This characteristic of the reinforcement paradigm is extremely crucial for e-learning. However, it also bears design and algorithmic challenges.

Generally, RL agents converge to a solution with a probability of 1 if they can visit all states infinitely. In practice, this would mean that every state should be visited multiple times. As long as we have a limited state space, this will not create any practical obstacle. However, the suitability of learning objects provided by the RL agent can be quite low if, due to a large state space, the agent does not have the possibility to receive *sufficient* feedbacks from the learner for relevant states.

Personalization can be hindered by the following obstacles:

Feedback reliability: The learner can, due to fatigue, provide the wrong feedback.
Feedback insufficiency: The learner rarely works with the agent.
LOID complexity: The learner works often with the agent but due to the large state space the agent cannot converge to an optimal solution.

The RL agent must be trained based on the specific learner's intentions and demands. We need to consider that one learner may not be able or willing to provide reward or punishment as a feedback to the system to train the agent. In addition, wrong feedbacks may be provided due to fatigue and/or not paying attention. The larger problem, however, is the number of feedbacks. Assuming we have $L'_R = 1000$ keywords to which the learner requests, L_R, can be mapped. Further, let's assume that there are $n = 1000$ learning objects in $m = 100$ different subclasses. Then, the private state vector $[L'_R, C_i, w_1, w_2, \ldots, w_n]$ will have $1000 \times 100 \times 1000 = 10^8$ different variations. Of course many of these possible states will not occur, but a large number of them should be *visited* by the RL agent in order to converge to an optimal solution. Expecting that one single learner can/will provide several million feedbacks to the RL agent is not realistic.

In the reinforcement learning literature a variety of modifications have been proposed to accelerate the learning speed in spite of high-dimensional state space. We propose the following approaches to solve this problem:

Off-line training: The RL agent could be trained off-line. The demands and needs of a *typical learner* can be learned off-line to minimize the on-line learning time for personalizing the agent.
A priori knowledge integration: Any knowledge about the learning objects and the learner's preferences can be considered before on-line learning begins.
Task distribution: A *main agent* communicates with the learner and distributes the required tasks among n other agents (Fig. 9.5).
Multiagent cooperation: Every learner has his/her own RL agent trying to adjust the learning objects' sorting weights. The agents cooperate among one another, exchange information, and learn faster.

In the last case a multiagent search environment could be implemented (Fig. 9.6).

In this framework we have several agents, each associated with one of the learners. Each learner has an RL agent in his/her personal computer connected to

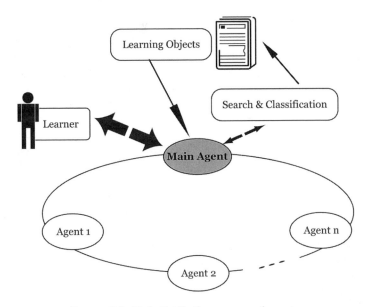

FIGURE 9.5. Task distribution among subagents.

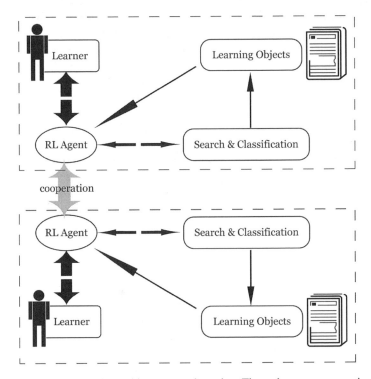

FIGURE 9.6. Framework of a multiagent search engine. Through agent cooperation, additional feedback can be acquired, resulting in a faster convergence.

a network. If the agent does not receive enough feedback from the user, then it contacts other agents to see whether they have knowledge of taking appropriate actions in similar states. Then the RL agent updates its value function based on the knowledge that it receives from other agents (which are the same type of agents with similar actions definitions and for similar states). The agents act independently but cooperate to exchange information. Clustering algorithms can be used to classify similar agents, similar states, and similar actions.

The major design issue in a multiagent system is the cooperation aspect. The designer must consider whether the agents ignore other agents and act independently or whether they cooperate with other agents. The agents may share the information or hide it and attempt to learn other agents' action values and strategies. Claus and Boutilier [5] present dynamics of RL in cooperative multiagent systems. To expedite the convergence, the cooperation of agents has a clear goal: updating more frequently than is possible by simply receiving feedback from the learner. The foremost condition for the cooperation is that collaborating agents are dealing with the same learning objects and ideally are accessing the same learning object repository.

Managing the tasks and resources is an other important issue. The resources (e.g., databases) could be equally distributed among the agents or optimally distributed based on the intensity of receiving queries by each agent. The agent must also consider the necessary time for coordination and calculate coordination costs in order to decide whether the benefit of coordination outweighs the cost.

In cooperative multiagent systems with global reward, there is the so-called "credit assignment problem" [3]. This is related to difficulty in gauging which of the agent's contribution has led to the reward. In some cases agents cannot observe the action of other agents and therefore the role of each agent in producing the reward is not determinable [3]. Chang et al [3] introduce a new approach to solve the credit assignment problem. They consider the reward signal as an observed global reward for the agent that is the sum of the personal reward for that agent and a random Markov process (which is a reward of other agents and the external source of the reward as noise). The on-line Kalman filter [32] is implemented to estimate these rewards. In this approach learning is based on the global reward, and the agents learn and converge faster to an optimal or near-optimal policy [3].

9.4.5 Example for Designing Human–Agent Interaction

In this section we provide an example of how the RL agent can interact with a human operator in order to learn a certain task. As an example we have provided a reinforcement agent that communicates with the learner (user) to binarize a digital image.

Image thresholding (or binarization) is a common task in computer vision. The evaluation of the quality of the binary image with respect to object visibility, however, is generally a difficult task that cannot be solved by quantitative measures. In contrast, the human observer can easily judge the image quality and provide the agent with evaluative feedback. The agent, on its part, will attempt to take proper actions (different levels of binarization) in order to satisfy the user and, by doing

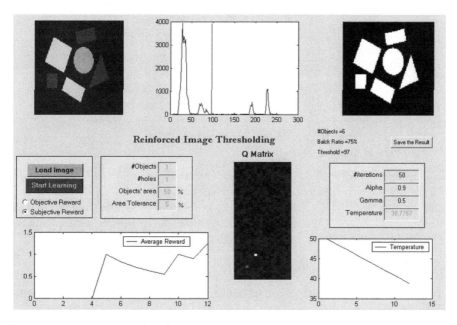

FIGURE 9.7. GUI for using RL technique: learning process based on interaction with user.

so, generate the optimal image. A graphical user interface must be designed to create an easy-to-use system interface [28] (see Fig. 9.7).

Using this GUI, the agent can communicate with an experienced operator. The agent takes an image from the set of images and thresholds it. The threshold is initialized with a constant value. This definition is arbitrary but has an impact on the learning speed. Inappropriate initial thresholds may lead to increase in learning time. The initial value could be a random number in the range of minimum to maximum gray level. One may select the initial threshold, using existing thresholding techniques or the average of several thresholds provided by several different thresholding algorithms.

Definition of States

The states can be determined by using the number of objects, n_O, and the ratio of black pixels n_B to the total number of pixels n after applying the threshold to the image. Concretely, the states are defined as follows:

$$\text{IF } c_1 \leq \frac{n_B}{n} < c_2$$
$$\text{IF } n_O == d$$
$$s = i$$
$$\text{END}$$
$$\text{END}$$

where c_1, $c_2 \in [o, 1]$, and $d, i \in N$.

TABLE 9.4. Definition of actions for Q-based image
thresholding: κ is minimum gray level, ν is maximum gray
level, and τ_{opt} is final threshold

$\Delta = (\nu - \kappa)/20$
$x = \kappa + a.\Delta$
$y = \kappa + (a+1).\Delta$
$\tau_{opt} = (x+y)/2$

Definition of Actions

The agent modifies the initial threshold τ_{opt} by taking an action a. A total number
of 20 actions were defined for this purpose, each increasing or decreasing the
current threshold by a certain amount Δ. Considering the scaling and interval of
the threshold values in the image, Table 9.4. shows how the threshold τ_{opt} can be
modified by taking action $a \in \{1, 2, \ldots, 20\}$ in each iteration.

Definition of Reward and Punishment

Two different kinds of reward can be defined, namely subjective and objective. In
the subjective case the reward is given to the agent by the experienced operator.
In the objective case the reward must be defined for the agent based on some
quantitative measure. In this example, the reinforcement agent receives one of
these two types of rewards according to the selected option. This task is handled
by interaction of the user with the agent through the GUI. The user is asked
whether the result of thresholding is *bad*, *fair*, or *good*. The user chooses one of
these options based on his/her knowledge and perception. The relation in equation
(9.4) shows these reward/punishment values:

$$r = \begin{cases} 0 & \text{if} \quad bad \\ 5 & \text{if} \quad fair \\ 10 & \text{if} \quad good \end{cases} \tag{9.4}$$

The objective reward is defined using the number of objects n_O and the area of
object A. The definition of objective reward appears in Table 9.5.

Q-learning and Policy

The Q-learning algorithm (see section 9.3.1) was selected as a learning algorithm.
The Q-matrix serves to accumulate rewards and acts as a value function indicating

TABLE 9.5. Objective reward for Q-based thresholding

If n_O within acceptable limits
if A is correct $r = 10$;
else
if A almost correct $r = 5$;
else $r = 2.5$;
else $r = 0$;

what is a good strategy for future states. The Q-matrix is initialized with random numbers. A proper policy makes action selection possible and enables the agent to map current states to appropriate actions. The Boltzmann function is a common action policy. Using Boltzmann distribution, the probability of taking action *a* (in a given state *s*) can be determined.

9.4.6 Reinforcement Reliability and Adjustable Autonomy

To reduce human error for the repetitive task of giving reward and punishment to the agent, a new solution is presented here. We developed a new reinforced image thresholding technique [27] whose autonomy can be adjusted by a human user. To reduce the user's error as a result of the interaction of the user with the agent for giving the reward or punishment, two different techniques are proposed in this section. The interaction of the user with the agent is based on using the given graphical user interface (see Fig. 9.7).

The first task is to design an RL agent to find the optimal threshold. This agent has interaction with the user by using a GUI [28]. Such a graphical user interface gives the user the choice to adjust the autonomy by choosing a subjective reward or transfer the autonomy to the agent by choosing an objective reward [28]. If the subjective option is chosen, an experienced operator must give the reward and punishment to the agent. However, there is a possibility of error for the operator to give punishment instead of reward or vice versa. To reduce this error, the objective reward is also calculated to be compared with the subjective reward for each episode iteration. Normalization may be necessary to produce the subjective and objective rewards with the same scale. The agent compares the objective and subjective rewards to see whether there is a conflict. If there is a difference between the values of objective and subjective rewards, corrective measures should be taken. The history of reinforcement signals can help find which of the rewards can be trusted and to what degree.

The concept of *trust* must be considered in conflict situations because there is the possibility of error for human operators when they are performing a repetitive task. There is also a possibility of error for objective reward because of different kinds of noise. Inappropriate choice of initialized variables could also affect the objective reward. The average reward strategy is proposed to deal with this situation [27].

In the *average reward strategy* the agent trusts the objective and subjective rewards equally and considers the average of the two. Consequently, the average value will be mapped to the appropriate reward or punishment scale. The weighted average can be considered as well if weights can be defined based on *the degree of the trust* for each reward value.

Confirm reward is another strategy [27]. In this strategy if there is a difference between the values of the objective and subjective reward, the agent ignores both rewards and asks the user for reevaluation. This process can be considered as a *confirmation* procedure, and the user may not be offended. The algorithm of the proposed technique is presented in Table 9.6.

TABLE 9.6. Proposed RL algorithm for reducing error in human-computer interaction

Initialize δ (limit for sum of the rewards), l_m (max number
of iterations), and number of objects; ϖ (threshold);
Choose subjective or objective options for reward;
Do
    Take The image;
    Take the threshold value ϖ;
    Threshold the image;
    Receive reward;
    If the reward (which has been chosen) is subjective
      Calculate objective reward;
      Compare objective reward with subjective reward;
      Use proposed strategy (Confirm Reward or Average Reward) to define the
      reward;
    End
    Observe states, ϖ and reward;
    Apply actions & Calculate $\varpi 1$;
    $\varpi = \varpi 1$;
    If δ reached, then exit
while $j < l_m$

In the mixed initiative systems defined in Section 9.2, the agent must consider the uncertainty about the user's goals/intentions [12]. If the agent receives reward from the user for performing a task and in the same situation receives a punishment from the same user for the same task, it may be related to human error or the user's uncertainty with respect to his/her request. In this case, the agent can use the suggested solutions presented in Table 9.6. The agent can· also use an efficient dialogue to learn uncertainties about the user [12] and monitor the user's reaction to judge whether the user has the intention to provide reward and punishment. This can be performed by calculating the feedback time that is consumed for receiving the reward from the user. The graphical user interface must be easy to use for learners in order for them to provide a reward or punishment. The agent can provide guidelines to the users before starting the learning process and ask them whether they are willing to provide evaluative feedbacks.

9.5 Advanced Issues in Reinforcement Learning

In Web-based applications there is a possibility that the agent has limited access to the states because of the noise or missing data. Partially observable Markov decision process (POMDP) can be applied to deal with this problem. The POMDP is like Markov decision process (MDP) with the difference that in POMDP there is no direct access to all or some of the states. Instead, the agent receives information about the states based on observation, which could be probabilistic. It yields a set of discrete probability distributions over finite states for POMDP. The observation is based on action and observation functions. The observation function presents the probability distribution over possible observations for each action and resulting state. The goal of the agent is maximizing the discounted long-term reward [15]. The probability distribution over all states must be maintained to provide a track of the history [20]. It yields more accurate results in partial observable environments. The transition and observation probabilities must also be updated. Keeping track of the entire history of the process makes the process non-Markovian [20] and also increases the computational complexity of the problem.

The paper presented by Littman's group [15] provides an algorithm for solving POMDPs off-line and provides discussions on the difficulty of finding exact solutions for MDPs. The POMDPs model can be applied for planning under uncertainty. Witness algorithm, for instance, provides a framework for "finite-state controllers" in continuous belief spaces. In the case of large problems, Littman's group also proposes the use of function approximation for calculating value functions and the use of simulation techniques for approximation on the frequently visited parts of the belief space. The authors suggest the extension of their techniques for large problems and acquisition of a world model. They also suggest using learning hidden Markov models to learn POMDP and the use of their proposed algorithm for learning.

There is a need for developing the algorithm that can be applied for approximate planning in large MDPs and POMDPs to deal with complexity of approximation of the value and Q-functions. Ng and Jordan [19] proposed a technique, PEGASUS, for a policy search method for large MDPs and POMDPs. The paper presents an algorithm for providing a policy search method for MDP and POMDP, given a model, by transforming (PO)MDP into equivalent POMDP to reduce the policy search based on POMDPs with deterministic transitions.

In e-learning environments we need a reliable speaker-independence system to recognize the dialogues in noisy and ambiguous situations for e-learning applications. Roy et al [24] use POMDP for dialogue management. Their proposed model has the ability to describe dialogue naturally and handles the noisy and ambiguous situations autonomously. Roy et al's proposed technique does not have access to states directly; it is developed for mobile robots with access to several knowledge domains and also has interaction with people. The state observation is based on speech utterances, and it is provided by a speech recognition system. A set of keywords extracted from speech utterances is used to represent observations. Actions are defined based on a set of responses. Rewards present "the relative value of accomplishing certain actions" [24]. POMDP policy has the ability to handle noisy situations by gaining the reward slowly in degraded recognition to reduce the number of mistakes from using blind guesses. To deal with computational complexity, the near-optimal policy is applied to perform faster. There is a localized assumption about the uncertainty to summarize the belief vector by a pair consisting of the most likely state and the entropy of the belief state [24].

As mentioned earlier, in POMDP, keeping track of the entire history of the process makes the process non-Markovian [20]. Most reinforcement learning algorithms are proposed to be applied on Markov decision problems. However, in more realistic problems the states are partially observable or hidden. Jaakkola et al [13] propose an algorithm to solve a class of non-Markov decision problem with a Markovian environment and restricted access to the state information by the user. Their algorithm is based on a combination of Monte Carlo policy evaluation and policy improvement methods (similar to Markov decision problems). This algorithm solves an RL problem in a POMDP setting, where the learner has limited access to the state of the environment.

In an e-learning framework we need to design a personalized search engine to provide information to learners according to their queries. On the other hand, data mining techniques can help discover complex relationships and patterns to detect trends in a large database so that it will help answer some questions about the design or query for specific applications [22]. Pham [22] presents perception-based HMMs as framework for data mining and knowledge discovery by combining human perceptions and the theory of hidden Markov models. Perception-based HMMs implement the model of statistical and fuzzy information to help satisfy the user's preferences. This also helps agents match the query with the information available in databases.

Ghahramani [8] introduces the hidden Markov model as a tool that represents distribution over a sequence of observations by having two properties: observation at time t generated by some process whose state s_t is (a) hidden from the observer and (b) satisfies the Markov property.

Smyth et al [30] discuss how we can model the hidden Markov probability models (HMM) as probabilistic independence networks (PINs). The relationship between the probability models and graphs is considered for this modeling. The graphical model is suitable for representing dependencies between random variables and conditional independency in the probability models for model assessment and revision [30].

Reinforcement learning provides a framework for solving Markov decision problems (MDPs) without using any prior knowledge [37]. Semi-Markov models are applicable for modeling the hierarchical Markov decision processes based on reinforcement learning [26]. One of the techniques that can be used in e-learning is information extraction. Sarawagi et al [26] propose an advanced technique based on semi-Markov model for information extraction. Semi-Markov decision Processes (SMDPs) are generalized MDPs by allowing actions to be history dependent and modeling the transition time distribution of actions [37].

9.6 Conclusion

The field of e-learning will certainly dominate many applications in the future. In this chapter we briefly outlined the potential and challenges of reinforcement learning for e-learning environments. The main benefit of using RL techniques is without doubt their ability to learn through interaction. Highly specialized RL agents can learn from users and adjust the e-learning parameters in order to save time and provide a more efficient learning environment. On the other hand, RL agents need to be designed carefully. Computational challenges appear to be the main obstacle in the way of creating personalized and highly specialized software for e-learning.

References

1. Ayesh, A. (2004) Emotionally Motivated Reinforcement Learning Based Controller. The Hague, The Netherlands: IEEE SMC.
2. Berenji, H.R. (1994) Fuzzy Q-learning: a new approach for fuzzy dynamic programming problems. Third IEEE International Conference on Fuzzy Systems, Orlando, FL.
3. Chang, Y.H., Ho, T., Kaelbling, L.P. (2004) All learning is local: Multi-agent learning in global reward games, Advances in Neural Information Processing Systems 16, Vancouver, (NIPS-03).
4. Chalkiadakis, G., Boutilier, C. (2003) Coordination in Multiagent Reinforcement Learning: A Bayesian Approach, AAMAS03, Melbourne, Australia, 1418.
5. Claus, C., Boutilier, C. (1998) The Dynamics of Reinforcement Learning in Cooperative Multiagent Systems, Department of Computer Science, University of British Columbia, Canada (American Association for Artificial Intelligence).
6. Dearden, R., Friedman, N., Russell, S. (1998) Bayesian Q-learning, Department of Computer Science, University of British Columbia, Vancouver, Canada Computer Science Division, University of California Berkeley.
7. Gadanho, S. (1999) Reinforcement Learning in Autonomous Robots: An Empirical Investigation of the Role of Emotions. Edinburgh: PhD Thesis, University of Edinburgh.
8. Ghahramani, Z. (2001) An Introduction to hidden Markov models and Bayesian networks. International Journal of Pattern Recognition and Artificial Intelligence, 15(1):9–42.
9. Glorennec, P.Y. (1994) Fuzzy Q-learning and dynamical fuzzy Q-learning. Proceedings of the Third IEEE International Conference on Fuzzy Systems, IEEE Press, Piscataway, NJ, pp. 474–479.
10. Glorennec, P.Y., Jouffe, L. (1997) Fuzzy Q-Learning. Proceedings of Sixth International Conference on Fuzzy Systems, Barcelona, Spain, pp. 659–662.
11. Hearst, M.A. (1999) Trends & Controversies, Mixed-Initiative Interaction, IEEE Intelligence Systems, September/October.
12. Horvitz, E. (May, 1999) Principles of Mixed-Initiative User Interfaces. Proceedings of CHI'99, ACM SIGCHI Conference on Human Factors in Computing Systems, Pittsburgh, PA.
13. Jaakkola, T., Singh, S.P., Jordan, M.I. (1994) Reinforcement learning algorithm for partially observable markov decision problems, In Advances in Neural Information Processing Systems (NIPS), 7.
14. Jouffe, L. (1999) Fuzzy inference system learning by reinforcement methods, IEEE Transactions on Systems, Man and Cybernetics, 28:338–355.
15. Kaelbling, L.P., Littman, M.L., Cassandra, A.R. (1998) Planning and acting in partially observable stochastic domains. Artificial Intelligence, 101:99–134.
16. Kaelbling, L.P., Littman, M.L., Moore, A.W. (1996) Reinforcement learning: a survey. Journal of Artificial Intelligence Research, 4:237–285.

17. Li, Y. (2005) Hidden Markov models with states depending on observations source, Pattern Recognition Letters Archive, New York, NY: Elsevier Science Inc. 26(7): 977–984.

18. Littman, M.L., Cassandra, A.R., Kaelbling, L.P. (1995) Learning Policies for Partially Observable Environments: Scaling Up, Proceedings of the Twelfth International Conference on Machine Learning.

19. Ng, A.Y., Jordan, M.I. (2000) PEGASUS: A policy search method for large MDPs and POMDPs, Uncertainty in artificial intelligence (UAI), Proceedinjgs of the Sixteenth Conference.

20. Online Tutorial, Brown University, Department of Computer Science, POMDPs for Dummies, Subtitled: POMDPs and Their Algorithms, Sans Formula!, http://www.cs.brown.edu/research/ai/pomdp/tutorial/index.html.

21. Pearl, J. (1988) Probabilistic Reasoning in Intelligent Systems: Networks of Plausible Inference. San Mateo, CA: Morgan Kaufmann Publishers.

22. Pham, T.D. (2002). Perception-Based Hidden Markov Models: A Theoretical Framework for Data Mining and Knowledge Discovery. Soft Computing, 6: 400–405. New York: Springer-Verlag.

23. Ribeiro, C. (2002) Reinforcement learning agent. Artificial Intelligence Review 17:223–250.

24. Roy, N., Pineau, J., Thrun, S. (2000) Spoken dialogue management using probabilistic reasoning, In Proceedings of the 38th Annual Meeting of the Association for Computational Linguistics (ACL-2000), Hong Kong.

25. Russell, S.J., Norvig, P. (2003) Artificial Intelligence: A Modern Approach. NJ: Pearson Education Inc.

26. Sarawagi, S., Cohen, W.W. (2004) Semi-Markov Conditional Random Fields for Information Extraction, NIPS 2004 (Advances in Neural Information Processing Systems 17 [Neural Information Processing Systems, NIPS 2004, December 13–18, 2004, Vancouver, British Columbia, Canada]).

27. Shokri, M. (2004) Adjustable Autonomy in Reinforced Image Thresholding, Report, Cs 886: Advanced Topics in Artificial Intelligence, University of Waterloo.

28. Shokri, M., Tizhoosh, H.R. (2003) Using Reinforcement Learning for Image Thresholding, Canadian Conference on Electrical and Computer Engineering, 1:1231–1234.

29. Shokri, M., Tizhoosh, H.R. (2004) Q(λ)-Based Image Thresholding, Canadian Conference on Computer and Robot Vision.

30. Smyth, P., Heckerman, D., Jordan, M. (1996) Probabilistic Independence Networks for Hidden Markov Models, Massachusetts Institute of Technology, Artificial Intelligence Laboratory and Center for Biological and Computational Learning, Department of Brain and Cognitive Science.

31. Sutton R.S., Barto, A.G. (1998) Reinforcement Learning: An Introduction, Cambridge, MA: MIT Press.

32. Thacker, N.A., Lacey, A.J. (1998) Tutorial: The Kalman Filter, Imaging Science and Biomedical Engineering Division, Medical School, University of Manchester, Stopford Building, Oxford Road, Manchester, M13 9PT.

33. Tsiriga, V., Virvou, M. (2004) A Framework for the initialization of student models in Web-based intelligent tutoring systems. User Modeling and User-Adapted Interaction, 14:289–316.

34. Walker, M.A. (2000) An Application of Reinforcement Learning to Dialogue Strategy Selection in a Spoken Dialogue System for Email, Journal of Artificial Intelligence Research (JAIR), 12:387–416.

35. Watkins, C.J.H. (1989) Learning from Delayed Rewards. Cambridge: Cambridge University.
36. Watkins, C.J.H., Dayan, P. (1992) Technical note, Q-learning. Machine Learning, 8:279–292.
37. Wang, G., Mahadevan, S. (1999) Hierarchical Optimization of Policy-Coupled Semi-Markov Decision Processes, Proceeding of the 16th International Conference on Machine Learning (ICML '99), Bled, Slovenia, June 27–30. (nominated for best paper award at ICML-99).
38. Yin, P.Y. (2002) Maximum entropy-based optimal threshold selection using deterministic reinforcement learning with controlled randomization. Signal Processing 82:993–1006.
39. Zhang, W., Dietterich, T.G. (1995) Value Function Approximations and Job-Shop Scheduling, Submitted to the Workshop on Value Function Approximation in Reinforcement Learning at ICML-95.

10
Secure Communication Layer for Scalable Networks of Learning Object Repositories

Marek Hatala, Griff Richards, Timmy Eap, and Ashok Shah

Abstract. The eduSource Communication Layer (ECL) defines a set of services, middleware, and communication conventions that enable repositories and tools to communicate with each other. ECL was designed and implemented within the scope of the recommendations in the IMS DRI specification. The ECL has been deployed worldwide and connects repositories in Canada, the United States, Australia, the United Kingdom, and Europe. In this chapter we describe the design of ECL, its architecture, and its middleware components. We also describe novel ECL security infrastructure (ECL-SI) for Web services that provide the security framework for object repositories based on a trust federation. The security solution defines security profiles, infrastructure services, and middleware component for a low-barrier adoption by existing repositories. Although this infrastructure can scale to large networks; it is particularly sensitive to the needs of medium-sized and small organizations, which have complex attributes and accessing policies.

10.1 Introduction

Over the last few years we have seen significant progress in the area of crucial technologies and standards for the Semantic Web's XML and Resource Description Framework (RDF). They have gained wide acceptance in the industry, and the semantic Web group at W3C is finalizing the recommendation for next essential semantic Web component—the Ontology Web Language. Metadata are in use across all vertical layers of the systems, and several large-scale initiatives are trying to build usable networked systems for object and knowledge sharing and to further our understanding of the related issues. All these activities promise to develop systems that can discover and share information with other systems in the near future.

One of the leading areas where integration and sharing are in high demand is education, particularly in e-learning. The wholesale adoption of Internet technology as a channel for education and training has resulted in an abundance of learning resources in Web-ready digital format. Typically, these digital learning objects [33] may be lesson content stored as text, audiovisual or interactive media files, or simply learning activity templates expressed in a learning design format [18].

Despite their apparent ubiquity, locating and reusing learning objects are hampered by a lack of coordinated effort in addressing issues related to their storage, cataloging, and rights management. Strident efforts have been made to create portal repositories by communities such as Merlot,[1] SMETE,[2] RDN[3] and, in Canada, by BCcampus[4] and CAREO[5]. Not surprisingly, each entity produces a rather individual reflection of its own perceived organizational needs, and the concept of making all these repositories work together, while laudable, has received less attention.

The e-learning community has seen fruitful initiatives in the standardization of learning object metadata by the Institute of Electrical and Electronics Engineers (IEEE) [16] and the emergence of specifications toward the standardization of other aspects of learning objects and learning processes by organizations such as IMS and ADL.[6] More recently, the e-learning community has been focusing on the ability to connect and use resources located in distributed and heterogeneous repositories. This process of federation closely resembles the initiatives in the domain of digital libraries, to the extent that there have been initiatives such as the IMS Alt-i Lab meetings to bring these two communities together.

We begin by examining how interoperability is handled in several significant interoperability initiatives and projects. Next we describe the main drivers of the eduSource project as an infrastructure for connecting different types of networks and people. This provides us with main issues when creating large and open networks and guides us in the development of the eduSource Communication Layer (ECL) and enabling middleware for easy connection within the ECL network and between eduSource and other networks. Later we present the design of the federated security layer that sits on top of the ECL. Our work defines the necessary infrastructure components and the profile to support the Web services security in the federation of Web services. Finally we discuss lessons learned in the context of the design and implementation choices, and we compare our approach with other approaches in the field.

10.2 Major Interoperability Efforts in E-Learning

OAI: Although not specifically oriented to education, the Open Archive Initiative (OAI) [32] develops and promotes interoperability standards for content dissemination. The Protocol for Metadata Harvesting (PMH) developed by OAI provides an application-independent interoperability framework for metadata harvesting.

---

[1] Multimedia Educational Resource for Learning and Online Teaching, http://www.merlot.org

[2] Science, Math, Engineering on Technology Education Digital Library, http://www.smete.org.

[3] Resource Discovery Network, http://www.rdn.ac.uk.

[4] http://www.bccampus.ca.

[5] Campus Alberk Repository of Educational Objects, http://www.careo.org.

[6] http://www.imsglobal.org and http://www.adlnet.org.

The protocol enables repositories (called harvesters) to selectively collect metadata from other sources (providers) and create cumulative and/or specialized collections of metadata. In addition to its protocol, OAI provides guidelines and community support. The protocol is used widely by other initiatives to support harvesting functionality.

NSDL: The National Science Digital Library (NSDL) project[7] is a major project funded by the National Science Foundation with the goal of building a digital library for education in science, mathematics, engineering, and technology. The potential collections for inclusion in NSDL have a wide variety of data types, metadata standards, protocols, authentication schemes, and business models [2]. The aim of the NSDL interoperability is to build coherent services for users from technically different components. NSDL aims to support three levels of interoperability:

1. **Federation** implements the strong standards approach with libraries agreeing to use specific standards.
2. **Harvesting** allows higher autonomy. The only requirement is to enable a limited set of services via a simple exchange mechanism. NSDL is using PMH developed by the OAI (described above). Harvesting is supported on the repository side by implementing a relatively simple wrapper communicated via PMH and providing metadata based on Dublin Core.[8]
3. **Gathering** uses the Web crawler technique to collect information from the organizations that do not formally participate in the NSDL program.

The NSDL has selected eight preferred metadata element sets for metadata storage. While member libraries can store the metadata in their original local format, they have to be able to serve the metadata in Dublin Core format. Effectively this solution establishes Dublin Core as the lowest common denominator for the NSDL. Through its active grants program NSDL has exponentially increased the number of affiliated searchable collections in a few short years and a vast variety of resources can be found through its portal.

IMS DRI: The IMS Digital Repository Interoperability (DRI) Group, in its specifications for the digital repository interoperability [17], provided a functional architecture and reference model for repository interoperability. Aiming at very broad application of the specification the DRI document makes recommendations only to a certain level and leaves the resolution of more operational issues to the system implementers. Five basic functions defined by IMS DRI are search/expose, gather/expose, submit/store, request/deliver, and subscribe/alert. For the search function, the specification recommends using either XQuery[9] with the SOAP[10] protocol or Z39.50.[11] For the gather function, the OAI's harvesting protocol is recommended. No recommendation is made for the other three functions in the

---

[7] http://www.nsdl.org.
[8] http://www.dublincore.org.
[9] http://www.w3c.org/XML/Query.
[10] http://www.w3c.org/TR/soap/.
[11] http://www.loc.gov/z3950/agency/.

current version of the specification. The current version of IMS DRI envisions but does not explicitly deal with heterogeneity of the repositories, and it is up to the implementers to ensure format compatibility. The DRI group recommends development of "search intermediaries" that will deal with multiple formats. IMS DRI was first implemented by our eduSource project in 2002.

POOL: The Portals for Online Objects in Learning (POOL) project ran from 1999 to 2002. One of its major goals was to build an infrastructure for connecting heterogeneous repositories into one network [25]. The infrastructure used a peer-to-peer model in which nodes could be individual repositories (called SPLASH) or community or enterprise repositories (PONDs). PONDs were connected to the POOL network using a specialized peer performing the functions of both a gateway and wrapper. The POOL network initially used the JXTA[12] peering protocol, but later a POOL peering protocol was implemented to improve network performance. POOL followed the CanCore/IMS metadata profile/specification[13] to exchange metadata. Connected PONDs communicate using wrappers either via HTTP and CGI or XML-RPC protocol. The wrapper also performs the metadata schema translation functions that are needed. The network supported high autonomy for the repositories, but this required creating a specialized wrapper to translate between the metadata schemas and communication protocols each time a new repository was added to the network.

ELENA/Edutella: This collaborative European project is creating Smart Spaces for Learning [28]. Smart learning spaces are defined as educational service mediators that allow the consumption of heterogeneous learning services via assessment tools, learning management systems, educational (meta) repositories and live delivery systems such as video conferencing systems. ELENA[14] builds a dynamic learner profile that is used as a basis for offering the learner the choice of a variety of knowledge sources. ELENA forms a layer on top of a learning management network built on Edutella [23]. Edutella is an RDF-based peer-to-peer (P2P) infrastructure that aims to connect highly heterogeneous educational peers with different types of repositories, query languages, and different kinds of metadata schemata.

OKI: The Open Knowledge Initiative[15] builds an open and extensible architecture that specifies how the components of an educational software environment communicate with each other and with other enterprise systems. The OKI provides a service-specific API called Open Service Interface Definition (OSID) that fosters an effective application development for higher education by providing definitions for data and common services. OSIDs cover a wide range of learning services from generic ones such as authentication and digital repository to services specific to education such as course management and grading. Currently OSID has few test implementations but has promising support from both the academic and industrial community.

---

[12] http://www.jxta.org.
[13] http://www.cancore.org.
[14] http://www.elena-project.org.
[15] http://web.mit.edu/oki/.

eduSourceCanada: Following the POOL project, the eduSourceCanada project[16] brought together major Canadian learning object repository (LOR) players to create an open infrastructure for linking interoperable LORs [26]. Within eduSource the authors led the development of an interoperability infrastructure to support a wide range of services and provide both ease of connecting and ease of using new and existing systems. For example, a repository using OAI's PMH protocol and Dublin Core metadata can either communicate with the eduSource network as a whole via the gateway mechanism or become a participant with access to wider range of services via the ECL interoperability connector. This chapter provides a full account of the robust, rapid, and flexible interoperability solutions developed within eduSource and the later projects.

GLOBE: Global Learning Objects Brokered Exchange (GLOBE)[17] is a consortium bringing together leading efforts in the e-learning federated search community. The initial partners in the consortium are the Ariadne Foundation in Europe, education.au in Australia, eduSourceCanada, the Merlot repository in the U.S., and National Institute of Multimedia Education (NIME) in Japan. The first four partners have already implemented their own interoperability solutions for federated searching across repositories. GLOBE aims to link these together to develop a worldwide distributed network of learning objects that meet high-quality standards. Ultimately those joining GLOBE would be required to make their technical alliances only once to the benefit of all partners worldwide.

10.3 IMS Digital Repository Interoperability

IMS is a global learning consortium developing specifications for a wide range of learning contexts. The specifications range from individual learning resource metadata specification, through specific learning specifications such as a question and test interoperability, to more generic digital repository interoperability specification [17]. IMS specifications are defined by three documents: the information model, the XML binding, and the best practices implementation guide.

The first version of IMS DRI specification (released in January 2003) provides recommendations for the interoperation of the most common repository functions. The specification does not make any assumptions about the technology or content of the repositories, and treats them as a collection of resources. The IMS DRI information model defines eight core functions (Table 10.1) where three functions are defined at the repository level (store, expose, deliver) and five functions are defined at the resource utilizer level (search, gather, submit, alert, request).

The reference model in the specification provides recommendations on functional architecture and recommends specific technologies. However, the level of recommendations is very high, leaving many specific details unanswered. The following five specifications are used for the combination of core functions:

---

[16] http://www.edusource.ca.
[17] http://globe.edna.edu.au/.

TABLE 10.1. IMS digital repository interoperability core functions.

Service	Description
Search	IMS DRI recommends XQuery as a query language. To enable connection of the repositories that do not support (full) XQuery, an ECL uses a set of XQuery templates. The repositories register their search service with an indication of supported templates or of their full XQuery search capability.
Gather	The gather service corresponds to the harvesting of metadata. IMS DRI recommends using the OAI protocol. ECL implemented Web services equivalent of the OAI protocol.
Expose	Expose service is provided by clients in the asynchronous communication. This service will be called by service providers to return the responses for search, gather, and alert.
Submit	This function moves an object (metadata and learning object) from a client to repository.
Store	When asynchronous messaging is required, this service is called by service providers to return the results of submit function (client function).
Request	This function asks to deliver objects to a client. The transfer protocol could be a successive SOAP request to download the object or an FTP transfer protocol.
Deliver	When asynchronous messaging is required, this service is called by service providers to return the requested objects (client service).
Alert	IMS DRI recommends Alert for push gather. Whenever repository has new metadata matching subscriber's parameters, it sends an alert message to the subscribers.

1. Search/Expose. Two query languages are recommended: XQuery for XML format and Z39.50 for searching library information.
2. Gather/Expose. No specific recommendation is made; the IMS DRI suggests that the OAI model will provide sufficient functionality.
3. Alert/Expose. No specific recommendation is made as Alert is regarded as being out of the scope of the first version of the recommendation.
4. Submit/Store. The specification recommends using the IMS package as a SOAP attachment.
5. Request/Deliver. The specification excludes several related issues from its scope, leaving implementers with the general guidance of using HTTP and FTP for different types of resources.

The IMS DRI Core Functions XML binding document specifies a SOAP messages over HTTP protocol as an initial message binding and defines the general message structure. Once again, the specification is not very specific and leaves many detailed questions open.

10.4 eduSource: An Open Network for Connecting Communities

To connect Canadian repositories into an open network, the eduSource project implemented the IMS DRI specification as closely as possible. To understand the motivation behind eduSource's strong requirements for interoperability, we need to analyze the reality of the Canadian educational space and the variety of communities to be served by eduSource.

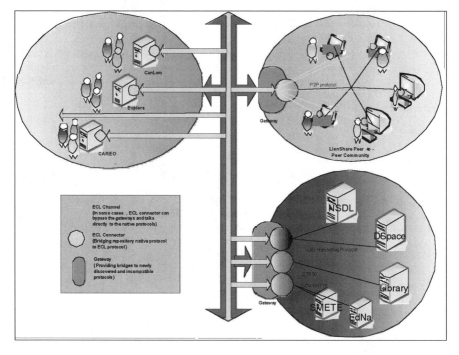

FIGURE 10.1. EduSource infrastructure supports three types of communities: server-type repositories and portals (top left) that already have their own user base, individual user tools and peer-to-peer systems (top right), and other existing system with already established protocols such as digital libraries, other repository projects, etc. (bottom right).

Server-type repositories: Figure 10.1 shows a schematic infrastructure of edu-Source network. The top left quadrant represents server-type repositories. The communities served by these repositories vary and can include governmental, academic, business, or special interest groups. Some of these repositories were created and managed by an organization expressly to serve their communities. For example, a university repository primarily serves its community of university students and professors; similarly, a provincial ministry of education might operate a repository of learning resources for the K–12 schools within its jurisdiction. Another type might be a commercial repository that licenses their content or charges fees per use. Another common type is informal repositories that are not tied to any formal organization but were simply set up by the community members themselves and are managed to further the community goals. In all these cases the repositories can be either public, or restricted to serve only its own community, or can provide mixed access with a blend of privileges depending on user identity and role.

The server-type repositories generally provide access to their functionality through a Web portal. This includes search and create functionality for metadata and view functionality for the resources. The metadata schema is determined by the repository developer and cannot be easily changed. One example of an interesting repository is CAREO,[18] which in addition to Web forms for metadata creation also provides a specialized application, ALOHA,[19] for metadata creation and uploading of metadata and learning objects to the appropriate repository. As community repositories provide the repository as a service to members, they typically insist on associating their identity with any objects retrieved or services provided.

Peer-to-peer repositories and end-user tools: The top right part of Figure 10.1 represents a network of end user tools and individual repositories that communicate with other repositories or with each other on the peer-to-peer basis. SPLASH [15] is an example of a peer-to-peer repository that was developed in POOL. Individual SPLASH repositories provide the storage and management functions for the learning objects used or collected by an individual user. SPLASH also enables its users to create metadata for the learning objects residing either on the individual's file system or on the Web. SPLASH uses peer-to-peer protocol to search for learning objects on other peers[20] and provides file swapping functionality to transfer learning objects between peers.

Peer-to-peer repositories serve the needs of the individual instructors and learners who may not have centralized repository support from their organizations. They are also of preference for those who object to the loss of control over their resources and imposed limitations when using centralized repositories, and they can serve as test sites for objects under construction either by content authors or as products of constructive learning activities. P2P repositories enable each individual to be included and contribute toward the community resources with minimal technical requirements. P2P repositories may lack the system support of the server-type repositories, but they often provide their users with additional object management functions and facilitate cross-repository searches. A side benefit typical of P2P systems is their potential scalability when high demand for a particular type of object occurs.

Repositories of harvested metadata: Metadata harvesting is an alternative to federated searches. Instead of constantly sending search requests out to all the primary repositories, harvesters collect metadata into a centralized database and requests scan the internal centralized collection. The objects themselves remain stored in their home repositories. To be efficient, a search engine might harvest metadata from external searches, and only conduct new external searches when insufficient objects are identified in the current database. In another scenario, a harvester might continually poll repositories for new metadata records. Frequent polling provides a better quality of service as the metadata will be up to date and provide few dead links. However, as the number of harvested records grows quickly to several hundreds of thousand records, refreshing the metadata collection can

---

[18] http://www.careo.org.

[19] http://aloha.netera.ca/.

[20] In the POOL network SPLASH also searches server-type repositories that were connected to the POOL network. In the eduSource network this functionality is being replaced by the more generic ECL approach.

become a heavy maintenance issue. Harvesting works well for repositories that use the same or easily mapped metadata schemas, as the queries are typically specified in one schema only.

It is important to note that not all primary sources (repositories) allow harvesting of their metadata. This is especially true of commercial repositories where their business model depends on the users visiting their repository directly. Some repositories only allow harvesting of certain metadata fields. In general, proprietary repositories prefer federated searches that generate results that direct potential users to the company's own Web site.

External repositories and networks: eduSource places an emphasis on connecting to other significant initiatives and networks. These connections can be bidirectional, enabling both eduSource users to search beyond the eduSource network and external users to find resources inside eduSource. Alternatively an external repository can use our preconfigured middleware to connect to the eduSource network.

10.5 ECL: eduSource Communication Layer

A communication protocol plays an important role in each of the major initiatives listed above. It allows the initiative to achieve its goals by enabling communication between its members, tools, and services. EduSource is a broad network aiming to support a wide range of services. At the same time, for eduSource to become an open network it has to build its protocol on existing standards and recommendations.

The eduSource Communication Layer (ECL) defines a set of services, middleware, and communication conventions that enable the four types of repositories and tools listed above to communicate with each other. ECL was designed and implemented within the scope of the recommendations in the IMS DRI specification. However, as noted in section 10.3, the IMS DRI recommendation is not specific enough for direct implementation, and the current usage of recommended technologies is not as widespread as assumed in the specification. Developing the ECL required interpretation of the IMS DRI using a variety of technologies beyond those suggested in the specification.

10.5.1 General Approach

The ECL architecture uses the Web services approach in which services communicate using the ECL protocol (Fig. 10.2). Although choosing the Web services approach was a straightforward decision, selecting associated technologies needed more consideration. The criteria for the protocol and its development process that affected our approach included:

- ECL connects a heterogeneous network consisting of existing and future institution repositories, peer-to-peer network, individual small repositories, and application interfaces.

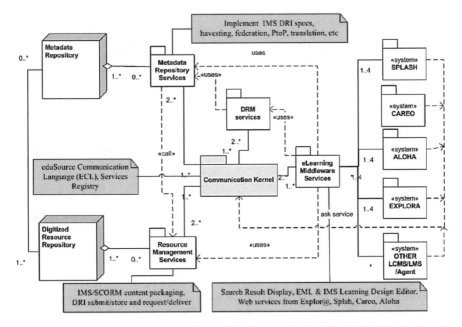

FIGURE 10.2. The ECL architecture. The architecture was designed for the highly distributed system of heterogeneous repositories and services. The architecture differentiates between the metadata repositories and resource repositories and makes an assumption that there are multiple instances of those. The repository services are using available standards.

- ECL will be evolving over the time, which makes all the parallel activities vulnerable to changes in the protocol.
- ECL supports many new services nonexisting in the current systems. Some of these services require asynchronous communication, such as search through peer-to-peer network or alert.
- ECL is a complex protocol. To achieve significant adoption, it has to be fast and easy to use and be supported with preconfigured middleware.
- A solution for connection between ECL and other initiatives has to be easy to maintain and easy to update if there is a change in the protocol used by the other initiative.

Extensive development team discussions led to document-style Web services [20] being selected as a method of the communication between services. ECL closely follows the IMS DRI specification and uses SOAP as a communication layer. IMS DRI core functions (see Table 10.1) are defined and implemented as ECL services. Repositories or tools connected to the ECL network can implement some of these services and register them in the ECL registry. Registration is a preferred way for discoverability of permanent services. However, in many cases user tools connected to the network do not register any service. For example, a search application does not provide any services on its own but needs to implement "delivery" service for asynchronous search results. This was made possible by using document-style Web services in preference to RPC-style.

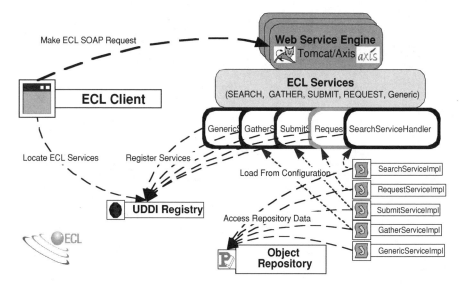

FIGURE 10.3. The ECL connector. The ECL connector is built on top of the Tomcat/Axis[14] platform for Web services. The connector defines ECL services in the form of specific handlers. To deploy a service at the repository a developer implements one or more of the handler implementations classes to communicate with their object repository. The ECL connector also manages the communication with the ECL registry. On the ECL client side the developer use the connector as the library to communicate with the ECL registry and facilitate processing and sending of ECL messages.

ECL is a complex protocol with communication patterns that may be challenging to implement. To lower the technical barriers for service providers to join the ECL network, it was essential to have a solution that made the ECL easy to implement. Hence we developed the ECL connector, a connecting middleware that facilitates the implementation of ECL services and tools.

10.5.2 ECL Connector

Since the complexity of the ECL protocol might be detrimental to its adoption, we are providing an "off-the-shelf" ECL connector that implements the ECL protocol, and ECL security (described below), and supports discovery and registration of services with the ECL registry. ECL connector is a middleware that exposes ECL services in the form of handlers and hides all the complexity of properly encoding XML messages and communicating with other ECL services.

The ECL connector provides a standard API to connect an existing repository to the ECL network. The ECL protocol only requires institutional repositories or repository tools to implement the connector handlers for those specific services the users want to expose to others (Fig. 10.3). Similarly, tool developers can use

---

[14] http://ws.apache.org/axis/.

```
public class SubmitServiceHandlerImpl extends SubmitServiceHandler{
  RepositoryBean rb;
  public SubmitServiceHandlerImpl(){
     rb = new RepositoryBean();
  }
  /*  init allows instantiator to initialize this class
     with user input parameters */
  public void init(Properties params){
  }
  public Store processSubmit(Submit request, DataHandler dh)
                                          throws SubmitException{
     try{
        String transId = rb.saveImsContent(
           request.getTransactionId(),
           request.getUsername(),
           request.getObjectAccessPermission(),
           request.getImsContentName(),
           dh.getInputStream(),
           request.isUnpack());
        Store store = new StoreImpl();
        store.setTransactionId(transId);
        return store;
     }catch(Exception e){
        e.printStackTrace();
        throw new SubmitException("Unable to process submit");
}}}
```

FIGURE 10.4. A repository specific ECL submit implementation. The `processSubmit` method is called by the `RepositoryBean` object, which provide `saveImsContent` method. The example shows how the data are extracted from the request object and passed to the repository, specific `saveImsContent` method.

ECL connector as a library that helps them to build and send queries and then extract results from the responses with very little programming effort. For example, Fig. 10.4 shows a snippet of the code that a repository developer has to implement to process an ECL submit message.

The second set of API functions allows the developers to communicate with the ECL registry (Fig. 10.3). The ECL connector registers services to the ECL registry as a part of the deployment process. This process is managed by the configuration wizard and does not require any programming effort. On the other side the API for querying ECL registry can be used by end-user tools developers to build tools that allow users to search and browse the ECL registry and to select repositories they want to communicate with.[15]

The ECL connector federates the communication to all selected repositories in the multithreaded fashion. It also provides multiuser support, which makes it suitable to be incorporated into multiuser environments such as portals.

---

[15] Alternatively, the end-user tools can be preconfigured to access only predefined repositories. This is desirable in specific applications such as in the K–12 environment where a set of specific repositories can be targeted instead of letting students select repositories manually.

The ECL connector also provides full support for the ECL security profiles and automatically selects the security profile appropriate for each repository.

The connector also facilitates version synchronization as the protocol evolves. Changes in the protocol itself rarely propagate to the API level. In most cases, repositories do not have to worry about the change in the protocol; they only need to update the connector's newer versions. Changes in the ECL protocol can be detected by the newer version of the connector and are dealt with automatically. This feature makes the implementation of the ECL protocol very attractive, especially in this early development stage where the implementation is still evolving.

It is important to note that an API is programming language specific while a protocol is language agnostic. Although the ECL connector with its API simplifies the connection process for those working in the same language, for example, Java, describing the protocol provides an opportunity for different programming language communities to implement and share ECL connectors in their preferred language.[16]

10.5.3 ECL Gateway

Although the ECL internal protocol provides a flexible and efficient solution, the reality is that well-established repositories and initiatives will continue to use their own protocols. Thus an ability of the ECL to connect to other established protocols and major initiatives is of the utmost importance to the ECL network participants. ECL addresses the problem of outside interoperability by providing a second type of mediator simply called the ECL gateway. The ECL gateway is modeled after the design pattern of an adapter [10] functioning at the network level. The main function of the gateway is to mediate between ECL and communication protocols used by the outside systems.

The ECL gateway provides a framework (Fig. 10.5) defining a chain of handlers that perform a conversion between ECL protocol and the protocol of the external network. The gateway framework enables us to define the mapping between protocols at four levels:

L1: Communication protocol (HTTP, SOAP, XML-RPC, peer-to-peer, etc.)
L2: Communication language (ECL, OAI, POOL, SQI,[17] CQL,[18] etc.)
L3: Metadata (IEEE LOM, IMS LOM, CanCore, Dublin core)
L4: Ontologies (vocabularies for metadata)

A separate gateway needs to be configured for each additional protocol; however, networks sharing the same protocol can share the same gateway. Typically, several

---

[16] At the time of writing, a stable version of the Java and partial version of Python connectors are available.

[17] Simple Query Interface, http://rubens.cs.kuleuven.ac.be/vqwiki-2.5.5/jsp/Wiki? LorInteroperability.

[18] Common Query Language, http://www.loc.gov/z3950/agency/zing/cql/.

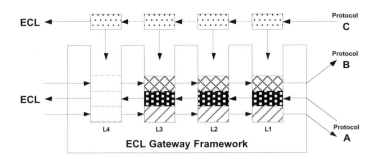

FIGURE 10.5. The ECL gateway framework is designed to easily build bridges between two protocols. The bridge consists of a chain of handlers that convert messages in one protocol to messages in another protocol. The four processing layers perform the conversion at the protocol transport layer (L1), protocol actions or language (L2), metadata (L3), and vocabulary or taxonomy semantics (L4).

ECL gateways run on a dedicated computer and provide services for all participants in the ECL network. After it is deployed the ECL gateway can be discovered and used by users in the same way as any other ECL service.

The main benefit of placing the mapping functionality for an outside network onto a gateway instead of with each participant is that it can be easily updated if the change in the outside network protocol occurs. In such a case, a chain of mapping handlers is updated at the one place, and all ECL network participants can continue to communicate with the gateway using ECL protocol without any change to the clients necessary. The ECL gateway is also scalable; there can be several ECL gateways for the same outside network if the traffic between the two networks is high.

10.5.4 ECL Registry

Although not essential, the ECL registry plays a major role in supporting the open nature of the ECL network. The main role of the registry is to enable discovery of the repositories and services by the end users as they become available. The secondary goal is to provide the end users applications with the information that will allow them to communicate with the discovered repositories immediately, without the need of modifying the application code.

Two sets of criteria, technical interoperability and content classification, are used to search the ECL registry. First, the technical criteria such as version of the protocol, supported metadata standards, required security profiles, etc. are used to select repositories that the user application is capable of communicating with. Second, each repository is classified with one of the available content classifications such as Dewey Decimal classification (three levels) [8] (DDC) and ACM classification [1]. The API in the ECL connector allows end users to select the classification system first and then use the terms within the classification system to discover repositories from their area of interest. The ECL registry supports semantic search within the classification hierarchy to facilitate search situations when direct string matches are not available.

The ECL registry is built on top of the UDDI[19] registry. It should be noted that although in ECL the repositories are accessible by Web services, the main purpose of the registry is not to share WSDL[20] descriptions of the Web services, as is common in Web services architectures, but rather to support the end users in their discovery of the services.

10.5.5 ECL Federated Searching Across Multiple Repositories

The ECL was designed as an open and highly distributed system of independent services. In ECL the end users can select the services they want to communicate with. Typically, users want to search through several repositories with a single query. This assumption is built into the ECL design and it is supported by the ECL federated search.

As mentioned above, the ECL connector in the *client application* provides the federated search to the selected repositories. This avoids potential scalability issues in other approaches to federated search such as EdNA[21] or Merlot,[22] where the federated search is provided by a specific centralized application.

A second interesting aspect of the ECL federated search is how the ECL gateways are treated by the search. As mentioned above, the main role of the ECL gateway is to transform between ECL protocol and the protocol used by another network or repository. As the transformation process is time-consuming, increasing traffic might create scalability problems. The ECL solved this problem by enlisting the help of the ECL connector that will also distribute and update the ECL gateway mapping code. When the user selects a particular ECL gateway in the ECL registry, the record in the registry indicates which class is responsible for transforming ECL messages to the messages of the network the ECL gateway bridges into. The ECL connector first checks whether that code is available on the local client and if it is, then the code is dynamically loaded and the client sends messages in the other network native protocol. If the code is not available, the standard ECL message is sent to the ECL gateway, where it is translated and sent to the target repository or network. This provides for the highly scalable solution that makes full use of the computing power on the client machines.

10.6 Scalable Security Solution

ECL security infrastructure (ECL-SI) is designed as a general security solution for the open network of Web services (such as ECL). The ECL-SI builds on the

---

[19] http://www.uddi.org.
[20] http://www.w3e.org/TR/wsdl.
[21] http://www.edna.edu.au/edna/search?SearchMode=Advancemode.
[22] http://fedsearch.merlot.org/main/search.jsp.

idea of a federation of services where trust exists between organizations providing the services. The main goal of ECL-SI is to support an effective sharing and interoperability in many sectors such as government research, education, and business in general. The solution supports greater interoperability by providing a scalable solution for secure access to resources.

ECL-SI makes extensive use of standards developed by the Web services (WS) security group at OASIS.[23] The WS security standard [22] defines how to send SOAP [4] messages over insecure transport by embedding security headers that include signatures, encrypted text, and other security tokens. WS-security policy [9] is another set of specifications that provides a standard format for specifying how Web service implementations construct and check WS security headers. There is a substantial body of research results available in the verification of the security policies [3,12,13], and generating implementation code based on policies and abstract protocol descriptions [19,24,29] as well as tools for generating policies [3,30].

The ECL-SI builds on the idea of federated security, which aims to provide an identity management and secure access to resources and services among multiple organizations [21]. The Liberty Project[24] is a consortium of over 150 organizations that is working to address the technical, business, and policy challenges surrounding identity and Web services or federated identity management. The project develops specifications, guidelines, and best practices. The Liberty identity federation framework proposes the use of a federated network identity to solve the problems of identity management [31]. The Shibboleth Project[25] has developed an open-source system that provides a federated security for Web-based applications. In Shibboleth, providers make an authorization decision based on the attributes issued to the users by their home organization. The attributes and their values are agreed upon by the federation members and exchanged in the form of Security Assertion Markup Language (SAML) assertions [27].

ECL-SI supports a security layer on top of the ECL digital repository interoperability layer. We defined and implemented multiple security profiles for both federated and repository-managed security. Our security infrastructure is designed with the specific goals of supporting the easy creation of new federations and having low barriers to adoption by new members joining the network. The ECL connector provides a full support for security that simplifies the connection of new nodes. The ECL connector communicates with two other infrastructure components: the certification authority and attribute authority. Similarly to the connector, both infrastructure components are easy to deploy and connect to an existing organizational infrastructure.

Our design is compatible with the Shibboleth solution by effectively extending the Shibboleth solution for Web-based applications to rich clients and Web

---

[23] http://www.oasis-open.org/.
[24] http://www.projectliberty.org.
[25] http://shibboleth.internet2.edu.

services. The implementation uses the latest standards developed by the WS security working group.

10.6.1 Motivations for Federated Security Solution

The learning repository networks, as they exist in their current form, are limited to sharing free learning resources. If any restrictions are imposed on the collection in the repository, then the repository does not participate in the learning repository network but rather requires users to obtain a user account and log in to the repository through the repository Web site. The security layer for ECL extends the repository's ability to not only share free material but also serve the material that has a certain level of access restrictions. The implementation of security will be of increasing importance as e-learning organizations add new types of services beyond content repositories. Our design of the security layer draws on two case studies that provide the motivation for our work.

10.6.1.1 Case Study: Course Management Systems

The Course Management System (CMS) at Simon Fraser University (SFU), Surrey, England, is used to manage and deliver courses that are structured into learning objects. The learning objects in CMS include material developed by faculty (documents, Web pages, media documents, applets, etc.); cached copies of material from the Web for which use has been cleared with the material owners; referenced materials from the digital library maintained by the SFU library with different licensing agreements with publishers; and material directly purchased from publishers for specific course offerings. To complicate the situation, learning objects quite often include resources with different access rights to the original resource. For example, a unit of instruction prepared by a professor who wants to share it with the community can contain an image from an image library with a license allowing access to any member of the academic community at a Canadian university and a scanned image from a book with access purchased from a publisher for a specific group of students taking a course. Although access to these resources can differ based on the user roles such as faculty-at-SFU, faculty-at-Canadian-university, general-public, undergraduate-registered-to-itec426-fall2005, etc. the current solution conservatively locks the whole repository, and only students and faculty directly associated with the courses can access the material after they log in to the system.

The access to CMS for the faculty at SFU could be easily accomplished by binding the access policies to the directory information available for SFU users. However, the external academic community that might benefit from access, to the substantial resources licensed for academic use has no access, as the attribute information is not available for the users external to SFU. Clearly a method for recognizing attributes of faculty and students in partner universities could promote cost-sharing of licenses and increase the overall availability of licensed content.

10.6.1.2 Case Study: Secure P2P Network LionShare

The LionShare project[26] is developing an authenticated peer-to-peer (P2P) system that uses Security Assertions Markup Language (SAML) attributes for controlling access to learning resources shared by other peers. LionShare also connects peer-to-peer users to the learning object repositories by using the ECL connector. To allow the LionShare users from different organization to access the resources in the protected repositories (such as the one described above), a solution utilizing a trust federation is needed. Our solution enables the repositories to accept attributes issued to the peer-to-peer users by their home organizations and allow them access to the resources based on the attribute values and the repository access policies. In the other direction, the repository users can use attributes issued by their organization to access resources available on the LionShare network via the ECL/LionShare bridge that converts between the protocols but maintains the security credentials.

10.6.2 Federated Security

Different organizations have different security policies with respect to the access to their resources. Some organizations want to maintain full control over users and their account management (e.g., Merlot). Other organizations are looking at the more scalable approach in the form of the trust federations (e.g., publishers).

10.6.2.1 Shibboleth

Shibboleth is an initiative by Internet2 working to develop security solutions that promote interinstitutional collaboration and access to digital content. It is a single-sign-on (SSO) and attribute-based exchange protocol consisting of two main components: Identity Provider (IdP) and Service Provider (SP). For the installation of the Shibboleth IdP, it is recommended to have a secure local authentication system and an LDAP[27] directory storing user attributes in eduPerson[28] organizational scheme. IdP is coupled with attribute authority (AA), which maintains a set of policies called Attribute Release Policies that govern the sharing of user attributes with Shibboleth SP sites [6].

In an SSO model, users sign on to their respective IdPs and can access all SPs in the federation. In Shibboleth, a *federation* is an association of organizations that use a common set of attributes, practices, and policies to exchange information about their users and resources in order to enable collaborations and transactions [5]. Shibboleth achieves SSO by using Web browser technologies: redirection and cookies. The first time a user accesses services on an SP, the SP displays a list

---

[26] http://lionshare.its.psu.edu.
[27] Lightweight Directory Access Protocol, http://tools.ietf.org/html/4510.
[28] http://www.educause.edu/eduperson/.

of trusted IdPs.[29] The SP redirects the user to the selected IdP with appropriate parameters necessary for IdP to validate the SP as a trusted entity and redirect the user back to the SP once the authentication is complete. The information is passed between the IdP and SP servers as a cookie, and a user's profile is then delivered directly to the SP from IdP as SAML attribute assertions. The profile is valid for the session duration.

10.6.2.2 Web Services and Federated Security

Web services differ from browser transactions in that they lack user interactions, redirection, and cookies. Since user applications access Web services on behalf of the users, the applications must determine the user profiles' attributes required to access a service before making the request. The applications request these attributes from IdP and use it to access the service on a SP. To make the operation safe a combination of security features such as certificates, signatures, and encryption has to be used and treated in a specific way that is defined in the security profile. Our work defines the necessary infrastructure components and the profile to support the Web services' security in the federation of Web services.

10.6.3 Security Infrastructure Components

The ECL security infrastructure (ECL-SI) is a lightweight integrated solution. It is flexible in the sense that it enables repositories to join the federation with the minimal effort. Technically, the ECL-SI allows repositories to use any IdP and to form their own circle of trust (federation). To provide this flexibility, the ECL-SI assumes that the repositories determine their own trust federation and their own access control policies while the ECL-SI provides the basic mechanisms and infrastructure components to support this trust. The ECL-SI is designed for Web services and provides three components: certification authority (CA), local attribute authority (LAA), and ECL registry.

10.6.3.1 Certification Authority

The ECL-SI solution depends on certificates to be issued to users and to repositories by trusted entities. Unlike a Web application, all members including users must have a certificate signed by a trusted CA. The ECL-SI accommodates both a commercial CA and its own ECL-CA. The ECL-CA can be integrated into the organizational authentication system to provide certificates to the organization members and services.

The ECL-SI supports establishing trust in a small group of organizations by organizing their CAs into a hierarchy and providing a mechanism for validating

---

[29] Trust is maintained by the federation. For example, in the InCommon federation sponsored by Internet2 to service U.S. higher educational institutions, all SPs and IdPs receive a list of all trusted sites and certificates to validate trust and authorize the access control to digital contents [5].

the trust for all members under the same CA umbrella. It should be noted, that the strength of the security depends on the authentication system, and it is up to the federation to decide what authentication level is appropriate for their federation. The ECL-CA can be integrated with a standard login module such as Kerberos[30] or simple login with username and password. However, the infrastructure also allows both repository and application developers to load and use their own login modules.

10.6.3.2 Local Attribute Authority

LAA is a component of the identity provider in the ECL-SI. Users obtain their required attributes assertions from LAA to access resources at an SP. An LAA can be coupled with a CA to avoid sending authentication to two different sites. The ECL-LAA is a modified Shibboleth IdP, which is adapted to work with Web services. Assuming that the user applications know the required attributes to access a service, the applications formulate a Shibboleth attribute query request and call LAA. The LAA is typically integrated with the organizational directory service where it obtains user attributes. Typically, the user certificate is also included in the SAML assertion, and then the whole assertion is signed by the LAA to guarantee the attributes are presented by their owner (so-called holder-of-the-key method[31]).

10.6.3.3 ECL Registry

The ECL registry was described above. It registry plays a significant role in the ECL-SI. The ECL registry holds information about SPs' supported security profiles, their certificates, a list of their trusted LAAs, a list of their required attributes, and their values needed to access resources on the SP. Based on this information, user applications can determine if they have the required security credentials to access a resource. First, the user applications begin determining if the SPs are trusted members of the federation they associate to, and then check if their LAAs are in the list. Finally, they determine if they have all the required attributes and if their attribute values match those in the list of possible values. These checks are done automatically and can be used to preselect a set of services the application is able to communicate with. The user makes the final selection only from the list of compatible services.

In the ECL scheme, the SPs do not have to be known in advance but can be discovered by querying the registry. This is different from the other federations such as InCommon [5], where the federation maintains the list of trusted entities and the list has to be distributed to all members of the federation.

---

[30] http://web.mit.edu/kerberos/.
[31] The method opens the SSL connection using a trust certificate only with the holder of the matching private key. As a result the connection is established only with the agent with the proven identity.

10.6.4 ECL Security Profiles

A *security profile* represents the description of the message exchange sequence and how it is supported by security information in the protocol messages. At the level of its SOAP-based protocol the ECL-SI defines two types of Web services security profiles: repository controlled and federated.

Both profiles use message level security as defined by WS security [22] involving a combination of the security headers in the SOAP message (certificates and signatures) with encryption of parts of the SOAP message itself. Different combinations of these security techniques within the profile allow us to achieve different levels of security. This differs from the pure SSL[32] approach, where the only security measure is to secure the communication channel. The messages in ECL-SI can be delivered over an unsecured wire and can be (partially) processed by the middleware services if required. The following subsections look at the two ECL security profiles in detail.

10.6.4.1 Repository Controlled Security Profile

In the repository controlled security profile the user has to have an account at the target repository. The repository manages its own user base, and users are responsible to negotiate with the repository for their access on individual basis. This typically means registering with the repository either for free or paid service. As a result, users obtain the username and password they use to authenticate themselves to the repository.

Figure 10.6 shows the flow of the messages and user's actions in the repository controlled profile. The user discovers the repository in the ECL registry and user clients obtain the necessary information for the profile. To obtain the user name and password, the information the registry record contains URL, where the users can register with the repository. The ECL-SI includes the username and password in ECL messages with appropriate encryption. When the repository receives the request, it validates the security parameters and grants access to the user.

If the repository requires the encryption and signature, the ECL client uses the repository's certificate to encrypt the message and its own certificate to sign the message.

10.6.4.2 Federated Security Profile

This profile supports security and privacy of communication between two parties that trust each other based on their membership in the trust federation. This means they provide access to their organizational resources based on the attributes issued by another organization.

Figure 10.7 shows the communication flow of messages and information passed among a client, a repository, and infrastructure services. The clients discover the

---

[32] Secure sockets layer, http://www.netscape.com/eng/ssl3/.

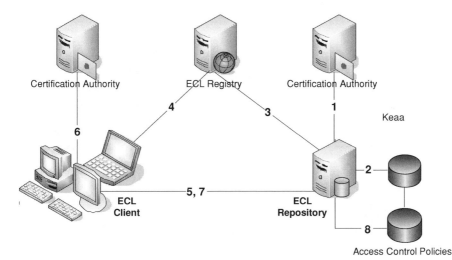

FIGURE 10.6. Repository controlled security profile. Upon installation the ECL repository authenticates with its certification authority (CA) and obtains its certificate (1). Repository stores the certificate in its key store (2) and registers/updates its information including the certificate in the ECL service registry (3). The ECL client retrieves the information about the repository from the ECL service registry (4) either after the user searches the registry or from the client's preconfigured list of the repositories. The information contains the repository certificate, the URL for obtaining the user account on the repository, and technical parameters to establish the communication. If the user does not have an account with the repository, it follows the URL and obtains the user account name and password (5). If the communication should be encrypted, users obtain their certificate from the generally trusted certification authority (6). Self-signed certificates can be used with a repository that does not require signed certificates. The username, password, and optionally user certificate are included into the ECL message and sent to the ECL repository (7). The message can be optionally encrypted, so only the repository can decrypt the message. The repository authenticates the user against its access control policies (8). The returned results can be encrypted so only the originator of the request can decrypt it.

services via the service registry. The client users authenticate and request attributes from their home institution. The repository validates the attributes and makes an authorization decision based on the user's attribute values and its access policies. As a result no users' information is kept outside of their home organization.

By default the security tokens in the profile are encrypted, to avoid the possible leak of the security parameters. The ECL-SI also allows the repository to request a mandatory time stamp and signature to be included along with the security token. The signature by itself avoids the hijacking of the security parameters before the ECL message is formed. The time stamp makes it impossible to reuse the token after it has expired.

To avoid the man-in-the-middle attack, a combination of the time stamp, signature, and encryption is used. The encryption ensures that the security parameters

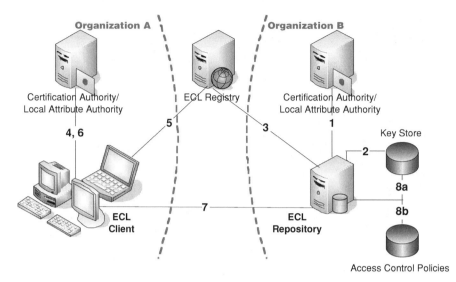

FIGURE 10.7. Federated security profile. Upon installation of the ECL repository in organization B the ECL repository authenticates with its certification authority (CA) and obtains its certificate (1). Repository stores the certificate in the keystore (2) and registers/updates its information including the certificate in the ECL service registry (3). The repository also contacts the trust federation and keeps its list of trusted CAs and LAAs up to date (not shown). When the ECL client in organization A initializes, it authenticates the user with its certification authority and obtains the user's certificate (4). The ECL client retrieves the information about the repository from the ECL service registry (5) either after the user searches the registry or from the client's preconfigured list of the repositories. The information contains the certificate, required attributes, and technical parameters to establish the communication. Before sending a message to the repository the ECL, the client contacts its LAA to issue the required attributes (6). The attributes are included in the ECL message and sent to the ECL repository (7). The message can be optionally encrypted so only the repository can decrypt the message. The repository retrieves the attributes from the message, and validates the attributes against the federation trust information (8a). If successful, the access policy engine authorizes processing of the request (8b). The returned results can be encrypted so only the originator of the request can decrypt it.

are not readable to someone who hijacks the message. If the time stamp is both encrypted and signed, any attempt to change the time stamp by a hijacker would result in the signature value not matching the modified time stamp. This combination of three features makes it very difficult to reuse the security tokens.

10.7 Implementation and Deployment

The ECL infrastructure was developed within the eduSource project in 2003. Initially it was deployed across the eduSource Canada partner organizations and then extended with ECL gateways to repositories in Australia and the United States. After the end of the eduSource project in March 2004, the ECL development continued within our group at the Laboratory for Ontological Research at Simon Fraser University. Currently over a dozen repositories in Canada, the U.S., Australia, the United Kingdom, and Europe are connected to the network.

We have developed several gateways between ECL and other networks and protocols:

- The ECL gateway for EdNA Online bridges between ECL and HTTP-based protocol in the form CGI.
- The ECL gateway to the U.K.'s resource description network (RDN) bridges between ECL and SRW/SRU protocols.
- The ECL gateway to the Ariadne Foundation bridges between ECL and another Web service-oriented protocol. This is true also for the ECL gateway to the SMETE repository.
- The ECL gateway to the LionShare peer-to-peer network bridges between ECL and Gnutella protocol.

The ECL has been also integrated with Open Knowledge Initiatives (OKI) open-system interface definitions. We have developed an ECL/OKI plug-in that we have integrated into OKI systems to provide ECL connectivity [14].

The ECL-SI profiles are implemented in the ECL connector. The connector uses the Axis SOAP engine and WSS4J[33] WS security implementation. Typically the ECL-SI profiles sit between Axis and WSS4J. The profile uses OpenSAML[34] implementation of the SAML specification. The ECL registry is implemented on top of the UDDI registry.

The ECL middleware is implemented using open-source tool technologies. The ECL technology is distributed under Lesser GPL License (LGPL).

10.8 Discussion

In this section we discuss several challenges that we faced in the design and implementation of the interoperability mechanism, especially as it is one of the first implementations of a specification that is not well articulated, and it recommends technology (IMS DRI recommends XQuery) that is not widely used in real-world applications. Of course early implementation allowed us to further inform the specification process and provide best-practice recommendations. Implementation and deployment also provide an opportunity to discover the synergies with other approaches and to define the next set of questions that need to be addressed through the specification process to achieve a higher level of interoperability.

---

[33] http://ws.apache.org/ws-fx/wss4j/
[34] http://www.opensaml.org.

10.8.1 Pragmatics of Following the IMS DRI

Following the recommendations from IMS DRI required making several pragmatic decisions. One major obstacle we faced was following the recommendation for using XQuery as a query language for search functionality. The reality is that there are very few products that currently support XQuery, indeed, many of the existing repositories of ECL stakeholders do not support XQuery. Two possible solutions to address this problem were:

1. degrade the query language to a less powerful but commonly supported language, such as XPath; or
2. use XQuery but provide a solution that will enable all repositories to participate in ECL.

Although the first option looked expedient, we opted for the second option mainly because of the potential long-term benefits of having a solution following the recommendation from IMS. We have implemented several template XQueries to satisfy the requirements of the major stakeholders.[35] Participants without XQuery support may implement as many templates as they want to support and register these services with their explicitly specified supporting format. ECL participants who support the full XQuery will support all defined templates through their XQuery engine.

10.8.2 Document-Style Web Services

As mentioned in section 10.5.1, we have chosen a document-style Web services approach over the more commonly used remote procedure call (RPC) style. RPC style is more common as people started to implement Web services using the familiar paradigm from RMI and CORBA for exposing server-side data and functions. The RPC method can also be easily supported by frameworks and tools. On the other side, document-style Web services offer a satisfying mix of well-defined structures and interoperability [11]. The benefits of document style for the development of complex interoperability protocols, such as ECL, include the full use of XML, the ability to validate request and objects using XML-schemas, and making object exchange more flexible.

By using document style, the ECL protocol is much richer than any framework expressible by RPC calls that require a rigid contract. RPC calls do not provide enough coverage for the variety of connections found in an evolving heterogeneous network. Specifically, ECL implements a whole set of new services that are now possible, such as "push gather," "subscribe," and "alert." Using document style Web services in ECL makes it easier to connect with asynchronous peer-to-peer networks. This is particularly important when the search results from

---

[35] Templates differ by their query capabilities and how they format their results. For example, one template specifies keyword-based search and formulates results in brief format. Another template specifies keyword search and returns full IEEE LOM records.

the broadcasted query arrive in batches. When processing large amounts of data, it is always more manageable to have asynchronous messaging deliver results in batches. Document-style Web services also make object exchange easier and allow making full use of XML. This is essential as we have to deal with the reality that different repositories will use at best, different variants of the metadata standards or, at worst, completely specific metadata that needs to be mapped to the standards or transferred unchanged.

10.8.3 Comparison with Other Approaches

Interoperability: Section 10.2 listed relevant projects and approaches to inter-operability in the current learning objects arena. They can be compared using different criteria:

- From the perspective of scope of functionality, the POOL project, Edutella/Elena, ECL, and OKI project all aim at supporting a wide range of interoperability functions.
- The NSDL meta-repository initiative is too broad to be easily categorized but does have several goals overlapping with our project.
- The OAI project focuses on dissemination, clearly addressing one part of the ECL goals. The approaches differ at the level that they address the problem of interoperability.
- The POOL and Edutella projects used peer-to-peer ideas to connect repositories and tools with different capabilities.
- The Elena project development is at an early stage, with early drafts suggesting that the project will not follow the IMS DRI specification as closely as has the ECL. Another difference between two projects is that Elena is using the Web services approach with the remote method invocation approach (see above) with all the consequences of tightly coupled system.

The comparison with OKI OSID is interesting as OSID aims mainly at the inter-operability between components within learning systems during its development, while ECL addresses the problem of interoperability between stand-alone learning systems and services. This makes the two approaches complementary, and we have integrated both in the ECL/OKI plug-in [14].

Security Infrastructure: The ECL security infrastructure has been deployed at the Simon Fraser University and can provide certificates and signed attribute assertions to SFU users. The trust network has been created with our LionShare partners at Pennsylvania State University. As a result LionShare and ECL users at SFU and Pennsylvania State can access resources in both the CMS and P2P network using the attributes issued by their own institutions.

To the best of our knowledge, similar work does not exist. However, in different aspects our work is closely related to several initiatives, including Shibboleth, the WS security group at OASIS, and the Liberty Project. Our approach extends Shibboleth from the Web environment into the Web services environment. The WS security group concentrates on the specifications, and we make use of their work. The Liberty Project [31] is much broader in scope than our work. In that respect our work can be considered lightweight, with the main focus on easy setup of new trust networks and low threshold enrollment of the new nodes into the trust network. Another difference is that the Liberty Project makes available only the specification, while the implementation is typically not available as it is done by the commercial partners of the project.

Finally, there are two other projects that attract our attention: GridShib[36] is developing a solution for multiple organizations that wish to form a virtual organization or grid. In the GridShib model, SP can authenticate users (grid clients) using GridLogon and request additional users' attributes from Shibboleth AA (pull mode). In a push mode, which is similar to our approach, GridShib users authenticate and obtain attributes from Shibboleth AA and use them to make the request to SP. MAMS Project[37] [7] at Macquarie University implements an inter-institutional authentication and authorization regime based on attribute exchange and XACML policies. Where the MAMS project is focusing purely on the Web browser environment, our ECL focus is on Web services.

10.9 Conclusion

In a perfect world there would be only one metadata protocol and we would need only one repository and one search mechanism. However, this would be a rather bland world. The reality of e-learning is a hodge-podge of legacy repositories, protocols, special interest groups, and self-serving communities. Rather than preach conformance, the ECL focused on the common functions desired by the owners and user of learning object repositories and strived to intermediate between the technologies involved. Our previous experience with POOL, POND, and SPLASH proved that heterogeneous repository types could and should coexist and serve a global interest in the reuse of learning objects. The ECL demonstrated that the technical barriers can be overcome and that robust solutions to interoperability are possible. However, the ultimate challenges to interoperability remain political—we can only interoperate with those repositories that wish to do so.

The ECL security infrastructure is a novel approach that is awaiting wider adoption. The infrastructure provides the security framework for object repositories to create a trust federation as well as to provide services with different levels of security. The solution defines security profiles, infrastructure services, and middleware component for a low-barrier adoption by existing repositories. Although this infrastructure can scale to large networks, it is particularly sensitive to the needs of medium-sized and small organizations, which have complex attributes and accessing policies.

---

[36] http://grid.ncsa.uiuc.edu/GridShib/.
[37] http://www.melcoe.mq.edu.au/projects/MAMS/index.htm.

The infrastructure uses WS security standards. It is compatible with Shibboleth infrastructure for Web applications, which enables developers to share infrastructure components such as attribute authority.

The infrastructure has been deployed in a pilot application to provide access to a repository of learning material with the complex intellectual property arrangements for individual resources. The access policies in the repository were based on the user attributes. The pilot successfully demonstrated the federated security for users from two different organizations.

Our current research focuses on bridging between our solution and attribute-based security that is being developed for peer-to-peer network within the Lion-Share project. The second area of interest is looking at further developing a trust management component of the infrastructure with respect to the ease of deployment for small communities and integration of our solution with the tools for management of access policies.

In the long term we hope the ECL will gain wider adoption as e-learning organizations begin to realize that interoperability expands from the simple exchange of learning objects to the growing world of e-learning services and constructivist knowledge collaborations. A flexible tool like the ECL will facilitate the interoperability of yet-to-be-defined functions across a semantically enhanced Web.

References

1. ACM. (1998) The ACM Computing Classification System 1998 version. http://www.acm.org/class/1998/.
2. Arms, W.Y., Hillmann, D., Lagoze, C., et al. (2002) A spectrum of interoperability: the site for science prototype for the NSDL. D-Lib Magazine, 8(1). http://dx.doi.ord/10.1045/jamlorg2002-arms.
3. Bhargavan, K., Fournet, C., Gordon, A.D. (2004) Verifying policy-based security for web services. CCS '04: Proceedings of the 11th ACM conference on Computer and Communications Security. Washington, DC, USA: ACM Press, pp. 268–277.
4. Box, D., Ehnebuske, D., Kakivaya, G., et al. (2000) Simple Object Access Protocol (SOAP) 1.1.
5. Carmody, S., Erdos, M., Hazelton, K., et al. (2005) InCommon Technical Requirements and Information.
6. Carmody, S., Erdos, M., Hazelton, K., (2005) Shibboleth-Architecture v09.
7. Dalziel, J.R., Vullings, E. (2005) MAMS and Middleware: the easily solved authentication, authorisation, identity, single sign-on, federation, trust, security, digital rights and automated access policy cluster of problems. Educause Australasia.
8. DDC Dewey Decimal Classification.
9. Della-Libera, G., Hallam-Baker, P., Hondo, M., et al. (2002) Web services security policy language (WS-SecurityPolicy).
10. Gamma, E., Helm, R., Johnson, R. and Vlissides, J. (1995) Design Patterns. Reading, MA: Addison-Wesley.
11. Gibbs, K., Goodman, B.D., Torres, E. (2003) Create Web services using Apache Axis and Castor. IBM Developer Works.

12. Gordon, A.D. and Pucella, R. (2002) Validating a Web service security abstraction by typing. XMLSEC '02: Proceedings of the 2002 ACM workshop on XML security. ACM Press, pp. 18–29.

13. Guttman, J.D., Herzog, A.L. (2005) Rigorous automated network security management, International Journal of Information Security, 4(1–2):29–48.

14. Hatala, M., Richards, G., Thorne, S., Merriman, J. (2004) Closing the interoperability gap: connecting open service interfaces with digital repository interoperability. Proceeding of the Ed-Media Conference, pp. 78–83.

15. Hatala, M., Richards, G. (2002) Global vs. community metadata standards: empowering users for knowledge exchange. In: Proceedings of the First International Semantic Web Conference on the Semantic Web. New York: Springer-Verlag, pp. 292–306.

16. IEEE. (2004) 1484.12.1: IEEE Standard for Learning Object Metadata, IEEE Learning Technologies Standards Commitee.

17. IMS. (2003) IMS Digital Repositories Interoperability—Core Functions Information Model.

18. Koper, R., Tattersall, C. (Eds.) (2005) Learning Design: A Handbook on Modelling and Delivering Networked Education and Training. New York: Springer-Verlag.

19. Lukell, S., Hutchison, A. (2003) Automated attack analysis and code generation in a multi-dimensional security protocol engineering framework. Proceedings of the Southern African Telecommunications Networks and Applications Conference.

20. McCarthy, J. (2003) Reap Benefits of Document Style Web Services. IBM Developer Works.

21. Morgan, R.L., Cantor, S., Carmody, S., Hoehn, W., Klingenstein, K. (2004) Federated security: the shibboleth approach. Educause Quaterly, 4:12–17.

22. Nadalin, A., Kaler, C., Hallam-Baker, P., Monzillo., R. (2004) OASIS Web Services Security: SOAP Message Security 1.0 (WS-Security 2004).

23. Nejdl, W., Wolf, B., Qu, C., et al. (2002) EDUTELLA: a P2P networking infrastructure based on RDF. Proceedings of the Eleventh International Conference on World Wide Web. ACM Press, pp. 604–615.

24. Pozza, D., Sisto, R., Durante, L. (2004) Spi2Java: Automatic Cryptographic Protocol Java Code Generation from spi calculus. AINA '04: Proceedings of the 18th International Conference on Advanced Information Networking and Applications Volume 2IEEE Computer Society, pp. 400–405.

25. Richards, G., Hatala, M. (2004) POOL, POND and SPLASH: portals for online objects for learning. In: McGreal, R. (ed.) Online Education Using Learning Objects, London: RoutledgeFalmer.

26. Richards, G., Hatala, M. (2004) Semantic cobblestones: an interoperability mechanism for learning object repositories. In: McGreal, R. (ed.) Online Education Using Learning Objects. London: RoutledgeFalmer.

27. Scavo, T. (2005) Shibboleth Architecture: Technical Overview.

28. Simon, B., Miklos, Z., Nejdl, W., Sintek, M., Salvachua, J. (2003) Smart space for learning: a mediation infrastructure for learning services. Twelfth International Conference on World Wide Web.

29. Song, D., Perrig, A. Phan, D.E. (2001) AGVI—Automatic Generation, Verification, and Implementation of Security Protocols.

30. Tatsubori, M., Imamura, T., Nakamura, Y. (2004) Best-practice patterns and tool support for configuring secure Web services messaging. ICWS '04: Proceedings of the IEEE International Conference on Web Services (ICWS'04) IEEE Computer Society, pp. 244–251.

31. Tourzan, J., Koga, Y. (2004) Liberty ID-WSF Architecture Overview. Version 1.0, Liberty Alliance Project.
32. Van de Sompel, H., Lagoze, C. (2003) Notes from the Interoperability Front: A Progress Report on the Open Archives Initiative. ECDL 2002 LNCS 2458. New York: Springer, pp. 144–157.
33. Wiley, D. (2001) Instructional Use of Learning Objects.

11
Quality of Service and Collaboration Aspects in a Distributed E-Laboratory Environment

Alejandro Quintero, Samuel Pierre, and David Tassy

Abstract. This chapter proposes an architecture for implementing e-laboratory environment by taking into account several aspects concerning not only the educational process, but also the network infrastructure, the collaboration and quality of service (QoS) requirements, the types of content, etc. This is a flexible, parametrical, and component-oriented architecture designed to support collaboration among different actors or entities of the e-learning environment. According to the diverse aspects of QoS that an e-learning service comprises, this architecture was tested with different network loads. Experimental results show that improvements caused by traffic differentiation, even without special network loads, become even more significant as the number of users increases.

11.1 Introduction

The emergence of the Internet in the late 1990s as a global and ubiquitous communication medium, coupled with the advances in the information and communication technologies, has spawned a wealth of possibilities in terms of application development and social collaboration (e.g., e-learning). Generally, e-learning refers to the use of computer networks for learning [4,11,16,36]. It allows for the supervision of students by trainers, tutors, and professors, all scattered in space and time. Thus, the support of learning activities in different scientific and technical disciplines requires distributed learning environments similar, as much as possible, to those in conventional laboratories. The overall aim of using Web-based learning is to facilitate student-centered learning and to support the flexibility of students' time [28].

One of the most important components of the virtual learning environment is the virtual laboratory. At the core of the virtual laboratory lies the concept of distance learning, where the learners, the teachers, and tools or equipment used in the learning process may be distributed over several geographical locations. Virtual learning environments (VLEs) refers to the components in which learners and tutors participate in on-line interactions of various kinds, including on-line learning [19]. A VLE is a web-based online environment that integrates tools for content delivery, communication, assessment, and student management [23]. One type of virtual learning environments is the collaborative virtual environments (CVEs). In this kind of VLE, some of the components in which learners and tutors participate allow collaboration between them.

Collaboration is an essential part of the learning process. It is defined as the set of processes and tools that make it possible for different actors (e.g., teachers, learners, etc.) to communicate with one another, to share know-how and knowledge, and to work together as a group [33]. The support of active collaboration is one of the main elements for the success of Web-based learning environments. Thus tools designed to ease communication exchanges between people, within CVE, must be able to support collective intelligence [32]. Collaboration using the World Wide Web is a broad research field that includes knowledge sharing and knowledge representation as well as technologies enabling information sharing and the creation of distributed environments [8,9]. Collaboration implies the use of many different tools, each having its specific quality of service (QoS) requirements [18].

Quality of service can be defined as a set of requirements that the network must meet or guarantee in order for an application to function properly. In the first days of the Internet, only best-effort services were offered. These services do not make special provision for QoS requirements as they treat all traffic types equally: packets pertaining to a real-time flow are treated in the same way (the same service level) as packets belonging to Web browsing or e-mail sessions. Hence, using best-effort services in collaborative environments may prove to be problematic, as the different tools used require different levels of service.

A networking environment QoS is generally expressed in terms of:

- Delay: time span from the emission of the first bit of a packet at the source to the reception of the last bit of the same packet at the destination
- Jitter: end-to-end delay variation
- Bandwidth or throughput maximum transfer between two extremities of a communication channel
- Availability: mean error rate of a link
- Packet loss rate: number of packets incorrectly transmitted in a given transmission

The virtual laboratory on which our work is based is a CVE. The idea behind the CVE technology is that computer networks can be used to create virtual workspaces that allow social interaction among participants.

This chapter proposes a CVE architecture supporting quality of service. Section 11.2 introduces the background and related work. Section 11.3 describes the proposed architecture. Section 11.4 presents and analyzes simulation results. Section 11.5 concludes the chapter.

11.2 Background and Related Work

Virtual learning benefited greatly from the variety of tools offered by information and communication technologies. The emergence of the Internet amplified to a certain extent this phenomenon, rendering possible the use of modern and powerful tools without imposing restriction in terms of geographical location. Furthermore, more often than not, these tools are less expensive to use than their traditional counterparts [31].

11.2.1 Electronic Learning Concepts

E-learning differs from the more traditional learning methods primarily by the fact that it does not limit the learning process to a single geographical location nor a specific previously predetermined meeting time. Up until recently, learners have experienced attending classes offered by certain colleges or universities. E-learning is a major innovative step, as courses and material are no longer bound by the physical location of learners and teachers. Furthermore, in most cases, learning institutions offer a limited number of classes on different subjects, at a single physical location and with little or no regard to the needs, capacity, and availability of learners and teachers. E-learning promises to change this by offering course material that can be tailored to the needs, strengths, and prior knowledge of each learner. Moreover, such a learning scenario allows learners to choose the time when and the place where they wish to complete their courses.

With the advent of new information and communication technologies, and more specifically the Internet, e-learning environments can now offer direct interaction, multimedia, on-demand evaluations, tailored learning modules [13,17,27], etc. In fact, the introduction of such technologies made it possible for the learning process to be automated. The possibilities offered by these technologies encouraged universities around the world to develop new educational approaches including virtual laboratories and more generally, distance learning. Some authors even introduced the concept of cyberversity in an attempt to explain this phenomenon [17].

Learning can be viewed in terms of scenarios [11,12], either by modeling the global organization of the teaching process, or by concentrating on the specific tools available to the learner [5]. Different models are used for distance learning [12]: independent of time, simultaneously distributed, and an independent study model. In the first model, traditional activities such as lectures, usually given in a classroom, are combined with homework and course material to be studied at home. A perpetual dialogue is established between the learners and the teachers but also among the learners themselves. In the second model, learners can hear and see their teacher, and hence the learners can establish a dialogue with the teacher at any time. Usually, this model uses such technologies as satellites, cable television, and video telephony. Furthermore, the wide accessibility of the Internet offers new possibilities such as networking (working inside a Web of collaboration). Finally, in the last model, the learner works alone (without consulting any teachers or peers) and acquires course material from a sequence of well-organized modules.

11.2.2 Virtual Environments and Learning Management Systems

The first virtual environment presented is INVITE (Intelligent Distributed Virtual Training Environment). The main goal of the INVITE project [8,9,25] is to develop a synchronous virtual learning platform capable of interacting with intelligent management systems.

JETS (Java-Enabled Tele-collaboration System) [34] is a Java-based virtual learning environment. The Java programming environment offers numerous advantages in terms of interoperability and portability. JETS aims to use Web search engines to execute applications.

The main problem with most of the tools used in virtual laboratories lies in the fact that their design does not take collaboration into account. Dorneich and Jones [14] introduced the concept of collaboratory. This concept can be defined as a virtual environment that uses information and communication technologies to enable communication and collaboration among users who are not geographically close to one another.

In some collaborative environments such as the Medical Collaboratory Project [25], actors distributed spatially and temporally need to share medical data and applications with one another in a secure and efficient manner. Since the flows associated with each window will probably have to migrate among many networks, they will be subjected to the delays, jitters, and packet losses that characterize those networks.

In some virtual environments there is a learning management system (LMS). An LMS becomes a VLE when it is in educational use (populated with content, communication, and learners) to facilitate complex learning interactions.

Oracle iLearning is a learning management system that provides effective, manageable, integrated, and extensible Internet-based training to anyone, anytime, anywhere [29]. The system is designed to train a widely dispersed staff that follows consistent corporate standards. Additionally, Oracle is managed from one central location, allowing more people in more places to receive the necessary training on-line. Oracle iLearning's unique permission model, browser accessibility, and content-management capabilities enable self-service content assembly and delivery, thus speeding the process of delivering information from the experts to the audience.

Web Course Tools (WebCT) is a software application for the management of World Wide Web (WWW)-based educational environments [37]. It can be used to take entire on-line courses, or to simply publish materials that supplement existing face-to-face classes. It is designed to require little technical expertise on the part of the professor or the student. WebCT courses are password protected to ensure privacy. WebCT can do the following:

- Provide course materials that include text, images, video, and audio
- Evaluate students with quizzes and assignments

- Communicate with students via discussions, email, real-time chat sessions, and an interactive whiteboard
- Manage grades
- Supply student feedback via an on-line grade-book, self-tests, and progress tracking
- Obtain data that allows us to analyze the effectiveness of the course

Blackboard's suite of applications are backed by the Blackboard Global Solutions team, providing integrated planning, implementation, and growth management solutions designed to meet our client's unique e-education objectives [6]. Blackboard's suite of enterprise applications includes the following:

- Blackboard learning system: enables organizations to use the Internet as a powerful tool for teaching and learning
- Blackboard content system: Enables all students and faculty members to manage their own Internet-based file space on a central system and to collect, share, discover, and manage important materials from articles and research papers to presentations and multimedia files; includes a set of Web applications for managing student career and evaluation portfolios, integrating content with campus course management systems, maintaining version control of digital assets; tagging, searching, and reusing learning objects; and more
- Blackboard portal system : powerful, easy to deploy portal technology for integrating Web-based services and building on-line communities of learning
- Blackboard transaction system: enhances the daily student experience through a seamless environment for on-line and off-line transactions.

11.2.3 QoS and Collaboration in Virtual Learning Environments

Commonly accepted from the Internet community, an e-learning service imposes a great burden on the underlying network in terms of bandwidth resources and nonelastic traffic. General end-user requirements underpin the argument that the network infrastructure should support QoS mechanisms, interpreting these mechanisms according to International Telecommunication Union (ITU-T) E.800 recommendation. E-learning applications generate nonelastic traffic that must be protected from the Internet's best-effort traffic. Thus, the provision of QoS classes is necessary. It would also be desirable that the QoS signaling could reach the machines of the end users. In this way, the QoS allocation of resources could be dynamic and therefore more adaptable to the changes of the state of the network [30].

The wealth of multimedia applications available, coupled with innovations in information and communication technologies, will eventually replace many traditional social and economical interaction models such as phone conversations or face-to-face meetings. To meet educational requirements and standards, distributed learning environments (DLEs), will have to offer to learners, instructors, and administrators many features that are [1,2,10,24]:

- interactive and engaging
- group-based, not solely used in isolation
- real-world input, not only simulations
- learner-centered, with individual needs addresseds
- available anytime/anywhere, providing wider access to education

Receptivity, defined as the delay between an information request and its associated response, needs to be as small as possible in order for the environment to provide a strong feeling of interaction to its users. Furthermore, group organization (learners are gathered into homogeneous groups) implies the safe and efficient sharing of laboratory resources between concurrent users. Hence, when dealing with virtual learning environments, concurrency is as important as security issues and real-time requirements.

11.3 The E-Laboratory Environment

A virtual laboratory can be viewed as a complex computer environment promoting coherent recasting of conventional experimentation rules and styles. Scientific simulations use existing and coming networking technologies for the transport and distribution of multimedia documents and sequences over different kind of telecommunication media. From this perspective, the telecommunication platform can be considered as a coordinating element halfway between the remote users and the experimental tools replicated on one or many servers. Thus, an efficient conceptual structure should take into account key issues such as openness, cross-media adaptation, and potential extensions' ability [31].

11.3.1 The Telecommunication Platform

The management of telecommunication networks mainly aims at providing a reliable and efficient infrastructure and means of transporting information among distributed and diverse applications and services. Nevertheless, when considering a network-based service, we cannot easily discriminate between the application and the underlying network infrastructure and isolate each one. Every day, new applications and services deploy telecommunication infrastructure as a vehicle to reach new clients, located in different and distant areas. The need for providing distributed services leads to an emerging need for managing these services as a whole, including the management of underlying network infrastructure [3].

Pierre and Kassouf [31] have proposed a telecommunication platform model that ensures interoperability among heterogeneous networks and serves as an access infrastructure to distributed virtual laboratories. Conceptually, this platform is a three-layered structure where a layer of basic tools and functionalities is framed with an adaptation layer that adapts them to specific tools and functionalities. The main idea, presented by Pierre and Kassouf, consists of modeling a generic laboratory node whose additional extensions will enable developing other specific

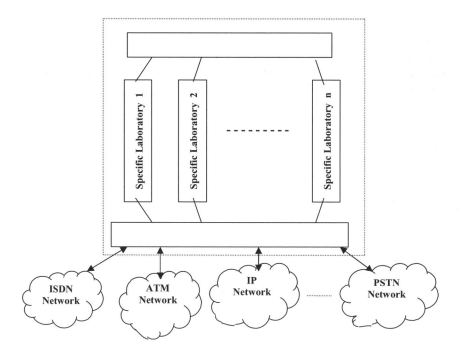

FIGURE 11.1. Proposed architecture for the virtual laboratories (Pierre and Kassouf, [31])

laboratories for diverse scientific and engineering disciplines. The proposed inductive methodology consists of defining and developing different laboratories according to characteristics that are specific to the corresponding knowledge fields or disciplines. Then, the tools and functions on which diverse laboratories are based are regrouped into two large sets: BTF (basic tools and functionalities) common to several types of laboratory, and STF (specific tools and functionalities) that are rather peculiar to one type of laboratory. The generic feature of the virtual laboratory model results from the development of a sufficient number of specific laboratories integrating a variety of functionalities and tools. However, this generic aspect is mainly built on a telecommunication platform, that is, the physical support of BTF, as shown in Figure 11.1.

A telecommunication platform could be seen as a regrouping of modules. Each of these modules is dedicated to a specific task. As shown in Figure 11.2, these modules carry out the following three tasks: adaptation to STF, integration of BTF, and adaptation to users' communication networks.

11.3.2 The Collaborative E-Learning Architecture

This section defines the architecture of a conceptual collaborative learning environment supporting quality of service (QoS) requirements that such environments must satisfy in order to be considered successful.

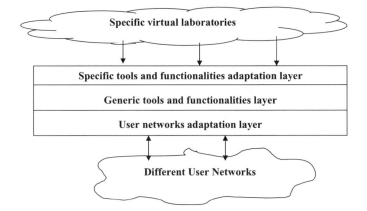

FIGURE 11.2. Triple-layered model for the telecommunication platform (Pierre and Kassouf [31])

As for quality of service, the main concern is the delay in accessing, transmiting, and displaying the (possibly multimedia) information that is exchanged in this type of environment. This aspect warrants particular attention in the context of virtual laboratories where interactive simulation, tele-measurement, and tele-experimentation are among the considered approaches and methods. Among other concerns, there are the quality of images and the precision of measures. These are directly related to the available bandwidth. In non–real-time situations, they can be traded against the transmission delay. Quality of service is something that can be negotiated and configured. When dealing with an human user, we must be careful to use a level of language that can be understood, given that most people involved are not and cannot be expected to be experts in networking. This is where the idea of QoS translation must be properly applied.

From an educational standpoint, it is essential to be able to reinforce theoretical material with practical exercises and experimentation. This is even more important in science, as various studies have shown that learners learn better and faster when they can experiment with what they have just learned. As shown in Figure 11.3, such components of the virtual learning environment architecture were integrated into our model.

The architecture suggested in this chapter implies collaboration among different actors or entities found in a given environment. Thus, according to the tasks that learners are asked to accomplish, they may need to interact with one or many actors, each playing various roles in the learning process. Our learning environment includes three types of actors or entities:

• **Coordinator (C):** This role is assigned to a teacher, a professor, a laboratory assistant, or anyone involved in the management of the learning process. The coordinator's duties include supervising and coordinating the set of resources, services, and tools offered by the virtual laboratory.

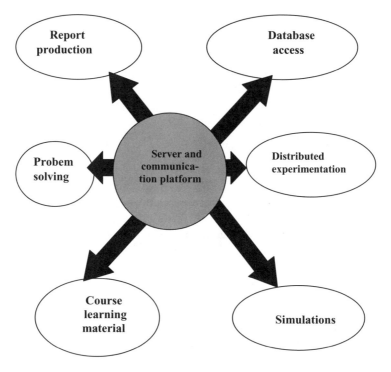

FIGURE 11.3. Nonhuman components of the learning environment.

- **Learner (L):** Learners are the central entities of the environment as the whole learning process is hinged upon them.
- **Group (G):** A group is a set of learners (the number of learners involved in a group is a function determined by the laboratory). The group entity represents the essence of collaboration as group members cooperate and communicate with one another within the environment.

The three entities—learner, group, and coordinator—make it possible to illustrate the interactions within a virtual laboratory. Thus, our collaborative learning architecture is designed around these entities (Fig. 11.4) and provides them with the tools and services required to collaborate efficiently.

11.3.3 Process in Collaboration

Collaboration is an integral part of the learning process. Furthermore, we hypothesized that collaboration can be broken down into two distinct but complementary process: cooperation and communication. We now address the three underlying levels (functional, structural, and technological) for each process of collaboration.

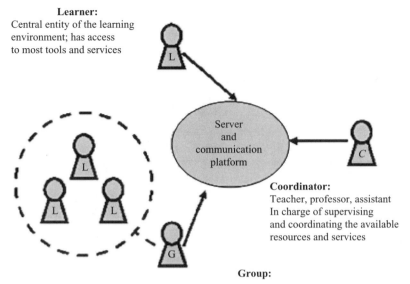

FIGURE 11.4. Actors or entities involved in the learning process.

A. Cooperation

Functional level: This subsection presents a detailed definition of the functional level, as well as an inventory of the actions performed by each actor. Hence, we separate the actions performed by the coordinator and learner roles. These two entities play distinct but complementary roles as illustrated in Figures 11.5 and 11.6.

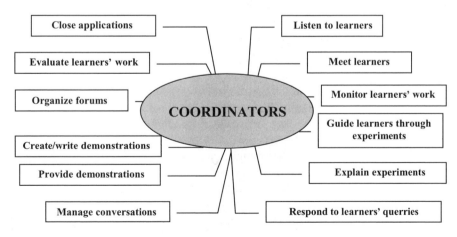

FIGURE 11.5. Coordinator's responsibilities.

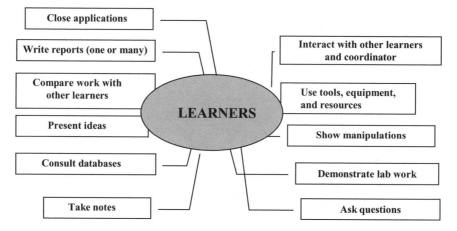

FIGURE 11.6. Learners' responsibilities.

Group activities: A group entity model is not illustrated as a group involved a given set of learners. Thus, we assume that a group would be associated with the actions performed by the learners composing the group.

Structural level: Now that the set of all possible cooperative actions performed in a virtual laboratory has been identified, we can list the collection of tools used to implement those actions. This basically constitutes the structural level of cooperation. The cooperation tools range from chat to videoconferencing applications, although they also include less interactive applications such as virtual lab books and exams.

Technological level: As for the transport layer, depending on the characteristics of the application, it is recommended to use Transmission Control Protocol (TCP) or User Datagramme Protocol (UDP) as the main transport protocol. As for the application layer, each application uses its own underlying technology and protocols. Thus, for the virtual lab book, we use HTTP, while Remote Method Invocation (RMI) and Real Time Protocol (RTP)/Real Time Control Protocol (RTCP) are used for the chat and videoconferencing applications, respectively.

B. Communication

Functional level: From the functional point of view, communication can be defined as the set of agreements and rules that govern the exchange of data, information, and speech among different actors in a virtual laboratory. Indeed, this set of permissible actions has to be properly defined in order for the exchange to be equally beneficial for all actors participating in the communicative events. The speech act [35] is a concept that summarizes this idea relatively well. Further, we present various virtual laboratory situations and learning processes where components of a speech act can be found:

• Question: at any moment, a learner is liable to ask questions about course material or experimental manipulations to his fellow learners (i.e., the group) or to the coordinator of the virtual laboratory.

- Answer: a learner seeking an answer to a question initiates a dialogue with another virtual laboratory actor who responds to the interrogation.
- Explanation: if experimental results do not match expected ones, learners must explain what went wrong (from their point of view). Moreover, the coordinator must explain to the learners what is expected from them.
- Argumentation: learners participate in group-wide discussions, sharing ideas about the lab project and convincing other learners of the validity of their ideas by presenting strong arguments.
- Hypothesizing: when preparing lab experiments, learners have to hypothesize before sharing their work and thoughts with other learners in the group.
- Justification: to support hypotheses, learners are asked to show realistic argument related to the course material.
- Conciliation: before submitting their work or lab results, learners consult one another to validate their work, and a group spokesperson is elected.

Finally, actions that are incumbent on the coordinator of the virtual laboratory are:

- Reformulation: the coordinator may need to reformulate in more precise terms previous lectures or explanations for the learners to better understand course material or lab experiments.
- Commenting: at the end of the learning process, the coordinator needs to comment on learners' work before evaluating them.
- Evaluating: the coordinator must evaluate the learners' work and progress.

Structural level: Now that we have listed all permissible communicative actions, we can identify the structural constraints associated with this process. Indeed, it is essential to notice that networked communications (Internet, LAN, etc.) are slightly more complex to manage than the more traditional voice or paper communications, as many different and competing data flows have to be considered at the same time. According to the number of participants and the time the connection is established, a communication will be classified into one of many possible categories. To describe all possible categories, we limit the scope of this chapter to two types of considerations: quantitative and temporal.

Quantitative considerations: Here, we classify communication according to the number of participants, the presence of a group or not, etc. There are three possible types of communication:

- Unicast: this is the simplest and most basic type of communication. In this case, only two entities (learner-learner or learner-coordinator) are involved in the communication process.
- Broadcast: this communication is used when the lab coordinator wants to reach (or provide access to) all learners participating in the lab. This communication can be labeled as one-to-many (the number of learners may be unlimited).
- Multicast: this communication occurs when the instructor wants to address specific groups of learners. This type of communication can also be labeled as one-to-many, but the number of learners reached is limited for each group.

Temporal considerations: The applications used in the virtual laboratory may have different temporal requirements. We classify these temporal considerations according to the type of connection used:

• Synchronous: for this method, applications are usually running at the same time (from identical origins) [22] and they must be mutually synchronized. Furthermore, all entities (i.e., people or applications) participating in the communication progress in parallel (e.g., chat).
• Asynchronous: this type of communication is used when the entities participating in the communication are not present simultaneously, at the same time (e.g., typically emails, discussion groups or forums) [21].

Technological level: The proposed architecture must be able to manage both multicast and broadcast communications (unicast being the default communication mode). The selection of network layer technologies is the most important aspect of our analysis. After a thorough analysis of several network layer protocols, we chose to base our architecture on the IPv6 protocol, as it meets all of our criteria (all types of communications defined so far are supported by IPv6), but also because it is a powerful and scalable technology.

11.3.4 Collaboration Scenarios

Now that all elements of the collaborative learning environment (CLE) have been presented and that all needs have been classified, we can justify some of the choices made. First, we explain these choices using some scenarios the CLE can support. Indeed, to better understand the role and usage of each module in the CLE, it is important to describe some of the activities involved in the learning process. Let us now delve into the details of what goes on in the problem solving and the distance learning activities.

A. Problem Solving

In the problem solving activity, we consider that a set of problems is given to n learners (L). The problems may be solved either synchronously or asynchronously. Moreover, in this activity, the coordinator (C) is present in class and assists learners while they solve the problems given to them (the asynchronous case will be treated later). A chat application is used by both learners and coordinator to communicate. That is, learners send questions to the coordinator while, he, in turn, sends back answers in real-time through the chat application (Fig. 11.7).

The first case considered here is when a question requires an individual answer to learner Li. In that particular case, the coordinator (C) can answer the question using one of three methods. Indeed, based on the complexity of the answer, the coordinator can contact Li using three distinct tools:

• Chat application: the question can be answered with a simple answer
• Videoconference: the answer includes a simple demonstration

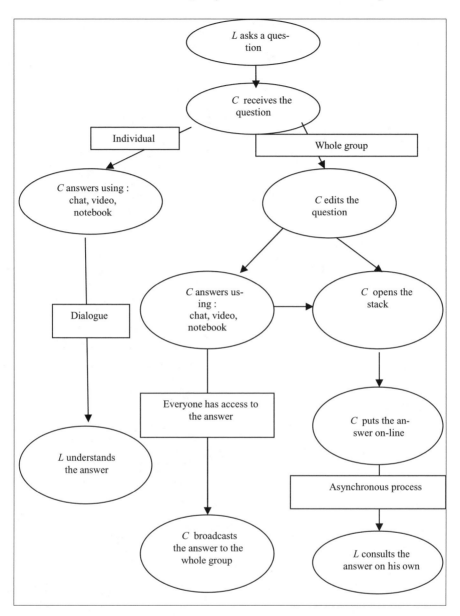

FIGURE 11.7. Steps involved in answering a question in the problem solving activity.

• Demonstration notebook: the answer includes a demonstration requiring some examples

Ideally, there would be coordination between two or more tools simultaneously.

In the second case, illustrated in Figure 11.7, the coordinator gives an answer to the whole class. Indeed, if the coordinator deems the question worthy and the answer profitable to the whole class, he can decide to give a common answer. The class may or may not be interrupted. As in the previous case, an answer can be given using one of the aforementioned tools, the difference this time being that the answer is broadcasted.

If the coordinator decides to answer the question for the whole class, a stack is used to circumvent any synchronicity problems. Moreover, to enable permanent viewing of class communications, and since learners may be absent on the day the class is given, we consider creating a list based on a discussion forum model. Thus, the coordinator having considered the question pertinent, he edits the question and its answer on the list and makes it available to all learners on a permanent basis. Hence, all learners enrolled in the course will have access to a permanent on-line list. As was the case before, the answers can take one of three forms.

B. Distance Learning

The second scenario, which is more representative of the collaborations going on in the CLE, is concerned with the distance learning activity. This scenario is illustrated in Figure 11.8. In the distance learning activity, we present collaborations occurring within a group composed of one or many sets of learners and a coordinator.

It is interesting to notice how group work is organized in the laboratory. As in the problem solving case, the main tool used to communicate is the chat application. We

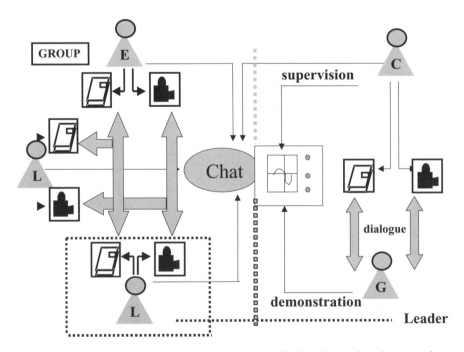

FIGURE 11.8. Interactions and collaborations involved in the distance learning scenario.

also consider the possibility of restricting its usage to a limited number or subgroup of learners. Thanks to this tool, students can share their ideas and communicate among themselves easily. Problems arising due to the complex nature of distance learning can be resolved using videoconferencing or the workbook.

During the time the distance learning tasks are performed, all learners belonging to a group have exactly the same status. Once the tasks are completed, a leader is elected and is responsible for presenting the group's work to the coordinator. Using multicasting or broadcasting, learners belonging to the group but also the coordinator can follow the demonstration given by the leader. If necessary, the coordinator can take control of the equipment used for the demonstration and apply the necessary modifications.

11.3.5 Collaborative Architecture Supporting Quality of Service

The architecture presented is based on a classical client-server model. As shown in Figure 11.9, our architecture is composed of two subsystems: a client subsystem, whose area is delimited by a dotted line, and a server supporting QoS, enclosed in a shaded rectangle. Components associated with the client are executed locally (by a learner), while all other components can be shared, used, and executed by all actors participating in the virtual laboratory. Notice that the QoS manager plays a central role in the architecture as it manages and controls the QoS level of the platform.

The remainder of this section describes, the components of this collaborative architecture, from both the client and server perspectives, while highlighting their interactions and the role they play in the collaboration process.

Graphical user interface (GUI): This is the main access to the virtual laboratory; all tools and services are available or accessible through the GUI. Note that laboratories have different GUI, depending on the services and tools available.

Registration module: The registration module provides laboratory access and identifies for every registered learner (learners who wish to use the virtual lab must register first) the parts of the system that are available to them.

Security module: The importance of security is even more critical in shared environments. This module offers authentication features (learners using the virtual lab must log in using a password) as well as security solutions pertaining to the confidentiality of data, applications, and communication within the virtual lab. Hence, only authorized actors (e.g., coordinators, lab assistants) can access learners' work.

Cooperation interface: The main objective of this component aims first to establish cooperation and, ultimately, collaboration. While ensuring the collaboration level required by the users of the virtual laboratory, the cooperation interface also manages QoS (speed, image resolution, throughput, etc.) and the efficient classification of learners into groups.

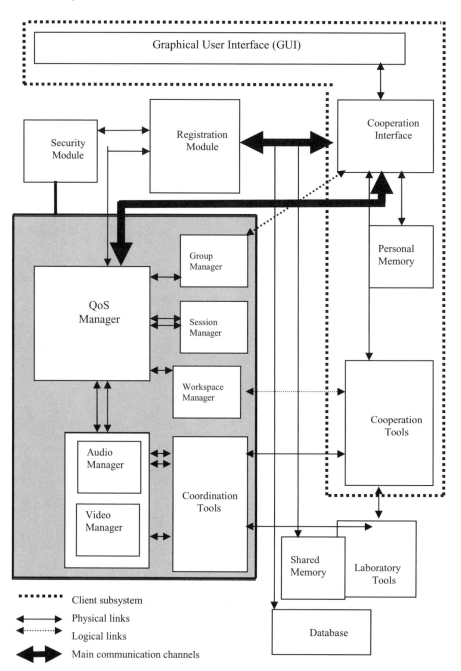

FIGURE 11.9. Global collaborative architecture.

QoS manager: This is the main QoS component. It links the users of the virtual laboratory (through the cooperation interface) to other QoS system components (session, group, and workspace managers). Indeed, by collecting information on the state of the platform and the traffic parameters, it informs the virtual lab users on the available QoS.

Session manager: Coordination is defined as the transition between the co-operation and communication processes. The session manager implements this coordination as it defines the roles (e.g., coordinator, learner, leader, etc.) and actions performed by every actor of the virtual laboratory.

Workspace manager: This module controls temporal access to the laboratory workspace as well as the applications and tools used by learners. This control is necessary due to the wide variety of configurations available for each laboratory.

Group manager: This module is used to manage the collaborative aspects within each group participating in the laboratory.

Audio manager: This module ensures efficient transfer of audio flows through-out the virtual laboratory.

Video manager: This module plays a role similar to the audio manager, although it is dedicated to video flows. However, efficiency is extremely important here since video interactivity makes all the difference between a collaborative and a noncollaborative platform.

Laboratory tools: Tools used mainly for experimental purposes.

Cooperation tools: These include chat (text and audio), browser, forum, questions and answers (Q&A), and videoconferencing applications. Cooperation tools are generic applications chosen by the laboratory designer according to the desired level of collaboration.

Coordination tools: Coordination is an important aspect of interactivity. The role of this module consists in synchronizing and parallelizing the usage of all lab tools and applications.

Shared memory: This memory area is shared, and hence can be used by all actors evolving in the virtual laboratory. As an example, the laboratory coordinator can use the shared memory area to store a discussion forum from which learners will retrieve answers to their questions. Notice that this type of storage is permanent.

Personal memory: Learners can save experimental data and personal information for future use in this memory area.

Databases: These databases provide access to a wealth of information on existing experimentations. They are also used as repositories for course material and encyclopedias.

11.4 Implementation and Results

The cooperation interface and other virtual laboratory components were implemented using a Java programming environment. Figure 11.10 shows the protocols used by several applications included in the virtual laboratory.

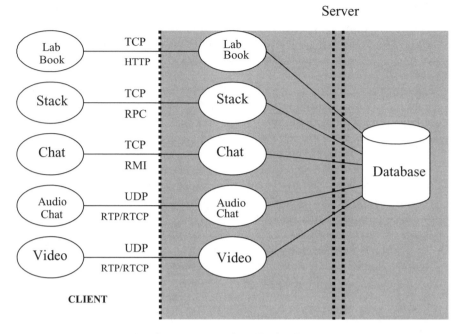

FIGURE 11.10. Transport and application layer protocols.

11.4.1 Implementation of QoS in the Collaborative Environment

QoS support is one of the two major aspects of our architecture, the other being collaboration. As mentioned above, users must be able to specify the desired level of QoS they expect from a platform. Since data flows transmitted by the virtual laboratories will potentially travel through several networks, from source to destination, the implementation of our QoS manager must take into account available QoS technologies. The two most popular QoS models are *integrated services* (IntServ) and *differentiated services* (DiffServ).

The DiffServ [7,26] model enables traffic differentiation into several classes of service. With this model, users can choose the class of service that best fits their needs from the various classes: best effort, excellent effort, standard, interactive voice, interactive video, etc. Moreover, for each class of service, the network guarantees the value of QoS parameters such as mean delay, jitter, throughput, etc. [15].

While the DiffServ model is used to classify services into different categories, the IntServ model is more granular as it offers the possibility to precisely specify the service requirements needed by a data flow. Once they are specified, the network reserves the resources needed to deliver the required level of QoS. As in DiffServ, several classes of service are offered, such as guaranteed services and controlled service. Furthermore, it is up to the network to decide if it can deliver the required QoS or if the flow will be treated as best effort traffic.

QoS is provisioned dynamically to the architecture by the network. Treating the architecture with QoS guarantees allows the end users to experience the differentiated QoS supported by the underlying network. Measurements are transferred throughout the network safely while commands to the instrument are securely passed and cannot be lost even if they experience a network congestion condition. Applications involving virtual instrumentation, data acquisition, and surveillance need to run over a QoS aware network, due to their intolerance to data loss.

Local demonstrations aim to illustrate the framework's capabilities since network-related conditions are easily controlled and the applications can be used to their full extent. For testing the architecture's QoS characteristics, these tests were also reproduced by adding extra "noise" traffic (best-effort class flows) and monitoring the network layer's ability to distinguish and protect the "useful" flows.

End-to-end demonstrations were subject to resource limitations such as bandwidth, and targeted at providing a way to evaluate the applications' capability to overcome difficult network conditions. To provide a full-range testing framework, both quality guaranteed and non–QoS-aware test cases were included.

11.4.2 Model Definition, Results, and Analyses

The OPNET network simulator was used to evaluate the performance of this architecture. The first step of the simulation process consists of selecting the metrics to evaluate. The three metrics selected for our performance evaluation are delay, jitter, and packet loss rate. Furthermore, to obtain the most realistic results possible, we have to define a networking environment, consisting of a network topology, traffic flows, and applications, which will best model real-world usage of our platform. We define two types of users: user A in a virtual laboratory supporting QoS, and user B in a virtual laboratory without QoS.

Network topology: The focus of our performance evaluation will be on the virtual laboratory users. We have modeled our topology according to the client-server model, where user A and user B are at one extremity of the system and a server is at the other, processing the flows generated by different users of the virtual lab. Furthermore, we use an Internet connection to link the two ends of the topology. The different network node connections are basic point-to-point links. Finally, user B is a standard user of the system without QoS, which will be used to compare results obtained from other users.

Traffic and applications: It is extremely difficult to model with precision the different traffic flows that will be generated by virtual laboratories, as these flows depend on the characteristics of the lab itself. Hence, we chose to use the trace file found in [20]. This file contains traffic data for voice, video, and HTTP (i.e., file transfer) flows. This traffic can be respectively associated with audio-chat, videoconferencing, and browsing applications. Now that we have defined a network topology and the different traffic types we wish to analyze, we can evaluate the performance of our architecture. Our performance evaluation is conducted in two steps:

- We first evaluate the selected metrics (delay, jitter, and packet loss rate) by applying traffic generated by a single user to the network. In other words, we create a standard, or baseline, from which we can compare results obtained from different configurations;
- In the second step, we evaluate the same metrics, but this time, we consider the number of participants in the virtual laboratory. Hence, we evaluate and compare the performance of our architecture with groups of 10, 25, 50, and 100 users.

The traffic generated in the network consists of the following protocols: VoIP for communications of voice over the Internet, and http for navigation on the Web and video. Every type of traffic is modeled by the successive juxtapositions of an active period and a period of inactivity. More exactly, we determine the distribution of interarrivals as well as that of the duration of the sessions.

Voice Model

A stochastic process can describe the voice traffic model, with arrival times corresponding to the beginning times of sessions. Each session describes a complete phone call and contains the ON-OFF period. ON periods occur when voice packets are generated, whereas no packets are generated, during OFF periods. To model both uplink and downlink, we can use two symmetric sources.

Quintero et al. have used an ON-OFF voice, with the ON period distribution following an exponential law with mean 352 ms and the OFF period also following an exponential law with mean 650 ms. Within the ON period, packets arrive at a fixed rate $1/\tau$. Therefore, $1/\tau$ is the sampling rate. For example, for the Global System for Mobile Communications (GSM) codec, τ is 20 ms. The call mean time duration is 5 minutes. The exponential distribution has the following probability density function:

$$f_{VoIP}(x) = \lambda.e^{-\lambda x}, x \geq 0$$

where $\lambda = (300x)^{-1}$, x represents the time.

Http Model

Quintero et al. describe the data traffic characteristics of individual WWW users. When a user requests a page, several URL (Uniform Resource Locator) requests may follow. The first one transmits the user's direct request to the server, and the browser program generates the following requests automatically. This requires a separate request to be sent automatically by the client program during the download of a page. The various parameters of the HTTP model are as follows:

- The size of the files is modeled by: a log-normal distribution whose corresponding normal distribution has a mean of 9.357 Kbytes and a standard deviation of

1.318 Kbytes for the body of the file size distribution, and a Pareto distribution with location 133 Kbytes and shape 1.1 for the tail of the distribution (93% of the files have their sizes drawn from the log-normal distribution).
- The number of embedded references follows a Pareto law with location (or scale) 1 and shape 2.43.
- The number of clicks per session can be modeled by a Pareto distribution with a location (or scale) of approximately 0.8 and a shape of about 1.16.
- Inactive OFF interarrivals follow a Pareto distribution with location 1 and shape 1.5.
- Active OFF interarrivals follow a Weibull distribution with scale 1.46 and shape 0.382.
- The duration of the sessions follows a Pareto distribution having the following probability density function:

$$f_{http}(x) = a \cdots b^a / x^{a+1}$$

We can calculate the relation between the parameters of the law of Pareto with its average m_{Pareto} and $a = 1.35$ [38]:

$$m_{Pareto}(a, b) = \int_b^\infty x \cdots (ab^a \cdots x^{-a-1}) dx \text{ with } a \in]1, 2[$$

It gives:

$$m_{Pareto}(a, b) = ab^a \int_b^\infty x^{-a} dx$$

or

$$m_{Pareto}(a, b)/ab^a = \int_b^\infty x^{-a} dx$$

then

$$m_{Pareto}(a, b)/ab^a = \left[\frac{x^{-a+1}}{-a+1} \right]_b^\infty$$

i.e.

$$m_{Pareto}(a, b)/a * b^a = \frac{b^{-a+1}}{-a+1}$$

We can conclude:

$$m_{Pareto}(a, b) = (a * b)/(a - 1) \text{ for } a \in]1, 2[$$

Knowing the parameter a and the average $m_{Pareto}(a, b)$, we can determine the parameter b.

Video Model

The video-on-demand model is more complex and it was taken from [38]. Video data are highly correlated. The correlations arise as a consequence of the similarities among images (interframe) or parts of images that are used as units of compression (intraframes). Due to the high bandwidth needs of uncompressed video streams, coding algorithms are used for the compression of the video stream. The most frequent is the MPEG (ISO-Moving Picture Expert Group) suite of coding schemes. In these schemes, a video sequence consists of a series of frames, each containing a two-dimensional array of pixels. For each pixel, both luminance and chrominance information is stored. The compression algorithm is used to reduce the data rate before the transmission of the video stream. In MPEG-coded streams, there are three types of frames, each using a slightly different coding scheme: I-frames use only intra frame coding based on discrete cosine transform and entropy coding; P-frames use a similar coding algorithm to I-frames, but with the addition of motion compensation with respect to the previous I- or P-frame; B-frames are similar to P-frames, except that the motion compensation can be with respect to the previous I- or P-frame or an interpolation between them.

Each frame type is fitted using a log-normal distribution, where parameters are estimated using the maximum likelihood estimators. The P- and B-frames size fits to log-normal distributions whose corresponding normal distributions have respectively a mean of 4 and 3, and a standard deviation of 0.6 and 0.46 approximately. However, we will use only the P-frame size distribution. This does not imply a big loss of generality as P- and B-frames size fits the same type of distribution and it has been shown that P-B-frames produce similar traces [38]. Moreover, we are on the safe side as P-frames are generally bigger than B-frames. According to [38], the P-frames size distribution is a log normal with mean 65.4 Kbits and standard deviation 43 Kbits. The I-frame size distribution also follows a log-normal distribution with mean 194.4 Kbits and standard deviation 81 Kbits.

The frame interarrival is constant and equal to 41.7 ms (24 frames per second). The number of frames in a session is proportional to the session length. A video on demand (VoD) session can be a movie session or a video-clip session. We will suppose that movie sessions are scarce. In a first time, we will ignore movies ordering and suppose that VoD transfers only video clips. Subsequent variations on the traffic distribution will introduce longer video sequences. A video clip lasts between 2 and 6 minutes with a mean of about 4 minutes. Consequently, the number of frames per session is distributed according to a triangular distribution with minimum 2880, maximum 8640, and mean 5760. The session arrival process will be modeled by an exponential law with parameter $\lambda 2$. This parameter will be adjusted to obtain the required traffic proportion [38].

The remainder of this section presents simulation results obtained for this architecture in terms of delay, jitter, and packet loss rate. Furthermore, the influence of the service level chosen to support the traffic flow and of network congestion will be addressed.

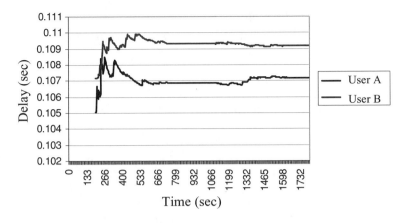

FIGURE 11.11. Comparing delays between user A and user B.

A. Voice Traffic

The first observation we can make about traffic is that, as with voice, there is a sensible difference between user A and user B in terms of delay. Indeed, as illustrated on Figure 11.11, even without network congestion, the interactive service decreases the delay by 0.025 seconds or 2.3%.

B. HTTP Traffic

For the response time per object or the losses, the results obtained are relatively similar and characteristic. Figure 11.12 shows the comparative results for two identical applications, with and without QoS. Hence, the application named user A supports Qos while the one named user B does not; it is simply best effort. It clearly appears that for user A the response time is significantly lower than for user

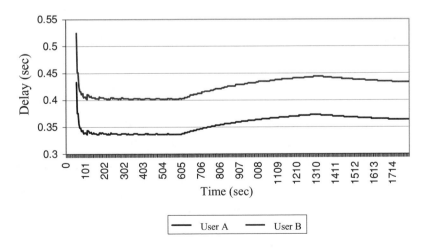

FIGURE 11.12. Comparative response times for user A and user B.

TABLE 11.1. Comparing performance delays

	HTTP	VOICE	VIDEO
Gross (sec)	0.0654	0.0019	0.1421
Relative (%)	19.4	1.85	86.1

B. If the general profiles are identical (slight influence of the video application, which somewhat increases the response time), the numbers are quite eloquent. Indeed, if we apply the standard treatment, we increase by 20%, on average. This increase, even though not significant (0,065s) cannot be considered negligible. Consequently, we can say that service differentiation seems to be beneficial to the user. Moreover, the tendency is confirmed and becomes ever more evident when we increase the network load by adding traffic Group Users. Hence, we can say that the difference between the two increases as the number of users increases.

Tables 11.1 through 11.3 facilitate the comparison of performance variations according to the service contract chosen, the considered applications, and the network congestion. Hence, Table 11.1 emphasizes the differences between an application running in privileged and nonprivileged modes, respectively.

C. Video Traffic

The last aspect of our simulation is concerned with the evaluation of service differentiation for video applications. Indeed, these applications constitute the last facet of the collaboration. Our analysis will follow the same plan as for the HTTP case. As shown in Figure 11.13, the difference is self-evident. There is a constant difference of 0.15 seconds between user A and user B. This difference is equal to a 96% improvement of the overall performance.

Tables 11.2 and 11.3 illustrate the results obtained for the delay metric (N/A indicates no results were obtained due to network saturation) for user A and user B.

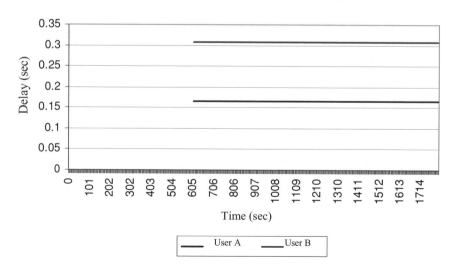

FIGURE 11.13. Delay comparison between user A and user B.

TABLE 11.2. Delay variation (jitter) for user B

		HTTP	VOICE	VIDEO
10 Users B	Gross (sec)	0.4155	0.7991	1.6273
	Relative (%)	97	740	530
25 Users B	Gross (sec)	0.6127	1.2941	0.9920
	Relative (%)	143	1197	323
50 Users B	Gross (sec)	1.4376	0.9083	0.8691
	Relative (%)	335	841	283
100 Users B	Gross (sec)	1.79 (saturation)	N/A	0.8742
	Relative (%)	418 (saturation)	N/A	285

Hence, by showing performance degradation as a function of the level of network congestion for user A and user B, we can clearly see the benefits brought by service differentiation. Indeed, without congestion, results obtained for user A are much better than those obtained for user B. Moerover, as we have already established that performance degradation is greater in the second case, it becomes clear that the greater the congestion, the greater the difference between the two.

The demonstrations performed indicated that the architecture developed can adapt to various network environments and that it can, even under stressed conditions, deliver an important subset of its full capabilities. More specifically:

- Chat and Whiteboard are lightweight applications that produce minimal traffic and can operate without QoS needs. Their operation proved to be efficient for a virtual classroom with many students even under a strained environment.
- File transfer performance was satisfactory taking into consideration the nature of material exchanged in the frame of a classroom, being mostly documents.
- Video conference could also adapt well to network impairments when used in audio-only mode in conjunction with a low-bit-rate codec. Video size and frame rate can be adjusted so as to constrain traffic to the available limit. Although the application benefits from resource reservation, even in non-QoS environment, it exhibited robustness and successfully recuperated from temporarily network disturbances.
- Video on demand, being by nature a network demanding service, cannot be exploited properly in a constrained environment. When bandwidth was available

TABLE 11.3. Delay variation (jitter) for user A

		HTTP	VOICE	VIDEO
10 Users A	Gross (sec)	0.0250	0.0134	0.0056
	Relative (%)	7.5	11.8	3.4
25 Users A	Gross (sec)	0.0197	0.0196	0.0052
	Relative (%)	5.9	18.2	3.1
50 Users A	Gross (sec)	0.0052	0.2100	0.005
	Relative (%)	1.6	195	3.0
100 Users A	Gross (sec)	0.0752	N/A	0.005
	Relative (%)	22	N/A	3.0

(e.g., LAN environment), it significantly enhanced the usability of the virtual classroom experiments. In such an environment, video conference could also be used to its extent, with full video and audio quality, supporting many students concurrently. When coupled with the architecture, these applications provided a robust and reliable framework for the deliverance of a high-quality e-learning service.

11.5 Conclusion

In this chapter, we have presented a distributed e-laboratory environment. The architecture presented is based on a classical client-server model, and it is composed of two subsystems a client subsystem and a server supporting QoS. Components associated with the client are executed locally (by a learner) while all other components can be shared, used, and executed by all actors participating in the virtual laboratory.

Our concern was to design a flexible, parametrical, and component-oriented architecture to support collaboration among different actors or entities for each request for e-learning service according to current context that depends on all the diverse aspects of QoS that an e-learning service comprises. To this effect, we listed several ideas to enhance the concept of virtual laboratories. We first focused on collaboration. We defined terminology by synthesizing virtual learning, traditional collaboration, and collaboration enabling technologies available today. A detailed analysis of these parameters enabled us to explicitly characterize collaboration. Indeed, we defined collaboration as two distinct but complementary processes: cooperation and communication. Moreover, to complete this definition, we added the concept of coordination as the glue joining cooperation and communication.

Furthermore, to facilitate the implementation of solutions adapted to the addressed problem, we completed this decomposition by providing several levels of analyses (functional, structural, and technological). One of the original contributions of this work is the definition of a cooperation interface controlling every aspects of cooperation, notably quality of service, by using several communication mechanisms to optimize the collaboration process. The usage of the tools designed best illustrates this originality. We attempted to find a solution to address the fact that tools used necessarily generate quality challenges.

To validate our implementation, we have carried out a series of simulations, involving different kind of users and different kind of traffic. Experimentation scenarios have been elaborated in order to evaluate the performance of communications during the use of the environment. Results indicate that improvements caused by traffic differentiation, even without special network loads, become even more significant as the number of users increases.

References

1. Alfano, M., Sigle, R. (1996) Controlling QoS in a collaborative multimedia environment. Proceedings of high performance distribute computing (HPDC-5), Syracuse, N.Y., USA pp. 340–342.

2. Allison, C., Lawson, H., McKechan, D., Ruddle, A. (2001) Quality of service issues in distributed learning environments. IEEE International Conference on Advanced Learning Technologies, Vol. 2, pp. 29–32, Madison, WI, USA.

3. Apostolopoulos, T., Kefala, A. (2003) An e-learning service management architecture. The 3rd IEEE International Conference on Advanced Learning Technologies, pp. 140–144, Joansuu, Finland.

4. Ausserhofer, A. (1999) Web-based teaching and learning: a panacea. IEEE Communications Magazine, 37(3):92–96.

5. Bates A. (1995) Technology: Open Learning and Distance Education. London: Routledge.

6. Blackboard. (2004) www.blackboard.com.

7. Blake, S., Black, D. (1998) An Architecture for Differentiated Services. Request for Comments (RFC) 2475.

8. Bouras, C., Triantafillou, V., Tsiatos, T. (2001) Aspects of a Collaborative Learning Environment Using Distributed Virtual Environments. Tampere, Finland: ED-MEDIA, pp. 173–178.

9. Bouras, C., Hornig, G., Triantafillou, V., Tsiatsos, T. (2001) Architectures supporting e-learning through collaborative virtual environments: the case of INVITE. IEEE International Conference on Advanced Learning Technologies-ICALT, pp. 13–16.

10. Choukair, Z., Retailleau, D., Hellstrom, M. (2000) Environment for performing collaborative distributed virtual environments with QoS. Seventh International Conference on Parallel and Distributed Systems, pp. 111–118.

11. Collis, B. (1997) Tele-Learning in a Digital World: The Future of Distance Learning. London: International Thomson Publications.

12. Collis, B. (1999) Applications of computer communications in education: an overview. IEEE Communications Magazine, 37(3):82–86.

13. Costabile, M., De Marsico, M, Lanzilotti, R., Plantamura V., Rosell, T. (2005) On the usability evaluation of e-learning applications. International Conference on System Sciences, HICSS '05. pp. 6b–8b.

14. Dorneich, M., Jones, P. (2000) The design and implementation of a learning collaboratory. IEEE International Conference on Systems, Man, and Cybernetics, Vol. 2, pp. 1146–1151, Nashville, TE, USA.

15. Gaidioz, B., Primet, P. (2002) The equivalent differentiated services model. INRIA, France, research report 4387.

16. Hamburg, I., Hamburg, A., Gavota, M., Lazea, M. (2004) Integrating wireless technology in e-learning for disabled. International Conference on Information and Communication Technologies: From Theory to Applications, Damascus, Syria, pp. 123–124.

17. Houstis, E., Joshi, A., Weeraawarana, S., Elmagarmid, A. (1996) Internet, education, and the Web. 5th International Workshops on Enabling Technologies: Infrastructure for Collaborative Enterprises (WETICE'96), Los Alamitos, CA, USA, pp. 27–33.

18. Hsin-Chuan, H., Chao-Tung, Y., Chi-Chung, C. (2004) Building an e-learning platform by access grid and data grid technologies. IEEE International Conference on e-Technology, e-Commerce and e-Service, pp. 452–455.

19. Joint Information Systems Committee. (2005) http://www.jisc.ac.uk.

20. Johnston, W., Agarwal, D., Lace, E. (1997) The Virtual Laboratory: Using Networks to Enable Widely Distributed Collaboratory Science. NSF & BNS and Networking and Application Researchers Workshop, LBNL report 37466.

21. King, F., Mayall, H. (2001) Asynchronous distributed problem-based learning. IEEE International Conference on Advanced Learning Technologies, Madison, WI, USA, pp. 157–159.

22. Licea, G., Favala, J., Garcia, J., Aaguilar, J. (1997) A pattern system supporting QoS for synchronous collaborative systems. IEEE Conference on Protocols for Multimedia Systems—Multimedia Networking, Santiago, Chile, pp. 223–228.
23. Littlejohn, A.H., Higgison, C. (2003) E-learning Guide for Teachers in Higher Education, Learning and Teaching Support Network Publications, LTSN Generic Centre e-Learning Series No. 3, York, England.
24. Liu, K., Tsaoussidis, T. (2000) Efficient Network for Collaborative Services and Application Development. IEEE International Conference on Multimedia and Expo, New York, NY, USA, vol. 1, pp. 53–56.
25. Mathur, A., Prakash, A. (1996) A protocol composition-based approach to QoS control in collaboration systems. Proceedings of MULTIMEDIA, pp. 62–69.
26. Medina, O, Bonnin, J., Toutain L. (2000) Service DiffServ pour les Flux Audio et Vidéo. Bretagne, France: ENST.
27. M'tir, R., Jeribi, I., Rumpler, B., Ghazala, H.H.B. (2004) Reuse and cooperation in e-learning systems. Fifth International Conference on Information Technology Based Higher Education and Training, ITHET, Istanbul, Turkey, pp. 131–137.
28. Nguyen, Q., Huang, M., Hawryszkiewycz, I. (2004) A new visualization approach for supporting knowledge management and collaboration in e-learning. Eighth International Conference on Information Visualization, London, England, pp. 693–700.
29. Oracle. (2004) www.oracle.com/ilearning.
30. Patrikakis, Ch., Karapetsas, K., Diakonikolaou, G. (2003) A QoS aware e-learning service framework: The MOICANE case, In: Spinellis, D. (ed.) Kluwer International Series in Engineering and Computer Science: Cross-Media Service Delivery. New York: Kluwer Academic Publishers, pp. 109–120.
31. Pierre, S., Kassouf M. (2001) Towards a telecommunication platform for supporting distributed virtual laboratories. International Journal of Educational Telecommunications, 7(2):157–194.
32. Raymond, D., Baudin-Thomas, V., Gayraud, K., Matsuura, K., Diaz M., Yano, Y. (2004) Distant e-learning using synchronous collaborative environment platine. IEEE Sixth International Symposium on Multimedia Software Engineering, Miami, FL, USA, pp. 88–95.
33. Ronchetti, M., Saini, P. (2004) Knowledge management in an e-learning system. IEEE International Conference on Advanced Learning Technologies, Joansuu, Finland, pp. 365–369.
34. Shirmohammadi, S., Georganas, N. (1997) JETS: a Java-enabled telecollaboration system. Multimedia Computing and Systems '97. International Conference on Proceedings, IEEE, Ottawa, ON, Canada, pp. 541–547.
35. Sitarama, S., Dong, A., Agonino, A. (2001) Speech acts and peer learning in product development case-study discussions. International Conference on Engineering Education, Oslo, Norway, pp. 18–23.
36. Virvon, M., Alepis, E. (2004) Mobile versus desktop facilities for an e-learning system: user perspective, IEEE International Conference on Systems, Man and Cybernetics, vol. 1, pp. 48–52.
37. WebCT. (2004) www.webct.com.
38. Quintero, A., Elalamy, Y., Pierre, S. (2004) Performance evaluation of a broadband wireless access system subjected to heavy load, Computer Communications, 27(9):781–791.

Part IV
Retrieving Resources and Knowledge

12
Quality Rating and Recommendation of Learning Objects

Vivekanandan Kumar, John Nesbit, Philip Winne, Allyson Hadwin, Dianne Jamieson-Noel, and Kate Han

12.1 Introduction

The unceasing growth of the Internet has led to new modes of learning in which learners routinely interact on-line with instructors, other students, and digital resources. Much recent research has focused on building infrastructure for these activities, especially to facilitate searching, filtering, and recommending on-line resources known as learning objects. Although newly defined standards for learning object metadata are expected to greatly improve searching and filtering capabilities, learners, instructors, and instructional developers may still be faced with choosing from many pages of object listings returned from a single learning object query. The listed objects tend to vary widely in quality. With current metadata and search methods, those who search for learning objects waste time and effort groping through overwhelming masses of information, often finding only poorly designed and developed instructional materials. Hence, there is a clear need for quality evaluations prior to making a recommendation that can be communicated in a coherent, standardized format to measure the quality of learning objects.

In the last few years, a number of quality rating standards have been developed. As different evaluation instruments are deployed in learning object repositories serving specialized communities of users, what methods can be applied for translating evaluative data across instruments to allow these data to be shared among different repositories? How can the large number of possible explicit and implicit measures of preference and quality be combined to recommend objects to users? To address these questions, we employ a Bayesian belief networks (BBN), a powerful probabilistic knowledge representation and reasoning technique for partial beliefs under uncertainty. Using BBN, we also tackle problems of insufficient and incomplete reviews in learning object repositories, as well as translating and integrating data among different quality evaluation instruments.

In this chapter, we argue that BBNs are a new way of collecting and analyzing the evaluation of learning object quality, and we present real-world BBNs that are constructed to probabilistically model relationships among different roles of reviewers, among various explicit and implicit ratings, and among items of different evaluation measurements. We also present results from a qualitative study and from simulated testing cases to show that the BBN model makes quantitatively reliable inferences about different dimensions of learning object quality.

12.2 Online Learning and Learning Objects

The competitive nature and ever-increasing productivity of our society creates a demand for "up-to-date," "just-in-time," and "just-enough" learning solutions. Unsurprisingly, the sheer volume and high availability of information on the Internet has led to new methods for learning and knowledge construction in education. Before the Internet era, education was much more reliant on school buildings, classrooms, and face-to-face interaction with teachers, books, and libraries. With the advent of the Internet, many of the educational functions provided by these resources and facilities are made available on-line. Students can learn anywhere, anytime by accessing the Internet. Through this ubiquitous medium, education has become more accessible.

Some regard on-line learning as "the use of Internet technologies to deliver a broad array of solutions that enhance knowledge and performance" [10]. Others accept a broader definition that includes learning through intranets and other electronic networks. Over the last decade, Web-based communication media such as asynchronous and audiographic conferencing technologies have led to important new methods for teaching and learning. The Web also allows access to an ever-richer array of multimedia resources that are mined for integration in Web-based courses. It is the challenges in this latter area to which the research reported in this chapter is addressed.

Substantial funding from both public and private educational and industrial organizations has poured into developing on-line learning resources. Examples of initiatives underway include the Curriculum Online project being undertaken for schools in the United Kingdom at a cost of approximately $500 million (www.curriculumonline.gov.uk), and the Australian Learning Federation, a project similar in emphasis with a $30 million budget (www.thelearningfederation.edu.au). To facilitate access to the many thousands of on-line, multimedia resources, we now require sophisticated databases, technical standards, and network infrastructure. These innovations reach beyond the provision of technical facilities needed to distribute resources. Indeed, the capacity of the Internet for allowing information to be easily shared is affecting the way that learning resources are designed and developed.

Digital resources created within one educational institution can now be distributed and reused on a global scale. However, to fully realize the potential for reuse, there is a need to resolve issues of portability across heterogeneous technical platforms and durability across evolving technologies. The technical standards and implementation criteria for learning objects [1] are intended to address these issues.

12.2.1 Learning Objects

Learning objects are digital resources such as images, documents, and simulations that are designed to meet explicit learning goals [5]. According to one Canadian group a learning object is "any digital resource that can be reused to support learning" [14]. Some sources have more narrow definitions that specify rarely met requirements. For example, at Cisco, the network technology giant, a learning object is composed of a learning objective, metadata, content, practice, and assessment [16]. Properties often attributed to learning objects are modularity, reusability, discoverability, customizability, and interoperability [52].

The modular design of learning objects echoes the "object-oriented" trend in modern computer software development. Object-oriented programming focuses on the creation of software objects that can be more easily aggregated into larger programs and reused within many programs. In principle, learning objects can be created that easily integrate into larger, more complex resources such that changes can be made within the learning object that do not require changes to the aggregating body. In theory, being able to unplug a learning object from its assembling unit, revise it, and replace it saves substantial effort compared to revising conventional course material. It is easier to update a small unit of learning material than it is to update an entire cohesive course. As a result, content management becomes easier. This innovation may become especially valuable as knowledge renewal continues to accelerate.

Closely related to modularity is the important attribute of reusability. Once developed, a learning object can potentially be used in multiple contexts for multiple purposes. Many thousands of schools, colleges, and universities offer similar courses, in which the fundamental knowledge to learned is more or less the same. Yet, most educational institutions develop their own course material. Duplicate investment does not make sense, but in the past, sharing course material was difficult, with time and physical distance constraints. Another difficulty is that all courses contain some elements that are local and not transferable to other contexts because courses are often aimed a specific learner groups and they operate within schools that have different academic and administrative structures. Therefore, courses themselves are not suitable candidates for sharing [18]. Reusable learning objects allow cost-effective sharing to occur at a lower level of granularity than the entire course.

Before a learning object can be reused, it must be discovered. Discoverability is enabled by metadata that describes the object in a standardized format. Discoverability is a nontrivial feature in a Web environment, where massive and all-inclusive information is presented. To aid retrieval, learning objects include, or are represented by, metadata composed of standard attribute fields. The LTSC (Learning Technologies Standards Committee) of the IEEE (Institute of Electrical and Electronics Engineers) has published a metadata standard, called LOM (Learning Object Metadata), that is a standard method for describing and cataloging learning objects to enhance learning object discovery. For example, if all learning objects in a repository have properties of *title*, *keywords*, and *language*, then a learning object search could be constructed as "find a learning object such that its *title* contains 'physics', *keywords* contains 'quantum', in the *language* 'English'." The descriptive and relational information in LOM identifies learning objects so that they can be referenced and searched. LOM is designed to describe any learning object, regardless of its size and content.

Ideally, learning objects are also customizable. Because they are modular, individual learning objects can be redesigned to fit the needs of local organizations and learner populations. Every time an object is customized it is subjected to scrutiny and improvement, resulting in a continuing cycle of quality improvement.

Finally, learning objects have the potential to interoperate with other objects, or with a learning management system using established standards. Interoperability standards are being developed by the IMS (Instructional Management System–Global Learning Consortium) organization that will allow learning objects to communicate basic assessment information to a learning management system through a standard interface [20].

12.2.2 Learning Object Repositories

So that they can be distributed and shared for learning, teaching, and course development, learning objects are stored and indexed in databases called learning object repositories or collections. Most repositories do not store the objects, but rather information about objects that are located on Web servers distributed over the Internet. A typical learning object repository consists of a database storing records that conform to the IEEE metadata standard, and Web forms for submitting and searching object metadata. Repository designers often use guidelines published by national or local organizations (e.g., CanCore, 2003 [55]) that show how to implement subsets of the IEEE standard.

Multiple repositories can be connected together to maximize the pool of objects discoverable through a single search operation. The largest of these federated search sites is the U.S. National Sciences Digital Library (NSDL), which offers federated search of several hundred repositories. Another federated search solution being developed centers around eduSource Canada, a Canadian consortium building a national interoperability framework for both academic and industrial contexts. eduSource Canada presents a framework that unites peer-to-peer and Web services models, and formal mechanisms for interoperability at the transactional and semantic levels. The core of the proposed framework is the eduSource communications layer, an open protocol that enables search, gather, and retrieval (and other IMS digital repository interoperability specifications IMS DRI [61]) within a community of eduSource servers, clients, peers, gateways, and other networks.

Some of the many active learning object repositories are the following:

- MERLOT (www.merlot.org), currently indexing about 12,000 objects, is a repository designed for postsecondary education.
- CAREO (careo.netera.ca) currently indexing about 4000 objects, provides multidisciplinary teaching materials for educators in the Canadian province of Alberta.

TABLE 12.1. Educational elements of IEEE LOM metadata

Interactivity type
Learning resource type
Interactivity level
Semantic density
Intended end user role
Context
Typical age range
Difficulty
Typical learning time
Description
Language

- Maricopa Learning Exchange (www.mcli.dist.maricopa.edu/mlx/index.php) currently indexing about 1200 objects, targeting electronic warehouse of ideas, examples, and resources (represented as "packages") that support student learning.
- Edna Online (www.edna.edu.au) hosts a directory about education and training in Australia along with a database of Web resources for teaching and learning.

12.2.3 Pedagogical Metadata

Table 12.1 lists the educational elements of the IEEE metadata standard as described by CanCore [55].

Some of these elements, such as "semantic density," are rarely used and have been dropped by organizations that set usage guidelines for repository developers [55]. Dissatisfaction with the educational category in the LOM standard has led to proposals for extended forms of pedagogical metadata to make more explicit the educational purposes and methods that learning objects are intended to serve [56, 58].

Carey et al [56] developed a suite of "educational rationale" metatags consistent with the principles of learner centered design. Authors used the metatags to communicate the pedagogical intent underlying the design of the learning objects they create. For instance, an author might incorporate an [apply] tag in a learning object that provides students with practice in the application of theory, or a [monitor] tag in an object that prompts students to evaluate their learning strategies.

Mwanza and Engestrom [58] proposed a taxonomy of seven educational metadata elements derived from activity theory. Examples of elements from their taxonomy are objectives ("subjects shared motives for engaging in activities"), and community ("the environment or context in which objects are created and used"). Although it is doubtful that any single theory of learning or instructional design could find sufficiently broad acceptance to form an international standard for pedagogical metadata, it may be possible to establish a more generalized structure that encompasses descriptive terms from a variety of theories and design practices. For example, there could be a standardized "learning goals" element that encompassed both traditional learning objectives [57] and the activity theory metadata for objectives and desired outcomes described by Mwanza and Engestrom. To extend this scheme, separate fixed vocabularies could be developed for different theories and practices.

Rather than collect pedagogical metadata from learning object authors, one can collect it from teachers and learners. Users of the MERLOT repository [7] are able to post "assignments" for an object that describe lesson plans or educational use cases incorporating the object. The assignment is submitted as a form that has some limited pedagogical metadata fields, such as "learning objectives" and "educational level." However, much of the information entered into MERLOT assignments is relatively unstructured metadata in open text fields. In general, information in Web-based repositories that describes how specific learning objects have been used is both sparse and unstructured. Although structured metadata, like that supported by the IEEE standard, can be used more precisely to formulate search queries, unstructured metadata may be more appropriate when there is no broadly accepted taxonomy, as is the case with pedagogical metadata.

12.3 Evaluation and Recommendation Systems

As learning object repositories continue to grow, and as more repositories are accessed through federated search facilities, users will become increasingly overwhelmed by the number of objects returned by a search query. Although IEEE-style, descriptive metadata are useful in narrowing search, a point is reached where well-specified searches of precisely cataloged objects return many more objects than can be individually assessed by the user. Pedagogical metadata may help to narrow the field, but ultimately even this additional form of cataloging will not protect users from the "hit shock" produced by viewing an avalanche of search results. The problem is that users do not have a precise enough understanding of what they want to formulate specific queries, and object catalogers can not predict many of the detailed requirements of users. To bridge the knowledge gap between the consumer and producer, we need to introduce additional information about the objects that is generated by third parties.

Third parties, such as other consumers and experts, can generate two important types of information. They can provide quality evaluation of an object, perhaps about how well it functions, or its effectiveness for learning. Or they can offer subjective statement or measures of preference regarding the object. When we purchase a car we might read quality evaluations of different cars that state how well the cars are built or how often they need repair. We also might study sales statistics that indicate the popularity of different cars, or ask car owners how well they like their cars. Quality and preference information provided by third parties will also assist learning object users to narrow their search and avoid hit shock.

In this chapter we regard evaluation systems as social computing tools that are used to create and share information about the quality of learning objects. Such systems may be used to evaluate several specific aspects of learning object quality, such as technical functioning, and usability. Recommendation systems are social computing tools that differ from evaluation systems in that they match learning objects to individual users using information about the users and the objects.

All users of learning objects stand to benefit from evaluations and recommendations. Students, especially, are in need of guidance in selecting appropriate resources. Hill and Hannafin [30] observed that often "students lack sufficient meta-cognitive awareness and comprehension monitoring skill to make effective choices on resources." Third-party information in the form of quality evaluation and recommendation can aid teachers and course developers because it efficiently distributes effort required to examine and compare objects, and it allows these users to draw from the expertise of others to select objects.

12.3.1 Evaluating Quality

Learning evaluation systems are fundamentally composed of (1) tools for generating and storing quality ratings, and (2) a search engine that sorts search results according to averaged ratings in best-first order. The evaluation tools in such systems [eLera, MERLOT] enable reviewers to enter comments and ratings in a Web form. The form is a questionnaire-like instrument that asks reviewers to rate and comment on a set of predefined quality dimensions. In the following discussion and throughout this chapter we use the MERLOT [7] and eLera [8] evaluation systems as examples.

In the MERLOT evaluation tool there are three quality dimensions: quality of content, potential effectiveness as a teaching-learning tool, and ease of use [7]. When evaluating a learning object on MERLOT, for each dimension reviewers comment and provide a rating on a five-point scale. In contrast, there are nine quality dimensions in the Learning Object Review Instrument (LORI) provided on the eLera Web site: content quality, learning goal alignment, feedback and adaptation, motivation, presentation design, interaction usability, accessibility, reusability and standards compliance [9]. In LORI, as in MERLOT, reviewers can comment and rate on a five-point scale.

Demand exists for evaluation instruments with different levels of detail and areas of emphasis. Some users and organizations need detailed quality information in areas such as accessibility for learners with disabilities or compliance with specific industry standards. In other settings, quick and easy evaluations are important to encourage participation. The MERLOT instrument is designed to gather quality evaluations from university faculty who have subject matter expertise and teaching experience, but may not have technical or instructional design expertise. LORI is designed to gather evaluations from a panel of users and specialists with complementary areas of experience and expertise.

Both MERLOT and eLera use quality ratings as a default order for search results. In obtaining the overall score for a learning object, the system can calculate a weighted average over the rated dimensions. Ideally the system could allow searchers to specify the weights used in calculating the quality metric used for ordering the search results. To provide features similar to a recommender system, users might also be able to store their preferred weighting schemes in a preferences tool. We are not aware of any existing evaluation systems with these user-customization capabilities.

In addition to differently weighting quality dimensions, an evaluation system might allow its users to differently weight reviewers. Ratings from reviewers who are more trusted, or are more similar to the user, could be assigned a higher weight in the calculation of an object's quality score. We expect that the measurement and application of *trust metrics* will come to play an increasing role in learning object evaluation, especially in the design of recommendation systems.

At present, there are several practical problems that impede the broad use of learning object evaluation systems. The greatest of these is a supply problem. Despite the benefits offered by high-quality reviews, there are no well-established incentive structures that have been successful in encouraging broad participation in review activities. There is a widening gap between the many thousands of learning objects that are coming on-line every year, and the number of subject-matter specialists, instructional designers, teachers, and learners who are willing to review them. Secondarily, reviewers are often interested in or qualified to review only a subset of quality dimensions presented by a review instrument. Consequently, published reviews may have ratings on only some of the quality dimensions. Finally, reviews created with different instruments (e.g., MERLOT and eLera) are presently incompatible. Even though they may offer comparable information, they cannot be automicaly combined to generate a single quality score for use in ordering a search. This failing will become increasingly apparent as users turn to federated search facilities that return results from multiple repositories that apply different evaluation criteria.

12.3.2 Recommendation and Trust

Given a set of users and items, where items could be documents, products, other users, etc., a system recommends items to a user based on past behaviour of this user and/or other users, and additional information on users/items [23].

Recommendation is a very common social activity with a broadly understood meaning. However, in social computing, an essential feature of good recommendations is that they are relative to the preferences and needs of the recommendee. The purpose of recommendation systems is to find items that match a specific person or requirement.

Essentially, a recommendation system tries to make the best prediction that a user will or will not like a certain item.

With learning object metadata, better filtering techniques have been developed and applied in learning object discovery, that is, collaborative filtering versus text-based indexing used in most of the Internet search engines. Collaborative filtering holds promise in education not only for the purposes of helping learners and educators find useful resources, but as a means of bringing together people with similar interests and beliefs, and possibly as an aid to the learning process itself [6]

There are two basic types of recommendation systems, content-based and collaborative filtering. There are also social software[1] and social data mining,[2] which are not of our concern here [24].

Content-Based

Content-based recommendation systems use data about the requested item and the information regarding only the active user [25]. Content-based methods, also known as search-based or item-based, treat the recommendation problem as a search for related items. Based on an item provided by a user, the algorithm constructs a search query to find other items with similar keywords or subjects. These items are combined into a recommendation list.

There are different algorithms to determine the most-similar match for a given item. A few popular ones are the vector space model, Bayesian classifiers, and two variants of the vector space model, which are content representation of items and support vector machine classifiers [25].

One of the main limitations with content-based recommendation is that, in a search space, some items' features are impossible to extract for computing predictions. Another limitation is that some important aspects of an item cannot be captured without human intervention. Also, when the search space grows bigger, additional algorithms need to be applied to narrow it down for computation performance purposes [25].

Collaborative Filtering

For collaborative filtering or cluster model, the recommendation is achieved using information about other users, rather than only the active user [26]. In fact, "a pure collaborative recommendation system is one which does no analysis of the items at all—all that is known about an item is a unique identifier" [27]. The main idea is to find a subset of users who have similar tastes to the given user, and use this subset for making predictions. In pure collaborative filtering, one does not need to know the content of an item, only the relationship between different users [25].

There are a number of approaches to implement collaborative filtering, including neighborhood-based, BBN, induction rule learning, and so on. The one most frequently used is the neighborhood-based approach[3] [25].

Traditional collaborative filtering does little or no off-line computation. Using collaborative filtering to generate recommendations is computationally expensive. It is possible to partially address these scaling issues by reducing the data size, either the number of users in the neighbourhood or the number of catalogues within

---

[1] Social software: the recommendation process is supported but not automated [23].

[2] Social data mining: mine log data of social activity to learn group preferences [23].

[3] Neighborhood-based: The main idea is to find a subset of users who have similar tastes to the given user, and use this subset for making predictions.

a user. Unfortunately, these methods also reduce recommendation quality in one way or the other.

In addition to computational difficulty, collaborative filtering methods also suffer from a few other problems, some of which we encounter in learning object recommendations under different contexts:

- *Cold start*: If there are not enough users, it is difficult to find a high similarity coefficient [28].
- *Sparsity*: Sparsity refers to the sparse matrix users/rates, which happens when there are many possible items. This problem is important especially for those similarity functions that take into account only items rated by both users. The sparsity of the matrix could generate only low similarity coefficients or none at all [29].
- *First rater*: It is difficult to give a rate to new items, since they are not rated by anyone [25].
- *Popularity bias*: The system tends to recommend popular items, while being incapable of recommending items to a user with unique taste [25].

People have tried to take the advantages of both content-based and collaborative filtering methods, combing them in a mixed approach. Pazzani [29] used the knowledge of the content for avoiding the problems typical of collaborative filtering, generating more accurate predictions.

Sorting the results list by their quality appears to be an obvious answer, with the highest quality learning object on top of the list. What displays at the beginning of a list naturally gains more attention. This is an intuitive way of communicating with a user for recommendation. Hereafter, for a learning object recommendation we refer to the mechanism to return a list of inquired learning objects, sorted by quality, and the one with the best quality on top of the list.

Another advantage of a learning object recommendation is that the "item," a learning object, is structured, under the supervision of LTSC, but regular recommendation systems have to deal with masses of unstructured, inconsistent information.

From previous reviews of recommendation systems, we can see that generally they have a concept of "trust neighbor." As to what is a "good" neighbor and how to find these neighbors, different recommendation systems apply different algorithms and business implementations. Nevertheless, along with a growing interaction between users and recommendation systems, most systems are able to build up a profile, be it for items in its search space or for individual users. Profiling improves the accuracy of predictions made by recommendation systems. However, a current learning object recommendation is operated differently. Learning objects are first filtered according to LOM, and then sorted by quality rating. Hence, it is not a user preference or taste-related recommendation. A user who is interested in a learning object in discipline X today is quite possibly searching for a learning object in discipline Y tomorrow. There is no preference as to what type of learning objects a particular user is in favor of. It is a completely unpredictable factor in learning object searches. Profiling or the trust-neighborhood approach is not suitable for a current quality-oriented recommendation. In spite of this, it does not stop us from applying collaborative filtering on top of the quality-wise recommendation to make a personalized recommendation.

In this section, we present some of the key features one would employ in the process of implementing a learning object recommendation system.

Quantity

An accurate quality rating on a learning object requires evaluations from different perspectives in a teaching–learning process based on a certain rating standards. It also requires a fair amount of reviews in order to construct a reasonably "true" rating result. More reviews are always desired.

In addition, the resistance of providing reviews also comes from the implementation of the current reviewing system. It is "hard" to use, in a way that if a quality review is not complete, it cannot be submitted. Learning object rating standards are developed by professionals. Very often one reviewer is unable to rate all of the items in a rating standard subjectively. For example, an instructor might not have an accurate rating for motivation, since it is more from a learner's point of view. Similarly, a learner might not have sufficient knowledge to rate standards compliance. This yields two possible results. One is that a user might recoil from submitting a review. The other is that a keen user still submits a review, with randomly rated items that he or she in fact has no opinion on. Therefore, due to a stringent reviewing system, we either lose a potential review, or even worse, we take in a fictional quality rating.

Fairness

Recommendation has always been associated with experts' opinion. This should also apply in a learning object recommendation. For instance, an experienced instructional designer's rating should be taken into more serious consideration than that of a rookie; a subject-matter expert's review should weigh more than that of an anonymous on-line user. Current learning object recommendation systems lack a weighting mechanism whereby evaluations submitted by different reviewers can be taken into account differently, rather than using a simple average value of all quality ratings for a particular learning object. This is especially important when the number of reviews on a learning object is limited. One unfair review could dominate the quality rating and distort the real quality of a learning object.

The other fairness issue is from the recommendation system toward learning objects. In MERLOT, the majority of learning objects are not rated. These unrated learning objects will be returned at the bottom of a result list when they fit the search criteria. They are at the bottom of the list not because of poor quality, but because no review is available. Newly submitted learning objects are not likely to get many reviews, due to short exposure time. If they are returned at the bottom of a recommendation list, they are less likely to be browsed or used. If they are not used, they will not be reviewed. Following this vicious circle, a recommendation system is prejudiced against new learning objects by not giving them a fair start to join the system. This is similar to the first-rater problem in collaborative filtering.

Portability

Much effort has been made to link multiple learning object repositories, for example, the eduSource project [35], whose goal is to build an open network to connect learning object repositories in Canada. This is an inevitable course to ultimately share learning objects over the Internet. With this movement, the recommendation is facing a new challenge.

Learning objects are rated under different measurements: LORI or MERLOT. Ideally, when a search request is sent to a learning object repository, it indexes not only its own storage but also that of connected repositories. The result list is generated, but the recommendation will be impeded by the heterogeneous quality ratings.

There are different ways to solve this problem. Certainly, an industry standard is able to unify quality rating. However, demands exist to have different rating instruments. For instance, LORI and MERLOT serve different levels of detail in rating learning objects. To avoid multiplying evaluation work, with each learning object rated with all available standards, a better solution would be using an invisible adapter that is able to translate one type of rating from the other on the fly. The conversion only needs to be done once, at the "adapter" level. If it requires adjustment in mapping different rating standards or to put in a newly emerged rating instrument, it will not affect any existing evaluation data. Update is also done at the adapter. As such, the rating conversion service for recommendation as well as rating standards mapping maintenance are transparent to learning object repositories, rating standards, and learning object users. This could largely increase the portability of quality rating data.

Integrity

Currently, recommendation relies on quality ratings submitted to a learning object repository. This is a type of explicit rating, where a user's purposeful evaluation is required.

On the other hand, observing how learning objects are used could also provide rich quality-related information, for example, how many times a learning object is requested, how long a user stays with it, how many users put bookmarks on a learning object, how often users come back to use this bookmark, how long it stays as a bookmark, etc. It is similar to using Web page hits to gauge the popularity of a Web site. To some extent, this type of information is more authentic. The preference for certain learning objects is revealed naturally in a relaxed manner. Besides, technologies now exist to make such user activity tracking a reality.

In general, an ideal evaluation system should be flexible and thorough enough to integrate information from varied sources. It should be able to combine data from explicit evaluations as well as implicit measures. Moreover, it is able to mitigate the quantity deficiency in learning object evaluation. With learning objects usage tracking, as long as there are activities on learning objects, whether users review them or not, these activities continuously help learning object repositories to collect quality-related information.

Collecting implicit quality rating data, however, imposes yet another challenge on learning object recommendation systems. That is, how should this implicit information is integrated into the current rating system, so that it could serve the ultimate purpose—quality oriented recommendation?

Based on the above impediment analysis in current recommendation systems, we put forward a few ideas on the general directions to deal with these problems.

Nifty Incentive Mechanism

If users generally do not volunteer to offer quality reviews, learning object repositories should implement some incentive features to encourage or stimulate them to do so, such as greater personal recognition. Although personal recognition sounds vague in a virtual environment like the Internet, there exists a very successful example—Slashdot (www.slashdot.org). It is a Web site where people post, discuss, review, and comment on the latest IT news, issues, and technologies. Its reviewing system applies a concept called "karma," which is a point reward to reviewers who have contributed constructive evaluation to this Web site. People in this Web-site community strive after karma. What can these karma points do? They allow people to review more postings! This is such a benign cycle that one cannot ask for more in a recommendation-dependent system. It is this evaluation system that makes Slashdot a very unique, healthy, dynamic, and informative on-line community.

Hence, to foster an attractive and vigorous electronic culture in the learning object community, this can be a viable solution to encourage more reviews from learning object users.

Effective Implicit Rating Mechanism

The key to evaluation system design is finding ways for explicit ratings and implicit reviews to weave together in a complementary fashion. Compared with what we have achieved in the explicit rating area, we have not done nearly enough in collecting and analyzing explicit reviews in learning object practices. This certainly leaves us with room to grow. To integrate implicit ratings into the current learning object recommendation system, much research and study must be expended in user behavior analysis.

User-Friendly Review System

As we mentioned, learning object rating standards are professionally formulated. This, in a way, intimidates users who are not educational professionals. One way of encouraging evaluation would be to lower the bar of difficulty in using the rating system, for example, installing a system that allows reviewers to rate the learning objects on the items that they are comfortable and confident with. In other words, the system accepts partially rated evaluations.

While review systems present lower barriers to use, they also introduce incomplete rating data into the system. How these values should be integrated into recommendations needs to be resolved.

12.4 Learning Object Quality Rating Using Bayesian Belief Networks

We employ Bayesian belief network [3] (BBN) technology in learning object quality rating and recommendation to address all the concerns listed above.

12.4.1 What We Propose

Quality reviews are quite rare because evaluating the quality of a learning object takes time, effort, and expertise. A reviewer may not be comfortable with evaluating learning objects using every evaluation item listed in a rating standard. Therefore, we designed a recommendation system that accepts partially completed reviews, where reviewers can submit whatever they feel confident about. This increases our confidence in the accuracy of the quality review and hence improves the recommendation performance of the entire system. In the meantime, the system should be able to process this partial review appropriately to augment the accuracy of the quality rating of a learning object.

A good recommendation system should be able to actively collect quality-related information instead of passively waiting for review submission only. Especially in a Web environment, a Web browser's (user's) behavior, which could be tracked by the system, is able to reveal many quality-related issues. These user activities implicitly reflect the quality of learning objects. Our recommendation system is designed to take in these implicit reviews in a proper manner to contribute to the quality rating of a learning object.

Learning objects are evaluated with different rating standards. There are needs for these standards to coexist, serving different disciplines and different user communities. Our recommendation system is designed to convert these different ratings into a unified value so that recommendation can be carried out accordingly. This ability not only facilitates sorting by quality when learning objects are rated with different standards, but also allows a learning object rated with one standard to obtain a quality rating under another. Thus, an on-line learning system with a learning object repository using one rating standard is able to recommend learning objects even if they are returned from an external repository, where a different rating system might be applied.

We also designed the system to weigh quality reviews differently when reviews are submitted from different types of reviewers. For example, a quality review from a group of experts should weigh more than that of a single expert, and an expert's opinion should weigh more than that of an anonymous user.

After studying existing BBN applications and performance in evaluation systems, we find that BBN appears to be a viable solution to equip a learning object quality rating and recommendation system with the features listed earlier. BBN is a powerful probabilistic knowledge representation and reasoning tool for partial beliefs under uncertainty. Uncertainty could be insufficient knowledge, for example lacking of certain quality aspects in a quality review. It combines graph theory and probability theory to provide a practical means for representing and updating probabilities (beliefs) about events of interest, such as the quality rating of a learning object. In addition to offering probabilities of events, the most common task using BBN is to do probabilistic inference, for instance, to infer quality rating from one standard to that of the other.

We present two distinct uses for BBN in our learning object quality rating and recommendation system. First, BBN is used in a single quality review construction to tackle the problem of "incompleteness" of current quality reviews and to unite reviews from using different rating standards. The result is called "unit quality rating." Second, BBN is used to obtain an aggregated rating by integrating reviews from different sources, called "integrated quality rating." This includes different ways of the evaluation system collecting the data, that is, explicit or implicit, as well as the different roles of reviewers who submit the data, that is, recognized experts or anonymous users.

We claim that, through these two BBN approaches, the availability and accuracy of quality ratings can be largely improved in a learning object repository, thus making better learning object recommendations.

The rest of this section presents an introduction to Bayesian belief networks followed by our methodology of quality rating of learning objects in two phases:

In the first phase, we analyze two prevailing learning object quality rating standards: MERLOT[4] and LORI. With consultation from educational experts, we map attributes in one standard to the other, from which we derive a correlation structure between MERLOT Peer Review and LORI. After that, a BBN is constructed from this correlated structure. In this BBN, each rating standard functions as it does individually, giving the closest rating value in one rating standard that has no user review, based on an existing rating of any other attribute rated in either MERLOT or LORI.

For example, we could infer how a learning object would be rated on MERLOT's ease-of-use item, given actual ratings on LORI's interaction-usability and accessibility items. Using probability calculus and Bayes theorem [41], BBN derives the implications of observed events, the rated attributes, by propagating revised probabilities throughout the network, when each attribute's value is updated.

This achieves three things. First, we are able to browse/scan/navigate across learning object repositories to search and recommend learning objects. If a user at the MERLOT Web-site sends out a learning object search request, the MERLOT repository starts its search engine to match the criteria; meanwhile, it sends out a request to a repository where learning objects are rated by LORI. External results come back, whose quality rating data is then entered into the BBN we proposed.

---

[4] MERLOT: In this section, MERLOT represents MERLOT peer review evaluation criteria.

The outcome from the BBN is the quality rating in MERLOT standard. Thus, these external learning objects can be combined with the MERLOT internal result set. A sorting based on one quality rating can be quickly carried out. The learning objects are returned to the user, and recommended in the order of their quality.

Second, learning object repositories are now able to accept partially rated quality reviews. For example, when using LORI, based on a rating on content quality of a learning object, BBN could produce an "intelligent guess" on what the rating would be for motivation. Although this intelligent guess could only come from a large amount of empirical study, data analysis, and experiment on this BBN, nevertheless the mechanism is set up.

Finally, when constructing the BBN for quality rating using MERLOT and LORI, we decide to give a learning object an initial quality rating value instead of a null value that is neutral, implying neither good nor bad. Any submitted quality review will update this value via BBN propagation. The more quality reviews it gets, the closer this rating value is toward its real quality. A direct result of this is that the newly submitted learning object without quality rating will be returned in the middle of a list rather than behind those that have already been rated poorly. As such, a recommendation system gives a good fair start for new learning objects to join learning object repositories.

In phase one, the quality rating we get out of the BBN is for a single learning object. We call it the unit quality rating. In the second phase, taking a step further, we put a unit quality rating into the bigger picture, regarding where it comes from, how this learning object is used, etc.

As a result, the second BBN is constructed. Through this BBN, a unit quality rating is refined. The weight of an opinion is taken into account depending on who the reviewer is. A panel rating from a group of experts weighs the most. Subsequently, there are individual expert ratings, user panel ratings, individual panel ratings, and anonymous ratings.

Additionally, how a learning object is used also contributes to its quality rating, for instance, how often a learning object is added to a registered user's bookmark list, assuming the on-line learning system has a user interface that allows users to place bookmarks; how long it stays in the bookmark list; how often it is requested; whether it is downloaded or browsed only; and so on. All these activities take a role in the second BBN. They drive a quality rating toward the "real" value from a full view. Thus, we call the result the integrated quality rating. The information from user activity may sound trivial and not very well focused, but the payoff is their high availability and sheer volume. For that reason, we can afford to be strict on what types of activity could contribute to a quality rating and how much they could contribute. This is able to balance out the chaos in user behavior when we use it for a specific purpose.

An integrated quality rating largely depends on how an on-line learning system is implemented and deployed, both on the learning tool itself and its rating mechanism. Therefore, the structure of this BBN is foreseen to be relatively dynamic. It should be built based on the functions and features of a specific on-line learning system.

12.4.2 Bayesian Belief Networks: A Quick Introduction

In this section, we embark on a journey to review Bayesian belief networks (BBNs), a mathematical theory that has been mainly used in knowledge-based planning and scheduling tools in the artificial intelligence domain.

Bayes theorem was developed and named after Thomas Bayes (1702–1761) [41], who first used probability inductively and established a mathematical basis for probability inference. Bayesian belief networks (also known as Bayesian networks, causal probabilistic networks, causal nets, graphical probability networks, probabilistic cause-effect models, and probabilistic influence diagrams) provide decision support for a wide range of problems involving uncertainty and probabilistic reasoning.

The underlying theory of BBN is Bayesian probability theory and the notion of propagation. Although this has been around for a long time, it is only in the last decade that efficient algorithms and tools to implement them have been developed to enable propagation in networks with a reasonable number of variables. The dramatic upswing is visible by looking at the number of books written on Bayesian analysis. During the first 200 years, 1769 to 1969, there were about 15 books written on Bayesian statistics. During 1990 to 1999, roughly 60 Bayesian books have been written, not counting many dozens of Bayesian conference proceedings and collections of papers [36]. The recent explosion of interest in BBN shows that for the first time BBN can be used to solve real-world problems. These recent developments make BBN an excellent method for reasoning about uncertainty. Bayes theorem is expressed as

$$P(H|E, c) = \frac{P(H|c)P(E|H, c)}{P(E|c)}$$

where we can update our belief in hypothesis H given the additional evidence E and the background context c [37]. In the frequentist approach, the probability P of an uncertain event A, $P(A)$, is the frequency of that event based on previous observations. For example, looking at the record of the current champion of badminton, who has a history of eight tournament wins out of 10 times, the probability of a win by the current champion in the next tournament, P (current champion's win) is 0.8. If no such historical observation data exists, Bayesian analysis can reason about beliefs under uncertainty. The expression P(Current Champion's Win | K) thus represents a belief measure, where K implies knowledge about this event (e.g., the player's endurance on the court, techniques of strokes, recent break-up with girlfriend, etc).

One characteristic of Bayes' theorem is $P(H|c)$, which is the probability of the hypothesis H in context c regardless of the evidence. This is referred to as the prior probability. The real power comes when we apply the above theorem to propagate consistently the impact of evidence on the probabilities of uncertain outcomes in a BBN, which will derive all the implications of the beliefs that are input to it. They are usually the facts that can be checked against observations [38].

From a mathematical point of view, a BBN is a directed graph, together with a set of associated probability tables. The graph consists of nodes and arcs. The nodes represent variables, while the arcs represent causal or influential relationships between variables [3].

The BBN is a powerful probabilistic knowledge representation and reasoning tool for partial beliefs under uncertainty. It combines graph theory and probability theory to provide a practical means for representing and updating probabilities (beliefs) about events of interest. The most common task we wish to solve using BBN is probabilistic inference. In addition to the probabilities of events (the probability table), the user knows some evidence, that is, some events that have actually happened, and wishes to infer the probabilities of other events, which have not as yet been observed. Using probability calculus and Bayes theorem, it is then possible to update the values of all the other probabilities in the BBN.

The BBN has an intuitive visual representation, very useful to clarify the opaque problem domain. It not only makes explicit the dependencies between different variables, but also reveals that many of the variables are conditionally independent. However, when the number of variables in the BBN increases, the propagation becomes NP-hard computation. The computational complexity of BBN calculations had severely restricted the number of variables or beliefs that could be modeled, and has prevented the application of BBN to realistic problems [39]. This was the reason that BBN could not be used to solve realistic problems, until later when efficient Bayesian probability algorithm implementation was developed, for example, the Hugin tool [39].

The BBN technology has been applied in various disciplines, including archaeology, economics, education, genetics, law, medicine, quality management, safety management, and risk, management. Well-known application samples include Microsoft Office Assistant Wizard, Microsoft operating system's Technical Trouble Shooter, and SpamBayes (spambayes.sourceforge.net), an anti-email spamming software application.

Human society's development has always been revolving around automating tasks using tools as much as possible. The same applies to recommendation systems. We try to let machines interpret information and do the recommendation for us. Up until now, however, for decision making, in many cases information is still better interpreted by people than by machines. Using BBN in learning object recommendation involves both experts and computers. We try to find a quantitative way to develop qualitative data about information on the Web, thus maximizing both people and computer resources.

12.4.3 Unit Quality Rating

Quality rating, in the scope of our work, is a measure that is used to quantify the quality aspect of a learning object. When we try to provide a tool for quality rating, it is inevitable that we would get involved with the topics in educational measurement and evaluation.

In this research, we do not intend to define learning object quality rating; instead, we simply use it as it has been used in the e-learning community. Hence, in terms of measurement, the conceptualization process is beyond the scope of this project; however, the operationalization process is determined on the participation of two

FIGURE 12.1. Unit quality rating structure.

prevailing rating standards, MERLOT and LORI. Both of them apply a scale of number 1 to 5 in measuring the quality of a learning object. As a result, the quality rating from our newly proposed rating mechanism also bears the scale of 1 to 5.

It takes two things to construct a BBN. One is the structure of how all variables or nodes are related—the graph topology. The other is the probability distribution for each variable, known as the node probability table (NPT).

The BBN graph contains a set of nodes and the arcs that link the nodes. As mentioned earlier, one of the difficulties in current learning object recommendation is that different quality rating standards are used to evaluate learning objects. We overcome this problem by integrating MERLOT peer review rating criteria and LORI to obtain a standard neutral quality rating.

In MERLOT, learning object evaluation is based on three dimensions: quality of content, ease of use, and potential effectiveness as a teaching tool. Here we use the notation of, M.QualityOfContent, M.Usability, and M.PotentialEffectiveness.

In LORI, learning object evaluation consists of nine items. Here we prefix with an "L." in front of these items, such as L.ContentQuality, L.Reusability, and so forth.

Figure 12.1 shows the unit quality rating structure that we use to construct the BBN, where MERLOT and LORI are mapped into one. Each item in both rating standards is a node in the BBN. They represent all variables in the learning object quality evaluation domain.

With the graph in Figure 12.1, we then fill the NPT for each node. The NPT contains all the possible values of this node and their distributions. In this case, all nodes, either from MERLOT or from LORI, have 1 to 5 integer values.

In BBN, the nodes that have arcs pointing to them are called child nodes. The source nodes of the arcs are called parent nodes. Each possible value for a node in NPT is contributed by its parents, in the permutation of all their possible values.

If a node has no parent node, for example, at one end of the graph, the NPT we use is a normal distribution.[5] The probability to obtain each value in the set of {1, 2, 3, 4, 5} is {0.05, 0.17, 0.56, 0.17, 0.05}, respectively.

---

[5] Normal distribution: A normal distribution in a variant χ with mean μ and variance σ^2 is a statistic distribution with probability function

$$P(x) = \frac{1}{\sigma\sqrt{2\pi}} E^{-(\phi-\mu)^2/(2\sigma^2)}$$

on the domain χ ™ $(-\infty, \infty)$. It is also called Gaussian distribution or referred to as the "bell curve."

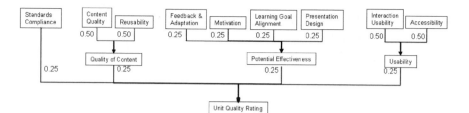

FIGURE 12.2. Unit quality rating BBN.

Thus, we obtain the BBN for unit quality rating, the topology of which is shown in Figure 12.2.

Figure 12.3 is a screenshot of the unit quality rating BBN constructed using JavaBayes [54], along with the NPT for L.ContentQuality node. The Unit_Quality_Rating node is the direct or indirect child of every other node in this BBN, whose value comes from other nodes' propagation of values. Other nodes' values come from quality review either using MERLOT (M) or LORI (L). The value of Unit_Quality_Rating is quality rating standard neutral.

Figure 12.4 is a screenshot of the unit quality rating BBN in JavaBayes with the NPT for the M.ContentOfQuality node. This is where things would get complicated

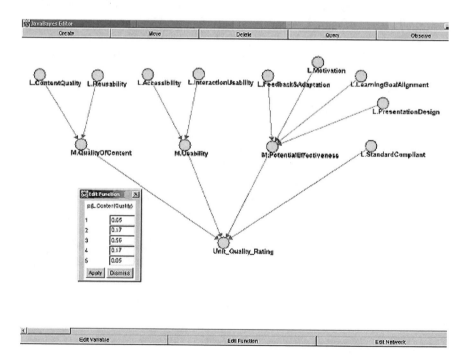

FIGURE 12.3. Unit quality rating BBN with NPT for L.ContentQuality node.

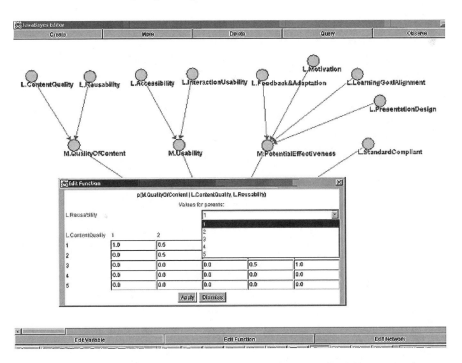

FIGURE 12.4. Unit quality rating BBN with NPT for M.QualityOfContent node.

without a tool like JavaBayes. The node M.QualityOfContent has two parent nodes, L.ContentQuality and L.Reusability.

JavaBayes picks one out of all the parent nodes to display all the possible values, which is 1 to 5. In this case, it is L.ContentQuality. The rest of the parent nodes are accessed via a drop-down list, whose options are all possible values of this parent node. The possible values are all 1 to 5 in this BBN. In Figure 12.4, there is only one drop-down list, L.Reusability. Therefore, the NPT for M.ContentOfQuality enumerates all the probabilities when L.ContentQuality is 1 to 5 under the condition of L.Reusability from 1 to 5. Each of the parent nodes contributes evenly toward the child node's value.

When a node has parent nodes, the NPT depends on whether or not we have empirical knowledge of its parent nodes. If we do, each parent node's influence on this child node can be translated into weight in percentage format. If we do not have any better knowledge about which one of these parent nodes should contribute more than the other, and how much more, as in our presented BBN, then NPT is evenly distributed among the parent nodes. For instance, if the value of L.ContentQuality and L.Reusability are 3 and 4, respectively, the value of M.ContentOfQuality is

$$3 \times 50\% + 4 \times 50\% = 3.5$$

L.ContentQuality and L.Reusability are the only parent nodes M.Content Of Quality has, and there is no prior knowledge of how much L.ContentQuality and

L.Reusability should influence child node M.ContentOfQuality. Therefore, the degree of influence is evenly distributed, which is 50% each.

In the future when we have sufficient quality rating domain knowledge, then parent nodes' influence on a child node can be specified rather than evenly distributed.

The other issue we want to address during constructing this BBN is the "first rater" problem. When a learning object is newly submitted to a repository, it is not likely to get reviews right away. In MERLOT, if this unrated learning object is returned in a search result, it is in the bottom of the list, which is a fundamental flaw.

Assume there are six learning objects, A, B, C, D, E, and Z, returned from one search. Five of them, A, B, C, D, and E, have ratings of 5, 4, 3, 2, and 1, respectively. The sixth one, Z, has no rating.

A user receives a list in the order of {A B C D E Z}. Z appears last due to lack of rating, not because of poor quality, but since it is in the end of the list, it is not likely to be selected by the user. Without being selected by the user, it is not likely to get any review. Without a review, it will remain at the bottom of the list. Thus, the system is biased against new learning objects. It does not get the equal opportunity to be exposed, reviewed, and used.

With BBN, it solves this problem by giving any learning object an initial value as a fair chance to start with. Since normal distribution is applied to the end nodes, the initial quality rating of a learning object will be 3. In a 1-to-5 scale system. Because rating value 3 has 56% out of 100%, all the other values, 1, 2, 4, and 5, have lower probabilities. In above scenario, the user will receive a list in the order of {A B Z C D E} or {A B C Z D E}. Any evaluation that Z gets, BBN then propagates its value and updates the quality rating, which eventually will become more and more accurate to reflect the real quality of this learning object.

12.4.4 Integrated Quality Rating

In current reviewing systems, there are expert panel ratings to differentiate reviews from those of regular users, but there is no mechanism to integrate them into one quality rating for a learning object.

In Figure 12.5, the BBN is composed of two types of rating: explicit and implicit. According to the roles of reviewers, we further break down the explicit rating into registered expert rating, registered user rating, and anonymous rating. Under each category some child nodes are listed based on our current understanding.

Note that this type of integrated quality rating largely depends on how a learning system is implemented. For example, some learning object repositories might not employ a group of experts to run a panel rating. It is even more so for implicit ratings. Implicit rating is an important means to get user feedback on learning objects and learning systems, yet how well a system is designed to allow users to expose their preference to learning objects is in the hands of system designers. For instance, certain learning systems' user interfaces allow users to bookmark a learning object. All these links are grouped together, called a bookshelf. When a

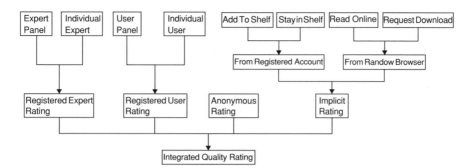

FIGURE 12.5. Integrated quality rating structure.

user comes back to this learning system, he can directly pull out a learning object from the "bookshelf" to use it, much like taking out a book from a real bookshelf. However, some learning systems do not have this mechanism.

Implicit rating not only depends on learning object reviewing and the recommendation system's implementation, but also the system capacity. Implicit rating data usually come from system logging. The more information that is logged, the more substantial analysis one can run on implicit rating, but intensive logging exhausts system resources and takes up database space. How much a system could sustain high-volume logging without impacting system performance varies tremendously. Logging data analysis is another issue. There is no standard logging format. Extracting data related to learning object quality requires a large amount of work in data formatting, sifting, and categorizing.

Above all, user behavior study is fundamental to learning object implicit quality rating. In Figure 12.5, we list items such as AddToShelf and RequestDownload. Certainly there are more user behavior aspects to reflect learning object quality. It requires further study to discover these aspects, as well as to quantify them in relation to learning object quality.

Hence, this part of the chapter describes a way of modeling integrated quality rating of learning objects. We have a long way to go toward obtaining an accurate and precise quality evaluation model.

For the NPT in this BBN, due to the topological structure, it does not make sense to evenly distribute the probability among the parent nodes, such as ImplicitRating and RegisteredExpertRating. For instance, a particular parent node can contribute more than the others. For those nodes that do not have parent nodes, normal distribution is still applied. Thus, by controlling the parent node contribution toward a child node, we ensure the data integrity of the evaluation system. The values in the NPT can be adjusted over time when more data are collected and better knowledge is gained about internode relationships.

Based on the topology in Figure 12.5, an integrated quality rating BBN is constructed, as shown in Figure 12.6.

Figure 12.7 shows split screenshots of the integrated quality rating BBN running in JavaBayes. Note that the darker nodes are with evidence, which means rating

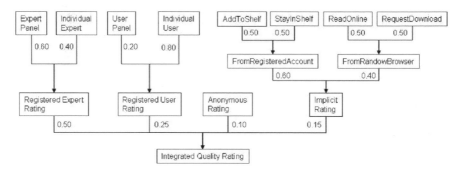

FIGURE 12.6. Integrated quality rating BBN.

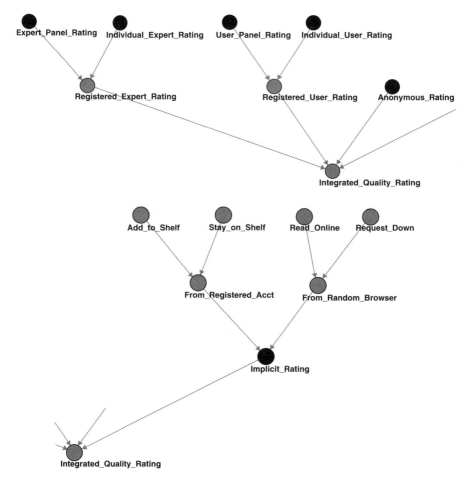

FIGURE 12.7. Integrated quality rating running in JavaBayes.

values are available. The value of other nodes can be inferred from evidence propagation, including integrated quality rating.

12.5 Discussion

We use Bayesian Belief Networks to overcome the incompleteness and absence of learning object quality reviews, as well as the divergence of applied quality rating standards and the monoculture of weighing evaluations from different reviewers. The ultimate goal is to improve learning object quality evaluation and recommendation.

12.5.1 Simulated Test Cases for Individual Rating

In BBN, the process of entering evidence and using it to update the probabilities is called propagation. After the BBN for unit quality rating is created, the inference, mainly the quality rating, can be obtained via the process of propagation.

In JavaBayes, under the "observe" mode, we input the incomplete quality rating we have, that is, the quality rating of three items out of nine items from LORI over a learning object. Then, switch to "query" mode, select Unit_Quality_Rating to observe. The output value, a probability distribution from 1 to 5, is printed out in the JavaBayes console window.

In addition, BBN can be used for both forward and backward inference. This means that if we have a unit quality rating but are missing the details, we can try to infer the quality rating of those items that compose the unit quality rating. What this can bring to us is the comparison and verification of the mapping between different rating standards. For instance, we could have an expert rate a learning object in both LORI and MERLOT. We first enter the LORI evaluation data into BBN, and obtain the detailed rating data for MERLOT rating items via BBN evidence propagation. We then compare MERLOT quality evaluation data from the expert's review and from BBN evidence propagation. If there is any discrepancy and the discrepancy is consistent, we could update the structure in Figure 12.1, or adjust the percentage weight of a parent node toward a child node in BBN in Figure 12.2.

Table 12.2 shows some simulated test cases with incomplete quality reviews as input, and the BBN inference result on various quality rating items.

What we achieved with the unit quality rating BBN was to alleviate the difficulty of quality evaluation by accepting incomplete quality ratings. Users can submit a review only on those quality aspects that they feel comfortable to rate on. Consequently, it leads to a more corresponsive quality rating. With a rating that complies with the actual quality of a learning object, a search result set can be properly sorted and returned in a prioritized manner.

By assigning normal distribution to leaf parent node, an un-rated learning object receives a default unit quality rating value 3, which has highest probability in a 1-to-5 set of probability distribution. Thus, we mitigated the first-rater problem. A learning object that is never rated will not be returned behind poor quality ones with

TABLE 12.2. Results from running unit quality rating BBN

Evidence	Result (inference probability)	Interpolated conclusion
No evidence (a learning object without any rating)	Unit_Quality_Rating: 2.1022165058413246E-4 0.13486437673298943 0.7298508032328528 0.13486437673298948 2.1022165058413246E-4	Unit_Quality_Rating: 3
M.QualityOf Content: 4 M.Usability: 4	Unit_Quality_Rating: 0.0 0.00212041825 0.49787958174999997 0.4978795817500001 0.00212041825	Unit_Quality_Rating: 3.5
M.QualityOf Content: 4 M.Usability: 4	L.InteractionUsability: 0.0 0.021562658548959918 0.3835616438356165 0.40969051243023846 0.18518518518518515	L.InteractionUsability: 4
Unit_Quality _Rating: 4 L.Standard Compliant: 2	M.Usability: 1.7025565641619698E-6 0.0041192137621463626 0.25868461836582135 0.6223689203228483 0.11482554499261993	M.Usability: 4
Unit_Quality _Rating: 4 L.Standard Compliant: 2	L.Motivation: 0.018327118400728655 0.10008038915613644 0.5248726734433744 0.24916289096414496 0.10755692803561545	L.Motivation: 3

rating lower than 3. It has a fair chance to be exposed, used, and eventually rated. With more evidence, such as quality reviews entering into the BBN, providing most reviewers have conformable evaluations, the initial default bell curve will become narrower and the rating values probability will be less distributed.

Additionally, using BBN's ability to conduct forward and backward inferences, we will be able to correlate the quality rating among different quality attribute nodes from different rating standards, such as MERLOT and LORI. Thus, a learning object query to a MERLOT-rated repository is able to obtain an estimated equivalent quality rating value for the learning objects returned from external learning object repositories that are rated with LORI, and vice versa.

Note that what we get after inference in BBN is a probability distribution among all the possible values, while what we want is one value that has the highest probability. In this project, the rules for interpolation for obtaining unit quality ratings are:

TABLE 12.3. Integrated quality rating BBN testing case

Reviewer Breakdown	Learning Object1	Learning Object2
Expert panel	5	
Expert individual		
User panel		
User		
Anonymous		5
Implicit		
Integrated rating	3.8	3.1

1. The rating that has the highest probability is the rating for the node that is queried.
2. If a few values share the same highest probability, the midpoint value of these values is the rating for the node that is queried.

This is a rough and basic way to interpolate the rating value. More refined and accurate interpolation can be explored and applied in the future.

12.5.2 Simulated Test Cases for Integrated Rating

To test the learning object integrated quality rating BBN, we designed an extreme test case. In this test case, we evaluated two learning objects, Learning Object1 and Learning Object2. For Learning Object1, we have an expert panel rating of 5; the other ratings for Learning Object1 are not available. For Learning Object2, we have an anonymous rating of 5; the other ratings for Learning Object2 are not available. Entering these two values into the BBN, we observed the node of Integrated_Quality_Rating.

Table 12.3 displays the data and result of this testing case.

Since normal distribution is applied to the nodes without parents, the root child Integrated Quality Rating has a value of 3 for a new learning object entering the learning object repository without any rating. In this case, Learning Object1's quality rating is increased from 3 to 3.8 by one expert panel rating of 5, while Learning Object2's quality rating is increased from 3 to 3.1 by one anonymous user rating of 5.

The inference of BBN takes evidence, an observed fact, to update the network with a prior built-in probability distribution. It will not dramatically change a node value with any single evidence entering the system, because we know the overall distribution, and we have control over it. This advantage appears to be more important for the integrated quality rating than for the unit quality rating.

From the above test case, we obtained the probability distributions of the integrated quality rating for these two learning objects. We then plot the resulting probability distributions. Figure 12.8 displays the plotting chart. It shows the positive shifting of the equality rating by these two different types of reviewers, compared to the default equality rating distribution. From a high expert rating, the overall quality rating is increased with an obvious margin, whereas a high anonymous rating has an insignificant impact on the overall rating.

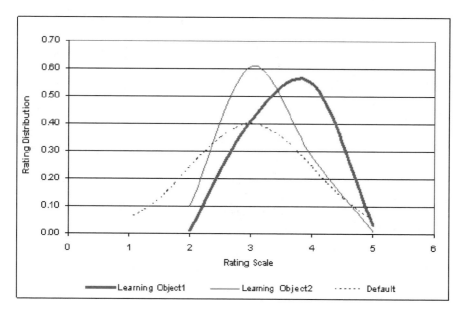

FIGURE 12.8. Analysis of an extreme test case.

This is a desired result when an irresponsible user, usually with anonymous identity, rates a particular learning object, which could be submitted by the user himself, with a high rate over and over again. BBN reduces the negative impact to learning object recommendation from distorted rating to a minimum degree.

This is an essential feature of an evaluation system, but many on-line rating systems do not have this type of behavior. For instance, on the "epinions" Web site (www.epinions.com), assuming two items A and B, under any category, based on a certain standard, A has one review rating of 5, which could be rated by the author or seller himself. B has a couple of ratings of 4, which come from various reviewers. As a result, A tops B when returned as a result of a query. This cannot be considered a healthy rating system.

Nowadays most on-line reviewing systems, as well as learning object repositories, implement a membership mechanism but accept anonymous reviews from unregistered users. It is a desirable feature to accept anonymous reviews for a learning object repository, but it also allows a user to abuse the system by rating a learning object again and again with an untruthful evaluation. However, in applying BBN, this impact can be minimized. With a membership mechanism, each member is allowed to submit one quality review per learning object; we assume registered members are less likely to behave improperly. An anonymous user or author has a higher possibility of rating his favorite item with the highest value, but that does not change the integrated quality rating much. On the contrary, the rating value will be strengthened more by members' evaluation. Hence, even if a learning object repository accepts anonymous reviews in which some are false, the BBN quality rating system still can maintain its integrity by controlling the NPT of anonymous peer ratings to a less influential degree in generating an integrated quality rating.

12.5.3 Reliability and Validity of Our Approach

Reliability is the extent to which we measure some attribute in a systematic and therefore repeatable way [42]. It means that the result would be consistently the same if a test were performed over again. When we use conventional methods to assess the reliability of the conceptual underpinnings of our work we have a promising outcome.

First, in the case of testing without directly involving human examinees, such as converting a quality rating from one standard to the other, the project has perfect test-retest reliability. In the case of testing involving reviewers, for example, accepting partially rated reviews into the system, we think that the reliability is determined by the quality rating standard being used rather than by the quality rating BBN itself.

Second, using internal consistency, the simulated test shows a positive consistency. For example, if "accessibility" has a low rating using LORI standard, the inferred rating of "usability" using MERLOT via the quality rating BBN is also low, and vice versa.

Third, using interrater, a valid testing case would have the same reviewers rate the same learning object using different rating standards, entering the reviews into the quality rating BBN and observing the unit quality rating that comes out, whether they are the same or close. Additionally, due to the empirical characteristic of this project, this type of testing case is supposed to be continuously conducted to help adjust the quality rating BBN.

Lastly, using alternate form, a valid testing case would be obtaining a complete quality review from a reviewer using one rating standard, for example, MERLOT, as well as a partial rating on a particular quality item using another rating standard, for example, LORI. The full quality review in MERLOT is then entered into quality rating BBN, and then an inferred rating on that particular quality item can be obtained in LORI. Comparing the rating from the reviewer and from BBN inference, the closer the values are in alternate form reliability verification, the better. This testing has been conducted as part of the quantitative analysis described earlier.

We would like to point out that, in our work, the interpretation of specific rating values is not important to the recommendation process; rather, the relativity among the learning objects ratings is important. In the test case (above), as long as the two values from different sources are close, it gives a good indication of the reliability of the BBN.

Validity is the extent to which the test being used actually measures the characteristic or dimension we intend to measure [43]. Results are positive when we use conventional methods to measure the validity of this project.

In terms of face validity, educational experts were consulted during quality rating BBN construction.

In terms of content validity, this links back to the quality rating's conceptualization and operationalization processes, which are beyond the scope of this chapter.

In terms of criterion validity, we have conducted a very successful simulated test case that is a typical problem in real-world on-line rating applications. The result shows an evident strength to solve this type of problem when using BBN. It will be discussed in later sections of this chapter.

Construct validity is known as the most difficult validity to achieve. According to Hunter and Schmidt [43], construct validity is a quantitative question rather than a qualitative distinction such as "valid" or "invalid"; it is a matter of degree. Therefore, in this work it will take a large amount of tests, experiments, and iterative modifications for a quality rating BBN to be more construct-valid.

12.5.4 Equating Scaling

Scaling is a study of developing systematic rules and meaningful units of measurement for quantifying psychological constructs and empirical observations, for example, assigning IQ to measure intelligence. Equating is a study of establishing equivalent scores of two tests [45]. In the BBN constructed to obtain unit quality rating in this project, we equate MERLOT ratings with that of LORI, based on experts' opinions.

In this study, to achieve a rating-standard-neutral unit quality rating, we simply trust experts' input in uniting different rating standards. BBN is a means to interpret the unison structure. Thus, we could make use of all ratings that are available for recommendation, not only those that are rated by reviewers, but also those that are not rated but inferred from the existing rating information.

In short, the exact equating scaling process of MERLOT and LORI is not of interest in this work; rather, the applicability of using BBN is of interest. We use BBN and verify that the quality rating yielded from the constructed BBN conforms to that of the reviewers' using whichever rating standard, so that it facilitates learning object recommendation by sorting learning objects in quality at its own applied rating value.

The tests were run on simulated data. They are designed to determine whether, given realistic incomplete evaluation data, the model could make qualitatively plausible translations between instruments, the model could treat the reviews appropriately to their sources, and that these estimates increased in certainty as more data was acquired. We are able to confirm that the BBN upgrades or downgrades the quality rating in a plausible and meaningful fashion consistent with the graph topology and the NPTs, and that the certainty represented in the model increases as evaluation data accumulates.

12.5.5 Personalised and Collaborative Recommendation and Distribution of BBN

The BBN is used to facilitate rating frameworks that are personalized to the preferences of individual reviewers. Different personalized BBNs focusing on a single learning object can be combined to provide a singular quality rating for that object. We present the application of a polytree algorithm to resolve ratings across distributed BBN.

In this study, we do not differentiate to whom a learning object is recommended. All people evaluate all learning objects using one BBN; all users get learning object recommendations using one BBN. However, the role information is often quite important in educational practice. For example, for a disabled learner, accessibility is more important than it is for the others; or for a language learning object, interaction usability is more important than it is for a mathematics learning object. Therefore, there is a need for different quality rating BBN to be constructed to serve different purposes. In other words, we expect a system to automatically form personalized recommendations that account for the demonstrated preferences of a user and the requested types of learning object.

"We are on the verge of being able to provide learning customised for each specific learner at a specific time, taking into account, their learning styles, experience, knowledge and learning goals" [49]. After adaptive selection of appropriate objects based on individual needs, context is the second path for personalization of learning objects. The key for deploying learning objects effectively is to provide ways for the learner to contextualize the information [50].

One topic that appeared in our project discussion is to distribute a BBN model to a client computer, whose user is searching for a learning object. With the advancing technology in distributed computing, letting the client computer build a customized BBN on the fly is not unreasonable. We briefly evaluated a distributed belief network application, RISO [51]. This application distributes a BBN over a TCP/IP network using RMI[6] technology. Due to the time frame of this project, we did not pursue the topic any further; however, it is certainly worth looking at in detail.

Where distributing BBN and client-side BBN customization are technically possible, the challenge is, Do we allow client to change the topology of the distributed BBN? If yes, how does an on-line learning system take a customized BBN to make a personalized recommendation? Should we integrate the customized BBN into the master one that standard recommendation uses? If yes, then we will face the mathematically unsolved problem of multiple BBNs integration besides any other issue; if not, we will still face the computational difficulty of ensuring the topology validity of a customized BBN. BBN is an acyclic directed graph. To compute using a customized BBN, besides checking the nodes and NPT to be mutually exclusive and exhaustive, we have to constantly check whether any cycle exists in the BBN, which is computationally difficult. Additionally, without an educational expert intervention, it is difficult to ensure the content validity of a customized BBN, that is, the relationship between nodes.

We certainly have long way to go to realize personalization in learning object recommendation.

---

[6] RMI: remote method invocation. RMI is the Java version of what is generally known as a remote procedure call (RPC), in which objects on different computers can interact in a distributed network.

12.5.6 Share Learning Objects Among Multiple Repositories

As mentioned, BBN is able to conduct forward and backward inference. After a certain amount of observation, we will be able to correlate the quality rating from different rating standards, for example, between MERLOT and LORI. Thus, an adapter can be developed between two or more learning object repositories. When a learning object query is initiated, the result list can be returned from multiple learning object repositories. Based on a converted universal quality rating, this result list can be returned with recommendation. As such, we not only share the learning objects in a repository, but also access learning objects across different repositories. It expands the search base so that the user has more opportunity to access a better learning object.

In conjunction with network solutions such as eduSource Architecture [35], applying a rating standard adapter will likely accelerate sharing learning objects across repositories.

12.5.7 BBN Drawback

Having chosen BBN as the learning object recommendation technical strut, we recognize that there are a few drawbacks of BBN.

BBN is used to deal with uncertainties. Ideally, there should be some prior knowledge of the modeled domain, to form the unconditional event probability distribution. In the learning object quality rating BBNs used in this project, other than the nodes, other factors are all assumptions, including the parent to child node evenly distributed influence and the leaf parent node normal distribution, because we do not have any better knowledge or empirical study in this area. This affects the accuracy or certainty of the quality rating that we want to infer from these two BBNs.

To find a suitable, out-of-box BBN tool for this project remains a difficult task, since there are domain specific requirements. Another key issue is the computational performance of BBN. When users keep submitting reviews, how often should we propagate BBN probabilities so that the quality rating of learning objects can be updated without hindering the normal tasks of the on-line learning system?

An ideal system would take input and output scale fallacy into account. In this project, we have certain output scaling fallacy control, by weighing different evaluation differently based on reviewers. However, we do not have any mechanism to handle the input scale fallacy. In fact, for any recommendation system based on user input, there will always be certain degree of input scale fallacy.

12.5.8 Further Research Angles

There are a few other interesting questions that we would like to raise at this time. Currently we use normal distribution for leaf parent node, which gives us an ideal rating value inference; what if after sufficient experiments and going through the BBN justification process, we find out that leaf parent node does not have a normal distribution? In that case, would the rating value inference and the default value for unrated learning object still remain valid?

In integrated quality rating BBN, we use one node to represent expert panel rating. Ideally, a group of experts reaches a consensus after individual evaluation and group discussion, which can be taken into the BBN. However, in reality, experts might not agree with each other. In that case, should the BBN consider certain variance coefficient for this type of panel rating? If yes, how is it implemented?

In current learning object quality rating BBNs all nodes are atomic events. What if through the BBN learning process, we discover that one of the nodes has its own microstructure, for example, a BBN. How can this be implemented? How will this affect the recommendation performance?

We assume that the quality rating structure and its NPT are all discovered. The BBN constructed in this project mainly uses evenly distributed probabilities among all the parent nodes for one child node, based on the fact that there is no prior experience or better knowledge available in learning object rating. Moreover, these probabilities are a fixed set of values. Once the BBN is constructed, the probability distribution remains the same unless they are manually updated based on better understanding of the problem domain.

On the other hand, BBN can also be used to represent and reason about the task of learning the parameters, weights, and structure of each of these representations [46]. BBN is known for its ability to take evidence and discover the nodes and/or its conditional probability distribution, in other words, the self-learning capability. There are algorithms available to discover both nodes and the probability distribution table.

A popular heuristic approach to search hidden nodes is to use the hidden Markov model[7] [46]. This is a useful tool to verify current learning object quality rating standards and whether they have caught all variables in the quality evaluation model. More importantly, it can identify new variables, for example, the learning object aging issue. With the astonishing speed of human knowledge advancement, should we consider a chronological property for learning objects, at least in some categories, for example, information technology?

Another algorithm, EM (Expectation Maximization) [48], can find optimal conditional probability distribution of nodes, based on the evidence. In the context of learning object quality evaluation, this can provide a mechanism to automatically revise the BBN nodes' probability distribution after a certain number of reviews.

Another point to note is that BBN not only can work with discrete value, for example integer 1 to 5 in this project, but also can take or produce continuous value. We could explore and adjust current BBNs structure and interpolation techniques to obtain fine-grained rating values, like 2.34, 3.56, etc.

---

[7] The hidden Markov model is a finite set of states, each of which is associated with a (generally multidimensional) probability distribution. Transitions among the states are governed by transition probabilities. In a particular state, observation can be generated, according to the associated probability distribution. It is only the outcome, not the state visible to an external observer. Therefore, states are "hidden" to the outside. [48]

These are promising techniques to enhance our current quality rating BBN. They ought to be explored further.

12.5.9 Conclusion

Our work explored a new way of obtaining the quality rating of learning objects. In applying Bayesian belief networks, a learning object repository is able to accept incomplete quality reviews. It also allows a learning object repository to obtain a standard neutral quality rating for learning objects, which facilitates sorting learning objects by quality upon learning object search request. Moreover, weight control over different types of evaluation increases the quality of the evaluations submitted to a learning object repository. The different types of evaluation include explicit and implicit ratings, as well as expert reviews and regular user reviews.

By proposing this new way of data measurement for learning object quality rating, it enhances the current learning object repository recommendation system, so that the entire on-line education efficiency can be improved.

Designers and developers of electronic learning today are being presented with a new content development landscape. Learning technology standards organisations are quickly moving toward open and industry-wide standards for learning objects. However, rather than preaching and waiting for conformance, we endeavor to create a mediator among technologies, owners, and users involved with learning objects. We seek an alternative way to satisfy a diversified on-line educational world.

Over the years it has become apparent that learning object repositories and the peripheral applications for learning object retrieval are of considerable international interest. Learning object recommendation is an inevitable course for on-line education to take. Our work is a small step toward a more effective on-line learning system. We expect the use of BBN to mature over time. We intend to provide richer case studies and examples and to continually reflect on our journey as we contribute a more intelligent learning object quality rating and recommendation system.

References

1. LTSC. (2000) Learning object. Learning technology standards committee Web site. ltsc.ieee.org.
2. Learning Object Metadata, LOM. (2000) http://ieeeltsc.org/wg12LOM/.
3. Fenton, N. (2000) What is BBN?, www.dcs.qmw.ac.uk/~norman/BBNs/BBNs.htm.
4. www.dei.isep.ipp.pt/docs/arpa.html.
5. Johnson, L.F. (2003) Elusive Vision: Challenges Impeding the Learning Object Economy, New Media Consortium.
6. Recker, M., Walker, A., Lawless, K. (2003) What do you recommend? Implementation and analyses of collaborative information filtering of web resources for education, Instructional Science, 31(4/5).

7. www.merlot.org.
8. www.elera.net/eLera/Home/About%20%20LORI/.
9. Nesbit, J.C., Belfer, K., Leacock, T. (2003) Learning Object Review Instrument User Manual version 1.5, eLera and POOL projects.
10. Rosenberg, M.J. (2001) E-Learning: Strategies for Delivering Knowledge in the Digital Age. New York: McGraw-Hill.
11. Friesen, N. (2004) Three objections to learning objects. In: Online Education Using Learning Objects. London: Routledge/Falmer, 2004.
12. ieeeltsc.org.
13. Wiley, D.A. (2002) Instructional use of learning objects. Agency for Instructional Technology.
14. cloe.on.ca.
15. Cisco Systems. (2003) Reusable Learning Object Strategy: Designing and Developing Learning Objects for Multiple Learning Approaches.
16. Hodgins, W. (2000) Into the Future: A Vision Paper. Technology and Adult Learning of the American Society for Training & Development, white paper.
17. Downes, S. (2001) Learning Objects: Resources for Distance Education Worldwide, International Review of Research in Open and Distance Learning, 2(1).
18. Wieseler, W. (1999) RIO: A standards-based approach for reusable information objects. Cisco Systems White Paper.
19. Longmire, W. (2000) Content and Context: Designing and Developing Learning Objects, Learning Without Limits, Volume 3: Emerging Strategies for e-Learning Solutions.
20. Downes, S. Learning object overview. http://www.learning-objects.net.
21. Marchionini, G. (1995) Information Seeking in Electronic Environments. Cambridge: Cambridge University Press.
22. Manning C., Raghavan, P. Text information retrieval, mining, and exploitation. www.stanford.edu/class/cs276b.
23. Levene, M. (2003) Recommendation system and collaborative filtering. www.dcs.bbk. ac.uk/~mark/download/lec7_collaborative_filtering.ppt.
24. Chesani, F. (2002) Recommendation systems. www-db.deis.unibo.it/courses/ SI2/Relazioni/RecSystems.pdf.
25. Goldberg, D., Nichols, D., Oki, B.M., Terry, D. (1992) Using collaborative filtering to weave an information tapestry. Communications of the ACM, 35(12):61–70.
26. Balabanovic, M., Shoham, Y. (1997) Fab: content-based collaborative recommendation. Communications of the ACM, 40(3):66–72.
27. Resnick, P., Lacovou, N., Suchak, M., Bergstrom, P., Riedl, J. (1994) GroupLens: an open architecture for collaborative filtering of netnews. In: Proceedings of ACM CSCW'94 Conference on Computer Supported Cooperative Work, pp. 175–186.
28. Melville, P., Mooney, R.J., Nagarajan, R. (2001) Content-boosted collaborative filtering. In: Proceedings of the ACM SIGIR-2001 Workshop on Recommender Systems, New Orleans, LA.
29. Pazzani, M.J. (1999) A framework for collaborative, content-based and demographic filtering. Artificial Intelligence Review, 13(5–6):393–408.
30. Hill, J.R., Hannafin, J.R. (2001) Teaching and learning in digital environments: the resurgence of resource-based learning. Educational Technology Research and Development, 49(3):37–52.

31. Nesbit, J.C., Belfer, K., Vargo, J. (2002) A convergent participation model for evaluation of learning objects. Canadian Journal of Learning and Technology, 28(3).
32. Reiser, R.A., Kegelmann, H.W. (1994) Evaluating instructional software: a review and critique of current methods. Educational Technology Research and Development, 42(3).
33. Vargo, J., Nesbit, J.C., Belfer, K., Archambault, A. (2003) Learning object evaluation: computer-mediated collaboration and inter-rater reliability. International Journal of Computers and Applications. 25(3).
34. Hatala, M., Richards, G., Eap, T., Willms, J. (2004) The interoperability of learning object repositories and services: standards, implementations and lessons. WWW Conference, ACM.
35. Berger, J.O. (2000) Bayesian Analysis: A Look at Today and Thoughts of Tomorrow. JASA.
36. Berry, D.A. (1996) Statistics: A Bayesian Perspective. Duxbury Press.
37. Technical Report. (2002) Basics of Bayesian networks. www.agena.co.uk.
38. Pearl, J. (1998) Probabilistic Reasoning in Intelligent Systems. Morgan Kaufmann.
39. www.hugin.com.
40. plato.stanford.edu/entries/bayes-theorem.
41. Walsh, W.B., Betz, N.E. (1995) Tests and Assessment. 4th ed., p. 49, Prentice Hall.
42. Walsh, W.B., Betz, N.E. (1990) Tests and Assessment. 4th ed., p. 58, Prentice Hall.
43. Hunter, J.E., Schmidt, F.L. (1990) Methods of Meta-Analysis: Correcting Error and Bias in Research Findings. Newsbury Park: Sage Publications.
44. Crocker, L., Algina, J. (1986) Introduction to Classical and Modern Test Theory. Forth Worth, TX: Harcourt Brace Jovanovich College Publishers.
45. Buntine, W.L. (1994) Operations for learning with graphical models. Journal of Artificial Intelligence Research, 2:159–225.
46. Rabiner, L.R., Juang, B.H. (1986) An Introduction to Hidden Markov Models. IEEE ASSP Magazine, January.
47. Dempster, A., Laird, N., Rubin, D. (1977) Maximum likelihood from incomplete data via the EM algorithm. Journal of the Royal Statistical Society, 39(B).
48. Schatz, S. (2001) Paradigm Shifts and Challenges for Instructional Designers.
49. Longmire, W. (2000) A Primer on Learning Objects. Learning Circuits, March.
50. Dodier, R. (1999) Unified Prediction and Diagnosis in Engineering Systems by Means of Distributed Belief Networks. PhD Dissertation. Dept. of Civil, Environmental, and Architectural Engineering, University of Colorado.
51. www.norsys.com/index.html.
52. Kumar V., Groeneboer C., Chu, S. (2005) Sustainable learning ecosystem. Tutorial, International Conference on Advanced Learning Technologies, ICALT 2005, Kaohsiung, Taiwan.
53. Hatala, M., Richards, G., Eap, T., Willms, J. (2004) eduSource: Implementing Open Network for Learning Repositories and Services. Special Track on Engineering e-Learning Systems held at ACM Symposium on Applied Computing (SAC).
54. www-2.cs.cmu.edu/~javabayes/Home/.
55. CanCore. (2003) CanCore guidelines version 2.0: educational category. www.cancore.ca.
56. Carey , T., Swallow, J., Oldfield, W. (2002) Educational rationale metadata for learning objects. Canadian Journal of Learning and Technology, 28(3):55–71.
57. Mager, R. (1975) Preparing Instructional Objectives, 2nd ed. Palo Alto, CA: Fearon.
58. Mwanza, D., Engestrom, Y. (2005) Managing content in e-learning environments. British Journal of Educational Technology, 36:453–463.

59. Greenberg, J. (ed.). (2000) Metadata and Organizing Educational Resources on the Internet. Binghamton, NY: Haworth.
60. IEEE-LTSC. (2002) IEEE Standard for Learning Object Metadata (1484.12.1-2002).
61. IMS Digital Repositories Interoperability: Core Functions Information Model, Version 1. www.imsglobal.org/digitalrepositories/index.cfm.

13
Data Mining in E-Learning

KHALED HAMMOUDA AND MOHAMED KAMEL

Abstract. This chapter presents an innovative approach for performing data mining on documents, which serves as a basis for knowledge extraction in e-learning environments. The approach is based on a radical model of text data that considers phrasal features paramount in documents, and employs graph theory to facilitate phrase representation and efficient matching. In the process of text mining, a grouping (clustering) approach is also employed to identify groups of documents such that each group represents a different topic in the underlying document collection. Document groups are tagged with topic labels through unsupervised key-phrase extraction from the document clusters. The approach serves in solving some of the difficult problems in e-learning where the volume of data could be overwhelming for the learner, such as automatically organizing documents and articles based on topics, and providing summaries for documents and groups of documents.[1]

13.1 Introduction

Resources in learning environments are authored for the purpose of transferring knowledge to the learner. The growth of learning repositories and the ease of publishing and accessing information has created an environment where finding and making efficient use of the available information can be overwhelming. It is the job of data mining to help the learners digest large amounts of data by leveraging sophisticated techniques in data analysis, restructuring, and organization.

Learning resources are mainly found in textual form, such as text documents, web documents, articles, and papers, among other forms. Due to the unstructured and unrestricted nature of text documents, a special field in data mining was coined "text mining." It is the field studying the nontrivial extraction of implicit, previously unknown, and potentially useful and significant information from text documents.

---

[1] Portions reprinted, with permission, from Khaled Hammouda and Mohamed Kamel. (2004). Efficient Phrase-Based Document Indexing for Web Document Clustering. IEEE Transactions on Knowledge and Data Engineering.16(10), 1279–1296. © 2004 IEEE.

Text mining is generally considered more difficult than traditional data mining. This is attributed to the fact that traditional databases have fixed and known structure, while text documents are unstructured, or, as in the case of Web documents, semistructured. Thus, text mining involves a series of steps for data preprocessing and modeling in order to condition the data for structured data mining.

Text mining can help in many tasks that otherwise would require large manual effort. Common problems solved by text mining include, but are not limited to, searching through documents, organizing documents, comparing documents, extracting key information, and summarizing documents. Methods in information retrieval, machine learning, information theory, and probability are employed to solve those problems.

Information extraction through text mining deals with finding particular data in text and Web documents. The approaches used in this area include document parsing, analysis, and restructuring. This allows for restructuring existing learning material into current standards. Other approaches include identifying and extracting significant semistructured information, extracting keywords and key phrases from documents using phrase indexing and matching. These methods have high potential in e-learning due to their ability to automatically extract useful information, and tag learning objects with certain metadata extracted from content.

Information organization through text mining provides an overview of the topics in a large set of documents without having to read the contents of individual documents. This can be achieved through data clustering and classification techniques. These techniques mainly rely on the analysis of keyword distribution in the documents. They also make use of similarity calculation through word and phrase matching. The end result is a more manageable grouping of documents tagged with topics and subjects.

While data clustering techniques are mainly used for content organization, they could be used to group learner profiles as well. In this case we can discover common interest groups of learners by judging the similarity between their profiles.

This chapter focuses on employing machine learning methods in finding relationships between text documents through phrase-based document modeling, similarity calculation, document clustering, and key-phrase extraction. Figure 13.1 illustrates the process of text mining in general, and refers to specific tasks as they are presented in this chapter. In particular, a set of documents is preprocessed through tokenization (identifying whole words and dropping punctuation symbols), removing stop words (very frequent words like *a*, *and*, and *the*), and stemming (reducing different forms of a word into a single form). Then a model of the data is built using a graph-based representation of phrases in the documents. Next, pattern analysis is applied to detect similarities between the documents based on shared and significant phrases followed by clustering the documents to form groups of documents, where each group contains only similar documents sharing the same topic. Finally, the process concludes by extracting key phrases from the clusters and identifying the topic of each cluster.

This chapter is organized as follows. Section 13.2 introduces the document model used throughout the process. Section 13.3 presents the phrase matching

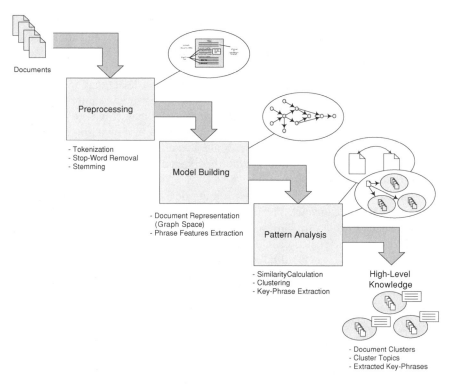

FIGURE 13.1. Text mining process.

capability of the model and the phrase-based similarity measure. Section 13.4 presents the document clustering algorithm. Section 13.5 presents the key-phrase extraction algorithm. Finally, section 13.6 concludes the chapter.

13.2 Phrase-Based Document Model

A process of data modeling is required to convert the input data into a form that is more suitable for processing by the data mining algorithm. In the case of text mining, input data are mainly text documents that do not necessarily obey a regular structure. The challenge is to convert the input space into feature space, where the features of the documents are expected to follow a fixed structure that can be manipulated by a text mining algorithm. The traditional document representation model, as well as the phrase-based model are introduced in this section.

13.2.1 Vector Space Model

By far the most common feature model in text mining is the vector space model, originally proposed by Salton et al in 1975 [1–3]. In this model, document features are the words in the document collection, and feature values come from different term-weighting schemes.

Each document is represented by a vector **d**, in the term space, such that $d = w_1, w_2, \ldots, w_n$, where w_i, $i = 1, \ldots, n$, is the weight of term i in the document. The weight of a term could be simply calculated as the *frequency* of the term in that document ($w_i = tf_i$), that is, how many times it appeared in the document. A more popular term weighting scheme is TF × IDF (Term Frequency × Inverse Document Frequency), which takes into account the document frequency of a term (df_i), the number of documents in which the term appears. A typical inverse document frequency (idf) factor of this type is given by $\log(N/df_i)$. Thus the TF × IDF weight of a term is $w_i = tf_i \times \log(N/df_i)$. In other words, terms that appear more frequently in a certain document but less frequently in other documents are given higher weights in that document, since it has higher correlation with that document than others. On the other hand, terms that appear frequently in all documents are penalized in all documents since they have less discrimination power.

To represent every document with the same set of terms, we have to extract all the terms found in the documents and use them as our feature vector. To keep the feature vector dimension reasonable, sometimes only terms with the highest weights in all the documents are chosen as the features. Wong and Fu [4] showed that they could reduce the number of representative terms by choosing only the terms that have sufficient coverage over the document set.

Some algorithms [4, 5] refrain from using continuous term weights by using a binary feature vector, where each term weight is either 1 or 0, depending on whether it is present in the document or not, respectively. Wong and Fu [4] argued that the average term frequency in Web documents is below 2 (based on statistical experiments), which does not indicate the actual importance of the term, thus a binary weighting scheme would be more suitable to this problem domain.

The simplicity of the model led to its wide adoption in the text mining literature. However, the independence between the words in the representation is one of its weaknesses. A more informed approach is to capture the phrase structure and word sequences in the document, thus providing context when comparing document features.

13.2.2 Graph Space Model

The model presented here for document representation is called the document index graph (DIG). This model indexes the documents while maintaining the sentence structure in the original documents. This allows us to make use of more informative phrase matching rather than individual words matching. Moreover, DIG also captures the different levels of significance of the original sentences, thus allowing us to make use of sentence significance. Suffix trees are the closest structure to the proposed model, but they suffer from huge redundancy [6]. Apostolico [7] gives over 40 references on suffix trees, and Manber and Myers

[8] add more recent ones. However, the proposed DIG model is not just an extension or an enhancement of suffix trees, it takes a different perspective on how to match phrases efficiently, without the need for storing redundant information.

Phrasal indexing has been widely used in the information retrieval literature [9]. The work presented here takes it a step further toward an efficient way of indexing phrases with emphasis on applying phrase-based similarity as a way of clustering documents accurately.

13.2.2.1 DIG Structure Overview

The DIG is a directed graph (digraph) $G = (V, E)$

where V is a set of *nodes* $\{v_1, v_2, \ldots, v_n\}$, where each node v represents a unique word in the entire document set; and

E is a set of *edges* $\{e_1, e_2, \ldots, e_m\}$, such that each edge e is an ordered pair of nodes (v_i, v_j). Edge (v_i, v_j) is from v_i to v_j, and v_j is adjacent to v_i. There will be an edge from v_i to v_j if, and only if, the word v_j appears successive to the word v_i in any document. A set of edges is said to be corresponding to a sentence in a document if they link the nodes corresponding to the sentence in the same order the words appeared in the sentence.

The above definition of the graph suggests that the number of nodes in the graph is the number of unique words in the document set, that is, the vocabulary of the document set, since each node represents a single word in the whole document set.

Nodes in the graph carry information about the documents they appeared in, along with the sentence path information. Sentence structure is maintained by recording the edge along which each sentence continues. This essentially creates an inverted list of the documents, but with sentence information recorded in the inverted list.

Assume a sentence of m words appearing in one document consists of the following word sequence: $\{v_1, v_2, \ldots, v_m\}$. The sentence is represented in the graph by a path from v_1 to v_m, such that $(v_1, v_2)(v_2, v_3), \ldots, (v_{m-1}, v_m)$ are edges in the graph. Path information is stored in the vertices along the path to uniquely identify each sentence. Sentences that share subphrases will have shared parts of their paths in the graph that correspond to the shared subphrase.

To better illustrate the graph structure, Figure 13.2 presents a simple example graph that represents three documents. Each document contains a number of sentences with some overlap between the documents. As seen from the graph, an edge is created between two nodes only if the words represented by the two nodes appear successive in any document. Thus, sentences map into paths in the graph. Dotted lines represent sentences from document 1, dash-dotted lines represent sentences from document 2, and dashed lines represent sentences from document 3. If a phrase appears more than once in a document, the frequency of the individual

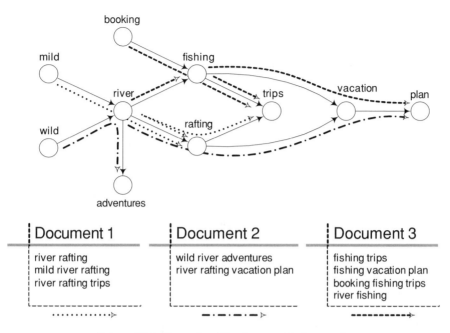

FIGURE 13.2. Example of the document index graph.

words making up the phrase is increased, and the sentence information in the nodes reflects the multiple occurrence of such phrase. As mentioned earlier, matching phrases between documents becomes a task of finding shared paths in the graph between different documents.

13.2.2.2 DIG Construction

The DIG is built incrementally by processing one document at a time. When a new document is introduced, it is scanned in sequential fashion, and the graph is updated with the new sentence information as necessary. New words are added to the graph as necessary and connected with other nodes to reflect the sentence structure. The graph building process becomes less memory demanding when no new words are introduced by a new document (or very few new words are introduced.) At this point the graph becomes more stable, and the only operation needed is to update the sentence structure in the graph to accommodate the new sentences introduced. It is very critical to note that introducing a new document will only require the inspection (or addition) of those words that appear in that document, and not every node in the graph. This is where the efficiency of the model comes from. Along with indexing the sentence structure, the level of significance of each sentence is also recorded in the graph. This allows us to recall such information when we measure the similarity with other documents.

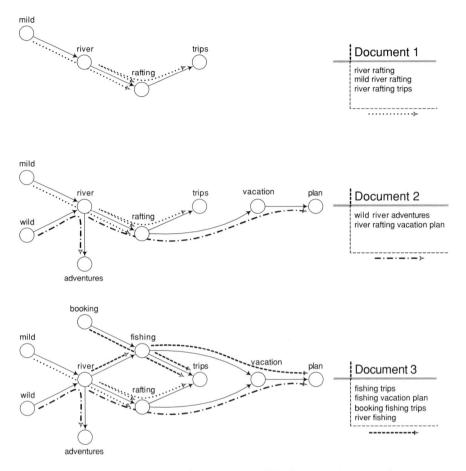

FIGURE 13.3. Incremental construction of the document index graph.

Continuing from the example introduced earlier, the process of constructing the graph that represents the three documents is illustrated in Figure 13.3. The emphasis here is on the incremental construction process, where new nodes are added and new edges are created incrementally upon introducing a new document. We now define the incremental DIG construction process formally in terms of graph properties and operations.

Document Subgraph. Each document d_i is mapped to a subgraph g_i that represents this document in a stand-alone manner (an example is the first step in Fig. 13.3.) Each subgraph can be viewed as a *detached* subset of the DIG that represents the corresponding document in terms of the DIG properties: $g_i = \{V_i, E_i\}$, where V_i is the set of nodes corresponding to the unique words of $\mathbf{d}_i$, and E_i is the set of edges representing the sentence paths of $\mathbf{d}_i$.

Cumulative DIG. Let the DIG representation of the documents processed up to document $\mathbf{d}_{i-1}$ be G_{i-1}, and that of the documents processed up to document $\mathbf{d}_i$ be G_i. Computing G_i is done by *merging* G_{i-1} with the subgraph g_i:

$$G_i = G_{i-1} \cup g_i \tag{13.1}$$

G_i is said to be the *cumulative DIG* of the documents processed up to document $\mathbf{d}_i$.

Phrase Matching. A list of matching phrases between document $\mathbf{d}_i$ and $\mathbf{d}_j$ is computed by *intersecting* the subgraphs of both documents, g_i and g_j, respectively. Let M_{ij} denote the such list, then:

$$M_{ij} = g_i \cap g_j \tag{13.2}$$

A list of matching phrases between document $\mathbf{d}_i$ and all previously processed documents is computed by intersecting the document subgraph g_i with the cumulative DIG G_{i-1}. Let M_i denote the such list, then:

$$M_i = g_i \cap G_{i-1} \tag{13.3}$$

Unlike traditional phrase matching techniques that are usually used in information retrieval literature, DIG provides complete information about full phrase matching between *every* pair of documents. While traditional phrase matching methods are aimed at searching and retrieval of documents that have matching phrases to a specific query, DIG is aimed at providing information about the degree of overlap between every pair of documents. This information will help in determining the degree of similarity between documents as will be explained in section 13.3.2.

13.3 Document Similarity Using Phrase Matching

Upon introducing a new document, finding matching phrases from previously seen documents becomes an easy task using DIG. Algorithm 1 describes the process of both incremental graph building and phrase matching. Instead of building document subgraphs and intersecting them with the cumulative DIG, the algorithm incrementally incorporates new documents into DIG while collecting matching phrases from previous documents at the same time.

13.3.1 Phrase Matching Using DIG

The procedure starts with a new document to process (line 1). Matching phrases from previous documents is done by keeping a list M that holds an entry for every previous document that shares a phrase with the current document $\mathbf{d}_i$. For each sentence (**for** loop at line 3) we process the words in the sentence sequentially, adding new words (as new nodes) to the graph, and constructing a path in the graph (by adding new edges if necessary) to represent the sentence we are processing.

Algorithm 1   DIG incremental construction and phrase matching

---

Require: G_{i-1}: cumulative graph up to document $\mathbf{d}_{i-1}$
      or G_0 if no documents were processed previously
1: $\mathbf{d}_i \leftarrow$ Next document
2: $M \leftarrow$ Empty list $\{M$ is a list of matching phrases from previous documents$\}$
3: **for** each sentence s_{ij} in $\mathbf{d}_i$ **do**
4:    $v_1 \leftarrow t_{ij1}$ {first word in s_{ij}}
5:    **if** v_1 is not in G_{i-1} **then**
6:       Add v_1 to G_{i-1}
7:    **end if**
8:    **for** each term $t_{ijk} \in s_{ij}, \ k = 2, \ldots, l_{ij}$ **do**
9:       $v_k \leftarrow t_{ijk}; \quad v_{k-1} \leftarrow t_{ij(k-1)}; \quad e_k = (v_{k-1}, v_k)$
10:      **if** v_k is not in G_{i-1} **then**
11:         Add v_k to G_{i-1}
12:      **end if**
13:      **if** e_k is an edge in G_{i-1} **then**
14:         Retrieve a list of document entries from v_{k-1} document table that have
            a sentence on the edge e_k
15:         Extend previous matching phrases in M for phrases that continue along
            edge e_k
16:         Add new matching phrases to M
17:      **else**
18:         Add edge e_k to G_{i-1}
19:      **end if**
20:      Update sentence path in nodes v_{k-1} and v_k
21:    **end for**
22: **end for**
23: $G_i \leftarrow G_{i-1}$
24: Output matching phrases list M

As we continue along the sentence path, we update M by adding new matching phrases and their respective document identifiers, and extending phrase matches from the previous iteration (lines 14 to 16). We first consult the document table of v_{k-1} for documents that have sentences that continue along the edge e_k. Those documents share at least two terms with the current sentence under consideration. We examine the list M for any previous matching phrases (from previous iterations) to extend the current two-term phrase match (on edge e_k). This allows the extension of previous matches, and can continue for any-length phrase match. If there are no matching phrases at some point, we just update the respective nodes of the graph to reflect the new sentence path (line 19). After the whole document is processed, M will contain all the matching phrases between the current document and any previous document that shared at least one phrase with the new document. Finally we update G_i to be the current cumulative DIG, and output M as the list of documents with all the necessary information about the matching phrases, which will be used in similarity calculation later.

The average number of the matching documents at any node tends to grow slowly. The actual performance depends on how much overlap of phrases there is in the document set; the more matching phrases the more time it takes to process the whole set, but the more accuracy we get for similarity, and vice versa. The trade-off is corpus-dependent, but in general for Web documents it is typically a balance between speed and accuracy.

This efficient performance of construction/phrase-matching lends itself to on-line incremental processing, such as processing the results of a Web search engine retrieved list of documents. The algorithm processed 2000 news group articles in as low as 44 seconds, while it processed 2340 moderate sized Web documents in a little over 5 minutes.

13.3.2 A Phrase-Based Similarity Measure

As mentioned earlier, phrases convey local context information, which is essential in determining an accurate similarity between documents. Toward this end we devised a similarity measure based on matching phrases rather than individual terms. This measure exploits the information extracted from the previous phrase matching algorithm to better judge the similarity between the documents. This is related to the work of Isaacs and Aslam [10], who used a pair-wise probabilistic document similarity measure based on information theory. Although they showed it could improve on traditional similarity measures, it is still fundamentally based on the vector space model representation.

The phrase similarity between two documents is calculated based on the list of matching phrases between the two documents. From an information theoretic point of view, the similarity between two objects is regarded as how much they share in common. The cosine and the Jaccard measures are indeed of such nature, but they are essentially used as single-term based similarity measures. Lin [11] gave a formal definition for any information theoretic similarity measure in the form of:

$$\text{sim}(x, y) = \frac{x \cap y}{x \cup y} \tag{13.4}$$

The basic assumption here is that the similarity between two documents is based on the ratio of how much they overlap to their union, all in terms of phrases. This definition still coincides with the major assumption of the cosine and the Jaccard measures, and to Lin's definition as well. This phrase-based similarity measure is a function of four factors:

- The number of matching phrases P
- The lengths of the matching phrases ($l_i : i = 1, 2, \ldots, P$)
- The frequencies of the matching phrases in both documents (f_{1i} and $f_{2i} : i = 1, 2, \ldots, P$)
- The levels of significance (*weight*) of the matching phrases in both documents (w_{1i} and $w_{2i} : i = 1, 2, \ldots, P$)

Frequency of phrases is an important factor in the similarity measure. The more frequent the phrase appears in both documents, the more similar they tend to be. Similarly, the level of significance of the matching phrase in both documents should be taken into consideration.

The phrase similarity between two documents, $\mathbf{d_1}$ and $\mathbf{d_2}$, is calculated using the following empirical equation:

$$\text{sim}_p(\mathbf{d_1}, \mathbf{d_2}) = \frac{\sqrt{\sum_{i=1}^{P}[g(l_i) \cdot (f_{1i}w_{1i} + f_{2i}w_{2i})]^2}}{\sum_j |s_{1j}| \cdot w_{1j} + \sum_k |s_{2k}| \cdot w_{2k}} \tag{13.5}$$

where $g(l_i)$ is a function that scores the matching phrase length, giving a higher score as the matching phrase length approaches the length of the original sentence; $|s_{1j}|$ and $|s_{2k}|$ are the original sentence lengths from document $\mathbf{d_1}$ and $\mathbf{d_2}$, respectively. The equation rewards longer phrase matches with higher level of significance, and with higher frequency in both documents. The function $g(l_i)$ in the implemented system was used as

$$g(l_i) = (l_i/|s_i|)^\gamma \tag{13.6}$$

where $|s_i|$ is the original phrase length, and γ is a sentence fragmentation factor with values greater than or equal to 1. If γ is 1, two halves of a sentence could be matched independently and would be treated as a whole sentence match. However, by increasing γ we can avoid this situation, and score whole sentence matches higher than fractions of sentences. A value of 1.2 for γ was found to produce the best results. The normalization by the length of the two documents in equation 13.5 is necessary to be able to compare the similarities from other documents.

13.3.3 Combining Single-Term and Phrase Similarities

If the similarity between documents is based solely on matching phrases, and not single terms at the same time, related documents could be judged as non-similar if they do not share enough phrases (a typical case.) Shared phrases provide important local context matching, but sometimes similarity based on phrases only is not sufficient. To alleviate this problem, and to produce high-quality clusters, we combined single-term similarity measure with our phrase-based similarity measure. Experimental results to justify this claim are given in section 13.3.4. We used the *cosine correlation* similarity measure [1], with TF-IDF term weights, as the single-term similarity measure. The cosine measure was chosen due to its wide use in the document clustering literature, and since it is described as being able to capture human categorization behavior well [12]. The TF-IDF weighting is also a widely used term weighting scheme [13].

Recall that the cosine measure calculates the cosine of the angle between the two document vectors. Accordingly our term-based similarity measure (sim_t) is given as

$$\text{sim}_t(\mathbf{d_1}, \mathbf{d_2}) = \cos(\mathbf{d_1}, \mathbf{d_2}) = \frac{\mathbf{d_1} \cdot \mathbf{d_2}}{\|\mathbf{d_1}\| \|\mathbf{d_2}\|} \tag{13.7}$$

where the vectors $\mathbf{d_1}$ and $\mathbf{d_2}$ are represented as term weights calculated using TF-IDF weighting scheme.

The combination of the term-based and the phrase-based similarity measures is a weighted average of the two quantities from equations 13.5 and 13.7, and is given by equation 13.8. The reason for separating single terms and phrases in the similarity equation, as opposed to treating a single term as a one-word phrase, is to evaluate the *blending* factor between the two quantities, and see the effect of phrases in similarity as opposed to single terms.

$$\text{sim}(\mathbf{d_1}, \mathbf{d_2}) = \alpha \cdot \text{sim}_p(\mathbf{d_1}, \mathbf{d_2}) + (1 - \alpha) \cdot \text{sim}_t(\mathbf{d_1}, \mathbf{d_2}) \tag{13.8}$$

where α is a value in the interval [0, 1], which determines the weight of the phrase similarity measure, or, as we call it, the *similarity blend factor*. According to the experimental results discussed in section 13.3.4, we found that a value between 0.6 and 0.8 for α results in the maximum improvement in the clustering quality.

13.3.4 Effect of Phrase-Based Similarity on Clustering Quality

The similarities calculated by our algorithm were used to construct a similarity matrix between the documents. We elected to use three standard document clustering techniques for testing the effect of phrase similarity on clustering [14]: (1) hierarchical agglomerative clustering (HAC), (2) single-pass clustering, and (3) K-nearest neighbor clustering (k-NN). For each of the algorithms, we constructed the similarity matrix and let the algorithm cluster the documents based on the presented similarity matrix.

The results listed in Table 13.1 show the improvement in the clustering quality using the combined similarity measure. We use the F-measure and entropy

TABLE 13.1. Phrase-based clustering improvement.

	Single-Term Similarity		Combined Similarity		
	F-measure	Entropy	F-measure	Entropy	Improvement
DS1 - UW-CAN					
HAC[2]	0.709	0.351	0.904	0.103	+ 19.5% F, − 24.8%E
Single Pass[3]	0.427	0.613	0.817	0.151	+39.0 % F, −46.2%E
k-NN[4]	0.228	0.173	0.834	0.082	+ 60.6 % F, −9.1% E
DS2 - Yahoo! news					
HAC	0.355	0.211	0.725	0.01	+37.0%F, −20.1%E
Single Pass	0.344	0.274	0.547	0.048	+20.3%F, −22.6%E
k-NN	0.453	0.163	0.733	0.022	+28.0%F, −14.1%E
DS3 - 20-newsgroups					
HAC	0.17	0.347	0.463	0.069	+29.3%F, −27.8%E
Single Pass	0.284	0.684	0.358	0.138	+7.4%F, −54.6%E
k-NN	0.197	0.398	0.349	0.09	+15.2%F, 30.8%E

evaluation measures for judging the quality of clustering. Better clustering should have higher F-measure and lower entropy. The improvements shown were achieved at a similarity blend factor between 70% and 80% (phrase similarity weight). The parameters chosen for the different algorithms were the ones that produced best results. The percentage of improvement ranges from 19.5% to 60.6% increase in the F-measure quality, and 9.1% to 46.2% drop in entropy (lower is better for entropy). It is obvious that the phrase-based similarity plays an important role in accurately judging the relation between documents. It is known that single-pass clustering is very sensitive to noise; that is why it has the worst performance. However, when the phrase similarity was introduced, the quality of clusters produced was pushed close to that produced by HAC and k-NN.

To better understand the effect of the phrase similarity on the clustering quality, we generated a clustering quality profile against the similarity blend factor. Figure 13.4 illustrates the effect of introducing the phrase similarity on the F-measure and the entropy of the resulting clusters. The alpha parameter is the similarity blend factor presented in equation 13.8. It is obvious that the phrase similarity enhances the quality of clustering until a certain point (around a weight of 80%), and then its effect starts bringing down the quality. As we mentioned in section 13.3.3 that phrases alone cannot capture all the similarity information between documents, the single-term similarity is still required, but to a smaller degree. The results show that both evaluation measures are optimized in the same trend with respect to the blend factor.

The performance of the model was closely examined to make sure that the phrase matching algorithm is scalable enough for moderate to large data sets. The experiments were performed on a Pentium 4, 2.0-GHz machine with 512 MB of main memory. The system was written in C++. Figure 13.5 shows the performance of the graph construction and phrase matching algorithm for the two different data sets. In both cases the algorithm performed in a near-linear time. Although the two data sets contain a close number of documents, the Yahoo news data set took about an order of magnitude more than the 20-news-group data set to build the graph and complete the phrase matching. This is attributed to two factors: (1) the Yahoo data set average words per document is almost twice that of 20-news-group data set, so we match more phrases per document; and (2) the Yahoo data set has a larger amount of shared phrases between documents on average than the 20-news-group data set. News group articles rarely share a large amount of phrases (except when someone quotes another post), so on average we do not need to match large number of phrases per document.

13.4 Document Clustering Using Similarity Histograms

In this section we present a brief overview of incremental clustering algorithms, and introduce the proposed algorithm, based on pair-wise document similarity, and employ it as part of the whole Web document clustering system.

The role of a document similarity measure is to provide judgment on the *closeness* of documents to each other. However, it is up to the clustering method how to

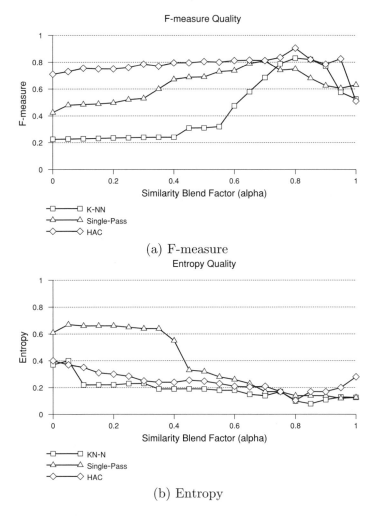

(a) F-measure

(b) Entropy

FIGURE 13.4. Effect of phrase similarity on clustering quality.

make use of such similarity calculation. Steinbach et al [15] give a good comparison of document clustering techniques. A large array of data clustering methods can be also found in [14]. Beil et al [16] proposed a clustering algorithm based on frequent terms that address the high dimensionality problem of text data sets.

The idea here is to employ an incremental clustering method that will exploit our similarity measure to produce clusters of high quality.

Incremental clustering is an essential strategy for on-line applications, where time is a critical factor for usability. Incremental clustering algorithms work by processing data objects one at a time, incrementally assigning data objects to their respective clusters while they progress. The process is simple enough, but faces several challenges. How to determine to which cluster the next object should be

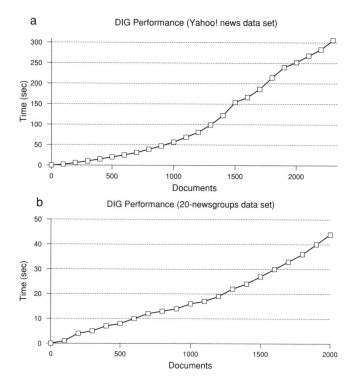

FIGURE 13.5. DIG performance. (a) DIG Performance using the Yahoo! news data set.
(b) DIG Performance using the 20-news group data set.

assigned? How to deal with the problem of insertion order? Once an object has
been assigned to a cluster, should its assignment to the cluster be frozen or is it
allowed to be reassigned to other clusters later on?

Usually a heuristic method is employed to deal with the above challenges. A
"good" incremental clustering algorithm has to find the respective cluster for each
newly introduced object without significantly sacrificing the accuracy of clustering
due to insertion order or fixed object-to-cluster assignment. We will briefly discuss
four incremental clustering methods in the light of the above challenges, before
we introduce our proposed method.

Single-Pass Clustering [17, 18]. This algorithm basically processes documents
sequentially, and compares each document to all existing clusters. If the similarity
between the document and any cluster is above a certain threshold, then the document is added to the closest cluster; otherwise, it forms its own cluster. Usually the
method for determining the similarity between a document and a cluster is done by
computing the average similarity of the document to all documents in that cluster.

K-Nearest Neighbor Clustering [18, 19]. Although k-NN is mostly known to be
used for classification, it has also been used for clustering (example could be found
in [20].) For each new document, the algorithm computes its similarity to every

other document, and chooses the top k documents. The new document is assigned to the cluster where the majority of the top k documents are assigned.

Suffix Tree Clustering (STC). Introduced by Zamir et al [21] in 1997, the idea behind the STC algorithm is to build a tree of phrase suffixes shared between multiple documents. The documents sharing a suffix are considered as a base cluster. Base clusters are then combined together if they have a document overlap of 50% or more. The algorithm has two drawbacks. First, although the structure used is a compact tree, suffixes can appear multiple times if they are part of larger shared suffixes. The other drawback is that the second phase of the algorithm is not incremental. Combining base clusters into final clusters has to be done in a nonincremental way. The algorithm deals properly with the insertion order problem though, since any insertion order will lead to the same result suffix tree.

DC-Tree Clustering. The DC-tree incremental algorithm was introduced by Wong and Fu [4] in 2000. The algorithm is based on the B^+-tree structure. Unlike the STC algorithm, this algorithm is based on vector space representation of the documents. Most of the algorithm operations are borrowed from the B^+-tree operations. Each node in the tree is a representation of a cluster, where a cluster is represented by the combined feature vectors of its individual documents. Inserting a new document involves comparison of the document feature vector with the cluster vectors at one level of the tree, and descending to the most similar cluster. The algorithm defines several parameters and thresholds for the various operations. The algorithm suffers from two problems though. Once a document is assigned to a cluster it is not allowed to be reassigned later to a newly created cluster. A second drawback, which is a consequence of the first drawback, is that clusters are not allowed to overlap; that is, a document can belong to only one cluster.

13.4.1 Similarity Histogram-Based Incremental Clustering

The clustering approach proposed here is an incremental dynamic method of building the clusters. We adopt an overlapped cluster model. The key concept for the similarity histogram-based clustering method (referred to as SHC hereafter) is to keep each cluster at a high degree of coherency at any time. We represent the coherency of a cluster with a new concept called cluster similarity histogram.

Cluster Similarity Histogram: A concise statistical representation of the set of pair-wise document similarities distribution in the cluster. A number of *bins* in the histogram correspond to fixed similarity value intervals. Each bin contains the count of pair-wise document similarities in the corresponding interval.

Our objective is to keep each cluster as coherent as possible. In terms of the similarity histogram concept this translates to maximizing the number of similarities in the high similarity intervals. To achieve this goal in an incremental fashion, we judge the effect of adding a new document to a certain cluster. If the document is going to *degrade* the distribution of the similarities in the clusters very much, it should not be added, otherwise it is added. A much stricter strategy would be to add documents that will *enhance* the similarity distribution. However, this could create a problem with perfect clusters. The document will be rejected by the cluster even if it has high similarity to most of the documents to the cluster (because it is perfect).

We judge the quality of a similarity histogram (cluster cohesiveness) by calculating the ratio of the count of similarities above a certain similarity threshold S_T to the total count of similarities. The higher this ratio, the more coherent is the cluster.

Let n_c be the number of the documents in a cluster. The number of pair-wise similarities in the cluster is $m_c = n_c(n_c + 1)/2$. Let $S = \{s_i : i = 1, \ldots, m_c\}$ be the set of similarities in the cluster. The histogram of the similarities in the cluster is represented as

$$H = \{h_i : i = 1, \ldots, B\} \tag{13.9a}$$
$$h_i = \text{count}(s_k) \qquad s_{li} \leq s_k < s_{ui} \tag{13.9b}$$

where B is the number of histogram bins,
h_i is the count of similarities in bin i,
s_{li} is the lower similarity bound of bin i, and
s_{ui} is the upper similarity bound of bin i.

The histogram ratio (HR) of a cluster is the measure of cohesiveness of the cluster as described above, and is calculated as

$$HR_c = \frac{\sum_{i=T}^{B} h_i}{\sum_{j=1}^{B} h_j} \tag{13.10a}$$
$$T = \lfloor S_T \cdot B \rfloor \tag{13.10b}$$

where HR_c is the histogram ratio of cluster c,
S_T is the similarity threshold, and
T is the bin number corresponding to the similarity threshold.

Basically we would like to keep the histogram ratio of each cluster high. However, since we allow documents that can degrade the histogram ratio to be added, this could result in a chain effect of degrading the ratio to zero eventually. To prevent this, we set a *minimum* histogram ratio HR_{min} that clusters should maintain. We also do not allow adding a document that will bring down the histogram ratio significantly (even if still above HR_{min}). This is to prevent a bad document from severely bringing down cluster quality by one single document addition.

We now present the incremental clustering algorithm based on the above framework (Algorithm 2). The algorithm works incrementally by receiving a new document, and for each cluster calculates the cluster histogram before and after simulating the addition of the document (lines 4 to 6). The old and new histogram ratios are compared, and if the new ratio is greater than or equal to the old one, the document is added to the cluster. If the new ratio is less than the old one by no more than ε and still above HR_{min}, it is added (lines 7 to 9). Otherwise it is not added. If after checking all clusters the document was not assigned to any cluster, a new cluster is created and the document is added to it (lines 11 to 15).

In comparison with the criteria of single-pass clustering and k-NN clustering, the similarity histogram ratio as a coherency measure provides a more representative

---

Algorithm 2   Similarity Histogram-Based Incremental Document Clustering

---

1: $L \leftarrow$ Empty list {cluster list}
2: **for** each document **d do**
3:    **for** each cluster c in L **do**
4:       $HR_{old} = HR_c$
5:       Simulate adding **d** to c
6:       $HR_{new} = HR_c$
7:       if $(HR_{new} \geq HR_{old})$ OR $(HR_{new} > HR_{min})$ AND $(HR_{old} - HR_{new} < \varepsilon))$
      then
8:          Add **d** to c
9:       **end if**
10:   **end for**
11:   **if d** was not added to any cluster **then**
12:      Create a new cluster c
13:      Add **d** to c
14:      Add c to L
15:   **end if**
16: **end for**

---

measure of the tightness of the documents in the cluster, and how the external document would affect such tightness. On the other hand, single-pass compares the external document to the *average* of the similarities in the cluster, while the k-NN method takes into consideration only a few similarities that might be outliers, and that is why we sometimes need to increase the value of the parameter k to get better results from k-NN. This was the main reason for devising such a concise cluster coherency measure and employing it in assessing the effect of external documents on each cluster.

13.4.2 Similarity Histogram-Based Clustering Evaluation

The SHC method was evaluated using two document sets (DS1 and DS2). We relied on the same evaluation measures F-measure and entropy.

Table 13.2. shows the result of SHC against HAC, single-pass, and k-NN clustering. For the first data set, the improvement was very significant, reaching

TABLE 13.2. SHC improvement.

	DS1			DS2		
	F-measure	Entropy	S^5	F-measure	Entropy	S
SHC	0.931	0.119	0.504	0.682	0.156	0.497
HAC[6]	0.901	0.211	0.455	0.584	0.281	0.398
Single-Pass[7]	0.641	0.313	0.385	0.502	0.250	0.311
k-NN[8]	0.727	0.173	0.367	0.522	0.161	0.452

over 20% improvement over k-NN (in terms of F-measure), 3% improvement over HAC, and 29% improvement over single pass. For the second data set an improvement between 10% and 18% was achieved over the other methods. However, the absolute F-measure was not really high compared to the first data set. The parameters chosen for the different algorithms were the ones that produced best results.

By examining the actual documents in DS2 and their classification, it turns out that the documents do not have enough overlap in each individual class, which makes it difficult to have an accurate similarity calculation between the documents. However, we were able to push the quality of clustering further by relying on accurate and robust phrase matching similarity calculation, and achieve higher clustering quality.

The time performance comparison of the different clustering algorithms is illustrated in Figure 13.6, showing the performance for both data sets. The performance of SHC is comparable to single pass and k-NN, while being much better than HAC. The reason for the gain in performance over HAC is because HAC spends so much time in recalculating the similarities between the newly merged cluster and all other clusters during every iteration, which brings its performance down significantly. On the other hand, SHC, single pass, and k-NN share the same general strategy for processing documents, without having to recalculate similarities at each step. Thus, while the SHC algorithm generates better quality clustering, it still exhibits the same, or better, performance as other incremental algorithms in its class.

13.5 Key-Phrase Extraction from Document Clusters

Document clusters are often represented as a membership matrix, where on one dimension are the document identifiers and on the other dimension are the cluster identifiers. An element in the membership matrix determines whether the document belongs to a cluster or not (if binary membership is used), or the degree of membership of the document to the cluster (if fuzzy membership is used).

This kind of cluster representation is useful for testing the accuracy of clustering, but not very useful for humans. An easier representation for clusters is to put labels to the clusters so that the end user can spot interesting clusters without having to look at individual documents in each cluster. That is where key-phrase extraction comes into play.

In this section we present a highly accurate method for extracting key phrases from document clusters, with no prior knowledge about the documents; that is, it is domain-independent. The algorithm is called **CorePhrase**, and is based on finding a set of core phrases that best describe a document cluster.

The algorithm leverages the DIG structure presented earlier to intersect every pair of documents to extract their shared phrases. A list of candidate key phrases for the cluster is then generated by consolidating all shared phrases in a cluster. The extracted candidate key phrases are then analyzed for frequency, span over the document set, and other features. Each phrase is assigned a score based on its

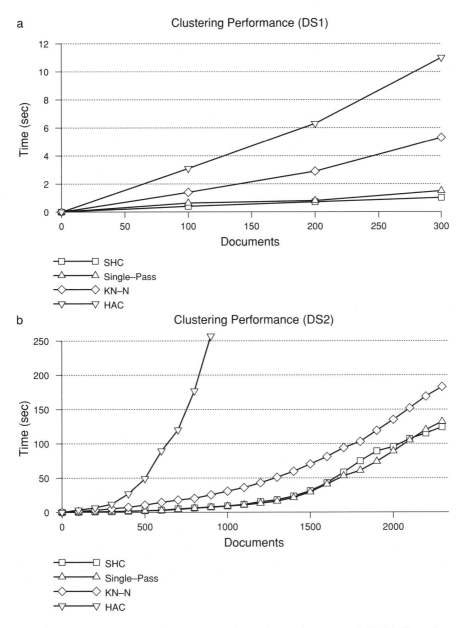

FIGURE 13.6. SHC cluster performance. (a) Clustering performance—DSI. (b) Clustering performance—DS2.

features, then the list is ranked and the top phrases are the output as the descriptive topic of the document cluster. Four scoring method variants are employed and their performance is analyzed. Figure 13.7 illustrates the different components of the key-phrase extraction system.

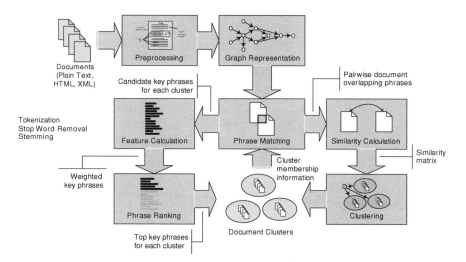

FIGURE 13.7. CorePhrase key-phrase extraction system.

13.5.1 Extraction of Candidate Key Phrases

A candidate key phrase that has the power to represent a set of documents in a cluster (rather than a single document) would naturally lie at the *intersection* of those documents. The CorePhrase algorithm works by first finding all possible key-phrase candidates through matching document pairs together, and extracting all matching phrases between document pairs. A master list of candidate phrases for the document cluster is then constructed from the pairwise document matching lists by consolidating the individual lists to remove duplicates. The resulting list contains all phrases that are shared by at least two documents.

This process of matching every pair of documents is inherently $O(n^2)$. However, by using a proven method of document phrase indexing graph structure, known as the document index graph (DIG), the algorithm can achieve this goal in near-linear time [22]. In DIG, phrase matching is done in an incremental fashion; all documents up to document $\mathbf{d}_i$ are represented by a graph structure, and, upon introducing a new document $\mathbf{d}_{i+1}$, the new document is matched to the graph to extract matching phrases with all previous documents. The new document is then added to the graph. This process produces complete phrase-matching output between every pair of documents in near-linear time, with arbitrary length phrases.

Figure 13.8 illustrates the process of phrase matching between two documents. In the figure, the two subgraphs of two documents are matched to get the list of phrases shared between them.

When a matching phrase, p_{ij}, is found between documents $\mathbf{d}_i$ and $\mathbf{d}_j$, we calculate its features with respect to each document, p_i and p_j, respectively, according to section 13.5.2.

Since this method outputs matching phrases for each new document, it is essential to keep a *master list*, M, of unique matched phrases, which will be

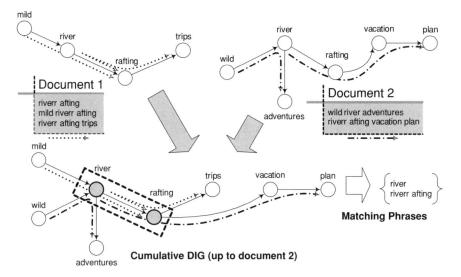

FIGURE 13.8. Phrase matching using document index graph.

used as the list of candidate keyphrases. The following simple procedure keeps this list updated:

Algorithm 3   Candidate Key-Phrase Extraction

1: {calculate M_i for document d_i using (13.3)}
   $M_{ij} = \{p_{ij}: 1 < j < i\}$: matching phrases between $\mathbf{d}_i$ and $\mathbf{d}_j$
   $M_i = \{M_{ij}\}$: matching phrases of $\mathbf{d}_i$
2: **for each** phrase p_{ij} in M_i **do**
3:    **if** phrase p_{ij} is in master list M **then**
4:       add feature vector $\mathbf{p}_{ij}$ to p_{ij} in M
5:       add feature vector $\mathbf{p}_j$ to p_{ij} in M if not present
6:    **else**
7:       add p_{ij} to M
8:       add feature vectors $\mathbf{p}_i$ and $\mathbf{p}_j$ to p_{ij} in M
9:    **end if**
10: **end for**
11: **for each** *unique* phrase p_k in M **do**
12:    calculate averages of feature vectors associated with p_k
13: **end for**

The set of matching phrases from all documents forms a pool of candidate key phrases. Each phrase in this pool is guaranteed to have been shared by at least two documents.

It should be noted that using the matching phrases from multidocument sets as candidate key phrases saves us from problems often faced by single-document key-phrase extraction, namely that of having to identify possible candidates using heuristic techniques, such as the case in the Kea [23] and Extractor [24] algorithms.

13.5.2 Phrase Features

To judge the quality of the candidate key phrases, we need to differentiate between them based on quantitative features. Each candidate key phrase p is assigned the following features:

df: **document frequency**; the number of documents in which the phrase appeared, normalized by the total number of documents.

$$df = \frac{|\text{ documents containing } p|}{|\text{ all documents }|}$$

w: average **weight**; the average weight of the phrase over all documents. The weight of a phrase in a document is calculated using structural text cues. Examples: title phrases have maximum weight, section headings are weighted less, while body text is weighted lowest.

pf: average **phrase frequency**; the average number of times this phrase has appeared in one document, normalized by the length of the document in words.

$$pf = \arg avg \left[\frac{|\text{ occurrences of } p|}{|\text{ words in document }|} \right]$$

d: average phrase **depth**; the location of the first occurrence of the phrase in the document.

$$d = \arg avg \left[1 - \frac{|\text{ words before first occurrence }|}{|\text{ words in document }|} \right]$$

Those features will be used to rank the candidate phrases. In particular, we want phrases that appear in more documents (high df), have higher weights (high w), higher frequencies (high pf), and shallow depth.[2]

The df feature can be regarded as the *support* of the key phrase; that is, from a frequent-set analysis point of view, df tells how many items (documents) support the key phrase. Since we are extracting key phrases that are shared by at least two documents, the minimum support is accordingly two. Although this may seem unnecessarily low support value, when the key phrases are ranked (as described in the next section), the top-ranking phrases usually exhibit high support.

---

[2] It might seem counterintuitive to look for phrases with high df to readers familiar with the TF-IDF term-weighting scheme. Remember that we are not scoring the phrase with respect to a particular document, but rather with respect to the whole document set. So the more common a phrase is across all documents, the better.

13.5.3 Phrase Ranking

In single-document keyphrase extraction setting, the above phrase features will be used as input vectors to a machine learning algorithm for training. The model is then applied to unseen documents to extract the key phrases. However, in our case we are looking at discovering "good" key phrases from multidocument data sets or clusters. Thus, we will use the features to calculate a *score* for each phrase, rank the phrases by score, and select a number of the top phrases as the ones describing the topic of the cluster.

There are two phrase-scoring formulas used, as well as two methods of assigning the score to the candidate phrases, for a total of four variants of the CorePhrase algorithm.

First Scoring Formula. The score of each phrase p is calculated using the following empirical formula:

$$\text{score}(p) = (w \cdot pf) \times -\log(1 - df) \tag{13.11}$$

The equation is derived from the TF $\times$ IDF term weighting measure; however, we are rewarding phrases that appear in more documents (high df) rather than punishing those phrases. Notice also that the first scoring formula does not take the *depth* feature into account. We will refer to the variant of the algorithm that uses this formula as CorePhrase-1.

Second Scoring Formula. By examining the distribution of the values of each feature in a typical corpus, it was found that the *weight* and *frequency* features usually have low values compared to the *depth* feature. To take this fact into account, it was necessary to "expand" the *weight* and *frequency* features by taking their square root, and to "compact" the *depth* by squaring it. This helps even out the feature distributions and prevents one feature from dominating the score equation. The formula is given in equation 13.12.

$$\text{score}(p) = (\sqrt{w \cdot pf} \cdot d^2) \times -\log(1 - df) \tag{13.12}$$

We will refer to the variant of the algorithm that uses this formula as CorePhrase-2.

Word Weight-Based Score Assignment. A *modified* score assignment scheme based on word weights is also used:

- First, assign *initial* scores to each phrase based on the phrase-scoring formulas given above.
- Construct a list of unique individual words out of the candidate phrases.
- For each word, add up all the scores of the phrases in which this word appeared to create a word weight.
- For each phrase, assign the *final* phrase score by adding the individual word weights of the constituent words and average them.

We will refer to the variants of the algorithm that use this method as CorePhrase-1M and CorePhrase-2M, based on the equation that was used to assign the initial phrase scores.

13.5.4 Key-Phrase Extraction Evaluation

For the evaluation of key-phrase extraction, in addition to subjective evaluation of the extracted key phrases, we relied on two other extrinsic evaluation measures that quantitatively assess how well the extracted key phrases relate to the topic of the original class or cluster. The name of each class represents the reference topic name against which the extracted key phrases are compared for evaluation.

The first measure is called *overlap*, which measures the similarity between each extracted key phrase to the predefined topic phrase of the cluster. The similarity is based on how many terms are shared between the two phrases. The overlap between an extracted key phrase p_i and the topic phrase p_t is defined as

$$\text{overlap}(p_i, p_t) = \frac{\mid p_i \cap p_t \mid}{\mid p_i \cup p_t \mid} \tag{13.13}$$

Evaluating each extracted key phrase alone might not give a good idea of how the whole set of top k phrases fit the topic. To evaluate the top k key phrases as a set, we take the average overlap of the whole set. This measure is essentially telling us how well the top key phrases, as a set, *fit* the reference topic.

The second evaluation measure is called *precision*[3], which gives an indication of how high the single key phrase that best fits the topic is ranked. The best key phrase is defined as the first key phrase, in the top k, that has maximum overlap with the reference topic. Thus, the precision for the set of top k phrases ($\mathbf{p}^k$) with respect to the reference topic p_t is defined as

$$\text{precision}(\mathbf{p}^k, p_t) = \text{overlap}(p_{\max}, p_t) \cdot \left[1 - \frac{\text{rank}(p_{\max}) - 1}{k} \right] \tag{13.14}$$

where $p_{\max} \in \mathbf{p}^k$ is the first phrase with maximum overlap in the top k phrases, and rank($p_{\max}$) is its rank in the top k. In other words, precision tells us how *high* in the ranking the best phrase appears. For example, if we get a perfect overlap in the first rank, precision is maximum. The lower the best phrase comes in the ranking, the lower the precision.

13.5.5 Key-Phrase Extraction Results

We have applied the CorePhrase algorithm on ten clusters produced from two data sets. The documents in each cluster were processed by the four variants of the CorePhrase algorithm. The extracted key phrases are ranked in descending order according to their score, and the top 10 key phrases were selected for output by the algorithm. In addition, a keyword-based extraction algorithm was used as a baseline for comparison. The algorithm extracts the centroid vector of a cluster

---

[3] This is not the same as the precision measure usually used in the information retrieval literature.

represented as a set of keywords and selects the top frequent keywords in the cluster. This method is considered representative of most cluster labeling methods.

Table 13.3 shows the results of key-phrase extraction by the CorePhrase algorithm variants for three of the classes (two classes from the first data subset, and one class from the second subset). The phrases in the results are shown in stemmed form, with stop words removed. In a real system the output of the algorithm would have to be in the original unstemmed form for presentation to the end user.

The key phrases extracted by the variants of the CorePhrase[4] algorithm are very close to the reference topic, which is a subjective verification of the algorithm correctness. We leave it to the reader to judge the quality of the key phrases.

A more concrete evaluation based on the quantitative measures, overlap and precision, is illustrated in Figure 13.9 (only CorePhrase-2 and CorePhrase-2M are shown). For each of the four variants of the CorePhrase algorithm, in addition to the baseline keyword centroid algorithm, we report the overlap and precision. The average overlap is taken over the top 10 key phrases/keywords of each cluster.

The first observation is that CorePhrase performs consistently better than the keyword centroid method. This is attributed to the key phrases being in greater overlap with the reference topic than the naturally shorter keywords. An interesting observation also is that CorePhrase-M, which is based on weighted words for phrase-scoring, and the keyword centroid follow the same trend. This is due to the link between the phrase scores and their constituent word scores.

The second observation is that the variants of the algorithm that use the depth feature (CorePhrase-2 and CorePhrase-2M) are consistently better than those that do not use the depth feature (CorePhrase-1 and CorePhrase-1M) in terms of both overlap and precision. This is attributed to the fact that some common phrases usually appear at the end of each document (such as "last updated," "copyright," the name of the Web site maintainer). If depth information is ignored, these phrases make their way up the rank (e.g., the phrase "roger watt" in **campus network** cluster, which is the name of the network maintainer that appears at the end of each document). If depth information is taken into consideration, these phrases are penalized due to their appearance at the end of the document.

Another observation is that the four variants of the algorithm were able to discover the topic of the cluster and rank it in the top 10 key phrases, which can be deduced from the maximum overlap value. CorePhrase is somewhat better than its word-weighted counterpart (CorePhrase-M) in extracting the best phrase and ranking it among the top 10, where it achieves 97% overlap on average for the best phrase. The word-weighted variant achieves 83% maximum overlap on average for the best phrase.

However, if we look at the set of the top 10 extracted phrases as a whole and not just the best phrase, the word-weighted variant achieves better performance in

---

[4] Throughout this discussion the name CorePhrase will refer to both CorePhrase-1 and CorePhrase-2, while CorePhrase-M will refer to both CorePhrase-1M and CorePhrase-2M; unless otherwise specified.

TABLE 13.3. Key phrase extraction results: top 10 key phrases.

	Core phrase-1	Core phrase-2	Core phrase-1M	Core phrase-2M
		canada transporation		
1	canada transport	canada transport	transport canada	canada transport
2	panel recommend	canada transport act	canada transport	transport canada
3	transport associ	transport act	road transport	transportact
4	transport associ canada	transport associ	transport issu	transportissu
5	associ canada	panel recommend	govern transport	recommend transport
6	canada transport act	unit state	surfac transport	transport polici canada transport
7	transport act	transport associ canada tac	public transport	canadian transport
8	road transport	associ canada tac	transport public	transport public
9	transport infrastructur	canada tac	transport infrastructur	public transport
10	transport associ canada tac	public privat sector	transport passeng	transport infrastructur
		winter weather canada		
1	winter storm	sever weather	new hampshir new	environment assess environment
2	winter weather	winter weather	new jersei new	program legisl
3	environ canada	winter storm	new mexico new	program hunt
4	sever weather	weather warn	new hampshir new jersei new	fund program
5	weather warn	sever winter	new jersei new mexico new	environment link fund program
6	freez rain	sever weather warn	new hampshir new jersei new mexico	environment assess environment link fund
7	new brunswick	sever winter weather	new hampshir	environment link
8	heavi snowfal	new brunswick	hampshir new	environment assess environment link
9	winter weather warn	environ canada	carolina new hampshir new	assess environment
10	warn issu	cold winter	carolina new	environment assess
		campus network		
1	campu network	campu network	network network	network network
2	uw campu network	uw campu network	network uw network	network level network
3	uw campu	uw campu	network level network	network uw network
4	roger watt	network connect	uw network	network subscrib network
5	roger watt ist	level network	network uw	level network level network
6	watt ist	high speed	network subscrib network	level network
7	ip address	uw resnet	network assign network	network level
8	ip network	connect uw	network uw campu network	network assign network
9	high speed	area campu network	network level	extern network level network level network
10	request registr	switch rout	level network level network	network level networkr out

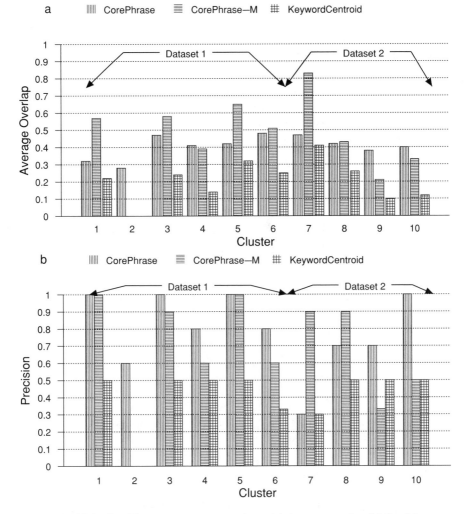

FIGURE 13.9. CorePhrase accuracy comparison. (a) Average overlap (b) Precision.

terms of average overlap (45% for CorePhrase-M against 40% for CorePhrase). This is attributed to the fact that key phrases extracted by the word-weighted version will always contain heavily weighted words, which often overlap with the reference topic. This means that CorePhrase-M will consistently extract phrases containing words found in the reference topic, but which do not necessarily constitute the best descriptive key phrases. This drawback manifests itself when there are few words that occur very frequently throughout the candidate phrases, but are not part of the reference topic. In this case the algorithm will rank up irrelevant phrases that contain those words due to their heavy weight. (An example is the **winter weather canada** cluster.)

A final observation is that CorePhrase consistently achieves better precision than CorePhrase-M (79% for CorePhrase against 67% for CorePhrase-M). This means that CorePhrase does not only find the best key phrase, but ranks it higher than CorePhrase-M.

To summarize these findings: (1) CorePhrase is more accurate than keyword-based algorithms; (2) using phrase depth information achieves better performance; (3) using word-weights to rank phrases usually produces a better *set* of top phrases; however, ignoring the word-weights usually produces the best descriptive phrase and ranks it higher; and (4) in most cases, CorePhrase is able to identify the reference topic in the top few key phrases.

13.6 Conclusion

This chapter presented a framework for text mining based on a phrase graph model of the underlying documents. The level of document representation and manipulation is shifted to its constituent phrases rather than individual words. Phrasal analysis of documents opened the door for more accurate representation, similarity calculation, and eventually higher clustering quality. Achieving the same results using traditional vector-space methods would be impractical.

The clustering framework is composed of four components. The first component is the DIG data structure, an efficient graph structure for representing and indexing phrases in documents. This structure is the underlying foundation upon which other components function.

The second component is the near-linear phrase matching algorithm, which is capable of generating all matching phrases between every pair of documents in near-linear time, with arbitrary-length phrases. The matching phrases are used to construct a complete similarity matrix for use by various clustering algorithms.

The third component is an incremental clustering algorithm based on similarity histogram distribution. The algorithm maintains tight clusters incrementally by keeping the similarity distribution in each cluster coherent.

Finally, the fourth component is the CorePhrase key-phrase extraction algorithm for labeling the generated clusters with key phrases. The algorithm accurately extracts the phrases that best describe each cluster using the DIG structure to extract the candidate key phrases, then rank the top representative phrases.

This framework is coherent, robust, and efficient, as demonstrated by experimental results. The underlying model is flexible and could be extended or enhanced to accommodate other phrase-based tasks for text mining.

The application of the model in e-learning environments provides a way to automatically group learning resources based on content, which can be overwhelming in very large learning repositories. Text mining can help reduce the load on the learner by offering a digest of the data that is accurate enough to acquire the desired information.

References

1. Salton, G., Wong, A., Yang, C. (1975) A vector space model for automatic indexing. Communications of the ACM, 18:613–620.
2. Salton, G., McGill, M.J. (1983) Introduction to Modern Information Retrieval. McGraw-Hill Computer Science Series. New York: McGraw-Hill.
3. Salton, G. (1989) Automatic Text Processing: The Transformation, Analysis, and Retrieval of Information by Computer. Reading, MA: Addison-Wesley.
4. Wong, W., Fu, A. (2000) Incremental document clustering for web page classification. In: 2000 International Conference on Information Society in the 21th Century: Emerging Technologies and New challenges (IS2000), Japan.
5. Jiang, Z., Joshi, A., Krishnapuram, R., Yi, L. (2000) Retriever: improving web search engine results using clustering. Technical report, CSEE Department, University of Maryland, Baltimore County (UMBC).
6. Kurtz, S. (1999) Reducing the space requirement of suffix trees. Software—Practice and Experience, 29:1149–1171.
7. Apostolico, A. (1985) The myriad virtues of subword trees. In: Apostolico, A., Galil, Z. (eds.), Combinatorial Algorithms on Words. NATO ISI Series. New York: Springer-Verlag, pp. 85–96.
8. Manber, U., Myers, G. (1993) Suffix arrays: a new method for on-line string searches. SIAM Journal on Computing, 22:935–948.
9. Caropreso, M.F., Matwin, S., Sebastiani, F. (2000) Statistical phrases in automated text categorization. Technical report IEI-B4-07-2000, Pisa, Italy.
10. Isaacs, J.D., Aslam, J.A. (1999) Investigating measures for pairwise document similarity. Technical report PCS-TR99-357, Dartmouth College, Computer Science, Hanover, NH.
11. Lin, D. (1998) An information-theoretic definition of similarity. In: Proceedings of the 15th International Conf. on Machine Learning, San Francisco: Morgan Kaufmann, pp. 296–304.
12. Strehl, A., Ghosh, J., Mooney, R. (2000) Impact of similarity measures on web-page clustering. In: Proceedings of the 17th National Conference on Artificial Intelligence: Workshop of Artificial Intelligence for Web Search (AAAI 2000), Austin, TX, AAAI, pp. 58–64.
13. Yang, Y., Pedersen, J.P. (1997) A comparative study on feature selection in text categorization. In: Proceedings of the 14th International Conference on Machine Learning (ICML'97), Nashville, TN, pp. 412–420.
14. Jain, A.K., Dubes, R.C. (1988) Algorithms for Clustering Data. Englewood Cliffs, NJ: Prentice Hall.
15. Steinbach, M., Karypis, G., Kumar, V. (2000) A comparison of document clustering techniques. KDD-2000 Workshop on TextMining.
16. Beil, F., Ester, M., Xu, X. (2002) Frequent term-based text clustering. In: Proceedings of the 8th International Conference on Knowledge Discovery and Data Mining (KDD 2002), Edmonton, Alberta, Canada, pp. 436–442.
17. Hill, D.R. (1968) A vector clustering technique. In: K. Samuelson, (ed.), Mechanized Information Storage, Retrieval and Dissemination. Amsterdam: North-Holland.
18. Cios, K., Pedrycs, W., Swiniarski, R. (1998) Data Mining Methods for Knowledge Discovery. Boston: Kluwer Academic Publishers.
19. Dasarathy, B.V. (1991) Nearest Neighbor (NN) Norms: NN Pattern Classification Techniques. McGraw-Hill Computer Science Series. Las Alamitos, CA: IEEE Computer Society Press.

20. Lu, S.Y., Fu, K.S. (1978) A sentence-to-sentence clustering procedure for pattern analysis. IEEE Transactions on Systems, Man, and Cybernetics, 8:381–389.
21. Zamir, O., Etzioni, O., Madanim, O., Karp, R.M. (1997) Fast and intuitive clustering of web documents. In: Proceedings of the 3rd International Conference on Knowledge Discovery and Data Mining, Newport Beach, CA, AAAI, pp. 287–290.
22. Hammouda, K., Kamel, M. (2004) Document similarity using a phrase indexing graph model. Knowledge and Information Systems, 6: 710–727.
23. Frank, E., Paynter, G.W., Witten, I.H., Gutwin, C., Nevill-Manning, C.G. (1999) Domain-specific keyphrase extraction. In: Sixteenth International Joint Conference on Artificial Intelligence (IJCAI-99), Stockholm, Sweden, Morgan Kaufmann, pp. 668–673.
24. Turney, P.D. (2000) Learning algorithms for keyphrase extraction. Information Retrieval, 2:303–336.

14
LORNAV: Virtual Reality Tool for Navigation of Distributed Learning Objects Repositories

ABDULMOTALEB El SADDIK AND M. ANWAR HOSSAIN

Abstract. Navigation in a 3D world has reached its pinnacle with the advent of several technologies like Java, XML, Web services, VRML, X3D, etc. Much effort has been given to visualizing and navigating in virtual mall, cities, digital libraries etc. We designed a virtual reality (VR) tool, called Learning Object Repository Navigator (LORNAV) that extracts learning object metadata (LOM) dynamically from distributed repositories, creates 3D representation of these objects and displays them in a 3D environment using several visualization metaphors. The proposed tool allows the user to navigate through the 3D environment, view the associated metadata of the 3D objects, read/play the content, and select the objects of interest to create a personal space within the 3D environment. The creation of personal space provides users with a familiar navigation space consisting of learning objects of their choice.

14.1 Introduction

Three-dimensional (3D) information visualization has quickly been gaining popularity in recent years. The widespread use of the Internet and the advancement of computer technology have made this journey even more viable. Learning, as a result, has been a common practice on the distributed network-based environment. More and more learning materials are constantly being added to repositories by the distributed learning communities. These huge sources of learning information, when organized according to standards instead of random ways, would create a huge learning base on the Web.

Considerable effort in the past few years has aimed to standardize metadata elements as a common method for identifying, searching, and retrieving Learning Objects (LOs) [23]. The IEEE Learning Object Metadata (LOM) [18] is one such effort toward more accessible, more reusable, and more interoperable LOs. The LOs are being stored over multiple distributed Learning Object Repositories (LORs). The metadata that describes those LOs are stored either with the LOs or in separate repositories.

With the steady increase of LOs and LOM-based repositories, the challenge has now shifted to novel access paradigms [8] in order to facilitate learners' or teachers' effectiveness in navigating, exploring, and searching LOs of their interest. The traditional form-based way of searching information might be helpful in this respect. However, other innovative approaches to information visualization such as 3D visual interface models may be explored. Three-dimensional visual interfaces would not substitute for the traditional ways; rather, they would help to augment the learner's experience in the intuitive visual environment.

Information visualization in general has become vigorous and thriving in the last 10 years [12,20]. Lots of visualization research has come into focus varying from scientific data visualization to more abstract data visualization. Unlike with scientific data where data are often ordered, there is no obvious way to visualize abstract data such as LOM.

This chapter focuses on the research of representing LOs in 3D virtual environment (VE) that leverages prior research on 3D information visualization and digital libraries. Several visualization metaphors and the 3D representation of LOs are also investigated here. Furthermore, several navigation and interaction tasks for exploring LOs are described. Finally, the design and implementation of a Web-based VR tool (LORNAV) including these functionalities are elaborated.

14.2 Learning Objects and Virtual Environment

LORNAV attempts to visualize LOs from distributed repositories in a 3D virtual environment, so at first the notion of LO, the metadata standard that describes LO, and the repositories that are used to store LOs and associated metadata are introduced in this section. This is followed by an overview of 3D visualization and the virtual environment, the virtual reality modeling language, and the necessity for 3D visualization.

14.2.1 Definition of Learning Objects

A learning object, according to the IEEE LOM standard, is "any entity, digital or non-digital, that may be used for learning, education or training" [18]. This is a very broad definition that encompasses everything related to learning as an LO. Hence an LO could be a picture of the Mona Lisa, a document on the Mona Lisa (that includes the picture), a course module on da Vinci, a complete course on art history, or even a 4-year master's curriculum on Western culture [8].

An LO can also be defined as an educational object used to enhance learning. It could include text, images, Web sites, videos, animation, audio, photographs, or presentations. For example, a module or object within an on-line course might consist of all of the objects listed above and yet be a learning object.

Other definitions have attempted to narrow the above definition. In [28], a learning object is considered a reusable digital resource to support learning. This also emphasizes those resources that can be accessed via network irrespective of its granularity. By excluding nondigital objects and classifying every digital resource as an LO, this definition, according to [23], undermines the primary concept of context and modularity.

Similarly, there have been many discussions on the granularity (e.g., size <1 KB, size ≤1 MB) and type (e.g., digital, nondigital) of the learning object. However, all the definitions and discussions aim at establishing a general framework of learning, where learners can share and reuse their learning resources and experiences.

14.2.2 Learning Object Metadata

Learning object metadata (LOM) [18] is a standard defined by the IEEE Learning Technology Standard Committee toward a common method for identifying, searching, and retrieving LOs. LOM is defined as a hierarchical structure consisting of nine broad categories. These are general, life cycle, meta-metadata, technical, educational, rights, relation, annotation, and classification. Under each of the categories, there are several metadata elements. However, all these data elements are optional as defined by the standard.

The LOM structure is extensible, which allows new data elements to be added to its hierarchy. It can be adapted to the needs of a specific community through the use of the application profile [8], yet preserving its original compatibility. The application profile can be defined by giving elements a mandatory condition, by restricting values for certain data elements, by imposing relationship between elements, by excluding some data elements, and by identifying taxonomies and classifications. For example CanCore [5] is an application profile of the IEEE metadata [18] scheme.

Without the use of the application profile, an LOM record probably would not contain any meaningful data (because of the optional characteristics of the LOM elements), thereby causing frustration to the user. However, the effort toward standardization of LOM remains unprecedented. It is the responsibility of the community that maintains the LOM repository to fill meaningful data in the LOM elements to be more usable and sharable by others.

14.2.3 Learning Object Repositories

Learning object repositories (LORs) typically contain LOs or references to them along with the metadata that define the LOs [22]. The process of storing LOs and their metadata may follow different approaches. They could either be stored physically together or separated yet providing a common interface. Hence, the terms LORs and LOM repository are sometimes used interchangeably.

An LOR allows searching and retrieving of LOs by either restricted or unrestricted users. The search could vary from a simple keyword-based search to an advanced element-level search. These kinds of searches may be applied against one single repository or multiple heterogeneous repositories. In the case of multiple repositories, the use of federated search may prove beneficial [8]. The federated search mechanism hides the underlying locations of the repositories and provides the user an interface of a single virtual repository.

There are several communities that maintain LORs to share and distribute knowledge. Examples of some LORs include ARIADNE [1,9], eduSource [11], and LORNET [19].

14.2.4 3D Visualization and Virtual Reality

Three-dimensional visualization is a way to represent real or abstract objects and information to be displayed in a computer-generated 3D environment that can be produced using several modeling languages such as VRML [27], X3D [29], etc. Objects within a 3D world are designed with the perspective and shadows somewhat similar to the real world, which change when the user moves around. This concept of 3D leads to virtual reality when extra senses for example, touch and motion, are involved.

Virtual reality (VR) or virtual environment (VE), as defined in [21], is an artificially created world that gives users a sense of presence in that world, moving around and manipulating the objects they are viewing. In a VR world, a user is able to walk, run, or even fly to explore the environment from different viewpoints that are not possible in the real world. The ability to touch, animate, move, and reposition objects is a true benefit for the VR user. This illusion of reality can be experienced by using different VR hardware like head-mounted display (HMD), data gloves, Binocular Omni-Orientation Monitor (BOOM), and other input and sensual devices.

An example of a VR world could be a virtual library where the users can navigate around, browse, choose books, and read the contents. Although the virtual library is designed by a computer program, the virtual books inside the library could represent real books. This eventually conveys the fact that the virtual world could be designed from data taken from multiple real repositories.

From the above definition and example it is obvious that user interaction tasks in a 3D environment are very important. These tasks can be divided into three main categories: navigation, selection/manipulation, and system control [3].

- Navigation is a very fundamental operation users perform in large 3D environment. Several issues can influence 3D navigation, such as support for spatial awareness, efficient and comfortable movement, and lightweight navigation. In general, the navigation tasks refer to exploration, search, and maneuvering. The exploration tasks are simple navigation without any defined purpose or direction. Unlike exploration, search is a more specific navigation task that a user performs to go to a particular location or view a particular item. The maneuvering tasks are performed by changing the viewpoint so as to get new insight or understanding of the environment.
- Selection/manipulation helps the user to select objects, position them at different locations, and rotate them at a different angle.
- The system control tasks are performed to change either the state of the system or the mode of interaction. These tasks are implemented using graphical menus,

voice commands, gesture interaction, or by any other combination of the different means.

14.2.5 Virtual Reality Modeling Language

Virtual Reality Modeling Language (VRML) [27] is a text-based language that enables us to create three-dimensional worlds consisting of 3D shapes, animations, image texture, light sources, sound effects, and other multimedia objects.

The VRML world can be displayed either from the local machine or from the Web. The delivery of the VRML files across the Web uses the "model/world" Multipurpose Internet Mail Extensions (MIME) type. The actual display of the VRML world requires a VRML browser that is configured as a plug-in for different Web browsers. There are several VRML browsers such as Cortona VRML Client [6], BS Contact VRML/X3D [4], etc. Using a VRML browser, users can navigate a 3D world, interact with the content, trigger an animation, and play a movie or sound from within the virtual environment. The support of hyperlinks from the 3D scene makes VRML even more powerful to be used with other server side technologies, such as Java servlets and Java server pages (JSPs).

VRML has been designed to be platform-independent and to work over low bandwidth connections. This has influenced many communities to use VRML for their virtual reality tool of choice.

14.2.6 The Need for 3D Visualization

The explosive growth of information repository has raised new challenges on how we present and understand information. The limitations of current visualizations [12] are pushing us to new visualization domain. A good amount of research has been performed to explore and find intuitive ways for information visualization in general and 3D visualization in particular. In summary, according to [14, 24], the following are some of the benefits 3D visualization offer:

- Abstract data can be represented using 3D visual attributes for improved perception of data.
- Large quantities of data can be comprehended more easily in 3D, as opposed to 2D textual presentation, in the fixed computer landscape.
- Navigation and exploration of the information space is easier than in 2D scrolling-type navigation.
- Additional direct intuitive interactions can be provided with the entities of interest in 3D environment.
- Relationships and structure among displayed entities can be more easily found and understood.

The above benefits formulate the need for a 3D environment to visualize LO repositories in order to navigate and identify learning objects in a natural way that is different from just "filling in electronic forms" [8].

14.3 Navigation of Learning Object Repositories

To visualize LOs in a 3D environment over the Web, LORNAV uses a 3D modeling language. As LOs are represented using the IEEE LOM [18] standard and are stored in distributed repositories, the 3D representation of each LOM record is created dynamically and visualized in the virtual environment, which encapsulates associated metadata and the link to the actual LO.

The 3D representation of a LOM record is a template 3D object that is replicated dynamically for each LOM record. Instead of considering all the LOM elements to be included with the 3D representation of LOM, a subset of elements (for example, title, language, format, etc.) has been taken into consideration. This is due to the fact that all the LOM elements are optional. Also not all elements are important to be visualized (described in section 14.3.3). Hence, selecting some important and necessary elements that are more likely to be filled by the learning community makes more sense.

There are thousands of LOM records in the repository that we use [11], and the number is increasing every day. This forced us to implement a user preference model. Based on the user preference, a query posed on the distributed repository is likely to return a limited number of records pertaining to user interest. In case the user profile is not yet set up, the system retrieves only a couple of hundred records. This approach is taken into consideration to reduce the load on the visualization engine and to speed up the rendering process.

To access LOM records from the distributed repositories, a data access mechanism is designed based on Web service technology. The choice is influenced by the Web service interface used at the individual repository level. The repository we use has a federated search interface that allows users to pose queries over all the repositories.

14.3.1 Use Case Model

In this section we describe the high-level user-centric functional requirements of our system using the UML-based use case diagram. The use case diagram in Figure 14.1 shows the interactions between external actors and LORNAV. The actors include system administrator, teacher, learner, and guest user.

Administration: The administration use case is included here to deal with different system administration tasks. Typical system administration tasks vary from assigning user roles, user profile and system preference maintenance, etc.

Create Account: This use case is used to refer to the creation of a user account. The security manager component of the system prompts the user to enter a username and password. Once the user is done, the system records the user account information, which can be used to log in to the system on subsequent visits.

Profile Entry/Edit: A learner or teacher can create or modify his/her profile. The security manager checks the user's credentials and for existing users it transfers control to the profile manager component, which prompts the user to enter a new profile or to edit an existing profile.

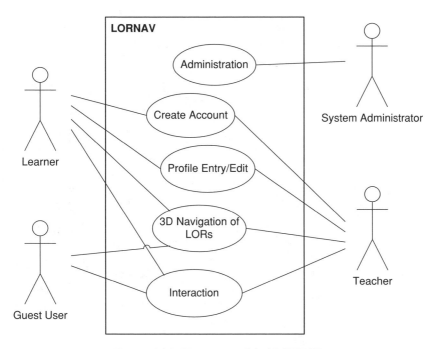

FIGURE 14.1. Use case model of LORNAV.

3D Navigation of LORs: The learner or teacher, once logged in, can navigate the 3D world that is generated by the 3D scene generator engine. The 3D world includes LOM records represented using 3D objects and are based on individual user profile settings. Navigation facilitates the user's performing several other operations such as visual exploration, metaphor selection, search, and maneuvering. These are described further in section 14.3.6.

Interaction: The system allows users to interact with the 3D virtual environment. The interaction includes several other operations such as touching an object, clicking to view the content, clicking to hide the content, selecting an object, rotating the container, and changing the background color. A detail of the interaction tasks are described in section 14.3.7.

14.3.2 Overall Architecture

The overall architecture of LORNAV consists of several functional modules as shown in Figure 14.2. In this figure, lines are used to show the connectivity between modules and we intentionally omitted arrows for clarity.

The system controller is the core component of the architecture. It intercepts all requests coming from the client, extracts request parameters, and maps to the appropriate model or view.

The session manager is responsible for managing a user's session that is used to track logged-in users for delivering personalized content.

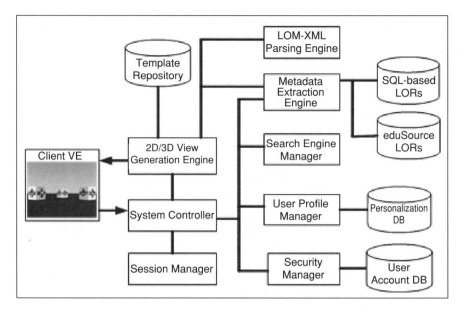

FIGURE 14.2. High-level architecture of LORNAV.

The security manager module is responsible for all security-related tasks, including managing user accounts, checking user's privilege, preventing hacking, and so on. The user account information is stored in the user account database (DB).

The user profile Manager is responsible for managing individual user profiles, which are stored in the personalization DB. Furthermore, the objects selected by the user while navigating in the VE are also stored in this DB and managed by the profile manager.

The search engine manager processes all the search-related operations. The search results are aggregated and stored in an XML file to be later used by the 3D view generation engine. The search engine manager is invoked by the search interface, which is a 2D user interface.

The metadata extraction engine is the module that actually extracts all the necessary metadata records from the remote or local repositories. LORNAV uses eduSource LORs [11] as the remote repository that holds the LOM records for LOs. These repositories are accessed using Web service interface. There are also JDBC-based SQL LORs that hold LOM records and are accessed via JDBC interface over HTTP. The metadata extraction engine receives the LOM records as XML streams and stores them in a XML file.

The LOM-XML parsing engine is responsible for parsing the LOM-XML file created by the metadata extraction engine. This module is invoked by the 3D view generation engine to generate the 3D world for the user.

The template repository holds the 3D templates designed for objects to be represented in a 3D environment. This is actually a file system that manages the template definitions that are created using modeling language like VRML.

The 3D view generation engine is responsible for creating a dynamic 3D environment and for populating that environment with the 3D representations of the LOM records. It also defines the interactivity of the 3D objects within the VE. This module uses the functionality of several other modules to receive the data from the repository and to create a final 3D view for the user.

The client VE is the client virtual environment rendered on the client machine on the browser. The clients need to install a special plug-in in their browser to actually view the 3D environment.

14.3.3 3D Visualization of Learning Objects

Like any other visualization system, 3D visualization demands suitable visual metaphors to visualize and understand information presentation. Visual metaphors are the mapping between data and visual models. Many researchers have stressed the importance of finding appropriate information space metaphors for effective information visualization [14,24,25].

The use of several metaphors has been investigated in LORNAV varying from a familiar real-life metaphor such as bookshelf and table to some new metaphors from the game industry such as car driving. One major concern is that the static metaphor cannot be used due to the large number of returned LOM records from distributed repositories. On the other hand, it is not quite feasible to display all the results in a 3D environment at the same time, which would cause visual clutter and heavily degrade the rendering performance. To address this issue, all the metaphors are generated dynamically in conjunction with several techniques provided by the modeling language are used, such as sensors, level of details, and links to control the number of displayed objects at a given time.

We use several templates of 3D objects to design the 3D environment. The use of template is a feature provided by the 3D modeling language. In our case, we use the capability of VRML to define prototype using PROTO [27]. PROTO is a way of reusing code to create reusable objects. This allows the encapsulation and parameterization of 3D objects and their behaviors. For example, if we need five boxes with different color we can create the box with a variable color parameter.

The definition of a PROTO can be instantiated from within the same VRML file or from outside the main VRML file. The use of PROTO within the same file is straightforward. On the other hand, PROTO defined outside of the main file can be accessed by VRML's EXTERNPROTO feature. In the following, the basic definitions of some PROTOs that LORNAV uses are provided.

protoLOM: This is one of the key templates that is designed to represent a single LOM record. Figure 14.3 shows just the header definition of this prototype along with the 3D object representation. It shows the use of several variables (initialized with some value) in the prototype definition that would ensure dynamic characteristics of the 3D objects.

The value of the parameters defined in the prototype comes from the distributed repositories during the dynamic scene generation process (described later in this chapter). There will be one 3D object for each LOM record retrieved from the

```
PROTO pLOM [
    field MFString title "Title"
    field MFString format "Format"
    field MFString location "Location"
    field SFVec3f pos 0 0 0        #translation
    field SFRotation rot 0 1 0 0   #rotation
    field SFColor dcolor 1 .5 .5   #object color
    field SFColor tcolor 1 1 .5    #text color
    field MFString logo "..\images\mcrlogo.jpg"
]
```

FIGURE 14.3. Prototype definition and sample 3D representation of LOM.

repository. Here title refers to the title element of the LO, format refers to the technical format of the LO (e.g., text/html, image/jpeg, etc.), and location refers to the http location of the LO. This is followed by pos, rot, dcolor, and tcolor for setting the spatial positions and some color properties. The remaining variable logo refers to the texture representation based on the value of format variable. Several predefined images have been used to represent different values such as text/html, image/jpeg, etc. of the format variable.

protoLABEL: This is another important template that is designed to show the selected metadata elements and their associated values in a LOM record from within the 3D environment. The header definition of this prototype along with the 3D representation is shown in Figure 14.4, where several variables correspond

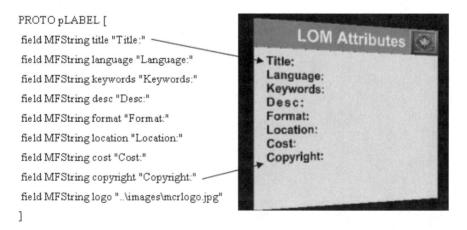

```
PROTO pLABEL [
    field MFString title "Title:"
    field MFString language "Language:"
    field MFString keywords "Keywords:"
    field MFString desc "Desc:"
    field MFString format "Format:"
    field MFString location "Location:"
    field MFString cost "Cost:"
    field MFString copyright "Copyright:"
    field MFString logo "..\images\mcrlogo.jpg"
]
```

FIGURE 14.4. Prototype definition and sample 3D representation of LOM attributes.

to different LOM elements. Here again the value of the variables come from the distributed repositories during execution.

In addition, LORNAV uses several other 3D templates such as box, book-shelf, table, etc. These templates are used to dynamically generate the visualization metaphor for the virtual environment presented later in the implementation section.

According to the IEEE LOM standard [18], nine base categories and more than 60 elements for these categories are used to define learning objects. This huge number makes it impractical for the learning community to properly tag the elements. This research identifies 18 LOM elements from all the element sets. The selection of these elements is influenced by our experience and work done by others in this area. From these 18 elements, another subset of eight elements is used for the purpose of visualization. The rest is left for other classification, search, and aggregation operations. These elements are listed in Table 14.1.

As shown earlier in Figures14.3 and 14.4, a number of variable fields defined in the templates are related to the visualization of LOM records. Those variable fields have a straight one-to-one correspondence with the LOM elements selected in Table 14.1, such as Title corresponds to 1.2 Title, Language corresponds to 1.3 Language, and so on. Hence, the virtual environment generated as a result of the user's search operation will display the search results by means of 3D representations of the LOs along with the respective metadata elements from the distributed repositories.

TABLE 14.1. LOM categories and selected LOM elements for visualization.

No.	Category	Selected elements	Used for visualization
1.	General	1.1.1 Identifier.Catalog	
		1.1.2 Identifier.Entry	
		1.2 Title	√
		1.3 Language	√
		1.4 Description	√
		1.5 Keyword	√
2.	Life cycle	2.3.1 Contribute.Role	
		2.3.3 Contribute.Date	
3.	Meta-metadata	3.2.1 Contribute.Role	
		3.2.2 Contribute.Entry	
4.	Technical	4.1 Technical.Format	√
		4.2 Technical.Size	
		4.3 Technical.Location	√
5.	Educational	5.2 Educational.LearningResourceType	
		5.5 Educational.IntendedEndUserRole	
6.	Rights	6.1 Rights.Cost	√
		6.2 Rights.CopyrightandOtherRestrictions	√
7.	Relation	—	
8.	Annotation	—	
9.	Classification	9.2.1 Classification.Keyword	

14.3.4 Data Clustering

Data clustering and categorization are major concerns in preparing 3D environments. LORNAV categorizes the returned LOM records based on keywords. The keywords are displayed on top of the object container that would hold LOM records according to its predefined capacity.

The other clustering techniques are used based on specific LOM elements, such as Technical.Format. The LOs that are similar in technical format are subgrouped under the main keyword-based category. There could be further grouping based on Educational.LearningResourceType or Educational.IntendedEndUserRole, or according to any classification system, for example, ACM or IEEE classification systems, to show similarities among objects. Furthermore, if considered semantically, the categorization could follow any given ontology for a particular domain.

14.3.5 Dynamic 3D View Generation

Generating a dynamic 3D world brings life to a 3D environment. Object representations in 3D VE can be based on repositories that are distributed over the network. Figure 14.5 is a sequence diagram that shows the algorithm for generating 3D view dynamically.

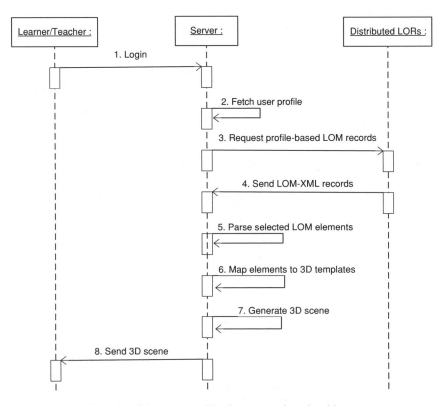

FIGURE 14.5. Dynamic 3D view generation algorithm.

Once a user logs into the system, the server fetches the corresponding user profile. The server then makes an XML-SOAP request based on the profile to the remote Web service interface of the distributed LORs in order to receive related LOM records. The remote Web service interface in reply sends the LOM records as a LOM-XML stream. Here is sample LOM-XML steam:

```
<lom xmlns="http://ltsc.ieee.org/xsd/LOMv1p0"
xmlns:lom="http://ltsc.ieee.org/xsd/LOMv1p0"
xmlns:xsi=http://www.w3.org/2001/XMLSchema-instance
xsi:schemaLocation="http://ltsc.ieee.org/xsd/LOMv1p0
http://explora2.licef.teluq.uquebec.ca/lomxml/schema/
lom.xsd">

  <general>
    <title>
      <string language="fr">
        Introduction au java</string>
    </title>
    <language>fr</language>
   <keyword>java programming</keyword>
  </general>
  <metaMetadata>
    <contribute>
      <role>
        <source>LOMv1.0</source>
        <value>creator</value>
      </role>
      <entry>BEGIN: vCard FN: Banville; Claire
            END: vCard</entry>
    </contribute>
  </metaMetadata>
  <technical>
    <format>application/pdf</format>
    <location>
      http://www.repository.ca/lornav.pdf
    </location>
  </technical>
  <educational>
   <intendedEndUserRole>
     <source>LOMv1.0</source>
     <value>Teacher</value>
   </intendedEndUserRole>
   <intendedEndUserRole>
     <source>LOMv1.0</source>
     <value>Learner</value>
   </intendedEndUserRole>
  </educational>
  <rights>
    <copyrightAndOtherRestrictions>
      <source>LOMv1.0</source>
```

```
      <value>yes</value>
    </copyrightAndOtherRestrictions>
    </rights>
  </lom>
```

Upon receiving the reply, the server parses the required metadata elements from the LOM-XML stream. It then uses the predefined 3D templates of LOs and metaphors, dynamically associates the metadata with the templates, and finally generates a 3D virtual environment scene. The 3D scene is then transferred back to the client browser for rendering.

14.3.6 Navigation Model

The navigation model focuses on client activities pertaining to the overall 3D environment. However, some client activities may require server interactions for processing requests, such as the search operation.

In LORNAV, learning objects retrieved from distributed learning object repositories are presented in the 3D environment over the Web. Users navigate the 3D world with the mouse input interface. The use of joysticks, gesture recognition, and other haptic devices would be interesting to explore in the future.

The navigation model of LORNAV includes several navigation tasks that a user currently performs. This model is shown in Figure 14.6. What follows is a brief description of each of the tasks.

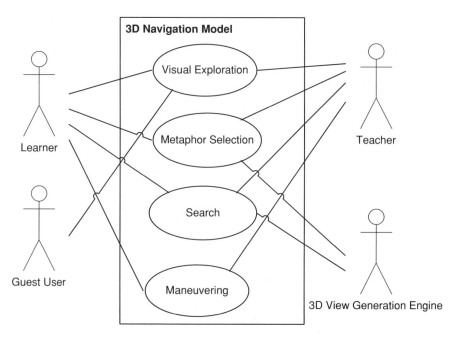

FIGURE 14.6. Use case of LORNAV navigation model.

Visual Exploration: This allows users to navigate around the 3D world without any predefined purpose or destination. Users often perform such exploration tasks to become familiar with the 3D world.

Metaphor Selection: LORNAV provides multiple visual metaphors to present the learning objects of interest. The use of multiple metaphors helps user to better understand the presented information.

Search: This operation is used to find specific learning objects. The search interface is a 2D-based interface. A user can perform two types of searches: keyword-based search and element-level search. In keyword-based search, the user types several keywords separated by commas and choose the target repositories on which to perform the search. Similarly in an element-level search, the user specifies search criteria for selected LOM elements and chooses the target repositories to carry the search operation. The server retrieves matching LOM records from the repositories and generates the dynamic 3D world for the user to navigate further.

Maneuvering: The maneuvering tasks are often performed to get new insight or understanding of the environment [3]. LORNAV defines several viewpoints while generating the 3D environment. Users are able to change these viewpoints at the time of exploring the 3D environment.

14.3.7 Interaction Model

The interaction model involves client activities performed on the 3D objects and artifacts displayed in the 3D environment. Interactions in the 3D environment with the objects may be challenging, especially when the user uses the 2D mouse interface [26]. LORNAV foresees the use of multiple haptic-based devices for better interaction in the future. Figure 14.7 represents a use case diagram for the current interaction tasks that a user can perform with the 2D mouse interface.

Touch Object: While navigating in the 3D world, a user can touch an object by putting the mouse on top of it. This allows him to see selected metadata attributes associated with that object. The metadata are shown in a 3D panel using the template in Figure 14.4. When the user removes the mouse from the object, the metadata panel disappears. LORNAV uses the capability of VRML's touch sensor to provide this functionality.

Click to View: While viewing the metadata of an object, a user can perform a mouse click to view the content of the learning object. The learning content may be viewed on an internal or external viewer based on the actual content type. Some of the media types such as movie, video, sound, image, etc. are played from within the 3D environment, while others such as pdf and html are viewed in external viewers.

Select Object: The clicking on an object is also treated as selection of that object. This idea behind this functionality is that the user becomes interested and hence clicks on that object to view its content. The object's metadata information is then stored in a separate database. In the next visit the selected objects are viewed in 3D within a personal space defined by the view generation module.

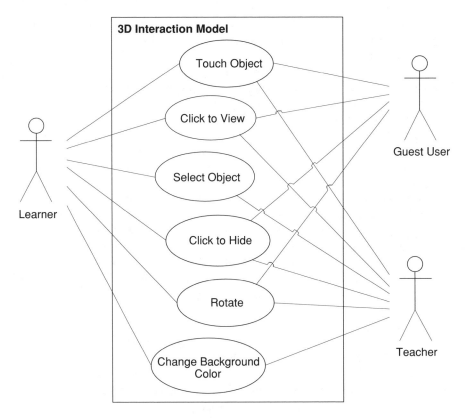

FIGURE 14.7. Use case of LORNAV interaction model.

Click to Hide: Both the click to view and the click to hide operations are similar to flip-flop events. The objects that are played from within the 3D environment by the mouse-click event are hidden by the subsequent mouse-click event.

Rotate: The 3D representations of LOs are organized in the 3D environment through the use of containers such as shelves, tables, or boxes. These containers can be rotated by the user to view objects that are arranged on the opposite sides of the user's current viewpoint.

Change Background Color: LORNAV uses several color properties for background color. A user is able to switch between different background colors for the 3D world by using custom-defined buttons.

14.3.8 Data Access

LORNAV attempts to visualize LORs that adopt LOM standard to describe LOs. The LORs may either be distributed over the network, or may reside in the server. To access distributed repositories, we use the eduSource [11] LORs that store and maintain LOM [18] records. The types (e.g., relational SQL DB, XML DB, etc.) of these LORs are unknown since they are maintained by the individual educational communities. However, they have a common Web service–based federated search interface to access the data. The federated search allows the user to pose a single query in order to receive data from multiple repositories. The local LOM repository is based on a MySQL database. It can be connected by using the Java database connectivity (JDBC) tool. The database connectivity parameters are stored in separate property files in text file format and are easy to update. The database platform is very transparent, meaning that one can easily change the database platform from MySQL to Oracle or SQL server simply by changing parameters in the property files. Search on this database can be performed only with standard SQL statements. Although this repository is locally stored in the server, it can be distributed as well because the access to this repository is done via HTTP.

The main aspect of the data access module is to keep the access interface completely separate from the view generation process so that any additional repository can be plugged in with little effort without affecting the views. This ensures smooth visualization of LOs even if some of the repositories are not active at a given time. Figure 14.8 shows a conceptual diagram of data access and aggregation

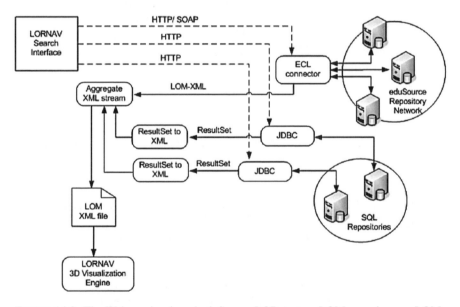

FIGURE 14.8. The Web service–based eduSource LORs return LOM records as an LOM-XML stream. On the other hand, the JDBC-based SQL LORs initially retrieve LOM records as ResultSet object by using SQL query. To aggregate these two kinds of data format, LORNAV first converts the ResultSet object into an XML stream of LOM records, combines these stream to those of eduSource stream, and stores them as an XML file. This file is used by the visualization engine and parsed to separate the required LOM elements by the LOM parser. The parsed element sets are then used by the visualization engine to generate the 3D virtual environment, which are transferred to the client's browser.

in LORNAV and the capability of the access module to handle multiple sources of repositories.

The eduSource LORs [11] are accessed using the eduSource Communication Layer (ECL) connector [10,15]. The connector provides standard API to connect and query existing repositories to the eduSource network. There are also relational SQL repositories that are accessed using the JDBC connectivity tool over the Internet.

In response to the data access request, the APIs of the repositories send replies with the matching LOM records. As the repositories are physically distributed, there is a need to aggregate the retrieved LOM records. The aggregate data then go straight into the LORNAV's 3D visualization engine to produce the 3D visualization in the virtual environment.

14.4 Implementation

The software architecture of LORNAV has been implemented using a standard software development process. It is a three-tier client-server–based tool that operates on the Web environment. Its architecture is based on the MVC [13] pattern, which has the potential to increase system performance, flexibility, maintainability, reusability, scalability, and interoperability. In Figure 14.9, we provide the actual software architecture of LORNAV as an extension of the high-level architecture previously shown in Figure 14.2. The following software has been used while implementing the system:

- Apache Tomcat 5.0.x as Web and application server (http://jakarta.apache.org/tomcat/).
- Java development kit 1.4.2_02 for building Java classes (http://java.sun.com/j2se/).
- MySQL database 4.1.7 as server database (http://dev.mysql.com/downloads/mysql/4.1.html).
- MySQL Java connector 3.1.x for database connectivity (http://dev.mysql.com/downloads/connector/j/3.1.html).
- VRML97 as 3D modeling language (http://www.web3d.org/x3d/specifications/vrml/).

The client tier provides a browser-based 3D virtual environment where the user navigates and interacts with the displayed learning objects. The 3D user interfaces are implemented using VRML97. The client browser requires additional plug-in to support rendering the VRML scenes. LORNAV uses the Cortona VRML plug-in [6] from parallel graphics.

While developing LORNAV, the VRML external authoring interface (EAI) [27] has been bypassed to communicate with the 3D scene and instead active server side components have been used to dynamically generate and manipulate the 3D objects. The reason behind this is that the VRML EAI only relies on Microsoft

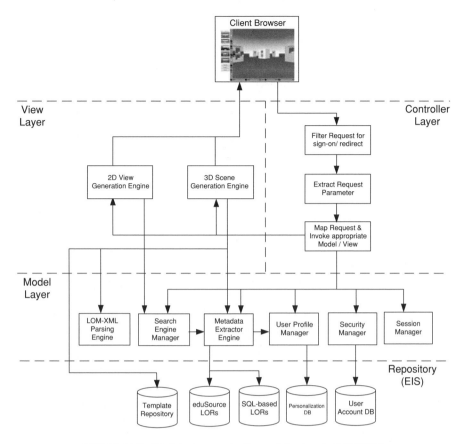

FIGURE 14.9. Model-view-controller architecture in LORNAV.

VM, which is based on Java 1.1 and does not support servlets, JSPs, and Web
services technology that we have used.

The web tier is based on the MVC pattern. The controller in this architecture
is the core component. It controls the flow of the application and serves as the
join between the model and view. We have used several active components (e.g.,
Java servlets) for processing HTTP requests coming from the clients. The model
layer encapsulates the business objects and API for the application's functionality.
There are several models in LORNAV architecture: security manager, session
manager, user profile panager, search engine manager, metadata extraction engine,
and LOM-XML parsing engine. These modules are implemented using a series of
Java classes and servlets. We have developed a custom-built LOM-XML parser
that uses the simple API for XML parser (SAXParser). The remaining functional
unit is the view layer that is mainly responsible for presenting data to the user. The
view layer includes the 2D and 3D view generation engine. This is implemented
using JSPs. The idea of generating 3D views as VRML scenes using JSP pages is

illustrated in [7]. The 3D view gdeneration engine uses 3D templates stored in the template repository and populates them with dynamic data to generate dynamic views.

The EIS tier is composed of several local and distributed LOM repositories, personalization DB, user account DB, and 3D template repositories. The dynamism of the 3D scenes is based on the data stored in the LORs. The software architecture of LORNAV supports both HTTP and HTTPs protocol for the communication between client and server. The HTTPs protocol takes care of secure communication between the LORNAV server and the client browser.

14.4.1 Example Interfaces

The implementation of LORNAV resulted in a number of user interfaces. This includes both 2D and 3D interfaces. The 2D interfaces are used for user input parameters such as entering login information, setting up the user profile, entering search parameters, and administering the system. The 3D interface is the 3D environment that is rendered on the client's browser. The 3D environment is populated with the LOs retrieved from the distributed LORs. All these interfaces can be classified into two types such as navigation interfaces and interaction interfaces. The classification comes from the fact that the user performs either navigation or interaction tasks in the 3D environment.

14.4.1.1 Navigation Interfaces

Figure 14.10 shows a sample screen shot when a user logs in the system using a metaphor containing square boxes. Each side of the box contains four objects representing four LOs. When users navigate in such an environment, they can rotate the box to see the objects in other sides of the box. As an alternative to this, they can walk through and see the objects in other sides. Each box represents the objects with similar keywords. However, if the number of objects related to a keyword is more than a box can contain, another box will be dynamically created to contain the additional objects.

The 3D environment shown in Figure 14.10 corresponds to the user profile settings of a particular user if the profile exists; otherwise, the first few hundred LOM records are displayed in this environment. In the figure, the user is given several choices including selecting a metaphor from the available metaphors, searching LOs of choice, entering or updating his/her profile, and administering if applicable.

Figure 14.11 shows the screen that appears after the user selects another metaphor created dynamically using familiar objects such as shelf and table. In this view, the user can rotate the shelf and table by walking close to it and use the mouse to go in the XY plane while holding it down. The user can also change the background color by using the 3D switch in the virtual environment.

Figure 14.12 shows a 2D interface when the user selects the search option. Users are able to search either by specifying multiple keywords or specific LOM elements such as title, format, and description and eventually on remaining LOM

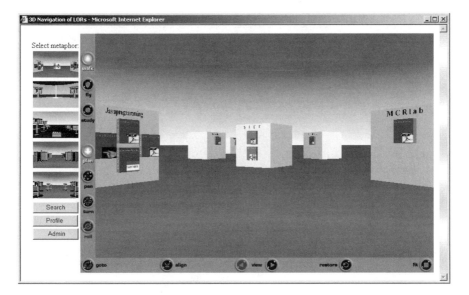

FIGURE 14.10. Sample 3D environment in a new box-type metaphor.

attributes. They can also specify which repository they wish to include in the search. After submitting their selection criteria, they are provided with the search results displayed in the 3D environment similar to Figures 14.10 and 14.11 or any other selected metaphor.

FIGURE 14.11. Sample 3D environment in a familiar metaphor.

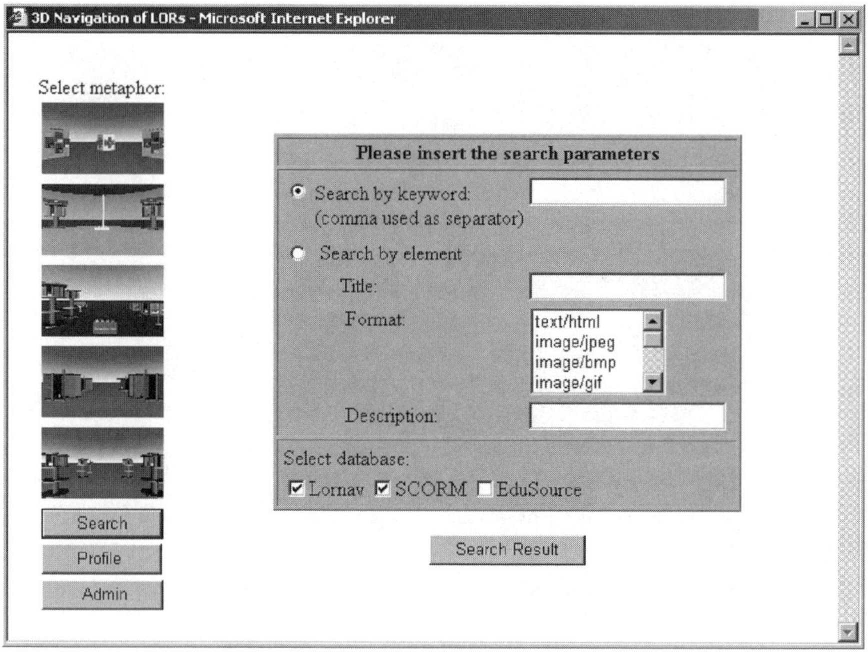

FIGURE 14.12. Sample search interface.

There are other navigation interfaces such as user profile entry interface, admin interface, and 3D metaphors. The sample screen shots of these interfaces are not presented here, but are available in the software prototype of LORNAV.

14.4.1.2 Interaction Interfaces

Figure 14.13 represents a sample interaction interface for touch and click interaction. There is a touch sensor attached to each of the 3D objects. When the user touches an object (by taking the mouse on top of the object) the touch sensor event is activated, which uses the protoLABEL (shown in Fig. 14.4) prototype to show the metadata associated with that object. If the user feels more interested in that object, he can click on that object to see the content. In the figure, the user touched an image object representing an LO and clicked on that to see the real image from within the 3D environment. The clicking also refers to the user's preference toward that object, and hence the metadata of that object are stored into a separate database to be viewed on subsequent visits. If the user moves the mouse, the metadata information will be hidden. In the case of an mpeg movie, the situation would be the same as the VRML browser supports playing mpeg movies from within the VE.

Figure 14.14 shows another interface for touch and click interaction in the case of an HTML document. Unlike an image, or movie object, the html document is opened in a separate browser. VRML does not support all types of media objects

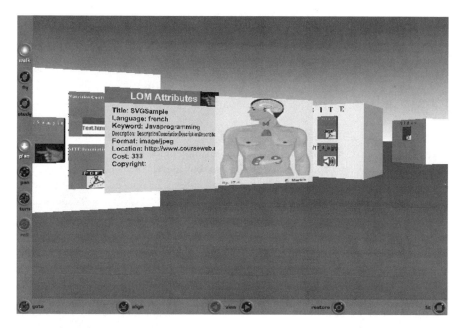

FIGURE 14.13. Sample interface for touching and clicking an LO of type image.

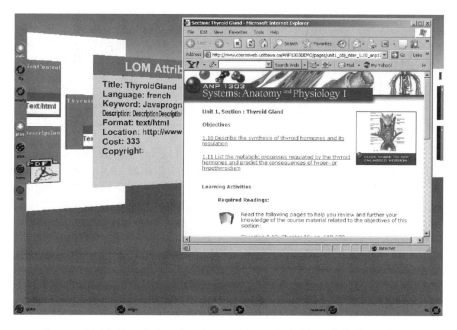

FIGURE 14.14. Sample interface for touching and clicking a LO of type html.

to be played or viewed from within the 3D environment. However, those objects can be viewed using an external plug-in such as a real player or windows media player.

14.5 Conclusion and Future Work

In this chapter, we have investigated the role of 3D information visualization techniques in the development of dynamic virtual environment based on learner's profile. LORNAV incorporates a Web service–based interface in addition to JDBC over http to access data from distributed repositories. The data access functionality has been made generic enough to be able to add or update any identical repositories using the LORNAV administrative control panel.

Our experience with LORNAV has been encouraging. User evaluation has been positive. Many learners have shown interest while navigating in the 3D environment in order to visualize and search learning contents. We believe that the enriched spatial model may play a significant role in attracting learners to visit, to interact, and to adapt LORNAV as a tool of choice to search and visualize learning objects.

In this work we addressed keyword-based or element-level search algorithms for retrieving learning objects from the repositories. This approach only returns those results that contain the keyword or element value within certain fields in the metadata records and does not reflect the actual closeness of the objects among each other. The aim is to address this issue in our future work by investigating several possible alternatives. One such alternative will be to use the semantic Web [2] to search and classify the learning objects. We performed preliminary investigations with the semantic Web tools, technologies and applications in [16,17]. However, more research is needed in this direction.

We also forecast the use of enhanced user control with the effect of haptic and auditory feedback while navigating the 3D environment. The new input technologies such as eye gaze, HMD, etc. will be exploited and tested in our virtual environment to provide the user a feeling of actually being in the environment.

Finally, new and intuitive visual metaphors will be investigated to present the learning objects in the virtual environment. Although in LORNAV we have several of such metaphors, the research in finding appropriate metaphor is never ending.

References

1. ARIADNE Foundation for the European Knowledge Pool. http://www.ariadne-eu.org.
2. Berners-Lee, T., Hendler, J., Lassila, O. (2001) The Semantic Web. Scientific American 284:34–43. http://www.sciam.com/article.cfm?articleID=00048144-10D2-1C70-84A9809EC588EF21.
3. Bowman, D.A., Kruijiff, E., LaVoila, J.J. Jr., Poupyrev, I. (2001) An introduction to 3-D user interface design. Presence, 10:96–108.
4. BS Contact VRML/X3D. http://www.bitmanagement.de/.
5. CanCore. http://www.cancore.ca/indexen.html.

6. Cortona VRML Client. http://www.parallelgraphics.com/products/cortona/.
7. Cowie, D. (2002) Use JSP to create your own VRML world. http://builder.com.com/5100-6371-1050067.html.
8. Duval, E., Hodgins, W. (2003) A LOM Research Agenda. Proc. 12th Int'l Conf. World Wide Web.
9. Duval, E., Warkentyne, K., Haenni, F., et al. (2001) The ARIADNE Knowledge Pool System. Communications of the ACM, 44:72–78.
10. ECL. eduSource Communication Layer. http://lore.iat.sfu.ca/ecl/.
11. eduSourceCanada, Canadian Network of Learning Object Repositories. http://www.edusource.ca/english/objects_eng.html.
12. Eick, S.G. (2005) Information Visualization at 10. IEEE Computer Graphics and Applications, 25:12–14.
13. Gamma, E., Helm, R., Johnson, R., Vlissides, J. (1995) Design Patterns. New York: Addison-Wesley Professional.
14. Gershow, N., Eick, S.G., Card, S. (1998) Information Visualization. Interactions, 5: 9–15.
15. Hatala, M., Richards, G., Eap, T., Willms, J. (2004) The EduSource Communication Language: Implementing Open Network for Learning Repositories and Services. Proc. 19th Ann. ACM Symp. Applied Computing, March, pp. 957–962.
16. Hossain, M.A., El Saddik, A., Lévy, P. (2004) Towards a Multi-domain Semantic Web Application. Proc. Canadian Conf. Electrical and Computer Engineering (CCECE04), Niagara, Ontario, Canada, May.
17. Hossain, M.A., El Saddik, A. (2004) Creating Knowledge and Semantic Web Applications on the Web. Proc. 2nd Intl. Symposium on Innovation in Information and Communication Technology (ISIICT), Amman, Jordan, April.
18. IEEE Learning Object Metadata, final draft standard, July 15, 2002 (IEEE 1484.12.1). http://ltsc.ieee.org/wg12/files/LOM_1484_12_1_v1_Final_Draft.pdf.
19. LORNET. http://www.lornet.org/eng/.
20. Ma, K. (2004) Visualization—a quickly emerging field. Computer Graphics, 38:4–7.
21. Manetta, C., Blade, R. (1995) Glossary of virtual reality terminology. International Journal of Virtual Reality 1(2):20–38.
22. Neven, F., Duval, E. (2002) Reusable Learning Objects: a Survey of LOM-Based Repositories. Proc. 10th ACM Int'l Conf. Multimedia, December, pp. 291–294.
23. Polsani, P.R. (2003) Use and abuse of reusable learning objects. Journal of Digital Information 3(4). http://jodi.ecs.soton.ae.uk/Articles/v03/i04/Polsani
24. Rohrer, R.M., Swing, E. (1997) Web-based information visualization. IEEE Computer Graphics and Applications, 17:52–59.
25. Santos, C.R.D., Gros, P., Abel, P., et al. (2000) Metaphor-Aware 3D Navigation. Proc. IEEE Symp. Information Visualization, October, pp. 155–165.
26. Tory, M., Mo¨ller, T. (2004) Human Factors in Visualization Research. IEEE Transactions on Visualization and Computer Graphics, 10:72–84.
27. VRML Specification. http://tecfa.unige.ch/guides/vrml/vrml97/spec/.
28. Wiley, D.A. (2000) Connecting learning objects to instructional design theory: a definition, a metaphor, and a taxonomy. In: Wiley, D.A. (ed.), The Instructional Use of Learning Objects, Online version, pp 1–35. http://www.reusability.org/read/chapters/wiley.doc.
29. X3D Documentation. http://www.web3d.org/x3d/.

Index

Printed in the United States of America.